THE WILLIAM WALTON READER

THE WILLIAM WALTON READER

THE GENESIS, PERFORMANCE, AND PUBLICATION OF HIS WORKS

EDITED BY
DAVID LLOYD-JONES

MUSIC DEPARTMENT

OXFORD
UNIVERSITY PRESS

OXFORD
UNIVERSITY PRESS

Great Clarendon Street, Oxford, OX2 6DP,
United Kingdom

Oxford University Press is a department of the University of Oxford.
It furthers the University's objective of excellence in research, scholarship,
and education by publishing worldwide. Oxford is a registered trade mark of
Oxford University Press in the UK and in certain other countries

First Edition published in 2018

Impression: 1

Published in the United States of America by Oxford University Press
198 Madison Avenue, New York, NY 10016, United States of America

British Library Cataloguing in Publication Data

Data available

Library of Congress Control Number: 2017963204

ISBN 978–0–19–341466–2

Printed in Great Britain by
Ashford Colour Press Ltd, Gosport, Hampshire

Contents

Foreword

In 1995 the contract between Sir William Walton (1903–83) and the Oxford University Press, which had published at least 95 per cent of his works, came up for renegotiation. Lady Walton and the lawyers of the William Walton Trust were considerably demanding, but eventually an agreement was reached; this included the stipulation that the publishers must embark on a newly edited William Walton Edition (WWE). This would have been called the William Walton Complete Edition were it not for the fact that some unpublished incidental music to theatre productions and broadcasts, and the film scores (most of which were no longer extant), were to be excluded, except for the Suites extracted from the four finest. Stewart Craggs, author of the indispensable *Catalogue of Works* (2nd edition, OUP, 1990), was to be Consultant, and I, who had conducted and recorded a number of his works, and met the composer several times, including at his Ischia home, was asked to be General Editor. I was generously given a free hand in the all-important matter of choosing suitable editors and of deciding which of the twenty-three music volumes I myself would edit. It is with considerable satisfaction that I can now look back at what I consider to be a total success in this respect, and the meticulous, scholarly, work of the editors (all but one of them executants) will surely stand the test of time. I should not fail to mention how invariably helpful and professional the staff of the OUP Music Department were during the twenty-year project.

Despite the existence of a number of books devoted to the life and works of Walton, most notably the late Michael Kennedy's perceptive *Portrait of Walton* (OUP, 1989), Stephen Lloyd's even more informative *William Walton: Muse of Fire* (The Boydell Press, 2001) and *The Selected Letters of William Walton*, edited by Malcolm Hayes (Faber & Faber, 2002), it has been thought appropriate to issue another publication devoted to the composer. The detailed research and scholarship that the WWE editors undertook, such as for the first time drawing on the rich store of information held in the OUP Archive, Oxford, resulted in a series of Prefaces that contained a wealth of new and up-to-date research on each of the Walton works published; detailed musical analysis was not included. It is these Prefaces that are now being republished (with the occasional correction or addition) to form an accessible, readable, yet authoritative account of Walton's numerically modest but consistently high-quality corpus of compositions, arranged chronologically as in the WWE volumes. In this connection, one small alteration has been made. Due to a technical error, Volumes 11 and 13 were juxtaposed, so that the Violin and Cello Concertos appeared before, not after, the Sinfonia Concertante.

The twenty-three Prefaces presented here, with any appropriate extra matter, are supplemented by the Selective Chronology from Stewart Craggs's third edition of his *Catalogue of Works*, which constitutes the concluding Volume 24 of the WWE, and by a General Index.

David Lloyd-Jones

Selective Chronology

1866
11 Oct   Louisa Maria Turner (mother) born at Herbert Street, Stretford, Lancashire

1867
28 Feb   Charles Alexander Walton (father) born at Albert Terrace, Hale, Cheshire

1898
10 Aug   marriage of Charles Alexander and Louisa Maria at the MacFadyen Memorial Congregational Church, Chorlton-cum-Hardy

1902
29 March William Turner Walton born at 93 Werneth Hall Road, Oldham. Siblings: brothers Noel (1899–1981) and Alexander (1909–1979), and sister Nora (born 1908).

1908   starts to learn piano, organ, and violin

1912   enters choir of Christ Church, Oxford, after his father sees a newspaper advertisement for choral scholarships

1914
4 Aug   war declared

1916
15 March confirmed in Christ Church Cathedral by Charles Gore, Bishop of Oxford. First known compositions performed in the cathedral.
The Dean of Christ Church arranges for him to stay on at the choir school.

1917
10 April   his March for organ (C104) is played at the wedding of Dr Henry Ley
June   meets Sir Hubert Parry

1918
11 June   as an undergraduate, passes the first half of his BMus examination at New College, Oxford
11 Nov   Armistice marking the end of World War I is announced
13 Nov   granted an in-college exhibition for two years by the governing body of Christ Church

1919
Feb   meets Osbert Sitwell
12 Feb   meets John Masefield and Siegfried Sassoon
June   fails Responsions
Sept   fails Responsions at second attempt
Dec   fails Responsions at third attempt

1920
spring   visits Italy for the first time with the Sitwells
8–9 June passes second part of his BMus

| 20 Oct | Christ Church governors postpone the renewal of Walton's exhibition |
| 10 Nov | Governors agree to pay Walton £150 'to clear him from his reasonable liabilities' |

1921

Sept	has lessons from Ernest Ansermet and E. J. Dent
24 Sept	tells his mother that 'Goossens has [his overture] Syntax'
Nov	starts to compose *Façade*, settings of poems by Edith Sitwell

1922

| 24 Jan | *Façade* given its first (private) performance |

1923

| 4 Aug | meets Schoenberg and Berg while attending the ISCM Festival in Salzburg |

1924 begins to compose the overture *Portsmouth Point*

1925

| 28 May | meets George Gershwin in London |
| 25 Oct | acts as best man at the wedding of Sacheverell Sitwell in Paris |

1926

| 30 Aug | Susana Gil Passo (Lady Walton) born in Argentina |
| Sept | signs a publishing contract for five years with Oxford University Press |

1927

26 June	attends an all-Elgar concert at Queen's Hall, London
autumn	meets Spike Hughes
10 Nov	Sacheverell Sitwell publishes *German Baroque Art* (London: Duckworth), which is dedicated to William Walton

1928

| 14 Sept | first European performance of *Façade* |
| Dec | starts work on the Viola Concerto |

1929

| 12 June | meets Imma Doernberg at the Daye House, Quidhampton, Wiltshire |
| 21 Aug | BBC commissions 'the writing of special music for broadcasting' |

1930

| March | approached by C. B. Cochran for music to one of his revues |

1931

| 8 Oct | first performance of *Belshazzar's Feast* in Leeds Town Hall |

1932

Jan	receives a lifetime annuity of £500 per annum in the will of Mrs Samuel Courtauld
	Hamilton Harty asks Walton for a symphony, for the Hallé Orchestra
	asked by Herbert Hughes to contribute a song to *The Joyce Book*. Refuses.

1933 working on the first symphony

1934

| spring | meets Alice Wimborne |
| 3 Dec | first performance of the first three movements of Symphony No. 1 |

1935

11 Aug mention of a ballet about Bath to a libretto by Osbert Sitwell for the de Basil Ballet

Oct moves to 56A South Eaton Place, Belgravia, London

1936

28 Feb report in *The Times* that Walton has been elected to membership of the Performing Right Society

March offered a contract for a René Clair film, *Break the News* (released in 1938). Refuses.

11 Aug conducts part of an all-Walton Promenade concert at Queen's Hall, London

Oct offered contract for *The Amateur Gentleman* (film). Refuses.

1937

12 May *Crown Imperial* played in Westminster Abbey before the Coronation service of King George VI and Queen Elizabeth

28 June receives an honorary DMus degree from the University of Durham

2 July receives an honorary Fellowship of the Royal College of Music

15 July attends a memorial service for Lady Ida Sitwell at St George's, Hanover Square, London

28 July meets Benjamin Britten

Aug approached for music for the film *The Last Curtain*. Refuses.

16 Aug approached for a test piece for the 1940 National Band Festival at the suggestion of John Ireland

1938

24 Feb Hubert Foss gives an interval talk about Walton on BBC radio

spring asked for a work for clarinet and violin by Benny Goodman and Joseph Szigeti. Refuses.

April approached for a choral work 'In honour of the City of New York' for the 1939 New York World's Fair. Also asked for music to the film *Pygmalion*. Refuses both offers.

June receives an honorary Fellowship of the Royal Academy of Music

July visited by Frederick Stock to discuss and confirm his proposed commission for the Chicago Symphony Orchestra

1939

20 June signs a contract to write an orchestral work for the Chicago Symphony Orchestra

3 Sept World War II begins; joins the Daventry Mobile First-aid Unit as an ambulance driver

7 Dec first performance of the Violin Concerto in Cleveland, Ohio

20 Dec considers writing an overture for Chicago about Monsieur Mongo (Nashe)

1940

Jan considers writing an overture for the Ministry of Information, having been offered the job of general music director of the MoI film unit

autumn	asked by the MoI to arrange a simple overture of popular music to run for about eight minutes

1941

March	is included in a new ENSA advisory music council established to promote the provision of good music for the forces and munition workers
spring	receives call-up papers from the Ministry of Labour
May	London home destroyed by enemy bombing
8 May	considers an opera about Carlo Gesualdo with Cecil Gray

1942

Jan	asked for music for a production of *Oedipus Rex* in the Royal Albert Hall. Refuses.
12 Feb	receives honorary DMus degree (with Malcolm Sargent) from Oxford University
24 March	Arthur Bliss (director of music, BBC) commissions Walton for a brass band suite
summer	approached for a choral work for St Matthew's Church, Northampton
27 Aug	report in *The Times* that a letter from English composers, including Walton, Bax, and John Ireland, had been sent in reply to one received from their Soviet contemporaries expressing mutual appreciation of their work
7 Nov	attends a reception at 13 Kensington Park Gardens, London, celebrating the 25th anniversary of the USSR

1943

Feb	offered a contract to write music for the film *The Bells Go Down*
	BBC asks Walton for a setting of the Te Deum to mark the 50th anniversary of the Promenade Concerts in Nov 1943
7 May	joins the music committee of the British Council

1944

May	completes composition of the music for the film *Henry V*
23 June	attends a lunch at Claridge's for Sir Henry Wood
20 July	named as one of the committee of five controlling the Royal Opera House, Covent Garden
6 Dec	contributes a manuscript which is included in the album 'Tribute to the Red Cross' and sold at Sotheby's

1945

5 April	contributes to a letter in *The Times* requesting British musicians take the lead in coming to the aid of the destitute 80-year-old Finnish composer Jean Sibelius
summer	considers writing a choral ballet about Agamemnon for the Sadler's Wells Ballet Company
29 sept	considers setting six verses of John Masefield's poetry for the Henry Wood memorial service
29 Oct	considers a setting of *Dream Play* by Strindberg

31 Oct	conducts part of an all-Walton concert on a British Council visit to Stockholm
5 Dec	elected an honorary member of the Royal Academy of Music

1946

Jan	considers music for the film of *King Lear*
20 April	appointed to the board of the Performing Right Society in place of the late Dr Thomas Dunhill
summer	joins the board of the Covent Garden Opera Trust
22 Nov	attends a lunch at the Savoy arranged on behalf of the Musicians' Benevolent Fund to commemorate the festival day of St Cecilia
31 Dec	nominated for Academy Award for scoring of *Henry V*

1947

Feb	considers an overture to celebrate the first anniversary of the BBC's Third Programme. Also considers an opera about Inez de Castro, with libretto by Cecil Grey, and another with libretto by Dylan Thomas
14 March	Imma Doernberg dies
31 March	*The Times* reveals that Walton had been appointed to Honorary Studentship of Christ Church, Oxford
20 May	visits Prague with Alice Wimborne, Alan Bush, and Gerald Abraham for the International Music Festival
15 July	decides upon the story of Troilus and Cressida for an opera
12 Aug	asked by the BBC to set one of six special poems for broadcasting
19 Nov	presented with the Gold Medal of the Royal Philharmonic society by Ralph Vaughan Williams at a RPS concert in the Royal Albert Hall

1948

30 June	receives an honorary DMus degree from Trinity College, Dublin
1 July	first performance of Alan Rawsthorne's first Violin Concerto, which is dedicated to William Walton
13 Sept	sails to Buenos Aires as a delegate to a Performing Right Society conference
13 Dec	marries Susana Gil Passo in a civil wedding ceremony

1949

20 Jan	marriage blessed in a church ceremony
2 June	asked to be visiting professor at the Yale School of Music for 1949–50 but declines
summer	moves to Ischia

1950

27 Nov	writes to *The Times* with other composers and musicians about the London County Council grant to the London Philharmonic Orchestra

1951

1 Jan	appointed a Knight Bachelor in the New Year's Honours List
March	considers writing a work for the Festival of Britain celebrations
30 July	writes to *The Times* with other composers about the rejected request for money to restore war-damaged Morley College

31 July	knighted by King George VI at an investiture, the king's first official engagement since his illness
21 Aug	Constant Lambert dies
23 Aug	appointed, with Benjamin Britten, to the National Arts Foundation of New York's Advisory Committee on Music
25 Aug	attends the funeral service for Constant Lambert at St Bartholomew the Great's Church, Smithfield, London
28 Sept	presents a tribute to Arnold Schoenberg at a memorial programme arranged by the London Contemporary Music Centre
7 Oct	contributes a talk about Lambert to the BBC's *Music Magazine*
22 Oct	writes to *The Times* with others including Benjamin Britten about the Arts Council's policy in the visual arts
25 Oct	publication of *Foyer*, a new quarterly magazine with Walton and Sacheverell Sitwell on the editorial board

1952

17 Jan	appointed an honorary member of the Royal Swedish Academy of Music
6 Feb	death of King George VI
Oct	declines a request to contribute a madrigal to *A Garland for the Queen*
31 Oct	formal commission from the Arts Council for *Orb and Sceptre*

1953

4 Feb	receives a telegram from George Neikrung in California asking for a cello concerto
20 May	receives an honorary DMus degree from the Victoria University of Manchester
2 June	*Orb and Sceptre* and *Coronation Te Deum* are performed at the Coronation service of Queen Elizabeth II in Westminster Abbey
8 June	attends the gala performance, at Covent Garden, of Britten's *Gloriana*; Walton's arrangement of the *National Anthem* is played before the start and at the end of the opera
Aug	sails to the USA and visits the West Coast; first American appearance as a conductor
Dec	approached for a score to the film *Antony and Cleopatra*. Refuses.

1954

3 Dec	first performance of *Troilus and Cressida*, Royal Opera House, Covent Garden, London

1955

27 April	attends the Royal Academy Dinner at Burlington House
10 June	receives an honorary DMus degree from the University of Cambridge
summer	considers writing music for the ballets *Macbeth* and *The Tempest* for Margot Fonteyn and Covent Garden
16 Nov	writes to *The Times* with other composers about the Copyright Bill; conducts an all-Walton concert in the Royal Festival Hall, organized by the RPS

| 24 Nov | receives an honorary DMus degree from the University of London |
| 7 Dec | writes another letter to *The Times* with other composers about further concerns over the Copyright Bill |

1956

10 Jan	interviewed by Felix Aprahamian (BBC Home Service) on the premiere of *Troilus and Cressida* at La Scala, Milan
spring	considers a Sinfonietta for the City of Birmingham Symphony Orchestra
summer	considers a double concerto for Heifetz and Piatigorsky
6 Nov	considers a flute concerto for Elaine Schaffer

1957

17 Jan	William and Lady Walton are involved in a serious car accident in Italy
Nov	considers a choral work about Moses and Pharaoh for the Huddersfield Choral Society
12 Dec	resigns from the PRS General Council

1958

| summer | considers adapting and expanding his music for *Macbeth* for a film directed by Laurence Olivier |

1959

| spring | moves from Casa Cirillo to San Felice in Ischia |
| 24 June | considers a piano concerto for Louis Kentner |

1960

Feb	visits the USA; considers writing music for the film *The Reason Why*; asked by David Lean for a joint score (with Malcolm Arnold) for his film *Lawrence of Arabia*
22 July	completes the composition of Symphony No. 2
17 Oct	considers a Concerto Grosso for George Szell
24 Nov	mention of the Koussevitsky Foundation pieces which 'could be a Suite Concertante for five solo wind and orchestra'

1961

21 March	conducts the Hallé Orchestra in a performance of Symphony No. 2
18 April	becomes the 14th honorary Freeman of the Borough of Oldham
Nov	work commences on the building of La Mortella, Ischia
27 Dec	the proposed Suite Concertante loses 'its priority'

1962

18 Jan	musical tribute to Walton is broadcast by the BBC from the Royal Festival Hall
4 Feb	appointed Accademico Onorario della Accademia Nazionale di Santa Cecilia in Rome
spring	asked by Erich Leinsdorf to write a piece for the Boston Symphony Orchestra
May	visits Canada for the first time
Aug	takes possession of La Mortella

23 Aug	considers writing an opera based on Oscar Wilde's play *The Importance of Being Earnest*
27 Aug	writes a letter to *The Times* about the RPS
9 Oct	conducts a performance of *Façade* at Edith Sitwell's 75th birthday concert in the Royal Festival Hall, London

1963

24 April	death of Christopher Hassall
July	visits Israel
Aug	visits the USA and conducts a concert of his works on 8 Aug at Lewisohn stadium, New York
Nov	Symphony No. 2 receives a nomination from the National Academy of Recording Arts and Sciences

1964

| Feb–April | visits New Zealand and Australia, conducting his own works; visits his sister, Nora Donnelly, and her family in New Zealand |

1965

| 19 July | asked to compose an anthem for the 1966 Southern Cathedrals Festival |

1966

| 10 Jan | has operation for cancer at the London Clinic |
| 4 March | promises Piatigorsky that 'it won't be too long before I start on the Double Concerto' |

1967

3 June	first performance of *The Bear*
summer	considers writing the music for Tony Richardson's film *The Charge of the Light Brigade*
10 July	Alun Hoddinott commissions a chamber work from Walton to commemorate the opening of the new building at University College, Cardiff
20 Sept	visits Expo '67 in Montreal
21 Nov	receives the Order of Merit from the Queen

1968

26 April	receives an honorary DLetts degree from the University of Surrey
25 May	BBC broadcasts *Workshop: William Walton* on BBC2, with script and narration by John Warrack
15 Aug	first American performance of *The Bear* at Aspen, Colorado
14 Nov	Alan Frank informs Walton that Gary Kerr, the American double bass player, wants to commission a double bass concerto from him

1969

| Jan | visits Houston, Texas |

1970

Jan	considers writing music for the film *Upon this Rock*, which he later refuses
10 July	Paul Dehn sends Walton a new suggestion for a one-act opera (*The Panic*)
autumn	considers a setting of a Cecil Day-Lewis poem for the Brighton Festival

1971

April   visits the USSR with the London Symphony Orchestra and André Previn

1972

17 Jan   awarded the Benjamin Franklin Medal

March   considers writing a third symphony for André Previn and the LSO

15 March   honorary membership of the Royal Northern College of Music conferred on Walton and Michael Kennedy

28 March   attends a 70th birthday concert in the Royal Festival Hall, London

29 March   attends a birthday dinner at 10 Downing Street, given by the prime minister, Edward Heath

April   considers setting some of the poems from the *Liber Basiorum* (*Book of Kisses*, 1541)

28 July   attends birthday celebrations at Aldeburgh, Suffolk

12 Sept   given honorary freedom of the Worshipful Company of Musicians

1973

31 May   elected member of the Athenaeum Club

15 July   considers a Te Deum for Chichester Cathedral

1974

3 March   considers writing a piece for the Bach Choir, including an elaborate version of *Cantico del Sole*

spring   interviewed and filmed for *William and our Gracie* (LWT)

23 April   receives the honorary degree of DMus from Universitas Hiberniae Nationalis

24 July   mention of a piece for Piatigorsky in the nature of *Chanson Poème*

autumn   invited to write a short orchestral work by the Greater London Council in celebration of the 25th Anniversary of the Royal Festival Hall, London

1975

12 March   Walton 'rather keen on the idea' of using *Anon. in Love* and the Bagatelles for guitar as a ballet

Sept   offered a commission to write a choral work for the 250th Three Choirs Festival (1977)

19 Oct   LWT broadcast a programme in the Aquarius series (*Sir William and our Gracie*) featuring the meeting between Sir William Walton (Oldham–Ischia) and Dame Gracie Fields (Rochdale–Capri)

1976

July   considers setting 'Peace', a poem by Paul Dehn, for the Queen's Silver Jubilee, 1977

25 July   considers a bassoon concerto for Milan Turkovic

Sept   commissioned to write an orchestral piece, entitled *The Prospect*, by Max Aitken

4 Sept   refuses to write a ceremonial piece for Nottingham County Council

| 12 Nov | *Troilus and Cressida*, revised version, performed at the Royal Opera House, Covent Garden, London |
| 30 Nov | collapses during a celebratory dinner at the Garrick Club in London |

1977

Jan	considers a work for the double choir of St Alban's Abbey
22 March	presented with the Incorporated Society of Musicians' 'Musician of the Year' award at the Park Lane Group 75th-birthday Gala for Walton in Fishmonger's Hall, London Bridge
28 March	London Mozart Players and Harry Blech present a birthday concert at the QEH, which includes *Façade*, narrated by Robert Tear
29 March	attends a 75th birthday concert at the Royal Festival Hall, London
14 April	prepares a setting of Psalm 130 for St Alban's Abbey
May	approached by the National Brass Band Championships of Great Britain with a commission to write a work for brass band
17 June	a celebration of British Music in Westminster Cathedral includes *Belshazzar's Feast*, conducted by Richard Hickox
29 June	agrees in principle to write a work for brass band
24 Aug	proposes to write Five Bagatelles for Brass Band
17 Nov	lunches (as a member of the Order of Merit) with the Queen at Buckingham Palace and attends a service for the Order in the Chapel Royal, St James's Palace
30 Dec	decides that he is unable to write the concert band work

1978

| 22 Jan | refuses to write the Berkeley 75th birthday piece, and a Mass for a San Francisco choir |
| May | honorary membership of the American Academy and Institute of Arts and Letters conferred on Walton |

1979

| 26 Feb | approached to write a setting of Horace's Odes for the 1982 Llandaff Festival |
| 5 March | confirmation that Walton would write an a cappella work for Llandaff |

1980

| 15 April | considers a companion piece for *The Bear*, with libretto by Alan Bennett |

1981

19 April	televising of Tony Palmer's film *At the Haunted End of the Day*
20 April	a new photograph of Walton by Lord Snowden appears in *The Times*
27 Sept	receives the Prix Italia winner's certificate for the film profile *At the Haunted End of the Day* (inscribed: 'in profound thanks for all the pleasure you have given me. Tony Palmer')

1982

| 29 March | attends his 80th birthday concert at the Royal Festival Hall, London, which is televised by the BBC |

1 April	attends a lunch for members of the Order of Merit, hosted by the Queen at Windsor Castle
22 July	filmed with Lady Walton as the King and Queen of Bavaria in Tony Palmer's film *Wagner*

1983

15 Jan	attempts to write a motet in the style of Palestrina
March	agrees to set the Stabat Mater for the 150th Anniversary of the Huddersfield Choral Society
8 March	dies at the age of 80
18 March	Frederick Ashton completes plans for a new ballet
20 July	memorial stone unveiled by Lady Walton at memorial service in Westminster Abbey, London

1985

30 May	the William Walton Trust is established to promote public education in the art of music and in particular the study, public performance and recording of Walton's work

1989 William Walton Foundation established

1990

12 Sept	inauguration of the Recital Hall at La Mortella

1995

21 May	a Solemn Mass of Thanksgiving is given at the church of St Alban the Martyr, Holborn, for church music through the works of Sir William Walton

1998

26 March	first volume of the WWE is published by OUP: Symphony No. 1

2002

31 March	Walton Day is held on BBC Radio 3 to mark the centenary of Walton's birth

William Walton Edition

General Editor: David Lloyd-Jones   Consultant: Stewart Craggs

1. Troilus and Cressida, edited by Stuart Hutchinson, 2003
2. The Bear, edited by Michael Burden, 2010
3. Ballets, edited by David Lloyd-Jones, 2014
4. Belshazzar's Feast, edited by Steuart Bedford, 2007
5. Choral Works with Orchestra, edited by Timothy Brown, 2009
6. Shorter Choral Works without Orchestra, edited by Timothy Brown, 1999
7. Façade Entertainments, edited by Stewart Craggs and David Lloyd-Jones, 2000
8. Vocal Music, edited by Steuart Bedford, 2011
9. Symphony No. 1, edited by David Lloyd-Jones, 1998
10. Symphony No. 2, edited by David Russell Hulme, 2006
11. Violin and Cello Concertos, edited by David Lloyd-Jones, 2011
12. Concerto for Viola and Orchestra, edited by Christopher Wellington, 2002
13. Sinfonia Concertante, edited by Lionel Friend, 2004
14. Overtures, edited by David Lloyd-Jones, 2002
15. Orchestral Works 1, edited by James Brooks Kuykendall, 2007
16. Orchestral Works 2, edited by Michael Durnin, 2012
17. Shorter Orchestral Works 1, edited by David Lloyd-Jones, 2009
18. Shorter Orchestral Works 2, edited by David Lloyd-Jones, 2007
19. Chamber Music, edited by Hugh Macdonald, 2008
20. Instrumental Music, edited by Michael Aston, 2003
21. Music for Brass, edited by Elgar Howarth, 2006
22. Shakespeare Film Suites, edited by James Brooks Kuykendall, 2010
23. Henry V: A Shakespeare Scenario arr. Palmer, edited by David Lloyd-Jones, 1999
24. William Walton: A Catalogue of Works, compiled and edited by Stewart Craggs, 2014

1

Troilus and Cressida *(Vol. 1)*

Stuart Hutchinson

Troilus and Cressida, William Walton's only full-length opera, received its premiere at the Royal Opera House, Covent Garden, on 3 December 1954. Walton produced a substantially revised and more compact version for a new production there in 1976, in which much of the soprano role of Cressida was transposed down, enabling it to be sung by a mezzo-soprano. In January 1995, nearly twelve years after the composer's death, the opera was restaged in Leeds by Opera North in the present form; this constitutes the revised 1976 version, but with the original soprano key structure of the 1954 version restored. It was in this 'Opera North version', which was commissioned jointly by the William Walton Trust and Oxford University Press, that the full score of the opera received its first publication in the WWE.

Genesis

In his 1936 critical analysis of the Viola Concerto, Donald Tovey declared, 'Walton's dramatic power has asserted itself in oratorio; but its unobtrusive presence in this thoughtful piece of purely instrumental music is more significant than any success in an oratorio', and went on to say that it was 'obvious he ought to write an opera'.[1] Walton had failed to respond to the challenge, partly because at that time the chances of success with a new British opera were slim.

By the late 1940s Walton was in danger of being overshadowed by Benjamin Britten, his junior by eleven years. From 1939 to 1942 Britten had lived in Canada and the United States, during which time he completed *Les Illuminations*, the *Sinfonia da Requiem*, the String Quartet No. 1, the operetta *Paul Bunyan*, and various choral works and songs. During the same period Walton mainly contented himself with writing music for the Ministry of Information's propaganda films, including *The Next of Kin* (1941) and *The First of the Few* (1942). In fact, though he had been celebrated for earlier success with *Façade* (1922–8), the Concerto for Viola and Orchestra (1929), *Belshazzar's Feast* (1931), Symphony No. 1 (1935), *Crown Imperial* (1936), and the overture *Scapino* (1940), the one major work that Walton had produced since the Concerto for Violin and Orchestra (1939) was the ballet *The Quest* (1943), thus far his only original work for the stage.

Britten returned to England in 1942, and there followed a succession of major first performances, culminating in the Sadler's Wells premiere of *Peter Grimes* on 7 June 1945, an event which brought him immediate international acclaim and aroused new hope for British opera. Britten built on this achievement by producing two further operas (albeit of chamber proportions) in quick succession, *The Rape of Lucretia* in 1946 and *Albert Herring* in 1947. In September 1949 the recently established Covent

Garden Opera Company gave its first premiere of a new British opera when Arthur Bliss's *The Olympians*, to a libretto by J. B. Priestley, was produced. Vaughan Williams subsequently scored a partial success with his long-contemplated 'morality' *The Pilgrim's Progress*, premiered in 1951. Walton clearly had to enter the field. In 1941 he had considered writing an opera to a libretto by the critic and composer Cecil Gray on the subject of Gesualdo, the sixteenth-century Italian composer who had supposedly arranged the murder of his first wife. This was abandoned, as was a later vague arrangement with Dylan Thomas.

It was the BBC that finally precipitated events when Victor Hely-Hutchinson, its director of music, wrote to Walton on 8 February 1947:

> The BBC has decided to commission an opera and would like you to compose it. I do not at all know how you are placed as regards time, but I very much hope that you will be interested in the idea.[2]

The BBC envisaged a work for studio performance, to be broadcast on the newly created Third Programme. It was to be delivered within eighteen months, and the fee proposed was £500. It was an offer that Walton felt he could not refuse.

Libretto

The opera's genesis was unusually protracted. Walton and his librettist Christopher Hassall experienced agonizing difficulties while collaborating on the first opera that either of them had undertaken. The somewhat surprising suggestion of Hassall as librettist was probably made by the conductor Stanford Robinson, at that time head of BBC Opera.

Hassall's collaboration and the choice of subject were encouraged by Walton's long-time companion Viscountess Wimborne, and an initial meeting was arranged in the early months of 1947. Another took place in mid-June, after which Alice Wimborne wrote to Hassall:

> It is important I believe that you should not be perplexed or worried at the unbounc-ing ball and equally that he [Walton] should think you are quite unmoved by procras-tination! so that he doesn't fear being, as it were, pushed in to anything because a decision is expected of him....I am positive that your views on what is required are right[;] the difficulty is to find the perfect subject. Many that would suit his music have other drawbacks, as a case in point, Byron. For apart from suitability for *him*, the story or plot must be so easy and clear and flowing and scenic. Troilus and C. has got that. And it's got, as we agreed, the Manon lady which he seems obviously to prefer to the Juliets![3]

News of Walton's opera, and the choice of subject, was announced in the press in January 1948. Three months later Alice Wimborne died, and in December of the same year Walton, while acting as a delegate to an international Performing Right Society conference in Buenos Aires, met and married the 22-year-old Susana Gil Passo. She was to find the first six years of their married life dominated by the composition of the opera.

After Byron, Volpone, Antony and Cleopatra, Duke Melveric, and other ideas had been rejected as possible subjects, Walton and Hassall finally chose the story of Troilus and Cressida.[4] Chaucer's epic poem *Troilus and Criseyde*—taken from Boccaccio's *Il Filostrato*—was preferred to Shakespeare's play as the primary source. Hassall's own introduction to the 1954 published libretto provides a valuable insight into the choice of subject and source.[5]

From its conception in the summer of 1947 to the completed orchestration, dated 13 September 1954, it took Walton and Hassall some seven and a half years to complete the opera. Much of this time was spent in an intensive reworking of the libretto (it was over six years before an ending was finally agreed) and in characteristically self-critical rewriting on Walton's part. Hassall's experience in stagecraft was chiefly that of an ex-actor and book writer for seven Ivor Novello musicals between 1935 and 1949; Walton was to make jibes about this on more than one occasion. Hassall was also author of some rather flowery poetry. Passages now regarded as among the weakest in the opera's libretto, for instance the love duet in Act II, took Walton the longest to compose. Hassall's writing—at once romantic, high-flown, and archaic—regularly posed a problem. One original line, later cut from the libretto, ran, 'There stand the satyr-faced plump urns that spill superfluous oleander for the sparrow rootling for grubs among festoons of flowers.'

Composition

Writing in 1955 of the opera's composition, Walton stated that he had wanted to achieve an 'English *bel canto*',[6] and he clearly drew upon models from the Italian grand opera tradition. When Hassall failed to provide either inspiring drama or text, or both, Walton would refer him to specific scenes and arias in Verdi's *Un ballo in maschera*, *Rigoletto*, *Otello*, *Aida*, and others—even to precise timings. He also repeatedly alluded to Cressida as a 'Manon figure'. Significantly it was this reluctance to break away from the set pieces, forms, and precedents of grand opera which was to become a recurrent theme in contemporary criticism. Some felt that Walton had denied his true self and produced an Italianate score of the post-verismo school. Cecil Smith, reviewing the premiere in *Opera* magazine, wrote: 'Perhaps the closest parallel to *Troilus and Cressida* in over-all treatment is the vocal-cum-symphonic style of such 1914 Italian poetic operas as Zandonai's *Francesca da Rimini* and Montemezzi's *L'Amore dei Tre Re*.'[7]

As work progressed, it became clear that the project was altogether too grand for a radio studio performance and in 1950 the BBC generously ceded the premiere to the Royal Opera House, Covent Garden, while paying Walton and Hassall their commission fees.

Following the death of George VI in February 1952 Walton wrote to Alan Frank, head of the music department at Oxford University Press, that he was unlikely to complete the opera before February 1953. He had scored some 80 pages of Act II, and his long-standing amanuensis Roy Douglas had begun making a piano reduction, but other interests were presenting themselves: 'Presumably I might get a Coronation March. When will it be? The title might be *Orb and Sceptre*. How useful is Henry V!!'[8]

Completion by February 1953 was optimistic. Walton worked steadily on Act II, all the while struggling with Hassall on the unresolved elements of the libretto. In April he wrote to Alan Frank: 'About the middle of June we go to stay in a cottage Larry [Laurence Olivier] has lent us and I hope to complete the score of Act I and possibly Act II....I've not proceeded with Act III and the libretto is still not at all satisfactory. When in the country Larry will be able to work at it with Christopher and myself and we should get it set.'[9]

In his desire to strengthen the libretto Walton even surreptitiously enlisted the advice of W. H. Auden who, with Chester Kallman, was a house guest from September to December 1953 at Casa Cirillo on Ischia, an island in the Bay of Naples, where the Waltons were then living. He wrote to Frank:

> I'll send some more of Act I in a few days, the scoring is progressing fairly fast in spite of having to do a lot of rewriting.
>
> The libretto of Act III is still not satisfactory but I'm having a 'go' at it with Auden who is here till Dec. & I think we shall at last get it [really] right.[10]

A draft of the Act III ensemble (a single sheet of typescript) was found by Edward Mendelson, Auden's literary executor, in the poet's posthumous papers:
The quintet opens this way—

> Among fierce foes, a maid,
> Weak, lonely and afraid;
> No succour ever came,
> No hope was to be seen.
> O what was she to do?
> When Diomede, she knew,
> Would take her for his Queen,
> And save her from worse shame.[11]

All of Act I had been despatched safely to England by January 1954 and Hassall, having at first been affronted by Auden's involvement, now produced a new version of Act III. Walton wrote to Frank, 'The Auden intervention seems to have put him on his mettle & he has produced something better than either A[uden]'s solution or the previous version.'[12] On 1 February 1954 Frank outlined the situation to Walter Legge (who was interested in the recording prospects for Columbia):
The position is as follows—

Act I   Entirely finished in full score
Act II   Scene 1—virtually finished in full score
          Scene 2—William hopes this will be scored by the end of February
Act III   A small part exists in score and a larger part is written but not scored. I think
          there is still quite a chunk at the end to be done, maybe 15–20 minutes, but
          William seems fairly confident that it will be finished and scored by end July.

But the truth was that Hassall's progress had been halted by a protracted illness, and it wasn't until 19 March that he was able to report to Frank, 'I've written to Wm. everyday for the last three days....I'm devoting my time exclusively to *Troilus*.'

Hassall visited Walton on Ischia some time between April and May 1954, knowing that an agreement had been reached between the Royal Opera House and OUP proposing 3 December 1954 as the date for the premiere. Walton subsequently reported to Frank, 'Chris' visit was very fruitful & he has now done a really splendid closing sc[ene] if the music will only come up to scratch. It's getting on, but there is quite a lot to do & some tough nuts to crack.'[13]

Meanwhile, between March and July 1954, Alan Frank organized a number of play-throughs in London of the material completed up to that point; these were given on two pianos (one of them certainly played by the composer Franz Reizenstein), with Viola Warr singing. Sir Malcolm Sargent, rather inexperienced in opera but very much associated with Walton's music, was by now engaged to conduct the premiere in December, and was present at a second play-through on 5 April. The sessions were recorded and the tapes dispatched to Walton on Ischia.

These recordings were incomplete, as a satisfactory conclusion to the opera had still not been found by librettist and composer. Walton had reported to Frank on 4 April 1954, 'At the moment of writing, I've completed about 15 mins of Act III which only means some 5 or 6 pages of score and [am] about to begin on the crucial and very difficult love scene between Cress and Dio.' Amazingly, it wasn't until July of that year that the libretto was completed. Sargent received the finished score of Act I only on 1 September; in October Act III had to be sent to him in Tokyo.

Walton finished his score on 13 September 1954 and shortly after wrote, with evident relief, to Alan Frank, 'Thank heavens I've finished, and by the date I gave you, in fact a few days sooner. We return to London on the 27th, leaving here on Sunday. I hope to contact Laszlo in Rome, and see how her English has progressed.'[14] Magda Laszlo was the Hungarian soprano who had been engaged to sing the role of Cressida.

The 1954 full score

Apart from the agonies experienced in finalizing the libretto, the practical aspects of the collaboration gave constant trouble to authors and publisher alike. Communication required copious correspondence, since Hassall lived in north London and Walton on Ischia, where there were no private telephones. OUP arranged for the construction of large cardboard boxes to send packages of Walton's manuscript between Ischia and London for photographing and copying. Transportation took up to six weeks, and Walton's nervous dispatches to Alan Frank were frequent:

> I'm worried, needlessly I hope, at not hearing of the arrival of the last 30–40 pages of Act I. I sent them at the end of Nov. & I need hardly say that we are properly sunk if they've got lost, as I've no notes of the last part as it was more or less entirely re-written....
>
> I've also not heard anything from Chris, which is now holding up the completion of Act II so I'm pottering around with bits & pieces of Act III.[15]

Having photographed the autograph full score of Acts I and II in London, OUP sent a copy to Walton on Ischia. On 21 January 1954 Walton reported to Alan Frank:

The last pages of Act I score arrived today. The box had come by steamer and I had a spot of bother with the customs and until I['d] written the staff were being a bit difficult, but a 100 lire settled it. I will continue to send the Mss as I've always done and not in the box. At the moment there is going to [be] a slight (?I hope only) hiatus. This Interlude (Act III:) [*recte* II] (which has always been my nightmare) is proving difficult, but once it is past the rest of the Act, all of which is musically (not scored) complete should not prove to be too arduous.... The alterations are considerable and I think a vast improvement.

Finally, despairing both of the boxes and customs officials, Walton resorted to simpler but more risky means: 'Please return the rest by ordinary registered book post, open both ends, much quicker and cleaner, as the Customs & Currency boys opened this lot in England, to see how many pound notes were between the sheets, left all the black sealing wax inside with a consequent ruin of many pages.'[16]

Sections of the manuscript were photographed as they were received by OUP in London. Walton's characteristic use of pencil did not make for clarity. When Guthrie Foote, OUP's production manager, observed diplomatically, 'Our production people are finding it difficult to produce your MS and it would be a great help if you could use a pencil that gives a rather clearer outline,'[17] Walton, ever practical, replied, 'If you would send me copies of the worst & best pages, I could possibly diagnose where the fault in my script lies.'[18]

A well-intentioned OUP solution soon proved to be the cause of the first of many subsequent problems. Prior to the photographic process, a number of people were employed to 'improve' the unclear noteheads in Walton's autograph, and this frequently compounded the problem of arriving at an accurate reading.

Preparation of the 1954 vocal score

The vocal score reduction was made by Roy Douglas and Franz Reizenstein, the latter working principally on the end of Act I, the first scene of Act II, and the beginning of Act III. Douglas began work on the reduction of his share of Act III in about June 1953. Following normal practice, Douglas's work on the vocal score was paid for by Walton himself, the publisher making deductions from the composer's royalties. An exception to this process was Walton's own reduction of part of Act III (original manuscript vocal score, pages 59–77). This was made on Ischia as late as August 1954 and copied in London. The urgency to complete the opera may well explain Walton's rare involvement in this way.

Indications of instrumentation were included in the first rehearsal copies. Remarkably, complete rehearsal material, including cuts and revisions, was printed by Halstan as late as October 1954.

Casting and production team

While composing the principal roles of Troilus and Cressida, Walton originally had Nicolai Gedda and Elisabeth Schwarzkopf in mind.[19] Schwarzkopf is mentioned in correspondence with David Webster, the general administrator of the Royal Opera House, as early as March 1953.[20] Although her availability was problematic, Walton was at first determined that she should sing the premiere: 'I want her [Schwarzkopf] even if only for the first three perfs. Gedda for Troilus (though I'm not absolutely sold on him, he seems to be just slightly lightweight—but Walter [Legge] swears he can get through everything). Uhde for Diomede, Parry Jones for Pandarus.'[21] But by January 1954, with the premiere now set for early autumn, it was clear that Schwarzkopf's commitments in America meant that an alternative Cressida was inevitable. Walter Legge, Schwarzkopf's husband, wrote to Alan Frank,

> I think it is only fair to warn you that if Willie wants Elisabeth to sing the first per-formance of his opera, there is no hope of it being done this year. She leaves England on 14 October for America, and will almost certainly be away from this country until March 1955. If you can get any information out of the Covent Garden nunnery, it might help.[22]

But Alan Frank had already learnt the truth independently and had written to Walton at Casa Cirillo,

> Through a leakage of information on Covent Garden's part, for which Webster blames someone else, I heard for the first time today that Schwarzkopf will not be available. It is perfectly true that she is going to America much earlier than you thought, i.e. about mid-October.[23]

Interestingly Frank goes on, 'You know of course about the Olivier situation ... which is simply that he may have a film at that time and therefore not be able to produce T and C.' The final choice of producer, on Christopher Hassall's recommendation, was the experienced George Devine, who that autumn was directing the premiere of Lennox Berkeley's *Nelson* at Sadler's Wells. The set designer was Sir Hugh Casson, with Malcolm Pride designer of costumes.

Walton, greatly disappointed by the Schwarzkopf predicament, at first considered delaying the premiere until May 1955.[24] Alan Frank was largely instrumental in propos-ing alternatives:

> I had long talks over the weekend about casting with Christopher, Legge (who was extremely helpful), Enid Blech in the absence of Harry, Urbach and Joan Ingpen ... with-out exception, all these opinions said that [Wilma] Lipp was an excellent light colora-tura, but absolutely unsuitable for a part written for Schwarzkopf. Everyone in fact seemed astonished that she should ever have been thought of. And the whole episode leaves one rather horrified at the casual way in which apparently Webster and/or his Covent Garden associates treat casting. Anyway, it is a lesson for us all. Apart from Enid's staggering but doubtless impracticable suggestion of Callas...[25]

After considering many alternative suggestions—including Lisa Styx, Hilde Gueden, Eleanor Steber, Hilde Zadek, Astrid Varnay, Martha Mödl, Sena Jurinac, and Gré Brouwenstijn—the Hungarian soprano Magda Laszlo was favoured to create the role of Cressida. Alan Frank and Lord Harewood, who was in charge of casting at Covent Garden, had recently heard Laszlo sing in a concert performance of Dallapiccola's *Il Prigioniero* at the Royal Festival Hall. By May 1954, under pressure to cast the role,

Walton telegraphed a decision: 'Please ascertain Magda Laszlo's English good enough for Cressida[.] If so fix her with Webster my first preference.'[26]

The Troilus situation was no less disappointing. Sections from Act I were sent to Nicolai Gedda in February 1954, but three months later Walton reported to Alan Frank: 'I had this cable from Walter [Legge] "Gedda wants to sing Tro[ilus] but has to do his forty days Military Service in Sweden. Suggest you write King of Sweden who loves music asking him to intervene on your behalf." '[27]

By the end of May, Peter Pears had been engaged to sing Pandarus (on the original joint suggestion of Malcolm Sargent and Christopher Hassall), and the Covent Garden company members Otakar Kraus and Frederick Dalberg were selected to sing Diomede and Calkas. Geraint Evans, Forbes Robinson, and Monica Sinclair, also members of the company, completed the cast. For the role of Troilus alternative choices to Nicolai Gedda were already being considered, including the distinguished oratorio singer Richard Lewis and the German Richard Holm. When Laszlo's contract was confirmed in August 1954, Walton was understandably nervous: 'I'm delighted about Laszlo but wish a tenor was forthcoming.' It was not until November 1954, one month before the premiere, that Richard Lewis was finally contracted to create the role.

Rehearsals and premiere

The date of the 1954 first performance was moved several times, first from January to mid-October, then to mid-November, before finally being fixed for Friday 3 December. Friday was not considered a good day for a world premiere; at that time it was too late for 'copy' in the Sunday press. Walton's supporter Ernest Newman, the revered music critic of the *Sunday Times*, who had advised on Hassall's libretto as far back as 1948, complained to Alan Frank, 'I'm planning a grand Romantic à la young Berlioz protest against Troilus and Cressida being produced on a Friday. My idea is to cut my throat in the foyer just before the performance begins. Or do you think that might hurt me more than Covent Garden?'[28] Frank replied, 'Two suicides in one evening, one on the stage, and one in the foyer, will certainly make a nice story for your colleagues of the press.'[29]

Walton was fully aware that between autumn 1954 and January 1955 three other new British operas would be produced for the first time—Britten's *The Turn of the Screw* (September 1954, Venice Festival), Berkeley's *Nelson*, and Tippett's *The Midsummer Marriage*. Walton, Berkeley, and Tippett, all in their fifties, were each writing their first opera. The 1954–5 winter season was a demanding one for the Royal Opera House, with company resources particularly stretched by the proximity of three large-scale productions: the world premiere of *Troilus and Cressida* on 3 December was followed only six days later by the first of four performances of Wagner's *Tristan und Isolde* (conducted by Rudolf Kempe), with the premiere of Tippett's *The Midsummer Marriage* on 27 January 1955.

Chorus rehearsals of Act I began in spring 1954. During ensemble rehearsals recordings were made and sent to the composer on Ischia. Walton possessed a primitive Grundig tape recorder that had originally belonged to Hans Werner Henze, an Ischian neighbour. The process was not entirely satisfactory, and Walton complained in a telegram: 'tape useless wrong tempi throughout'.[30]

As rehearsals progressed in London, Walton made a number of revisions and cuts in order to create greater tension and swifter progress in the action. Many of these revisions, particularly those to Act I, are evident in the autograph full score.[31] Orchestral rehearsals began on 29 October. The one on 2 November was devoted to a first read-through of Act I, and Walton, Roy Douglas, and OUP's Christopher Morris (in the absence of Alan Frank) attended. Douglas had copied the parts for the early part of the act, and while that section was played all went well. But the moment that a second copyist's work took over, mistakes came thick and fast, and pandemonium broke out. Eventually Sargent gave up and the rehearsal came to a halt. Four days later the composer vented his displeasure in an eloquent letter to Geoffrey Cumberlege, secretary to the delegates of OUP.[32] The situation was saved by the staff of the Covent Garden Library, who immediately prepared an alternative set of parts to replace those of the defective copyist.

Matters were further exacerbated by Sargent's demanding changes to the orchestration. Richard Temple Savage, librarian at the Royal Opera House and bass clarinettist in the orchestra, recalled that the alterations were legion:

> Every afternoon after the rehearsal all the material…had to be carried up four flights to the library where Walton would join me with the score to look through all Sargent's recommendations and make alterations which we then had to transfer to the parts. Sargent had a particular aversion to anything written for two harps and was constantly cutting out bits of the second harp part. One day Walton came upstairs looking particularly disgruntled and suddenly burst out: 'I'm not making any more alterations. It's my fucking opera and I'm going to write some *more* for the second harp!' which he proceeded to do and this seemed to have the desired effect.[33]

OUP sent copies of the rehearsal vocal score in advance to leading critics, a number of whom were also invited to the final dress rehearsal. Seven performances in all were given between 3 December 1954 and 14 January 1955, two of which were relayed by the BBC.[34] The reaction of the musical press was highly respectful, even enthusiastic, but flecked with misgivings. It was widely acknowledged that Walton had produced a skilled and effective opera in the grand manner, but his reliance on old formulae and uncertain response to the drama came in for adverse comment, as did aspects of Hassall's libretto.

Revisions and 1955 revival

Following the first run of performances at Covent Garden, Walton made further revisions to the opera. While revising the score Walton stayed at Lowndes Cottage, the London home left to him by Alice Wimborne. Between January and February 1955 OUP engaged a team of copyists to transfer the revisions into the parts. They were led by Roy Douglas, who wrote to OUP on 7 March:

> Herewith pp. 67 to 100, being the remainder of Act II Sc. 1 of Vocal Score. This is the scene that was supposed to contain few alterations! As you will see, there are very few pages that haven't some tiny change in expression marks or tempo, or words.…Also some of the pages include a little revision in the accompanying harmonies.[35]

During March and April 1955 the Royal Opera took its production of *Troilus and Cressida* on tour to Glasgow, Edinburgh, Leeds (broadcast), Manchester, and Coventry, under Reginald Goodall, one of its staff conductors. It was at the Manchester performance on 6 April that the complete set of revisions was implemented. Frank had reported to Lyle Dowling at OUP, New York, on 3 February: 'Walton has only just completed making quite extensive revisions to the whole work. Especially Act I is much improved by what he has done in the way of tightening and increasing the tension. The revised version of the opera will not be heard in London until April.' New sets of vocal scores and chorus parts, incorporating the revisions, were promised for the forthcoming American premieres.

The revised score, with cuts in each act, was given at a second group of performances at the Royal Opera House on 25 and 28 April and 3 May 1955. Alan Frank was able to report to Dowling, 'The performance last night took approximately two minutes off each Act, and Sir William likes this shorter duration.'[36] Further revisions were made in May to three sections of Act III, including a reworking of the final moments which, as the autograph and BBC recording of the premiere reveal, originally ended *pianissimo*.

Two additional performances took place at Covent Garden in July 1955, again conducted by Reginald Goodall. Alan Frank advised David Webster of further changes:

> I think that Sir William may already have told you about the new ending, but I think I ought to send you a written note. The soldiers are entirely eliminated, so that Cressida is alone on the stage at the end of Act III. Your orchestral material has already had the new ending put in, or is in the process of having it done now.[37]

On 15 July Frank wrote encouragingly to Walton on Ischia: 'Your scored up revision of the last pages has a noticeably beneficial effect on "audience reaction", which after all is quite important.'[38] But previously he noted that he had found the revival 'pretty rough and not very ready'.[39]

Five further performances were given at Covent Garden between December 1955 and February 1956; Ernest Newman reviewed the December revival and declared it 'first-class'. A second tour followed, visiting Cardiff, Birmingham, Liverpool, and Manchester. It is interesting that W. H. Auden who, after all, had given substantial advice on the libretto, had not seen a performance of the opera by August 1955—at least, he declined to write an article about it on those grounds.[40]

America and Italy

Walton and his wife attended the American premiere on 7 October 1955 in San Francisco. Conducted by Erich Leinsdorf, it was tremendously well received by the press. On the same trip, Walton lectured on 'Opera in England' at the University of Southern California, and was present at the final rehearsals for the New York premiere at City Center in October, conducted by Joseph Rosenstock. The New York Music Critics' Circle voted *Troilus and Cressida* the best new opera heard during the 1955 season. In the New York production an optional cut in Act III was approved by Walton; the cut was marked in the orchestral parts, and instructions were subsequently sent to the Royal Opera, La Scala, and Sir Malcolm Sargent for its future implementation. Walton attended the final rehearsals for the Italian premiere (in Italian) at La Scala in December 1955, at a time when he was already at work on the Concerto for Violoncello and Orchestra. In Italy 'local' changes were made to the score without Walton's involvement, including excisions from the Act II trio.

At the time of the Milan premiere on 12 January 1956, *Troilus and Cressida* and Britten's *Peter Grimes* were the only two British operas to have been performed at La Scala in its 150-year history. Walton reported that the performance had received a 'normal mixed reception from the first night audience with some whistles, but not many in evidence' and that it was 'much better on the second night'.[41] He was impressed by the conductor Nino Sanzogno, but Alan Frank later recalled: 'Of all the conductors who have done this opera, he was best pleased by [Erich] Leinsdorf.'[42]

Publication of the 1955 vocal score

All the revisions made following the Covent Garden premiere were incorporated in the engraved vocal score, published by OUP on 15 December 1955. This carries the credit, 'Vocal score by Roy Douglas and Franz Reizenstein'. Engraving had begun two months after the premiere, in February 1955, and Roy Douglas read the proofs; Walton preferred only to answer questions. On his instruction, details of the instrumentation were not included. This continued until September 1955, when Douglas wrote to OUP: 'Here are the first and second proofs of the vocal score … this seems to complete my work on "Troilus" after more than three years, but I can hardly believe it.' OUP ordered that copies of the original hand-copied rehearsal vocal scores should be destroyed.

Walton's 1954 full score was never engraved. Mysteriously, many of the discrepancies that had bedevilled the first orchestral rehearsals remained uncorrected in the autograph, in photocopies of the autograph (used as hire material), and in the orchestral parts. The published libretto, however, was completely revised and reprinted.

About this time Alan Frank drily noted to a colleague, 'As you know, I am interested in, and rather worried by, the problems that arise over the financial aspect of publishing and launching a new Opera under present day conditions.'[43]

Revisions 1955–1963

Walton's correspondence with OUP from 1957 to 1960 reveals a deep despondency over the fortunes of *Troilus and Cressida*. For a concert given by the Los Angeles Philharmonic Orchestra, conducted by Alfred Wallenstein, in the Hollywood Bowl on 8 August 1961 he made concert endings for two of the three Cressida arias, 'Slowly it all comes back' (from Act I, figs. 69–84), 'How can I sleep?' (Act II, figs. 22–31), and 'Diomede!' (Act III, fig. 98 to the end). For a revival of the work in five performances at Covent Garden in April 1963, Walton made further revisions to all three acts, cutting some eight minutes of music. These cuts, together with subsequent alterations, were retained in the 1976 revision of the opera. In this connection, Walton wrote in August 1962 to Christopher Morris:

> I enclose a sheet of proposed cuts in 'T&C' [Act III]. I've sent it also to M[alcolm] S[argent] & Chris[topher] Has[sall] to see if they approve. Some time you & Alan

[Frank] might look into them also. Personally I think they may be a great help in tightening up the opera.[44]

At the same time Walton also ratified the cuts in Act II that had been made in 1956 at La Scala.[45]

For the OUP proofreaders Roy Douglas and Michael Rowland, who were preparing material for the 1963 revival, the prospect of tinkering with the orchestral parts yet again was daunting. As Douglas wryly observed to Christopher Morris: 'Whoever makes the adjustments to the parts is going to have a tricky time, because I have been obliged in some instances to include a few bars before and after the actual cut or the new scoring.... Oh, these composers with their second thoughts, what a lot of complications they cause.'[46] But Walton and Sargent were both well pleased with this revival. Christopher Morris wrote to Michael Rowland: 'I went to a rehearsal and Sargent told me that the cuts were absolutely accurate.... The composer has made one further small cut. The two bars before figure 43 in Act II are to be taken out.'[47]

The Australian soprano Marie Collier sang Cressida in the acclaimed Covent Garden revival of 1963. Walton was 'tremendously impressed with her' and was keen that she should be engaged for the Adelaide Festival in the spring of the following year; Alan Frank thought her 'the best Cressida so far'.[48] Tragically, Christopher Hassall collapsed and died while travelling to one of these performances.

Revisions 1972–1976

For the composer's 70th birthday celebrations in 1972, the Royal Opera planned a new production of the opera. Once again, it proved impossible to find a suitable Cressida and the occasion was postponed. Walton, however, began more revision at this time. Act II was the first to be revised, and was performed at a Henry Wood Promenade Concert on 14 September 1972, with André Previn conducting the London Symphony Orchestra and the soprano Jill Gomez singing Cressida. During 1973 Walton made more revisions and cuts to Acts I and III. Some were downward transpositions in the role of Cressida for the distinguished mezzo-soprano Janet Baker, who had now been cast in the planned Covent Garden production. The majority were more significant changes affecting about half an hour of music. These included straightforward 'clean' cuts; cuts, with some minor rewriting of linking passages; 'partial' cuts, such as the removal of a chorus element while other material remained the same; vocal rewriting for improved dramatic effect, often reducing repetition; and text changes. In particular, the role of Cressida's father, the priest Calkas, was greatly diminished.[49]

In making these revisions, Walton was frequently guided by the producer Colin Graham who has recalled:

> I would say that at least 75 per cent of the alterations (apart from soprano v. mezzo) were William's second thoughts and improvements: the essential tightenings-up, etc.; I remember well our lengthy discussions on all those.... I guess that many things happened because of discussions over 'hold-ups' and red-herrings: moments that were too elongated, that went nowhere, or required people to stand about and just sing to no dramatic purpose.

Graham remembers the Act II love duet as a stumbling-block:

William got very uptight over the libretto for this: he felt it was just a series of literary statements that followed no course, that the characters were not developing their burgeoning love interest through the words *and* that they were darned difficult to set.[50]

This was all part of Walton's reworking process that had been going on since the opera's initial completion in September 1954. In total, some 930 bars of the original version were affected: 517 in cuts, 195 in rewriting, and 218 in direct transposition. The 1976 version contained only 17 bars of wholly new material. Walton's one personal regret was the loss of the ensemble 'Put Off the Serpent Girdle' at the start of Act II; with Cressida's handmaidens having been cut elsewhere in the scene it was hard to justify this beautiful number. Happily, he later ensured that it survived as a separate publication, with a second verse provided by Paul Dehn, the librettist for his only other opera, *The Bear*.

John Rutter, another OUP composer, was engaged to incorporate the changes for the 1976 new production, supplying revised full score pages for parts of Acts I and III. Meeting Walton at the Ritz Hotel, London, for just one hour, Rutter found the composer to be 'laconic' about the process, adding just a few slurs and accents. Walton later wrote to Rutter, thanking him for his 'expert carpentry'.[51]

The origination of the full score of the '1976' version was in progress by October 1974, while the proofreaders and copyists brought the orchestral parts up to date. Even at that stage they unveiled yet more problems.

In December 1975 Colin Graham visited Walton on Ischia, prompting further changes from the composer. Walton subsequently wrote to Graham: 'Here are I hope the last of the corrections and alterations for T.C.... I'm full of gloom at the prospects of T & C. There's not enough rehearsal time and worst of all there's no tenor unless Cov. gar. are going to hold out against Solti about [Alberto] Remedios.'[52]

Once again, there was a crisis in finding a suitable Troilus—even by February one had not been found. More revisions followed in April. As Robin Langley of OUP reported: 'Walton and Janet Baker have been in touch over the upper range of her part. Unfortunately this has resulted in yet another crop of cuts and transpositions.'[53]

In July 1976 Langley informed André Previn, who had been engaged to conduct the new production, that the composer appeared to have finished his revisions and that he now enclosed a 'fully corrected and up-to-date score'.[54] In the event, illness prevented Previn from conducting the performances of this revised version, which opened at Covent Garden on 12 November 1976. His place was taken by Lawrence Foster in the new production by Colin Graham, designed by Christopher Morley and Ann Curtis.

1976 version full score and vocal score

The vocal score of the 1976 version was published in 1980. After listening to the EMI recording, made during live performances at the Royal Opera House in 1976, Walton introduced further minor changes, and one or two pages were restored to the original soprano register. Even after the first proofs had been read he was still making changes. Little wonder that OUP were again nervous about the expense! As Christopher Morris wrote to Walton:

I had to make a summary of expenses to date for the revival of *Troilus and Cressida* and you will see from the enclosed that OUP are doing their bit towards making it a success. By the time we have dealt with the final revisions and the orchestral parts, it will be up to £10,000.[55]

The WWE edition

At the time of the 1976 Covent Garden staging it was widely considered that Walton had succeeded in creating greater dramatic tension in the revised version. However, commentators also noted the adverse effect of dispensing with one significantly strong ingredient of the original version, the dramatic soprano tessitura. In certain instances it seemed that transposition or rewriting had compromised the score. For example, in the love duet at the end of the second act, the original had had the voices overlapping in canon ('There howls the wind...'), yet essential changes for the mezzo range destroyed this. In 1955 Paul Müller had written, 'With this Cressida the opera stage has acquired a soprano role to rank with the great ones of the past.'[56] After the revised version of 1976, Walton's respected biographer Michael Kennedy wrote, 'Walton made a cardinal error in transposing the part for mezzo. If Cressida is to have any credibility, it must be as the dramatic soprano of his original conception.'[57]

Though encouraged by the favourable critical reception of the new version of his opera on dramatic grounds, Walton remained sensitive to the question of Cressida as soprano or mezzo-soprano. The vocal score of the 1976 version might well have been considered to represent his final thoughts on the opera in all respects. Yet, even after its publication in 1980, Walton (and publisher OUP on his behalf) sanctioned the restoration of substantial sections of the soprano tessitura. Replying to enquiries from the conductor David Lloyd-Jones at Opera North, Christopher Morris wrote in April 1981, 'The first version no longer exists and all Walton's cuts are permanent as in the new vocal score.' But he went on to say, 'As you know Walton has pushed up one or two of the passages that were put down for Janet Baker.'[58] Sir John Pritchard canvassed the use of soprano for a possible production in Cologne or at La Monnaie, Brussels, and Tony Palmer's ITV film profile of Walton, *At the Haunted End of the Day*, featured the soprano Yvonne Kenny as Cressida. In 1981 restoration of the original 1954 keys was allowed for the soprano Jill Gomez when the opera was given concert performances by the Chelsea Opera Group.

This history of revision led the William Walton Trust and OUP to commission yet another version in 1994. This version takes the 1976 full and vocal score as its basis, but restores the original soprano tessitura of Cressida, and is representative, therefore, of the composer's wishes, prior to his death in 1983. In 1995 it was used by Opera North for a major new production, and for the subsequent recording, by the English Northern Philharmonia and Opera North Chorus, conducted by Richard Hickox. It thereafter became the only version of the opera authorized by the William Walton Trust and OUP for performance. The 1976 material (unpublished full score and published vocal score) has been taken as representing Walton's final wishes as to musical text, libretto, stage directions, and tempo and dynamic markings. Where changes in 1976 had been made solely for the downward transposition of Cressida's part, the 1954 soprano text is restored, using the autograph (and photocopies of it) as the source, but consulting also the 1954 vocal score.

The British Library possesses a copy of the full score material prepared by OUP at the time of the rehearsals for the premiere. This mixed set of conductor's scores includes Act III as used by Sir Malcolm Sargent, who conducted the premiere, and Act II as used by Reginald Goodall.

NOTES

1. Donald Francis Tovey, *Essays in Musical Analysis*, Vol. 3 (London, 1936), pp. 220–226.
2. BBC Written Archives, Caversham.
3. Michael Kennedy, *Portrait of Walton* (Oxford, 1989), p. 138.
4. Writing in 'New English Opera', Alan Frank observed that the story of *Troilus and Cressida* was proposed to Walton as a possible operatic subject many years before the war by Sir Thomas Beecham, but that his suggestion referred to Shakespeare's play.
5. None of Chaucer's text is used, and his setting in the Middle Ages has been replaced by that of legendary Troy. The last part of the scenario is entirely original; Shakespeare and Chaucer both leave Cressida's fate and final action undecided.
6. Sleeve note to Walton's 1955 recording of highlights of the opera (Columbia CX1313).
7. Cecil Smith, *Opera*, No. 5 (January 1955), pp. 58–59.
8. 15 February 1952, OUP Archive, Oxford (except where stated, all subsequent quotations are from the OUP Archive). Walton was commissioned to write not only a March, but also a Te Deum with orchestra.
9. 27 April 1953.
10. To Alan Frank, September (?) 1953.
11. Letter from Edward Mendelson to Walton, 17 October 1976. The quintet to which Auden refers became a sextet in the opera.
12. 16 January 1954.
13. 21 May 1954. For fuller details of the writing of the libretto see Scott Price, '"A Lost Child": A Study of the Genesis of *Troilus and Cressida*', in Stewart R. Craggs, ed., *William Walton: Music and Literature* (Aldershot, 1999), pp. 182–208; see also *The Selected Letters of William Walton*, ed. Malcolm Hayes (London, 2002), pp. 183–255.
14. Undated letter, September (?) 1954.
15. 14 January 1954.
16. Walton to Alan Frank, 10 March 1954.
17. 9 April 1952.
18. Undated postcard, postmarked 15 April 1952.
19. Letter from Walton to Alan Frank, 4 April 1954: 'Having written the part with him [Gedda] a great deal in mind partly accounts for the tessitura (his low notes are weak).'
20. Letter from Walton's agent, Ian Hunter, to David Webster, 17 March 1953.
21. Letter to Alan Frank, 16 January 1954.
22. 17 February 1954.
23. 9 February 1954.
24. Letter to Alan Frank, 27 February 1954.
25. 1 March 1954.
26. To Alan Frank, undated (3–17 May 1954?).
27. 21 May 1954.
28. 20 September 1954.

29. 22 September 1954.
30. 1 March 1954.
31. Now housed at the Beinecke Rare Books and Manuscript Library, Yale University.
32. See *Selected Letters*, pp. 255–257.
33. Richard Temple Savage, *A Voice from the Pit: Reminiscences of an Orchestral Musician* (Newton Abbot, 1988), pp. 151–152.
34. The performances were broadcast on 3 December 1954 and 4 January 1955.
35. Letter to Christopher Morris, 7 March 1955.
36. 26 April 1955.
37. 9 June 1955.
38. Letter to Walton, 15 July 1955.
39. Letter to Walton, 11 July 1955.
40. Letter from Walton to Alan Frank, 3 August 1955.
41. Undated letter, probably to Alan Frank.
42. Letter to Lyle Dowling.
43. Letter to Dr Ernst Roth, 16 December 1955.
44. 19 August 1962.
45. See letter from Walton to Alan Frank, 21 September 1962.
46. Letter, 29 January 1963.
47. 19 April 1963.
48. Letter to John Bishop of the University of Adelaide, 23 April 1963.
49. For a fuller account of the 1973 revisions and the 1976 performances, see Kennedy, *Portrait*, pp. 186–189.
50. Fax to Stuart Hutchinson, 8 November 1994, private collection.
51. Letter in the possession of John Rutter.
52. 14 January 1976.
53. Letter to Alan Boustead, copyist, 28 April 1976.
54. 15 July 1976.
55. 26 March 1976.
56. Paul Müller, 'Troilus and Cressida: Two Further Opinions', *Opera*, No. 6 (February 1955), pp. 91–92.
57. Kennedy, *Portrait*, p. 190.
58. 24 April 1981.

PROGRAMME NOTES

The 1954 libretto, published by OUP, contained the following introduction by Christopher Hassall:

The chapter on Chaucer in *The Allegory of Love*, a study of medieval tradition, by C. S. Lewis, provided the first hint for the subject of this Opera. 'Fortunately Chaucer has so emphasised the ruling passion of his heroine that we cannot mistake it', writes the author in his analysis of the character of Criseide. 'It is Fear—the fear of loneliness, of old age, of death, of love, and of hostility.... And from this Fear springs the only positive passion which can be permanent in such a nature, the pitiable longing, more childlike than womanly, for *protection*, for some strong and stable thing that will hide her away and take the burden from her shoulder.' With this one should quote Hazlitt—'a grave, sober, considerate personage, who has an alternate eye to her character, her interest, and her pleasure', and add something of the 'ill-divining soul' of a Cassandra, to compose the elements of the Cressida in this libretto.

Though Troilus first appeared as the lover in the Latin work of the fourth century A.D., his story as part of a triangle with Diomede did not begin to evolve until about the year 1160, when Benoît of Sainte Maure, a troubadour who lived near Poitiers, wrote his contribution to the *Chansons de Geste*. In the middle of the fourteenth century Boccaccio borrowed and developed the story further when he invented Pandarus (then a young man, a cousin of Troilus) in his narrative poem *Il Filostrato*. Soon after this, in the early thirteen-seventies, Chaucer came upon the Italian work and was moved to write his masterpiece *Troylus and Criseide*. Thus the legend as we know it in English had taken almost a thousand years to evolve. If the Opera owes a broad outline of its action to Boccaccio, its greatest debt is to Chaucer—the creator of Pandarus as a light-hearted middle-aged schemer, of 'sudden Diomede', and of the Criseide whose personality (so different from Shakespeare's heroine) first drew attention to the theme.

Despite his Homeric names the world of Chaucer's poem is medieval England with its conception of 'courtly love', a code of manners between the sexes too remote from present-day custom for its followers easily to engage the sympathy and understanding of a modern audience. As I lifted the story out of the Middle Ages and retold it in a setting of legendary Troy, all that was essentially Chaucerian fell away; so that, in addition to the actual text throughout, some of the action would strike Chaucer as not only unfamiliar but foreign to the spirit of his poem.

The rules of courtly love required a go-between in the ordinary course of events. Transfer the story to another period and Pandarus must have a new justification or lose his office. So Cressida is here shown as disillusioned with life and a novice in the temple where her father is high priest. This reinforces her natural diffidence, places her apart from Troilus, and makes needful once again the intervention of a resourceful friend.

The rise of the curtain was suggested by the 23rd stanza of *Troylus and Criseide*, Book One, where a gathering of the people before the Temple of Pallas is described. In the 10th stanza we first hear of Calkas who 'in science so expert was' that he 'knew wel that Troy should destroyed be'. A little later we learn that 'to the Grekes ost ful prively he stol'. That is all we are told about him and his motives. To the situation suggested by these stanzas the libretto adds a new episode, Calkas's elaborate and disastrous attempt to awe the Trojans into submitting while they can still hope for some advantage. This serves to precipitate the crisis in his career, his desertion, from which the tragedy stems, and establishes at the outset the tumultuous public life with which the private life thereafter will be shown in conflict.

Thus launched on a course of its own the libretto was developed, with the order of Chaucer's events rearranged, new details introduced, and the whole compressed within much narrower limits of time, until the latter half of Act III where the Opera bears no relation to the medieval poem. There is nothing of Shakespeare in the libretto, beyond a similarity of situation here and there inevitable in two works derived from the same source.

The sleeve of the 1955 Columbia LP recording of highlights from the opera, under the composer, contained the following note by him:

The theme of this opera commended itself to me because of the human situations which, though set in prehistoric times, are of a universal kind. The story also presents a pattern of contrasted characters such as modern audiences can believe in, which is surely an essential for a contemporary dramatist of any sort, most especially a composer working for the opera house with its demand for clearly defined musical characterization. The conflict, not only between certain of the characters themselves, but by implication between the worlds of private and public life, also lends itself to musical treatment and as a background or climate of feeling likely to engage the sympathetic interest of people today.

Though the score contains what are commonly called motifs, such as the music representing Cressida's scarf (the symbol of her affections—which are transferred from one man to another and back again—which reappears in the tissue of the Interlude in Act II) and the nervous figure symbolizing her instinctive fears, the score is not conceived in the symphonic manner—in the sense that one must apply that term to the music dramas of, say, Wagner or Strauss. The voices follow the fluctuations of mood in the text with a minuteness more characteristic of the Italian than German opera. This closeness of vocal line and verbal phrase has led in many places to orchestration which is relatively light for a work on this scale. If my aim here was a close union of poetic and music drama, it was also my concern to recreate the characters in my own idiom of English *bel canto*, the parts carefully designed to bring out the potentialities of each voice according to its range—in the hope of adding another 'singers' opera' to the repertory.

The programme for the premiere of the 1976 version at the Royal Opera House, Covent Garden, contained the following brief note from Walton:

The part of Cressida was originally written for Elizabeth Schwarzkopf, and therefore contained tessitura too high for Janet Baker, so I have transposed parts of the opera down. In addition, this new production at Covent Garden provided a golden opportunity to make a few small cuts which I have had in mind for some years.

2

The Bear *(Vol. 2)*

Michael Burden

The Bear is the second of Walton's two operas and his only comedy. Based on the vaudeville of the same name by the Russian playwright Anton Chekhov, it had its premiere at the 20th Aldeburgh Festival, in the Jubilee Hall, on 3 June 1967.

In the first half of the 1960s, Walton was emerging from his 60th birthday celebrations, and from almost a year of travel: his visits in 1963 took him all round the world—Israel, USA, New Zealand, and Australia—during which period he wrote little. When, on his return, he began composing again, things did not go smoothly. The results of an attempt to write a small orchestral piece for George Szell were met with negative comments from both Szell and Oxford University Press's Head of Music, Alan Frank. Walton himself was not enthusiastic about it, and the sketches were put aside. However, commissions for an anthem *The Twelve* for his old college, Christ Church, Oxford, and a Missa Brevis for Coventry Cathedral seemed to lift his spirits, as did a visit to London in December 1965 to conduct the premiere in Westminster Abbey of the orchestral version of *The Twelve*. During this time he was diagnosed with lung cancer, but after an operation and recuperation he was back at his Italian home on Ischia by March 1966, with *The Bear* in prospect. Walton was keen on the project, despite the less than enthusiastic reception of his first opera *Troilus and Cressida* when it had been premiered in 1954. The staging of that work at the Adelaide Festival of Arts, which he saw on his travels, was, in his own words, 'lively, spirited, and dramatic', and must have shown him that in the right circumstances, he was quite capable of writing successful opera. Once completed, *The Bear* was a considerable success, and since its premiere it has been consistently popular, given in performances throughout the world.

Walton's commission

The Bear has its origins in a commission from the Serge Koussevitzky Music Foundation. The brainchild of the Russian conductor Serge Koussevitzky (1874–1951), famous for his leadership of the Boston Symphony Orchestra, the Foundation was formed in 1942, and by the time Walton was approached as a possible composer, its activities had resulted in works by Bartók, Copland, and Messiaen, and its opera commissions included Benjamin Britten's *Peter Grimes* and Douglas Moore's *The Ballad of Baby Doe*. Walton had originally been contacted through his publisher on 6 October 1958,[1] but had clearly put the matter to the back of his mind, for by March 1965 John Ward, OUP's music representative in New York, was writing to Alan Frank that Olga Koussevitzky, the late conductor's daughter, was very perturbed about the delay in the completion of the commission. The OUP music staff were adept at dealing with Walton's delays; Ward told Frank, 'Of course I made the usual remarks about Walton's perfectionism and so on', but it was clear that things were not progressing, and there was potential for embarrassment on all sides. There was an extra dimension to the project; Madame Koussevitzky wanted to use the piece to celebrate the 25th anniversary of such commissions, which would fall in 1967. And the timing of completion was not the only difficulty in prospect, for it became rapidly clear that Walton was not interested in fulfilling the commission as awarded. The Koussevitzky proposal was for an orchestral work, but by May 1965 Walton had begun to think of making a one-act opera, which he was considering writing for Britten's English Opera Group, do double duty as the commission piece. Some time after May, Walton and OUP agreed that the EOG opera and the Koussevitzky commission could be the same piece. Alan Frank wrote rather off-handedly to Walton: 'At some stage or other I suppose you should tell the Koussevitsky Foundation that this is "their work"', although, even then, Walton felt that this should not 'stand in the way of getting something out of the E.O.G. even if it only covers the cost of the parts'. John Ward later telephoned the long-suffering Madame Koussevitzky and told her that 'the work is a one-act opera, and she didn't seem to mind, though she pointed out that the commission did specify an orchestral work'.

Once this was agreed, the commission fee became a problem. The standard Koussevitzky fee was $1500, which Alan Frank and John Ward thought 'a bit on the miserable side'. There was general agreement that it ought to be increased by between $500 and $1000, but as John Ward succinctly pointed out:

> The difficulty of course is that no-one asked for an opera in the first place: an opera was presented in the place of the short orchestral work offered, and the idea was accepted. It isn't easy on the face of it immediately to claim a larger sum because it's a larger work.

But as it happened, the Koussevitzky Foundation independently offered an increase of $1000 in the 'honorarium', and the matter was settled. Walton was keen that the commission fee be paid as a prize so that he could avoid the Italian tax authorities, but in the end, it was paid as a grant.[2]

The libretto

The possibility of Walton's using Chekhov's short vaudeville *The Bear* (1888) as the subject for this new opera had been under discussion since January 1965. The tenor Peter Pears, co-founder of the Aldeburgh Festival, had approached Walton with the idea that 'Aldeburgh'—that is, the English Opera Group—would like an opera. He suggested, with no apparent preference, either *The Bear* or another short play by Chekhov, *The Proposal*, also of 1888.[3] On 12 February Walton sent Frank a telegram: 'Please send express airmail two copies Penguin Bear William'.[4] After reading both, Walton was much keener on *The Bear*; he felt the action could be put into the 'Hunting Shires'. Alan Frank felt that structurally it was superior because it offered 'such a good part for the woman as well as the man'. In fact, Frank was intrigued and also highly perceptive:

> My only doubt is whether the humour is too straightforward, almost knockabout, for you, though perhaps this wouldn't matter much in a one acter. When we have spoken

about your doing a comedy, I had always thought of something more sardonic and devious even, if not exactly black!

The librettist eventually chosen, Paul Dehn (1912–76), was someone Walton had already met;[5] when his name was proposed, the composer 'jumped at the idea'.[6] In many ways Dehn was the perfect choice; he had long been connected with the English theatre and had penned, among other things, the libretto for Lennox Berkeley's *A Dinner Engagement* of 1954, and the lyrics for the films *Moulin Rouge* (1952) and *The Innocents* (1961). He also scripted *Goldfinger* (1964), *The Spy Who Came in from the Cold* (1965), and *The Taming of the Shrew* (1967), which suggested skill and facility in the adaptation of complicated literary models and an understanding of dramatic pacing.

Chekhov's vaudeville was written in February 1888 and first published in the journal *New Time* on 30 August of the same year. It was premiered at Korsh's Theatre, Moscow, on 28 October, and appeared in book form with minor alterations in the 1897 edition of his plays. Dehn's text closely follows Chehkov's play. The 'bear' of the title is the boor Grigory Stepanovich Smirnov, 'landowner and retired lieutenant of artillery', to whom the promiscuous husband of Madam Popova, now deceased, owed thirteen hundred roubles for oats to feed his favourite horse Toby. Smirnov arrives at Madam Popova's house to collect the debt, and is shown into the drawing room by Popova's servant, Luka, a part that is a mixture of comic and censorious traits. However, while Smirnov is trying to extract the money from Popova, he falls in love with her; he is attracted not only by her good looks, but by her spirited response to his appalling manners and financial demands, one that culminates in her challenging him to a duel. Popova's final capitulation, witnessed by Luka and two mute parts, the Cook and the Groom, is encapsulated by her last remark 'tell the groom not to give Toby any oats at all today'; she now has no need to keep her husband's memory alive by looking after his horse.

Once he was under way, Dehn worked fast; by 11 October 1965 Walton was writing to him, 'How splendid of you to have written such "smashing" verses—& how quickly—if I could only set them so quickly'.[7] This was a reference to the ten (originally eleven) inserts to the play that Dehn had written specially for the opera. By November 1965 Walton was able to report to Frank: 'Paul Dehn has been here & the libretto has taken on very nicely. It could turn out to be a winner on a small scale. He's going to ring you on his return from Rome & report progress.' By February of the following year, the libretto was substantially complete; Dehn visited Walton on Ischia at the end of the month to 'repolish' the end of *The Bear*, cutting several of his inserts in the process. Whether Walton was ever entirely happy with the overall result is unclear; certainly the music of the last pages gave him difficulties and he did not think he had 'managed to bring [it] off'.

It was during Dehn's visit that the title and the ascription were finally settled. The title page gained the descriptive title 'an extravaganza', instead of 'vaudeville', their choice being based on a dictionary definition which gave the meaning of 'extravaganza' as 'a wild burlesque or farce; an irregular or fanciful composition'; Walton was heard by Dehn to mutter 'it's no good pretending it's *The Three Sisters*'.[8] They also agreed the final formula for their labours: 'libretto adapted by Paul Dehn and William Walton, lyrics by Paul Dehn'. But more work was required; Walton felt that the 'whole thing needs tightening up from p. 18 [of the manuscript libretto]', that is, the last part of the opera. At this point there had been an inserted aria for Smirnov after Popova's 'Let us fight', and a duet for them before her 'Keep away!'. On Walton's behalf, Frank raised the issue further with Dehn, who proved more than willing to redo the passage in question; at the end of February the newly condensed ending was sent to Walton, who wrote Dehn an ecstatic letter congratulating him on the revision. The final draft of the libretto was then sent to the OUP Music Department for copying; it is clear that publication for the first performance was already intended, for which OUP required 'an exact finalised copy'.

In taking Chekhov's play, Dehn's approach to the libretto was to cut unnecessary verbiage and insert ten quasi-operatic numbers, often in rhyme. These included 'I lent him the sum out of friendship and pity', 'Grozdiov is not at home', 'Mud in my hair! Muck on my boots!', 'Madame, je vous prie', and the show-stopper 'I was a constant, faithful wife'. Dehn's texts for each of these did, however, take their cues from Chekhov. In the case of 'I was a constant, faithful wife', for example, the very memorable refrain 'Mourning, mourning, mourning' derives from Chekhov's 'I won't take off this mourn-ing till my dying day'. He also removed a number of colloquialisms and references that implied specificity: the substitution of 'perfect gentlemen' for 'proper lollipops', 'call on the neighbours' for 'visit the Korchagins and the Vlasovs', 'typical feminine logic' for 'proper petticoat logic', and 'The Lord save us' for 'Holy fathers!' being only a sampling of these. The designated period 1890 is Dehn's addition,[9] but the dramatis personae and the description of the characters are Chekhov's; these include the walk-on mute parts of the Cook and Groom which inessentially bolster the final scene in which the servants discover Popova and Smirnov engaged in a prolonged kiss. Even a number of Chekhov's stage directions are carried over and reused, in both their original and new positions; an example is Smirnov's 'He clutches the back of a chair which breaks', which in Chekhov's original text falls in an earlier, very lengthy, and otherwise cut speech directed to Popova. Some of them became less like Chekhov's, with Walton having tinkered with Dehn's version of them during the compositional process.

Dehn was generally pleased with his efforts, as was Walton, but the composer was also worried. Dehn had followed Elisaveta Fen's translation in the Penguin edition very closely, especially the section during which Popova and Smirnov brandish pistols at each other. Dehn's working method had involved pasting the pages of the edition onto A4 sheets and annotating Fen's text, with the result that although many of the phrases had been altered, the essence of her work was (and, indeed, is) apparent. Walton was greatly concerned about copyright, having previously run into trouble when working on *Façade* and *Henry V*. As it happened, this matter had occurred to OUP earlier, but no action had been taken.[10] Such was the potential problem in this case, however, that *not* printing the libretto for the performances was a serious consideration; Frank did 'not want to run the risk of fomenting trouble at this stage in case of other copyright claimants'. Walton's response was to say that they had 'altered every sentence to avoid any copyright problems with the translations' and that 'the only word for word simi-larities are those between [figs] 17 and 20'. This was slightly disingenuous; it is true that the section of Popova's text from 'You shall see, *Nicolas*' to 'alone for weeks on end!' is not much changed, but Dehn's and Walton's technique here doesn't differ from that used elsewhere in the libretto, and there are other passages with as few alterations.

Ultimately OUP took the risk, and the libretto, on sale on the night of the premiere, was officially published on 8 June 1967. One last matter was to commission a German translation; Walton was keen that this be done by Frank's friend Dr Ernst Roth of Boosey & Hawkes, who had translated *Troilus and Cressida*, and he did indeed accept OUP's offer. There was also a subsequent Italian translation, which Bruno Rigacci undertook for a production at the 1976 Barga Festival.[11]

The opera had clearly been a happy collaboration for both Dehn and Walton, but was short-lived. Dehn went on to provide Walton with a second verse for 'Put Off the Serpent Girdle', when that short chorus for female voices was excised from *Troilus and Cressida* and published separately, but sadly died in 1976. Walton was thus robbed of any further opportunity to work with someone whom he clearly found congenial, and who was willing to mould his efforts to suit the composer.

Partnering The Bear

Almost from the very first discussions of the opera, the question of a partner for *The Bear* was an issue, playing a role in the selection of the story and of the orchestration. Walton himself felt that it fell awkwardly into the category of a curtain-raiser, and initially could not see more than 45 minutes' worth in the piece—accurately, as it turned out.

By November 1965 the intention was to partner it with another new work being written for the EOG by the OUP composer John Gardner. The delays on this commission led Alan Frank to ask Peter Pears if it was 'out of the question to make up the bill with a new production of FAÇADE, with you or Peter Ustinov?'.[12] Frank told Walton about this proposal, and rather to Frank's surprise, the composer was interested, and felt that Ustinov would be a big draw. The orchestration of the opera gave him some concern; he felt that the EOG might 'jibe at the extra Sax and Trumpet' of *Façade* (which he probably also intended to use in *The Bear*) and offered to pay those fees himself.

The next contender for the other half of the bill was a new piece by Harrison Birtwistle, his opera *Punch and Judy*; Frank described it to Walton as an 'extremely interesting sort of grotesque melodrama based on a Punch and Judy story by an American'. Pears thought it 'rather savage & curious & could well do with a laugh to go with it'.[13] Walton established the details of the orchestration of *Punch and Judy*, but told Frank that he objected to the idea for another reason:

> I'm not entirely happy about the coupling with Birtwistle. I feel the 'B' won't on its own draw in much of a public & I'm dubious about Birtwistle's drawing power, but I may be wrong. It might be better to suggest waiting until J. G.'s is ready.

While it is true that *The Bear* on its own may not have been good box office, it is unlikely that either Birtwistle or Gardner had at that point any power at all in terms of attracting an audience. The EOG, though, still intended until quite late in the day that *The Bear*'s partner should be Birtwistle's opera, but ultimately the work with which it was double-billed was Lennox Berkeley's *Castaway*, also receiving its first performance. That the libretto of *Castaway* was also by Dehn doubtless added to the perceived compatibility of the two operas.[14] (*Castaway* had originally been designed as a companion piece to another work, Berkeley's and Dehn's 1954 opera *A Dinner Engagement*.) The length of the opera was of importance throughout these discussions; apart from Walton's worry about the sustainability of the story, the EOG were interested in balancing their evening. John Tooley, the director of the EOG (by then under the management of the Royal Opera House), was looking for something to complement the length of the Birtwistle, which he estimated at an hour and a quarter.[15]

After *The Bear*'s premiere, OUP themselves began to cast around for suitable works for a double bill, to ensure that there would be a steady flow of further performances. There was a particularly amusing exchange between Alan Frank and John Ward in July 1967; Frank proposed that it be coupled either with Purcell's *Dido and Aeneas* in an evening called 'Landmarks in British Opera', or with *Façade*, a billing described as an 'evening of good clean British fun'. Ward, listening to a recording in New York, replied:

> Not sure about the 'Clean Fun': 'Flaunting her tail' produces here a gasp of incredulity, after which everyone rolls around on the floor, and the evening is off to a good start.

While subsequent partnerships (both actual and proposed) obviously did not feed into the composition process in quite the same way as had, say, the orchestration of Birtwistle's *Punch and Judy*, Walton's preoccupation—and the concern of the publisher—with the issue emphasizes the importance of getting it right for the subsequent life of the work.

Composition

The first sketches for *The Bear* appear to have been made in the summer of 1965. In November of that year, Walton told Alan Frank: 'I shall have a good shot at finishing at least in sketch before I come to London about Dec 27th.' Walton's sketch was essentially an embryonic piano score. The total length of the opera at this stage was to be 40 minutes, about 30 of which were to have been completed by the time the visit took place. But Walton's potentially fatal illness intervened. His recovery was slow and interrupted by a return of the cancer, this time in the left shoulder, which required radiation treatment in London's Middlesex Hospital. Although in theory he continued to work throughout his convalescence, his comment to the critic Peter Heyworth that by the end of April he had 'even looked a piece of Mss paper in the face!—not with very promising results however. But it's wonderful to have an excuse not to work!' suggests otherwise.[16] However, progress was certainly made, and in October OUP was able to send some of the autograph full score (probably pages 1–85) to be photographed. But Walton was dissatisfied; on 11 December, he wrote to Frank:

> The Bear moves slowly but steadily and if my next check-up is satisfactory I shall doubtless finish it in time, But I find a lot of what I did this time a year ago needs drastically re-writing.

Commenting on his health in the same letter, he claimed to be getting easily tired, although he dismissed it with the characteristically whimsical remark: 'That may be allergia to the "Bear"!'

Walton's approach to the composition of the opera was to work on pages of the full score, and then to prepare a rough vocal score. These were then sent to Walton's occasional assistant copyist Roy Douglas, who prepared the official vocal score. The composer's full score therefore precedes the vocal score, and explains the context of the preparatory material that survives in the Beinecke Library at Yale University. So by 4 January 1967, when things were well under way, Walton sent pages 86–117 of the autograph full score to OUP, by which time, however, only pages 1–36 of the vocal score had been completed. By 2 February he reported that he had only ten or fifteen minutes' work left, which he would do before his 65th birthday (29 March) 'if left in peace'. Walton's sketch version of the vocal score was completed on 19 April; at the same time, he was working on the orchestration, aiming to finish the full score for 3 May, the date on which Roy Douglas was due to go away on vacation. As was his custom, Douglas sent regular lists of queries to Walton during the copying process. On receiving pages 117–28, Douglas knew that 'we must be within sight of the end now, because Popova has gone to fetch the pistols'. The orchestral parts, at least those up to page 150, were also produced by Roy Douglas; the remainder involved Dennis Sheridan, and all were proofread by Dennis Morrell.

Walton, who had told Frank at the end of April that he felt that the opera was 'pretty awful—not at all funny & rather boring!', sent him the last of the full score, commenting with a characteristically self-critical assessment:

> I have found these last pages v. difficult […] But if the worst comes to the worst I have found a 'cut' from the top of 2 (new ending) to the top of p. 3 which would avoid a lot of embarrassing horror, but one [had] better leave it as it is till one sees it on the stage.

Throughout the compositional process, Walton discussed not only the voice ranges and types, but also casting possibilities, providing insight into the way in which he conceived the roles. The tessituras were settled by December 1965, Walton making Popova a mezzo-soprano (G3 to A♭5); Smirnov a baritone (A2 to G4), with a falsetto on B4; and Luka, a bass (G2 to E♭4). Given that the opera was intended for performance by the EOG, it might have been expected that the lead male role—in this case, Smirnov—would be a tenor, to accommodate Peter Pears, but Walton had decided otherwise, presumably because even the suggestion of an heroic side to the character undermined the buffo nature of the role.[17] The EOG's choice for Smirnov was Thomas Hemsley, who was often associated with Britten's music. However, Hemsley's contractual arrangements with Dortmund Opera ruled him out of consideration, and it then became a choice between John Shaw, an Australian member of the Covent Garden company, and favoured by Colin Graham, and Raimund Herincx, who was regarded as a good interpreter of *Belshazzar's Feast*, and recommended by the editor of *Opera*, Harold Rosenthal, because of his good diction. Walton, who had heard Shaw, didn't think he could reach the notes, and favoured Herincx. Ultimately, Walton must have been won over, since Shaw both created the role and undertook the first recording.

The role of Madam Popova was much more straightforward. Using the mezzo voice for Popova was an especially happy choice, for, at a stroke, Walton had turned a rather lightweight role into one with an automatic gravitas. The handsome and characterful Monica Sinclair, also a member of the Covent Garden company, was soon booked with no more discussion. Like Shaw, she also sang the role on the first recording. Although Walton had chosen a high tessitura for Luka, the role was thought from the start to be a true bass role, a part for which Norman Lumsden was under consideration. Lumsden had sung in each of the first thirteen Aldeburgh Festivals from 1948 to 1960, and had appeared in a number of Britten operas, including *Albert Herring* and *Billy Budd*. Further, Britten had written the role of Peter Quince for him in his version of Shakespeare's *A Midsummer Night's Dream*. Walton clearly wanted to discuss Lumsden with Britten, but, in the end, seems to have felt that the part's high E♭ would not present a challenge, given that Lumsden had been the original Superintendent Budd in *Albert Herring*, a role with a long high E.

Walton had made great efforts to establish the orchestration of Birtwistle's commission in order to develop its counterpart in *The Bear*, but this was, in any case, that of most of the works written for the EOG, and was limited by the small size of the Jubilee Hall. He described it as the 'standard BB' [Benjamin Britten for the EOG] orchestra of '4WW, Hn, Str5tet, Hp, Pf, 1 perc', but, faced with the possibility of *The Bear*'s being partnered with the new opera by John Gardner and feeling 'confined' by the orchestral requirements, he added a trumpet, a trombone, and second percussion. Walton agreed to accept the original solo string quintet in later performances, but declared that he would prefer that the strings be a group of 'tutti'; a note in the full score says, 'Although *The Bear* was originally scored for solo strings, the composer wishes it to be known that he considers it preferable for a larger body of strings to be used whenever possible.' As it happens, Britten himself found the 'standard BB' orchestra equally restricting, making a similar stipulation in the case of *A Midsummer Night's Dream*.

As far as the music itself was concerned, Walton himself saw the work as parodic, and not just admitting these parodies, but rejoicing in them. Early in the compositional process in 1965, he wrote to Alan Frank that the opera was 'full of parody's [*sic*] anything from Tchaikovsky to Stravinsky via Massenet etc. & maybe will be quite funny if it's not a damp squib'. Eighteen months later he told Frank that his view was that 'musically, [*The Bear*] is getting dottier and vulgarer! each progressive bar'. Walton even stretched this magpie approach to including four bars from *The Dance of the Seven Veils* from Richard Strauss's opera *Salome* in Smirnov's French pastiche aria to accompany the lines 'Put off those widow's weeds. Unveil, as did Salome!'; the sentiments of this aria Madam Popova dismisses as 'rude and not at all clever or funny'. The Strauss quote was to cause Walton some difficulties. Roy Douglas picked it up while working on the score, and alerted OUP. Writing to Walton from the firm in February 1967, Christopher Morris asked if there was 'anything else they should be told?!'. OUP and Walton agreed that copyright should be sought for this for the rather curious reason that 'it would look good to have B&H's name in the score'. However, it was not to be: Boosey & Hawkes, who asked for the exact context, since presumably 'the object of the reference is to make some particular point',[18] refused to give official permission and later added that 'it would not be advisable to ask Dr Franz Strauss, the composer's son, for his consent'. In the end, both parties agreed by phone that the matter should be ignored, and that there should be no acknowledgement or any mention of it in a press context. As Alan Frank finally concluded: 'I wonder how many people will in fact notice the reference.'

First performances and reception

The first performances of *The Bear* took place in the Jubilee Hall at the 1967 Aldeburgh Festival, starting on 3 June. As the opera was a part-EOG commission, Aldeburgh was always the logical place, with the Jubilee Hall the obvious venue, and the intention was to stage it in London immediately afterwards in an EOG season at Sadler's Wells. This was not, however, a foregone conclusion; when the word first got out that Walton was writing an opera, the EOG had had an approach from the Brighton Festival, interested in a double bill of *The Bear* and *Façade*. It was a matter for concern that the premiere would be in Brighton and not Aldeburgh, but by October the notion of Brighton was dead and the concentration was on Aldeburgh and Sadler's Wells.

The production was by Colin Graham, the in-house director of the EOG, and designed by Alix Stone. James Lockhart, a member of the music staff of Covent Garden, was designated conductor. Its reception was almost entirely positive. Two days later in *The Guardian* Edward Greenfield declared that Walton gave the audience 'the sense of security which comedy, from a music-hall turn upwards, unfailingly requires...there is a similarity of idiom too, but the wonder is that the more eclectic Walton is, the more he remains himself.' William Mann in *The Times* was even more upbeat, writing that 'The Bear...is an instantaneous winner, expertly abstracted from a short Chekhov comedy set to high-spirited, often mocking (indeed self-parodying) music that never flags from start to finish.' But a week later Stanley Sadie, also in *The Times*, felt just the opposite: 'Whether the slender joke...can sustain a piece of this length, and whether Dehn's libretto is too wordy by half, seemed on last night's evidence at best not proven: the fact is that the piece soon began to drag, and that the jokes—musical as well as verbal—became embarrassingly predictable.' He did go on to suggest that a 'more soubrettish' singer than Monica Sinclair might have lightened the piece, a comment echoed privately by all those involved, as problems with the singer's diction were discussed prior to the first studio recording.

On the back of this immediate success, Frank wrote to William Glock, suggesting *The Bear* for the Proms,[19] and by February 1968 he was advising Ward in New York to look out for a good opportunity to stage a United States premiere. There were no plans for the EOG to visit America—this had been hoped for by OUP in early 1966—and in any case, arrangements were well advanced for a premiere in Montreal at the 1967 International and Universal Exposition (or Expo 67). However, this left all parties in an awkward position. They had organized themselves what was dubbed a 'North American' premiere, but as a Koussevitzky commission the opera needed a United States premiere, and none was even planned. In the end Ward agreed to look for an American group to perform it, preferably a touring company so that there would be a series of performances, and then to make a clean breast of the matter to Olga Koussevitzky. Even then, OUP, grasping at all possibilities, split the United States in half, so that a request from Walton's sister-in-law Jo, 'the David Webster of Vancouver', to stage the 'West Coast' premiere could be considered. Walton himself attended the Canadian premiere in Montreal on 20 September; Freda Ferguson, the head of OUP Music in Canada, found Madame Koussevitzky very charming and reported that Walton seemed very pleased with the reception of the opera. The United States premiere finally took place on 15 August 1968 at the Wheeler Opera House in Aspen, Colorado, conducted by Leonard Slatkin; the producer was Madeleine Milhaud.

Recordings, broadcasts, telecasts

Alan Frank's assessment of *The Bear*—that 'they had a really big success on their hands'—and the opera's initial positive reception meant that enormous efforts were made from the outset to broadcast and record it. The first broadcast, by the BBC on 10 June 1967 from Aldeburgh, was fixed early on, and was to include its double-bill partner. Becoming more committed to the project as time went by, the BBC then approached OUP, asking for transcription rights for this broadcast to distribute it throughout the world. Fees were agreed, but the early commercial recording of Walton's opera caused this part of the enterprise to be scrapped. For the recording Frank's first port of call was John Culshaw at Decca: 'Are you interested in recording *The Bear*? Walton's new opera is sure to be a hit, unless I'm wildly out.'[20] Culshaw, a record producer of great discernment, was interested, though, not surprisingly, he wanted to hear the work first. He could not, however, attend any rehearsals, and this short delay lost him the recording; two days before the 10 June broadcast, EMI snapped it up to record at the end of the following month. The recording, by the original performers, and with Walton in attendance, duly took place from 30 July to 2 August.

At the same time there was a determined effort to get the opera televised. Initially OUP decided to approach Granada Television on the grounds that it would bring in twice the BBC fees, so Frank wrote to Lew Grade. But the commercially minded impresario showed no interest in the project,[21] and apparently expressed himself more forthrightly in direct communication; Frank wrote to Walton that Grade would 'not touch it with a barge-pole'. On 1 February 1970 BBC TV broadcast a studio production with Regina Resnik, Thomas Hemsley, and Derek Hammond-Stroud in the main roles. Walton conducted the English Chamber Orchestra in a corner of the studio, while James Lockhart conducted the singers, relaying the beat to them by means of monitor screens slung high in the set. The process seems to have been fraught. Walton was unused to conducting for the conditions television required and despite being told not to worry, he kept stopping whenever the singers and orchestra were out of time. As Susana Walton has recounted, 'the television producer [Rudolph Cartier] was soon spitting with rage, shouting that only he was allowed to stop the filming'.[22]

Adjustments and cuts

Once the opera premiere was over, there was time for second thoughts. This was not always a good thing where Walton was concerned: even during the run-up to the first staging, he was considering a number of cuts to the score to cover what he supposed was his incompetence. The producer Colin Graham wanted specific additions and cuts. One, the addition of Popova's 'That reminds me, Luka' passage in bar 284, was a sensible attempt to reiterate the joke about feeding Toby oats, in effect making it a topos of sorts. This was agreed by Dehn and Walton, but the second—cutting the last five lines of Smirnov's French parody aria 'Madame, je vous prie', after 'Unveil, as did Salome'—was contested by them, and seems not to have been agreed but was nevertheless included in the longer optional cut of bars 765–93.

After the premiere, a number of reviewers, who had noted problems of different sorts, were approached for details. Edward Greenfield was one, Desmond Shawe-Taylor of the *Sunday Times* another. The latter seems to have complained about 'smothered jokes' although, when approached by Dehn, was 'predictably' unable to point to a single one. Dehn himself wrote Walton a very thoughtful letter on a number of details, mostly on issues of length and audibility of the text. It is clear that Monica Sinclair's diction, referred to in a couple of reviews, caused problems; Dehn claimed that if he had not known the story, he would not have been able to follow it. There was even discussion of cutting the verse 'The dark, the fair' to 'all, all, all' (bars 860–70) from 'I was a constant, faithful wife' to shorten the aria, although Walton's comment—'I'm in several minds about "I was a constant" [we could] leave it alone and get MS to sing without so much exaggeration (it would save at least a minute)'—indicates that the reception was as much to do with Sinclair's performance as it was with the aria itself. In the end, there was just a suggested cut (never made) of the verse 'What could a poor' to 'neighbours' nieces' (bars 882–92). There were also one or two small alterations to the libretto at the suggestion of Richard Taubner (an attendee who must have known Chekhov's *The Bear* well), who wrote to Walton and Dehn after the first performances. There is a set of later alterations which reflected certain changes and adjustments made for the television performance conducted by Walton. Writing to Frank on 10 July 1972, the composer commented: 'Don't use the parts & Sc. which were used in the T.V. prod, as they contain alterations possible [only] for that purpose.'

One extra group of details relating to the staging of *The Bear* is, sadly, not available. In the initial euphoria of the premiere, Frank wrote to Colin Graham saying what a 'hit' they had had and that, given that much of this was due to Graham's production, he and Walton wanted to include some of his production details as notes in the vocal score, about to be published.[23] The notion was that these should be inserted as an appendix, but despite Graham's positive response, this idea did not materialize.

NOTES

1. John Ward to Alan Frank, 24 January 1966, OUP Archive, Oxford. All other quotations from the unusually extensive correspondence between OUP and Walton, and between members of the OUP staff, are to be found in this archive.
2. Even this did not represent the truth of the matter; Mr Brett-Smith, of the Library of Congress, pointed out that the 'fee' was, in fact, a payment for the sale of the manuscript.
3. Alan Frank added a note to the file that suggests that the idea had come from Eric Crozier, librettist of Britten's *Albert Herring* and a great admirer of Chekhov. In a letter to Crozier about *The Bear* of 1 February 1967 Frank says: 'I have the feeling that the whole operatic conception stems from some remark of yours' (OUP Archive).
4. See *The Selected Letters of William Walton*, ed. Malcolm Hayes (London, 2002), p. 357.
5. According to Susana Walton, this was while Dehn was a guest of Terence Rattigan, who was staying in one of their villas on Ischia; Susana Walton, *Behind the Façade* (Oxford, 1988), p. 197.
6. Michael Kennedy, *Portrait of Walton* (Oxford, 1989), p. 229.
7. *Selected Letters*, ed. Hayes, p. 357.

8. Paul Dehn, note to record sleeve, HMV Angel SAN 192.

9. This is alluded to as '1888' in the published vocal and full scores, but is merely the date of the original vaudeville.

10. In fact, at the outset of the project in the spring of 1965, Alan Frank had asked the Russian-speaking General Editor of this edition if he would be prepared to do an entirely new translation. But Walton had become impatient to start, and had chosen the Penguin translation and himself amended it, and had composed the first ten minutes before Paul Dehn joined as librettist (David Lloyd-Jones in conversation).

11. Susana Walton, *Behind the Façade*, p. 202.

12. Alan Frank to Peter Pears, 25 November 1965.

13. Peter Pears to Alan Frank [Christmas, 1965].

14. In April 1966, Keith Grant, the general manager of the EOG, assured Alan Frank that it would be performed with the Birtwistle, but by 8 May OUP was negotiating broadcast fees of a double bill of *The Bear* and *Castaway*.

15. Note of meeting between Alan Frank and John Tooley, 3 December 1965.

16. *Selected Letters*, ed. Hayes, p. 363.

17. Alan Frank to Peter Pears, 25 November 1965.

18. Muriel James to Alan Frank, 28 March 1967.

19. Alan Frank to William Glock, 13 June 1967.

20. Alan Frank to John Culshaw, 1 May 1967.

21. Lew Grade to Alan Frank, 2 August 1967.

22. Susana Walton, *Behind the Façade*, p. 202.

23. Frank to Colin Graham, 8 June 1967. In this, OUP probably took their cue from Faber and Faber's 1964 publication of Britten's church parable *Curlew River*, which included Graham's production notes.

3

Ballets *(Vol. 3)*

David Lloyd-Jones

Two factors account for William Walton's close connection with the ballet scene in Britain. The first was his fortunate position on coming down from Oxford to become a protégé and permanent guest of the Sitwell brothers in their London house. The worldly Osbert and Sacheverell were total devotees of the Russian Ballet which, since 1911, had been all the rage in the capital, and were on familiar terms with Diaghilev and those connected with him. This explains why the 24-year-old Walton, undoubtedly urged on by the Sitwells, wrote a prospective three-movement ballet score which he and the pianist Angus Morrison played to the great man after a luncheon at 2 Carlyle Square in 1926. Diaghilev politely declined to take the bait, and Walton subsequently transformed the work into the Sinfonia Concertante.[1]

Second, and ultimately far more important, was his friendship with Constant Lambert, who was three years his junior and, by chance, a close neighbour; for several formative years they lived virtually on opposite sides of the King's Road in Chelsea. Unlike Walton, Lambert did have an early ballet score accepted by Diaghilev but, more significantly, he soon became acquainted with two of the leading lights of the burgeoning British ballet scene, Ninette de Valois and Frederick Ashton. These two, together with Lambert as conductor, were central to the formation of the Camargo Society in 1930, and it was due to Lambert's negotiations with Walton that one of Ashton's earliest ballets (1931) was based on the five numbers of the 1926 orchestral suite from *Façade*, plus 'Scotch Rhapsody' and 'Popular Song', both orchestrated for the purpose by Lambert.[2] Over the years the ballet *Façade* became further extended with extra numbers (which were published as the Second Orchestral Suite in 1938), and it still retains its great popularity worldwide. In this way Walton became closely associated with the personnel of the Vic-Wells/Sadler's Wells Ballet (which had subsumed the Camargo Society), and he clearly enjoyed the alluring and stimulating companionship that they offered. During the war Walton must have derived a considerable income from the numerous performances of his three ballets in the Vic-Wells repertoire.[3] On account of Lambert's early death, Walton's most enduring friendship was with Ashton; indeed the very last music that he wrote four days before his death was at Ashton's request—a nine-bar short-score alternative ending to the shortened repeat of the first movement of *Varii Capricci*, on which he based his 1983 ballet.[4]

The Wise Virgins

It was during a touring visit of the ballet company to Cambridge in the last week of January 1940 that Ashton and Lambert spent an evening at King's College with its eminent choir director and organist Boris Ord. At one point the conversation turned to the music of J. S. Bach, and Lambert joined Ord at the piano(s?) playing transcriptions of various numbers, including some from the cantatas. One of these was the famous 'Sheep may safely graze' which, not surprisingly, made a deep impression on Ashton. During the war he had set himself the task of reading the Bible (sometimes out loud to company members when on tour), and the evening sowed the germs of his biblical ballet based on the music of Bach. For this, Lambert selected eight numbers (one was repeated in a shortened and reorchestrated version), and the highlight was to be 'Sheep may safely graze'. He himself could well have undertaken the task of orchestrating them for a modern symphony (i.e. ballet) orchestra, but it was probably the strain he experienced as music director of the company during wartime while on tour (male company members were increasingly being called up for military service), not to mention playing one of the two pianos that were used instead of an orchestra, that made him turn to his friend Walton to undertake the assignment. Orchestrating other people's music was something that Walton had hardly ever done before, but he appears to have enjoyed the experience, and he produced a much-admired score.

The Bach numbers

In view of Bach's vast output of instrumental music, it may seem odd that seven out of the eight pieces that Lambert selected were vocal numbers from the cantatas, but this was doubtless because of the importance attached to 'Sheep may safely graze'. Those that he chose are so diverse as to suggest an encyclopedic knowledge of the cantatas on his part, which would be a reasonable supposition about someone with his exceptionally wide culture and learning. However, the truth is more prosaic: the choice was dictated rather by the availability of a number of arrangements for two pianos that had appeared in Britain in the early decades of the twentieth century due to the revived enthusiasm for Bach, and especially for the little-known cantatas.[5] The OUP Music Department's founder, Hubert Foss, was particularly involved because the launch in 1923 of the Oxford Choral Songs series, edited by the Bach scholar and choral conductor William Gillies Whittaker, is regarded as the official beginning of the Bach revival. Whittaker became a major influence at OUP, and his editions of Bach cantatas, sinfonias, arias, and transcriptions for two pianos and piano solo became a regular feature of their growing catalogue. It is known that Lambert consulted with Ashton over the choice of numbers, but it is doubtful if, in the first instance, he would have done so with Walton, although later they may have discussed the final selection.

The following list gives notes on the sources that Lambert provided for Walton, together with any further points of interest.

I. Final four-part chorale (No. 7) of Cantata 140 'Wachet auf, ruft uns die Stimme', usually known in English as 'Sleepers, wake'. The choice of this cantata for the 27th Sunday after Trinity was especially appropriate, as the Gospel for the day was the first thirteen verses of Matthew 25, which is the only biblical source of the parable of the wise and foolish virgins. Bach's key for the accompanied chorale is E flat. Excluded from the Suite.

II. Bass aria (No. 2) 'Dein Geburtstag ist erschienen', from Cantata 142 'Uns ist ein Kind geboren'. Although the music is attractive, this number was an odd choice on Lambert's part since the cantata had long been considered to be spurious. Writing in 1912, the musicologist and editor of the *Bach-Jahrbuch* Arnold Schering had suggested that it was the work of Johann Kuhnau, Bach's predecessor at Leipzig as cantor of the Thomasschule, best known for his 'Biblical Sonatas'. Bach's contribution to this Christmas Day cantata, if any, is considered to be in the reshaping of the arias. The aria is accompanied by two violins and continuo. Excluded from the Suite.

III. Opening chorus of Cantata 99 'Was Gott thut, das ist wohlgethan'. This is an extended instrumental movement, with minimal chorale entries, which has been reduced from Bach's 116 bars to 70. It is scored for flute, oboe d'amore, horn (doubling sopranos), strings, and continuo. The use of the past tense in the English translation of the title is surprising.

IV. Chorale prelude for organ 'Herzlich thut mich verlangen', BWV 727. There can be no surprise at the choice of this number (commonly known as the Passion Chorale), the only one not to come from a cantata. It was the piece chosen by Walton to transcribe for piano solo that was included, with those by another eleven contemporary British composers, to make up *A Bach Book for Harriet Cohen*, published by OUP in 1932.[6] The chorale tune was in fact the work of Hans Leo Hassler (1564–1612) and was harmonized by Bach no fewer than eight times.

V. Tenor aria (No. 5) 'Seht, was die Liebe thut', from Cantata 85 'Ich bin ein guter Hirt'. In the Bach original the key is E flat, and the scoring for first and second violins and violas in unison, plus continuo. Walton alternates the vocal line between flute and oboe and mutes the strings.

VI. Opening chorus of Cantata 26 'Ach wie flüchtig, ach wie nichtig'. Lines 3 and 4 of the chorale text compare man's life to a mist that quickly forms and then, just as quickly, disappears, which could explain the continuous swirling semiquavers. Bach uses flute, three oboes, horn (doubling sopranos), strings, and continuo. In Walton's orchestration, woodwind and strings do not have even a half-bar's rest throughout the 53 bars.

VII. Recitative and soprano aria (Nos. 8 and 9), from Secular Cantata 208 'Was mir behagt, ist nur die muntre Jagd'. This is the earliest music of the ballet score, written in Weimar probably in 1713. Bach and the prolific Salomo Frank (librettist) were commissioned by their employer, Duke Wilhelm Ernst of Saxe-Weimar, to write a congratulatory birthday cantata for Duke Christian of Saxe-Weissenfels, who was holding a hunting festival. Frank provided a suitably sycophantic text with solo parts for Diana (soprano 1), Endymion (tenor), Pan (bass), and the goddess of flocks and herds Pales (soprano 2). This last deity was possibly included because of a pun on the Duke's name; Weissenfels is strictly translated as 'white rock' but can also be rendered as 'white fleece' by the addition of an extra letter l. The soprano's *secco* recitative (i.e. Walton's octave higher violin solo line) has the following loosely translated text: 'Shall the offering of Pales then be the last? No! no! I also will present my allegiance, and as the whole countryside rings with "Vivat", so does this beautiful field stir with joy [coloratura runs] and delight to honour our Saxon hero.' Walton's tempo indication 'Adagio' should surely refer to the aria rather than the recitative. The aria 'Schafe können sicher weiden' begins

'Sheep can safely graze where a good shepherd watches'. Many people, possibly including Walton and Ashton, have assumed that the good shepherd is Jesus (as it has been in V), whereas in fact it is the thoroughly secular Duke Christian. Bach scores for two recorders and continuo.

VIII. This is a much shortened and rescored version of III without the chorale. It was used in the ballet to represent the late arrival of the foolish virgins after the central door (through which the wedding procession has just passed) has been shut. Excluded from the Suite.

IX. Concluding extended chorale (No. 5) of Cantata 129 'Gelobet sei der Herr, mein Gott'. Bach's brilliant orchestration is for flute, two oboes, three trumpets, timpani, strings, and continuo.

Orchestration

On 26 February 1940 Lambert wrote to Hubert Foss from the Lyceum Theatre, Sheffield, telling him that he was 'busy working out a religious ballet for Ashton', and saying that he intended to use Mary Howe's OUP transcriptions for two pianos of 'Thy birthday is come' and 'Sheep may safely graze' along with Foss's own 'See what his love can do'. He adds, 'I am hoping to get Willie to do the scoring. A good idea, don't you think?'[7] Lambert failed to mention two other OUP publications that were needed, 'Sleepers, wake', arranged for two pianos by Whittaker, and Walton's own 'Lord hear my longing' for piano solo. The other arrangements to be used (i.e. for Nos. III, VI, and VIII) were those by W. Rummel, published by Chester. This was clearly the most convenient way of showing Walton the texts that were required to be orchestrated, but the transcriptions were also going to be necessary for when the company was again on tour, and later in London, with only two pianos (Lambert and Hilda Gaunt) after the season with orchestra at Sadler's Wells.

On 4 March Walton wrote to Alan Frank at OUP: 'I've let myself in for scoring a "Bach" ballet for the "Wells" so could you send me the following transcriptions [list follows]. You don't happen to know where or from whom I could borrow a Bach Gesellschaft [Complete Edition] so I could look at the originals, as the transcriptions Constant showed me are rather obscure in places as to where the parts come from and go to.' OUP were concerned about the question of copyright in the arrangements, but on 7 March Frank (in London) wrote to Foss (temporarily evacuated to Oxford with most of his staff): 'I have now seen Walton who assures me that as far as the orchestration is concerned he will be working from the original and not from our transcriptions.' Walton had clearly by then had access to the necessary Gesellschaft volumes.

Ashton's ballet

For his new ballet Ashton chose the parable of the wise and foolish virgins as found in Chapter 25 of the Gospel according to St Matthew. He extended the story into a form of morality ballet and, apart from the biblical five wise and five foolish virgins, created a new set of characters—the bridegroom (mentioned in the parable), the bride, her father, and her mother—as well as five angels and four cherubs. This subject had already been selected in 1933 by Ninette de Valois, who provided new choreography for the 1920 Swedish ballet *Les Vierges folles* to a score by Kurt Atterberg. As Walton's compositional personality was not involved in the creation of the score of *The Wise Virgins*, it is unnecessary to give further details of Ashton's scenario, but a detailed description of the action and production of the ballet can be found in Cyril W. Beaumont's *The Sadler's Wells Ballet*, first published only six years after the original production.[8] The ballet was choreographed mainly on a provincial tour. The premiere was given on 24 April 1940 by the Vic-Wells Ballet at Sadler's Wells Theatre, London, during their wartime spring season, with opulent and much admired baroque sets and costumes by Rex Whistler. Margot Fonteyn and Michael Somes were the bride and bridegroom, and Constant Lambert conducted.[9] The ballet was dedicated by Ashton to Edith Sitwell, though this fact was never published. Ashton's devout and serene handling of the story was generally admired (except for his choreography for the foolish virgins, which provoked laughter), but his choice of Bach's music for theatrical purposes came in for some pedantic opprobrium. However, Walton's stylish orchestrations were much approved; as the composer Humphrey Searle later wrote: 'This arrangement was tasteful but effective, successfully avoiding both archaism and over-modernity.'[10] Indeed, the ballet may truly be rated as one of his most subtle and imaginative efforts as an orchestrator, all the more so since he was not scoring his own music. The ballet received a further nine performances at Sadler's Wells, but London did not see it again until the company was obliged to move to the New Theatre in January 1941, the Sadler's Wells Theatre having been taken over as a rest centre for air-raid victims. As the stage of this venue was smaller than that of Sadler's Wells, it was not able to accommodate the Whistler sets, so instead the ballet was danced before gauzes until May 1942, when adapted Whistler designs were introduced. It achieved 83 performances in London (58 on tour) and was last given there on 13 January 1944.

The Suite

Three months after the first night, Walton recorded the six numbers that now constitute the Suite from the ballet with the Sadler's Wells Orchestra in HMV's Abbey Road Studios. The two-record set was released in September 1940.[11] The Suite received its first public performance when it was given on 13 November of that year at an afternoon concert of the Royal Philharmonic Society in Queen's Hall, with the Society's orchestra conducted by Dr Malcolm Sargent.

Publication

Ten days after the first performance of *The Wise Virgins*, the Vic-Wells company was sent by the British Council on a rather foolhardy mission to perform in Holland, Belgium, and France as a 'cultural propaganda' exercise. It would have seemed sensible to include the most recent new production as one of the six that they presented there, but the Whistler sets were considered too bulky to take on tour. This was fortunate because the company famously became caught up in the sudden German blitzkrieg invasion of Holland and, in their prolonged and ignominious sea journey back to Britain, had to abandon sets, costumes, scores, and orchestral parts.[12]

So this is not the reason why Walton's autograph score (from which Lambert had conducted) has not yet been found, as has sometimes been suspected.[13] This is demonstrated by the fact that OUP fortuitously arranged for a copy to be made in November 1940, and this was sent out by the Music Hire Library to conductors performing the ballet score in full or in part. It was this copyist's score that was marked up by the printer when, in 1942, OUP eventually decided to publish the ballet. The need for 92 pages is shown in his blue crayon castings-off, but it was probably due to the severe wartime paper shortage that it was finally decided to engrave only the suite that Walton had recorded in 1940 (although OUP had already adopted this procedure in 1938 with Lambert's ballet *Horoscope*). Consequently numbers I, II, and VIII were dropped, and the engraved suite was published as a study score in December 1942, reduced to 68 pages.

Unfortunately even the 1940 copy soon became mislaid so that, with the autograph and the original set of parts misssing, it became impossible to reconstruct the authentic full ballet. However, a breakthrough occurred in 2010 when the editor chanced to find the original 1940 copy, and so the full ballet score in Walton's orchestration can now be published for the first time.

The Quest

Ashton followed *The Wise Virgins* with *The Wanderer*, to Schubert's piano Fantasy in C, D.760, which was premiered at the New Theatre, London, on 27 January 1941. In June he found himself called up for service in the Royal Air Force. After a period in the ranks, in October he was commissioned as a Pilot Officer. Eventually posted to Edinburgh as an Intelligence Officer, and later to Newcastle-upon-Tyne and Catterick, he found himself railing to friends against the waste of his talent. This feeling of artistic impotence was further fanned by reports of the activities of his colleague Robert Helpmann who, in Ashton's absence, had achieved considerable success with *Comus*, *Hamlet*, and *The Birds* and, in so doing, had become the resident choreographer of the Sadler's Wells Ballet in all but name. A crisis point came when Constant Lambert threatened to resign unless Ashton could be allowed to return in order to bring matters under firmer artistic control. Sir Kenneth Clark, a friend and admirer of the company since its early days, wrote a minatory unofficial letter to the recently established Council for the Encouragement of Music and the Arts (CEMA, the forerunner of the Arts Council), warning that the Sadler's Wells Ballet might break up unless Ashton was returned to them.[14] This did not fully happen, but as a result of Clark's letter, Ashton was granted six weeks' leave of absence from the RAF to create a new ballet for the dispirited company.

The Faerie Queene

Choosing a subject for this much-desired return, Ashton was to revert to the idea of a ballet that, according to his biographer Julie Kavanagh, had been suggested to him five years previously by his friend Doris Langley Moore.[15] Mrs Moore was a wealthy South African scholar, writer, and fashion historian who, since 1925, had become a close friend of the artist Edward Burra. Through him, she had been involved in the growth of the ballet scene in London and especially with William Chappell, the Polish designer Sophie Fedorovich, and Frederick Ashton. In 1926 she had married and moved to a large house in Yorkshire near Harrogate, where Ashton used to stay when on tour in the district. In his 1946 study of the Sadler's Wells Ballet, Cyril Beaumont says (almost certainly quoting Ashton's personal reminiscences): 'When Ashton was a guest at the home of Miss [*sic*] Langley Moore [probably in 1939], he was attracted by a fine edition of [Edmund] Spenser's [*The*] *Faerie Queene*, which he noticed in her library. His hostess observed that it was a book well worth his attention, since it offered several possible themes for ballets. Indeed she would contrive a scenario for him and send it on.'[16] After Ashton had shown interest in the project and suggested Walton as the most suitable composer, Langley Moore went so far as to ask her friend Viscount Hastings, who had got to know Walton through the Sitwells, to broach the subject with him, saying that 'Freddy himself suggested it would be just the thing for music with that humorous quality which Walton writes better than anybody living'.[17] Eventually Ashton had second thoughts, and returned the synopsis that Langley Moore had prepared in the meantime because he considered it 'too literary'. However, he did not forget it, and in the dark days of early 1943 he had come to believe that the long-forgotten scenario, which concerned the conquest of evil forces by England's patron saint, contained elements of uplifting patriotism that would be appreciated by both the company and audiences. Walton was to write the music for the ballet and John Piper (probably at Clark's suggestion) to design the sets and costumes.[18] Later Langley Moore was to provide a concise synopsis of the action of the ballet, titled *The Quest*, for its programme, which was as follows:

> **Scene I Outside the House of Archimago** St. George and Una, lost in a storm, fall under the spell of Archimago, who transforms his female servant into an evil semblance of Una. St. George is deceived and leaves in disgust.
>
> **Scene II Near the Palace of Pride** Duessa chooses Sansfoy as her cavalier. St. George challenges him to battle and kills him. Duessa throws herself at St. George's mercy, and they leave together. Una, searching for St. George, is deceived by Archimago, who enters disguised in similar armour.
>
> **Scene III The Palace of Pride** [Langley Moore fails to mention the 'Seven Deadly Sins' episode at the start of this scene.]
>
> **St. George enters the Palace of Pride** with Duessa. Sansjoy follows him and they fight. Duessa takes the side of the Saracen Knight and reveals her love for him when he is killed. St. George, doubly disillusioned, sees the Palace of Pride and Duessa in their true light.
>
> **Scene IV Near the Palace of Pride** Sansloy is mourning for his two brothers. Archimago enters, still disguised as St. George, and Sansloy kills him. Una realises that she has been deceived by the Magician. Sansloy makes violent love to her. St. George enters, kills Sansloy and is re-united to Una.
>
> **Scene V The House of Holiness** St. George brings Una to the House of Holiness. After pledging himself to England, St. George bids farewell to his beloved Una and departs on his quest.

Creation

It is difficult to pin down the date when Ashton was informed about the granting of his six-week leave to return to the Sadler's Wells Ballet, and to know precisely when Walton was commissioned to provide the sizeable score—'45 mins' music in less than 5 weeks' as he wrote in a letter to John Warrack in 1957.[19] Some idea that this could have been around the end of 1942 is given in a letter of 24 January 1943 from Walton to Norman Peterkin, by then head of the OUP Music Department, in which he says: 'I've already been in touch with [the theatrical management] Linnit & Dunfee (Mr Clifton) about the ballet & they have arranged terms with [Bronson] Albery [manager of the New Theatre]. £4 a performance I believe. It is a bit awkward as I hadn't realised that the O.U.P. were agents for my stage works. Perhaps you could ring Clifton at Mayfair 0111 & see what can be arranged as regards splitting the boodle. It looks as if there won't be much by the time it gets to me.'[20] Another signpost is provided by Walton's piano sketch of Scene II which Lambert, on tour with the company, has signed 'C. Lambert/Queens Hotel Birmingham'. This points to the week of 8–13 March, although this is not necessarily the period of time in which the scene was first received.[21]

Walton was not a fast worker and would normally have required at least half a year for an orchestral work of more than forty minutes. But on this occasion he surpassed himself in committing to the task. Ashton had been reading the recently published scenarios that Marius Petipa had prepared for *The Sleeping Beauty* and *The Nutcracker*, with their precisely designated number of bars and type of music required. He consequently did much the same thing in terms of timings for Walton, who, with his by now considerable experience of film music, must have positively relished the challenge of being put into this form of straitjacket—even though his finished score surpassed Ashton's minutage by nearly ten minutes. Ashton's detailed instructions for *The Quest* can be found in the Appendix.

As remarkably few of Walton's composition sketches for any of his works survive, it is fascinating to be able to study the one he made for *The Quest*. This was done for piano in pencil on two, occasionally three, staves, and is a model of clarity, which was necessary as it had to serve as the basis for a copy from which the ballet rehearsal pianist(s) would play. The ballet was being created at the same time as the company was making a provincial tour, and Walton sent his piano score piecemeal to Ashton and Lambert (who was to conduct), requiring his original to be copied and then returned to him. As *The Star* newspaper was to report on 2 April 1943, this gave rise to risible situations:

> Senior boys at Repton school have had a hand, I hear, in getting out the music composed by William Walton for the new ballet 'The Quest', which the Sadler's Wells dancers are to produce at the New Theatre next Tuesday.
>
> The company were receiving a piano script from Walton almost page by page as they toured the provinces. Each slip received for rehearsal had to be copied out and the original returned to the composer for orchestration. At Derby, no professional copyist could be found, and some of the Repton [school] boys volunteered to do it.

Towards the end of the composition process timing became so tight that, having been given reasonable instructions as to what lay ahead, the rehearsal pianist Hilda Gaunt had to improvise an extended number of bars in slow 3/2 tempo to enable Ashton to create his choreography of the passacaglia Finale. Thanks to the foresight of Stewart Craggs, who in 1976 asked Margot Fonteyn, Beryl Grey, Moira Shearer, and John Piper for their reminiscences for his Walton Archive, we have short accounts of the rehearsal period by the dancers. It is a miracle that not only was the substantial score fully sketched but also orchestrated, and the parts copied, in time for the week of London rehearsals and the premiere. Walton dates the completion of his autograph full score 'March 29th 1943' (his 41st birthday); the premiere was on 6 April!

Walton had only achieved this by resorting to a couple of time-saving procedures. As the 'Seven Deadly Sins' episode at the start of Scene 3 was self-contained, he asked his friend, the film conductor and composer Ernest Irving, to undertake the task of orchestrating it. Roy Douglas is surely mistaken in claiming in a letter to Stewart Craggs that, in addition to Irving, he himself scored some 200 bars of this section (all seven 'sins' are only 170 bars); his distinctive writing is nowhere to be seen in the parts of the autograph score of this section not in Walton's hand, whereas it is easy to authenticate that of Irving.[22] The only exception is in the seventh variation, 'Pride'. Irving orchestrated this, and it is clear from the original set of orchestral parts that it was rehearsed, if not actually performed. However, his scoring was at some point replaced in the autograph score and parts by a new, heavier, and less imaginative orchestration. Why this was done, and by whom, it is not possible to say; the writing is without doubt not that of Walton, Irving, or Lambert. Perhaps Ashton asked for greater weight of sound, and perhaps the associate conductor Julian Clifford or the orchestral librarian obliged; it is certainly in the same hand as the person who copied the horn parts of the revised version, and the score is written on the same paper as that of the parts. This is the orchestration shown in the present edition. It would appear that Roy Douglas did, nevertheless, play a part in the ballet's orchestration, amounting approximately to the 200 bars that he mentioned. His writing can be seen in Scene III from the last 45 bars of the Hermaphrodites' Dance up to the 'Seven Deadly Sins' and from bar 20 of Scene IV up to rehearsal figure 16 of Scene V, though Walton has added a number of extra dynamics.

Clearly, the whole undertaking had been a close-run thing, especially considering the vicissitudes of wartime. With the clock ticking ominously, Walton has to be admired for the general accuracy of his autograph and for his refusal to take shortcuts in the matter of orchestration. For example, the section in Scene III (bars 359–72), depicting St George's disgust following the killing of Sansloy, could have been largely achieved by resorting to labour-saving shorthand devices, but the composer writes out the florid orchestration in admirably full and clear detail, which must have been time-consuming. At 1,224 bars (almost exactly the same number as the chamber opera *The Bear*), *The Quest* is Walton's fourth-longest work for orchestra (incidental and film music excepted), after Symphony No. 1 and the two operas.

Walton was fortunate that Constant Lambert was again in charge of musical matters. Doubtless due to wartime, Walton (living near Rugby) did not attend any rehearsals of the Sadler's Wells Ballet other than the very final ones,[23] although an important alteration towards the start of the ballet seems to indicate that he remained closely involved with the musical preparations.

Premiere

The Quest, sandwiched between *Les Sylphides* and *Façade*, was duly premiered at the New Theatre, London, on Tuesday 6 April 1943, and was a wild success.[24] This seemed to indicate not only that Ashton was much welcomed on his return to the company, but also that he had correctly judged the mood of the times. There were nearly twenty curtain calls, and five days later the critic of the *Sunday Times* referred to 'the almost frenzied enthusiasm of the audience'. The overnight review by Ferruccio Bonavia in the *Daily Telegraph* declared that 'the orchestra, under Constant Lambert, tackled the difficult score with confidence, ability and rare spirit'. Ashton's choreography was said to contain fine moments and serene quietness (in the final scene), but it was generally felt that, as Mary Clark later put it, 'masterpieces are not created to order within a given time limit'.[25] A full account of the action and production, written three years later by Cyril Beaumont in his book *The Sadler's Wells Ballet*, can be found in Appendix II.[26]

Walton's score received much praise. As one critic fancifully put it: 'It is impossible to judge Mr Walton's music from a single performance, but certainly it is a *tour de force*. Brilliant and buoyant, it supports the dancers like galleons on its bold, glittery, varicoloured, Mediterranean waves'.[27] However, Dyneley Hussey was more critical: 'He is rather inclined to fall back on somewhat commonplace Waltz-tunes, and when, in the finale, there is a call for a great noble melody, he is content with an ostinato bell-theme'.[28]

Walton must have enjoyed being back in a stimulating theatrical atmosphere after spending many wartime months living in rural (yet elegant) Northamptonshire and seems to have approved the production, although he found that, because of his distinctive flaring nostrils, Robert Helpmann looked 'more like the Dragon than St George!'.[29] The company, led by Margot Fonteyn as Una, also featured the exquisite, red-headed Moira Shearer as Pride, which was her first important creation, and the vamp Duessa gave the striking 15-year-old Beryl Grey a notable newly choreographed leading role. John Piper's sets were considered to be more successful than his costumes.[30] *The Quest* was given 93 times in London and 33 on tour before it was dropped from the repertory in August 1945 and never revived.[31]

Cuts

Writing to Roy Douglas in a letter simply dated 'May 1943', Walton said: 'About the ballet—when I've time I shall rescore the "7 deadlies"[,] also make some cuts in all the scenes. Having seen it three times I think I know just what is needed to tighten it'.[32] The cuts he suggested were never introduced into the production, doubtless because, as *The Tatler and Bystander* of 5 May reported, 'Ashton returned to the Air Force four days after the premiere'. The cuts, indicated in this edition by the conventional Vi = de signs, are those marked on two sheets of manuscript paper by Walton after the premiere. He found the few cuts he wanted to make in Scene II difficult to indicate exactly (indeed he has made a few mistakes) because he lacked access to the full score and parts when making them. Eventually all is self-explanatory except for what he writes about Scene V, which is as follows: 'from change into C major cut bars 15, 16, 17, 21, 22, 23, 24, 34, 35,

36, 37'. This is perplexing, as the whole movement, until eleven bars before the end, is essentially based on a three-bar, nine-note passacaglia theme. He adds, 'It needs a further cut in the A♭ section but again I can't do it without the score.' In the Suite, Tausky reduced this movement from 145 bars to 91; due to this, the E major and A flat sections are excluded in toto. It is tentatively suggested that, in order to avoid the unalloyed C major of the Suite, conductors might experiment with alternative cuts in this movement, if cuts are needed at all.

Loss of score and parts, and recovery

Wartime conditions must account for the casual approach that the company took over the preservation of the score and parts of the ballet, though Walton's lack of interest in their fate is harder to explain. At all events, nothing more was heard of *The Quest* until the habitually curious Alan Frank wrote to Walton on 3 November 1952 requesting information: 'I know I've asked you this question before . . . but what is the music of THE QUEST, and is there something peculiar about it? I just wonder why I have never seen it and why it is never heard.' On the 23rd of that month Walton replied from Casa Cirillo in Ischia: 'About the Quest. I suppose the score is somewhere but I don't know where. It would have to be drastically re-written before anything was done about it as it was composed in a terrific hurry[—]45 mins. in 4 weeks [*sic*] during the war, and though it may have its moments I doubt if it is worth doing unless there is a revival of the ballet. The whole thing[,] scenery—choreography—music was all too rushed & suffered in consequence.' This is a somewhat negative assessment of a ballet that received in all 126 performances.

And there matters rested until the writer and critic John Warrack, at that time assisting Frank at OUP and equally curious about the score, undertook a search for the missing material in November 1957, and came up trumps. He has kindly provided the following account of it for this edition:

> William himself, to whom I'd written in Ischia [in August 1957], had no idea what had happened to the score and wasn't all that keen on it being unearthed. Sadler's Wells music library knew nothing. Eventually I learnt from someone at the Wells that there was a storage warehouse in North London [a disused cinema off Dalston High Street] where they'd dumped old scenery and costumes and other junk that they didn't need but hadn't got round to destroying. On a hunch, I went up there, and the warehouseman in charge let me look round, to no avail, then showed me a cupboard which contained a lot of stuff, including some filthy dirty large brown envelopes of a very recognisable kind for keeping orchestral parts. In one of them, there indeed were the parts of 'The Quest', but also William's MS [and a copy of it]. I looked it through and checked that it appeared to be the complete score, and went back with it to OUP's Conduit Street office, feeling, I must say, as I clutched the envelope on a bus, quite excited.[33]

On 23 December 1957 Alan Frank wrote to Warrack at home: 'This is really a most dramatic piece of modern musical research work.' For some reason Frank waited until 17 October 1960 to inform Walton of this discovery: 'You will be amused to hear that by sheer persistence we have now recovered the score and material of THE QUEST.'

The Suite

Alan Frank eventually decided on a modest commercial exploitation of this rediscovery. The idea of extracting a suite from the ballet had been discussed between Walton and Norman Peterkin as far back as 1943, but nothing had come of it. Knowing well Walton's reluctance to make suites from his theatrical scores (which had become more pronounced with his Shakespeare film scores), Frank wisely proposed Vilem Tausky, conductor of the BBC Concert Orchestra, as someone who could reliably inspect the score, make suggestions for those sections that might form a suite, and 'normalize' the scoring. Having studied the copy of the autograph and discussed his selection with Frank, Tausky agreed to undertake the relatively simple task of concocting a four-movement suite (with appropriately modified opening and closing bars) and filling out the brass parts. Having done this to OUP's satisfaction, he performed the Suite at a BBC Light Music Festival concert with the Concert Orchestra at the Royal Festival Hall on 3 June 1961, which so satisfied Frank that on 6 June he wrote to Walton: 'I think it would be quite safe for us to go ahead with Tausky and prepare a fair copy full score which we could show to you and then, if you don't disapprove, publish . . . Will you give me the OK to go ahead so far anyway?' Walton gave his agreement on 11 June, and Ronald Finch was engaged to originate the score.

Tausky gave a second performance of the Suite on the BBC's Home Service on 13 July, and Frank arranged for a private recording of it to be made which he sent out to Walton in Ischia. On 18 August Walton wrote to Frank: 'THE QUEST has arrived. Good on the whole. T. seems to have done a good job with scoring. I must say the Valse stinks a bit but it's mercifully short! But I can't remember what it is about especially the opening— witches?—bats? Does it need a programme note? At any rate it's ballet music and the finale is quite presentable.' It is not known how much Walton corrected the proofs of the Suite, and to what extent, if any, he made changes; whether it was he, for example, who deleted the tremolo strings in the two bars before the final bar, which Tausky had not originally done.

The details of the four movements of the published 15-minute Ballet Suite are as follows:

1. INTRODUCTION (Storm) *and*
   THE MAGICIAN AND THE TRANSFORMATION (Allegro malizioso) from Scene I, bars 1–10, 124–239 (plus extra bar by Tausky), 284–90, 297–344

2. SICILIANA (The Spell)
   Scene I, bars 79–123 (introductory bars and short concert ending arranged by Tausky)

3. THE CHALLENGE
   Scene II, bars 8–90

4. THE REUNION (Passacaglia)
   Scene V, bars 1–66, 104–10, 126–36, 140–5

Publication and recording

The study score of the Ballet Suite, with a note saying that it had been 'adapted by Vilem Tausky . . . with the cooperation of the composer', was published on 3 May 1962. Walton conducted the Suite with the BBC Symphony Orchestra on the opening night of that year's Proms on 21 July. It attracted favourable reviews as being a new work representing Walton in his much-admired lighter vein. As a result of this performance, a few corrections were made by hand to the hire scores and parts of the Suite in the month that followed. On 14 April 1970 Walton recorded it for Lyrita with the London Symphony Orchestra, and the disc was released in June of the following year.[34] In 1972 the Suite, together with the Viola Concerto, was used by the Royal Ballet for Joe Layton's ballet 'O.W.' [Oscar Wilde].

NOTES

1. See Preface to the WWE Vol. 13, p. v.
2. See Preface to the WWE Vol. 18, p. vi–vii. Ashton also choreographed Walton's music for the film *Escape Me Never* and for the revue *The First Shoot*.
3. It has to be assumed that Walton was not paid for the numerous wartime performances of *The Wise Virgins* given with two pianos.
4. See Preface to the WWE Vol. 16, p. xvi. and Facsimile 3. David Vaughan, in *Frederick Ashton and his Ballets* (London, 1999), p. 291, says that 'At the end of the 1954–1955 season [of the Royal Ballet] de Valois had announced in a curtain speech that there would be a three-act ballet by Ashton and Walton in the following year. The subject was to be *Macbeth*, but nothing came of the project.'
5. After being advised of this fact, William McNaught wrote in the *Musical Times* (June 1940, p. 279): 'The vision of Mr Lambert wading through two hundred cantatas is one that we abandon with regret.'
6. See Preface to the WWE Vol. 20, p. vii. *A Bach Book for Harriet Cohen* was reissued by OUP in 2013.
7. All references to correspondence with OUP are to be found in the OUP Archive, Oxford.
8. Cyril W. Beaumont, *The Sadler's Wells Ballet: A Detailed Account of Works in the Permanent Repertory with Critical Notes* (London, 1946, rev. edn, 1947), pp. 163–169. Opposite p. 164 is a black and white photograph of a scene from the production. Another, of the final tableau, can be seen in Alexander Bland, *The Royal Ballet: The First Fifty Years* (New York, 1981), p. 59.
9. In her *Autobiography* (London, 1975, p. 85), Margot Fonteyn relates: 'There was a lot of mirth when we saw it advertised on a billboard as "The Wise Virgins (subject to alteration)".' Whistler's costume design for the bridegroom is on display at the Brighton Museum and Art Gallery. Other designs, including that of the initial drop-curtain, are believed to be owned by the descendants of Laurence Whistler, the brother of Rex.
10. Humphrey Searle, *Ballet Music: An Introduction* (London, 1958; rev. edn, 1973), p. 149.
11. HMV C3178–9; Victor (USA) 18752/3. Walton re-recorded 'Sheep may safely graze' with the Philharmonia Orchestra in March 1953; Columbia 33C 1016 (LP), released in June 1953.
12. A full account of the whole debacle can be found in Meredith Daneman, *Margot Fonteyn* (London, 2004), pp. 146–154.
13. Perhaps the autograph was destroyed when Walton's flat in South Eaton Place was bombed in May 1941. However, the ballet continued to be performed up until January 1944, and the OUP copyist's score does not contain any markings made by Constant Lambert.
14. See Julie Kavanagh, *Secret Muses: The Life of Frederick Ashton* (London, 1996), pp. 288–290.
15. Beaumont, *The Sadler's Wells Ballet*, p. 178.
16. Kavanagh, *Secret Muses*, p. 289.
17. Kavanagh, *Secret Muses*, p. 289.

18. In Helen Wallace, *Boosey & Hawkes: The Publishing Story* (London, 2007), p. 41, it is recorded that Ashton first offered the commission to Benjamin Britten, newly returned to London from the USA.

19. Walton letter of 27 August 1957 to John Warrack, quoted in Michael Kennedy, *Portrait of Walton* (Oxford, 1989), p. 122.

20. *Selected Letters*, ed. Hayes, p. 145.

21. In fact, the company was performing in bomb-damaged Coventry that week, but Lambert was clearly staying in nearby Birmingham.

22. Roy Douglas letter to Stewart Craggs, 24 June 1987 (Craggs Archive).

23. A letter to Stewart Craggs of May 20 [1976] from Moira Shearer says: 'William Walton never appeared at all when we were working—but came to the dress rehearsals &, of course, the opening performance' (Craggs Archive).

24. The bottom of the front page of the programme stated, 'The entire proceeds of this performance have been donated to the Lady Cripps' "Aid to China Fund". This was the position in which the name of the conductor(s) was normally placed; as a result, Constant Lambert's name was omitted entirely.

25. Mary Clark, *The Sadler's Wells Ballet: A History and an Appreciation* (London, 1955), p. 177.

26. The book also contains three black and white photographs from Scenes 2, 3, and 5. However, the finest published photographic record of the production is to be found in *The Tatler and Bystander* issues of 28 April 1943, and 5 and 12 May.

27. *New Statesman & Nation*, 10 April 1943.

28. *The Spectator*, 16 April 1943.

29. Walton to John Warrack; see Kennedy, p. 122.

30. In his letter to Stewart Craggs of 20 July 1976, Piper says: 'Fred Ashton was in constant touch, and many of the design ideas—especially the costumes—were his' (Craggs Archive).

31. In his letter to John Warrack of August 1957, Walton said: 'However there have been quite persistent attempts to revive it, but both Freddy and I, perhaps wrongly, have fought shy of it.'

32. William Walton Archive, Ischia.

33. A copy of the email that John Warrack sent to the editor is now in the OUP Archive.

34. Lyrita, SRCS49. The Compact Disc SRCD224 was released in June 1992.

APPENDIX

Ashton's synopsis and minutage for *The Quest* as given to Walton

Scene 1

1	St George and Una in storm approach home of Archimago[;] as Archimago sees them servants take off his magician's robe and two bats fly from under it and dance round him. Archimago then walks up and down telling his beads devoutly.	1 ¾ min. storm.
2a	Archimago makes them welcome, drinks passed round?	½ min.
2b	Una exhausted does dance suggesting fatigue, lullaby?	1 min.

3	Bats flutter round Una and St George and make them sleepy. They fall asleep.	½ min.
4	Archimago whirls around in an ecstasy of malice.	½ min.
5	Archimago summons his female servant, changes her into Una and leads her to St George.	1 min. or less.
6	St George awakes and rises, does dance with false Una, at end of which he rejects her and retires into the chapel.	1 min.
7	Archimago, angry at his failure, calls his male servant and makes him lie with false Una. Brings St George out to watch spectacle.	½ min.
8	St George takes his helmet and exits in disgust. Archimago retires.	½ min.
9	Interlude suggesting dawn[,] bats in belfry, at end of which Una comes out of the house and searches for St George[;] unable to find him goes on her way.	¾ min.
10	Archimago comes out of hermitage to find Una gone, curses servants for letting her go. Servants bring him armour like St George. He exits preceded by bats and with noise of distant thunder like in Symphonie Fantastique?	1 min.
	Total	9 mins.

Scene 2

1	Sansloy and Sansjoy on stage, are joined by Sansfoy and Duessa[;] all knights compete for hand of Duessa and should each do a dance suggesting their various characters. Sansfoy most appealing[,] Sansloy heartiest and most brutal[,] Sansjoy poetic and most attractive but unscrupulous.	3 mins.
2	Enter St George[;] challenge and fight and kill [Sansfoy] and exit with Duessa.	1 min.
3	Enter Una searching for St George, weary and falls asleep.	½ min.
4	Bats flutter preceding Archimago who enters dressed like St George (St George theme distorted here) closes his visor wakes Una and exits together.	1 min.
	Total	5½ mins.

Scene 3

1	Curtain rises on Pride sitting on throne surrounded by Deadly Sins, and six hermaphrodites standing ready to begin dance.	1 min.
2	At conclusion of Hermaphrodite dance each sin does short dance.	about 4 mins.
3	At conclusion of Sixth Sin Queen Pride does her dance, at end of which she is joined by other Sins, so as to finish the Sins in a grandiose fashion.	1 min. or more.
4	Small fanfare and entrance of Sansloy.	½ min.
5	Rhapsodic dance for entire court.	¾ min.

6	Fanfare for St George. Intro challenge, separation by Queen who descends from throne and begs them to fight like Gents.	¾ min.
7	Fight.	1 min. or ¾.
8	Defeat of Sansloy, Duessa throws herself on his body. St George disillusioned. Cobwebs descend. Music here should be harsh and discordant to suggest disgust (dust and ashes) and then slow down as St George exits slowly and sadly.	1 min.
	Total	3¾ mins.

Scene 4

Scene same as scene 2[—]a rocky place towards evening.

1	Sansjoy (poetic one) alone[;] dance of mourning (like the beginning of Pathetic symphony last movement lacrimoso strings and slow?).	½ min.
2	Enter Archimago preceded by bats, gets killed by Sansjoy[.] Una runs away[,] is caught.	¾ min.
3	Sansjoy does impassioned dance with Una of seduction. (Towards end of dance St George enters and watches Una defending her virtue, is moved.)	¾ min.
4	St George rushes to Una's defence and kills Sansjoy, and is re-united with Una [;] their themes come together in the most movingly lyrical passage you have ever written.	1¼ mins.
	Total	3¾ mins.

Scene 5 House of Holiness

1	Short prelude to scene perhaps a single bell tolling.	
2	Curtain rises on Faith, Hope, Charity and their attendant virtues.	
3	Half a min. of Faith and Virtues[,] aspiring, religious music.	
4	½ a min. of Hope and Virtues. Broad visionary music.	
5	½ a min. of Charity and her Girls. Compassionate music.	
6	Combined effort of virtues leading to Entrance of Una and St George who are welcomed by F H & C.	1 min.
7	Pas de deux of Una and St George (wonderful music[,] high spot of ballet).	2 mins.
8	At end of pas de deux Una and St George are separated and he is reminded of his duties to his country.	½ min.
9	Music for Virtues who dress St George in his Armour again.	½ min.
10	Farewell of Una and St George.	½ min.
11	Exit of St George with banner, triumphant exalted music.	½ min.
12	Apotheosis. 1 min.[;] sense of suspended action like your March with all the bells in England ringing.	
	Total	7½ mins.

4

Belshazzar's Feast *(Vol. 4)*

Steuart Bedford

The first reference to a project that was to culminate in one of the twentieth century's finest choral works is to be found in the archives of the BBC:

> With reference to the suggestion we discussed recently concerning the writing of special music for broadcasting, I should be much obliged if you would let me know at the earliest possible moment the results of your cogitations, as the matter has now to be dealt with officially.[1]

This is part of a letter dated 21 August 1929 from Edward Clark to William Walton. Clark (1888–1962) was a particularly enlightened programme planner in the early years of the BBC; he was personally acquainted with many of the leading composers and artists of the day, and his interests were by no means confined to England. On 27 July 1929 there took place in Baden-Baden the first performance of *Der Lindbergh Flug*, a radio cantata by Paul Hindemith and Kurt Weill. The work would have been of particular interest to the BBC, not only because it was written specifically for radio, but also because it used small forces—four soloists, small orchestra, small chorus—which at that time were considered more suitable for broadcasting than large-scale works. Clark, who had already suggested that Hindemith be engaged as soloist in the first performance of Walton's Viola Concerto in October 1929, was almost certainly present at this performance. It can be no coincidence that within a few days he was actively seeking to commission works on a similar scale from three young British composers—Constant Lambert, Victor Hely-Hutchinson, and William Walton. In this context Clark's follow-up letter to Walton of August 1929 falls neatly into place.

Although no reply has survived, on 12 January 1930 Clark was able to report to his BBC colleagues that the three composers approached had all decided on their subjects, and accepted the limited forces at their disposal. Walton's was to be *Nebuchadnezzar* [sic] *and the Writing on the Wall*. A fee of 50 guineas was proposed.

Since 1919, when he was virtually adopted by the Sitwell family, Walton had been living in Chelsea with the brothers Osbert and Sacheverell, the latter always known as Sachie. It was therefore natural for Walton to turn to Osbert for advice on the BBC project; perhaps he preferred to avoid Sachie, as it was one of his poems that Constant Lambert had used in the previous year for his very successful choral work *The Rio Grande*. Be that as it may, it was Osbert who suggested 'the writing on the wall' and, as he tells us in *Laughter in the Next Room* (the fourth volume of his autobiography), he spent ten days over Christmas 1929 in Venice 'partly in sight-seeing and partly in composing and putting together for William Walton the words of our oratorio Belshazzar's Feast'.[2] Meanwhile, in a letter to his mother dated 23 December 1929, Walton says that he is 'off to Amalfi to join Osbert to work on Belshazzar'.[3] By Amalfi is meant the Albergo Cappuccini Convento, a converted monastery situated halfway up the town's cliff edge, with spectacular views across the Gulf of Salerno. It was a favourite resort of the Sitwell brothers, whose love of Italy and all things Italian they passed on to Walton in great measure. It can be assumed that Walton was the first to arrive at Amalfi, but once Osbert appeared he was able to hand over his (as he thought) completed libretto. At Walton's suggestion various passages were later changed and others substituted, and by January 1930 work on the composition had begun. In a letter to Siegfried Sassoon of 17 January Osbert describes the situation:

> [William] is rather depressed, sits long at the piano and does little work. But it is a stage thru' which he always passes, if he could only recognize it. Also C. Lambert's success with Rice Grands [*Rio Grande*] has, I am sorry to say, tinged a little their carefree friendship with a certain acerbity. In fact, I thought the other day that I distinctly heard him referred to as 'that little beast.' But do not mention it.[4]

Progress was slow, and in April Walton opted for a change of scene, installing himself in a small *pensione* at Ascona in Switzerland at the northern end of Lake Maggiore. This appears to have done the trick, for on 30 May 1930 Clark was able to report to Adrian Boult, who was just two weeks into his appointment as musical director of the BBC, 'I saw Willie Walton on Wednesday, who has just returned from abroad where he has completed the composition of *Belshazzar* . . . Whilst abroad he has shown this work to various people whom it has evidently much impressed.'[5] This finally spurred the BBC to issue an official letter of commission, almost six months late, which spelled out the terms: duration 20–30 minutes, small orchestra and chorus, two soloists, and a fee of £50. The original guineas had been rounded down.

Walton's reaction is contained in a long letter to Hubert Foss, founder of the Oxford University Press music department and by then a close friend, which is of considerable interest as it appears to contradict Clark's report to Boult.[6] He claims that the BBC seems to have misunderstood the length and nature of the work that they had commissioned. He is 'about half way through' and predicts that it will last 30–40 minutes. The forces required will be small chorus and orchestra, two soloists, and a speaker who will connect the four sections. These are:

Speaker foreshadows the captivity of Israel

1 The Hebrews in captivity
  Speaker describes Babylon (chorus with baritone solo)
2 Description of the feast including the worship of the various gods (orchestral variations), leading to
3 A song of the Hebrews (duet for baritone and mezzo with chorus in the background)
  Speaker narrates the 'writing on the wall', the destruction of Belshazzar and the capture of Babylon
4 Song of thanksgiving (chorus)

The contradictory accounts as to whether the work was finished, or not, have never been satisfactorily explained. However, a letter from Walton to the pianist Harriet Cohen dated 3 May 1930 would seem to confirm that Clark had not been misinformed. Walton writes in answer to one of Cohen's letters asking about the progress of *Belshazzar*: 'Bloody awful. Anyhow that is what I think about it, though Sir Thos B & Sir Hubert Foss think otherwise, but they haven't seen the last part yet, which contains two or three minutes of boredom unsurpassed by any of the AB's (this is not to be repeated) or anybody & it is all quite unsingable.'[7]

This clearly indicates that the first version of the work was complete at least in vocal score, and this must have been the version that was 'shown to various people' and which Walton declared 'went down the drain' when he wrote to his biographer Michael Kennedy about it in 1976.[8]

The work that Walton is describing to Foss can only be the beginnings of a second version, expanding the material of the original (there would hardly have been time to reach the halfway point otherwise) but still retaining the small orchestra and chorus. Foss must have known all this, but for diplomatic reasons had to tread very carefully to avoid putting Clark in an awkward position.

He had, of course, no choice but to relay the contents of Walton's letter to the BBC, and their reaction was predictably negative. The fact that Walton had exceeded the specified 30 minutes was heavily censured, but the issue that caused virtual uproar was his request for a commissioning fee of £25 for each section, thereby doubling what was on offer. After much huffing and puffing the BBC decided in September 1930 that the work had grown to such proportions that it could no longer be considered to have been specifically written for broadcasting; accordingly they withdrew from the project. However, they did at least make partial amends by subsequently mounting the first London performance (the work's second) in November 1931.

None of this deterred Walton from ploughing ahead, even though for some time there was no prospect of a performance. At one point (fig.26+3) he came to a grinding halt, which he described three years later in a much-quoted letter to Hubert and Dora Foss: 'I got landed on the word gold—I was there from May to December, perched, unable to move either to the right or left or up or down.'[9] Compositional blocks were not unknown to Walton, and sadly were to remain a feature of his life; even so it is hard to take this one entirely at face value.

In November 1930 Walton installed himself in Sachie's home, Weston Hall, Northamptonshire, where he was given the run of the stables so that his work at the piano would not disturb the rest of the family. Another letter to Harriet Cohen describes his wretchedly slow progress. By January 1931 he was pulling himself out of his trough, no doubt encouraged by the proximity of one of his relatively recent female companions, Imma Doernberg, Princess of Erbach-Schönberg. However, it must have come as a great relief, as well as providing a real stimulus to the unlocking of his creative energy, when Sir Thomas Beecham, who had already seen the work in its early stages, suddenly stepped in and claimed the premiere for the Leeds Triennial Festival that was to take place in October 1931.The minutes of the festival management committee of 17 December 1930 do not mention any new work by Walton, but those of the next meeting on 19 February 1931 indicate that much had happened in the meantime. They record that 'Belshazzar would be ready by April which would be quite early enough. The secretary had offered a fee of 20 guineas for the first performance and undertook to purchase 320 copies of the vocal score. Mr Walton was suggesting a slightly larger fee but no difficulty in settling terms was anticipated.'[10] No doubt this aspect was greatly facilitated when Walton's composer friend Lord Berners offered to pay £50 for the dedication. Walton never forgot this kindness, and when Elizabeth Lutyens was going through a lean patch in her composing career he offered her £100 to write anything she liked and dedicate it to him; the result was her 1945 dramatic scena, *The Pit*. This gesture was particularly appropriate as her husband was Edward Clark, the originator of the *Belshazzar* project.

The final reference to *Belshazzar* in the Leeds Festival minutes is of a meeting on 15 April 1931 when it was recorded that 'Walton had changed his mind and cut out the contralto solo. He needed only a baritone and says that Mr Dennis Noble would be admirable in the part.'[11] No trace of what the contralto was to do has survived; she is mentioned only in section three of the description Walton gave to Foss in June 1930, and at some point this part was jettisoned. Could Walton have originally intended her to sing in section one, 'The Hebrews in captivity', a passage that is now given to the baritone and constitutes the only time he does not act as narrator?

In January 1931, revivified by the prospect of a performance at a major venue, Walton returned to Ascona with Imma Doernberg, ostensibly for her to help with the German translation. There he experienced one of those 'moments of great exhilaration when things are going well',[12] and by 8 March 1931 he was on to the final chorus, expecting to finish by 26 March, when he had promised to attend Lionel Tertis's performance of his Viola Concerto at Queen's Hall, the first time that Tertis was to play the work in England. In April, 320 early printed copies of the first section of the vocal score were rushed to Leeds. Now Walton could settle down and attend to the orchestration, which was conceived on an unusually large scale and included two optional brass bands.[13] This was completed by the end of May.

The text

Osbert Sitwell's text is described as 'arranged from biblical sources' in the published orchestral score and, more clearly, as 'selected and arranged from The Bible' in the vocal score. The final section of this Preface gives the text separately, together with the biblical references, and indicates where Sitwell either abbreviated the original or added lines of his own. However, this is not always easy to show with absolute precision, as Sitwell often plundered widely different sections of the Bible for use in close succession for a single passage of text. For example, in lines 25–9 excerpts from Psalm 137 and Revelation read like one continuous text; lines 43–92 are principally from Daniel 5: 1–5, but also incorporated are verses from Daniel 3, which deal with the story of Nebuchadnezzar and the Burning Fiery Furnace. A sprinkling of Sitwell's own lines completes the mix, which may well seem clumsy in the description but in practice reads quite naturally. To judge from the care with which the verses are laid out in the early editions of the vocal score Sitwell must have felt that his work had literary merit in its own right. In an interview which he gave to the *Yorkshire Evening News* the day before the premiere, he stated somewhat simplistically, 'The libretto as it stands is almost wholly taken from the Bible. I myself have merely added certain words to assist the music and the poetic flow.'[14]

In 1942, eleven years after the premiere, Sitwell suddenly woke up to the fact that he had never received any royalty payments for his work. Although one cannot help wondering whether this awakening was stimulated by the prospect of a commercial recording scheduled for January 1943, it was nonetheless a perfectly reasonable proposition, and accordingly he wrote to OUP to open negotiations. Foss, however, reacted rather testily, querying whether he had any real claim to collect fees for the use of words from the Bible, drawing from Sitwell a letter in which he asserted, among other things, that at least a quarter of the libretto was his own.[15] Quite apart from the fact that this does not match what he had told the newspaper in 1931, his claim is demonstrably untrue. Of the 119 lines that comprise the complete libretto, no more than 12 are by Sitwell.

In the circumstances he was probably wise not to respond to Foss's request for a marked-up copy of the text showing his original work, choosing to sit tight and await the publisher's consultations with Walton. The outcome was a three-way financial split between composer, librettist, and publisher, an amazing agreement considering the disparity of the work undertaken by the composer (15 months) and librettist (ten days in Venice). Perhaps Walton was genuinely mindful of how much he owed to the Sitwells in his early years, and sensed that here was an opportunity to repay some of that debt and even to do something to heal his relationship with Osbert, which had been more or less ruptured since 1936. His generosity resulted in the royalties from *Belshazzar* performances eventually becoming the most profitable item in the accounts of Osbert Sitwell's estate, a situation that continues to this day.

A curious postscript to the affair emerged in 1972 when, in a letter of 2 October to Stewart Craggs, Christabel, Lady Aberconway, dedicatee of the Viola Concerto and a former close friend of Osbert, claimed that she did most of the research for the text. While it is strange that this is the only time that she made this claim and that she chose to make it three years after Sitwell's death, the substance of her claim is entirely credible. Considering how widely the text ranges over the various books of the Bible, one can well imagine that Sitwell would have welcomed some help in its assembly, even if a biblical concordance might have served just as well. There is only one period of time possible for her collaboration and that falls between the decision to set the Belshazzar story and Sitwell's departure for Venice—roughly speaking, September to December 1929. However, a letter from Sitwell to Christabel dated 13 January 1930 states, 'I have finished a biblical libretto for Willie.' The use of the indefinite article seems to imply that she is hearing about it for the first time, which would make nonsense of her claim. Difficult as it is to believe that a close friend of Osbert would have known nothing about his participation in the *Belshazzar* project until after its completion, this is the inevitable implication, and unless further evidence comes to light we are unlikely ever to know the truth.

First performance

The Leeds Festival was founded in 1858, but it was not until it became triennial in 1880 that it began to gain a reputation as one of the most prestigious of all the choral festivals that proliferated in provincial England in the late nineteenth and early twentieth centuries. Commissions included works by Barnby, Sullivan, Stanford, and

Mackenzie, and the festival mounted an impressive number of first performances that include Dvořák's *St Ludmilla* (1886), Elgar's *Caractacus* (1898) and his symphonic study *Falstaff* (1913), and Vaughan Williams's *Toward the Unknown Region* (1907) and *A Sea Symphony* (1910).

The 1931 festival offered a programme that would have tested the endurance of the most avid concert-goer, to say nothing of the stamina of the Leeds Festival Chorus, which was taking part in premieres of works by Eric Fogg (*The Seasons*), Frederick Austin (*Pervigilium Veneris*), as well as the Walton, together with performances of Handel's *Solomon*, Cherubini's Requiem Mass in D minor, Delius's *A Mass of Life*, Berlioz's *Requiem*, and Bach's Mass in B minor. A liberal sprinkling of symphonies and concertos completed the programmes, all of which took place within a period of four days. No wonder that the critics were beginning to complain of overload and that audiences were showing signs of falling off.

Sir Thomas Beecham, who had been in charge of the festival since 1928, had assigned the conducting of *Belshazzar's Feast* to his recently appointed assistant Dr Malcolm Sargent. Then aged 36, Sargent had already gained considerable renown as a choral conductor elsewhere, and was now making his Leeds debut. The Festival Chorus had been rehearsing regularly since April with their chorus master Norman Strafford, organist and choirmaster at Holy Trinity Church, Kingston-upon-Hull, and regarded by Beecham as the best chorus master in England.[16]

They were also lucky to have as rehearsal pianist Herbert Bardgett, another distinguished Yorkshire figure, who was soon to take charge of the Huddersfield Choral Society and later assemble and train it, with all the difficulties created by wartime, for Walton's 1943 recording of *Belshazzar*. Sargent would undoubtedly have found them well prepared when he took his first choral rehearsal on 29 August; he returned on the next two Saturdays to consolidate his work. The often-repeated story that he was sent prematurely to Leeds to quell an incipient revolution, due to the chorus members reacting adversely to the difficulties of the choral writing, is not supported by any evidence, effective though it might have been for the purposes of 'spin'. No choir, or orchestra come to that, is without a core of hardliners who display an ingrained resistance to anything new, but this seldom represents anything more than a minority. Charles Reid, Sargent's first biographer, sought out some of the choristers from the original performance, and all denied finding the music impossibly difficult. Moreover, an unsigned article in the *Yorkshire Post* of 14 September, entitled 'Composer attends rehearsal', which reports on Sargent's third rehearsal, states 'from scraps of song heard in the vestibule afterwards one gathered that the fall of Babylon was the happiest thing that had ever happened'. Sargent too was clearly enjoying himself when he announced, 'This tenor lead is the most difficult in music', then turning to Walton with, 'Curse you!'

The first performance took place as part of a marathon programme (by today's standards) on Thursday 8 October 1931 at Leeds Town Hall. The London Symphony Orchestra was led by Elgar's old friend Willy Reed, and Dennis Noble was the baritone soloist. Beecham had come to the rescue by agreeing to some extra orchestral rehearsals.

The programme was:

> Vaughan Williams: Toward the Unknown Region
> J. S. Bach: Concerto for Two Violins
> Eric Fogg: The Seasons (conducted by the composer)
> Walton: Belshazzar's Feast
> Rimsky-Korsakov: 'Antar' Symphony

The chorus had already sung Austin's *Pervigilium Veneris* and Delius's *A Mass of Life* at the morning concert and were to precede *Belshazzar* with the Vaughan Williams and the Eric Fogg premiere. Nonetheless their rendering of Walton's work set the festival ablaze. 'This was a great performance of a work which bears the indubitable stamp of greatness,' wrote the critic of the *Yorkshire Observer*,[17] while the anonymous reviewer in *The Times* (actually Frank Howes) commented, 'We shall be surprised if *Belshazzar's Feast* does not create another landmark in the history of the Leeds Festival.'[18] The *Yorkshire Evening News* noted the spontaneous outburst of cheering from the chorus when Walton ascended the platform.[19] Though delighted by his success, Walton is said to have found the performance too slow. As it happens there exists some supporting evidence for this claim. Herbert Thompson, the distinguished music critic of the *Yorkshire Post*, was in the habit of timing virtually everything he heard, including rehearsals. His diary entry for 8 October 1931 records 'Belshazzar 38 minutes'—definitely on the slow side; Walton's own 1943 recording is four and a half minutes shorter.[20]

Subsequent performances

On 25 November 1931 a second performance took place at Queen's Hall, London, with BBC forces under Adrian Boult. Despite the excitement aroused, the general feeling of those who had attended the premiere at Leeds was that this performance did not have the same impact—the tempi seemed slower and the chorus was considerably less secure. Boult was happier with his second performance a year later but Walton, writing to Hubert and Dora Foss after listening to the broadcast in Berlin, found 'the slow part too slow and the fast . . . too fast'.[21] This is neither the first nor the last time that we find Walton adversely criticising conductors of this work.

Boult programmed *Belshazzar* twice more with his BBC forces before the war and eventually introduced it to the Proms in 1946. In 1947 Walton himself conducted the work.

It comes as no surprise that it was Sargent, the supreme choral conductor, who made the work very much his own. In January 1932 he gave three performances in London at the Courtauld–Sargent concerts, and thereafter contrived to programme the piece throughout his career, often performing it on his extended worldwide tours. He was in charge of the first performance of the revised version on 8 March 1950, and in 1951, as newly appointed chief conductor of the BBC Symphony Orchestra, he programmed the piece at the Proms, this time allowing Walton to conduct. Thereafter he treated the promenaders to a performance virtually every year, and between 1956 and 1966 it appeared nine times at these concerts. A tenth was scheduled for 1967, but in the event Sargent's final illness compelled him to hand over the performance to John Pritchard.

Second only to Sargent in the number of performances conducted was Walton himself. His first was on 2 January 1943 in Liverpool, a run-in for the recording on the following day. As we have seen, both Boult and Sargent invited him to conduct the work at the Proms and, like Sargent, Walton took the piece on extended tours—Australia, New Zealand, and the USA—and even gave four performances in Israel in Hebrew. Between 1965 and 1971 Walton's conducting of his oratorio became a regular feature of London's concert programmes. It is fortunate that the performance that he gave for the Commonwealth Arts Festival at the Royal Festival Hall in August 1965 has been issued on CD.

British conductors of note such as Wood, Harty, Coates, and Raybould were not slow to programme the new choral sensation. Performances were by no means confined to England. On 1 June 1933 Constant Lambert conducted the European premiere at the ISCM Festival in Amsterdam, having survived the indignity of having to rehearse his chorus from behind the counter in the Rotterdam central post office, as nowhere else large enough to accommodate them could be found. America was very quick to take up the challenge, and both Koussevitsky (Boston, 31 March 1933) and Eugene Goosens (Cincinnati Spring Festival, 1933) actually anticipated the European premiere. Stokowski (Philadelphia, January 1934), for whom the work would seem tailor-made, was not far behind. Gradually the number of performances snowballed to the extent that between March 1954 and June 1957 there were 19 performances in the USA, adding up to almost one every two months.

Although every publication of the vocal score has included a German translation, it was some time before this was actually heard. Herbert von Karajan's two performances in Vienna on 13 and 14 June 1948 were certainly among the first to use it, and the occasion moved Walton to tears, causing him to say privately that he could not believe that he had ever been capable of writing such marvellous music.[22] Eventually performances in the vernacular reached Budapest in 1956, Paris in 1957, Rome in 1958, and Buenos Aires in 1991.

Back in England *Belshazzar* was becoming such common fare that even schools were beginning to tackle it. What had once seemed daunting in its difficulty had now become part of everyday musical language, and in a letter of 14 April 1962 to Helga Cranston, editor of the *Henry V* film, Walton writes, 'No choir can call itself a choir these days unless it can sing "Belshazzar" almost by heart!'[23] One can only hope that in 1983, the last year of his life, Walton realized that his work had received the crowning accolade by being selected as a set work for GCE O-level music.

Revisions

In the second volume of his autobiography Spike Hughes gives a tantalizingly brief glimpse into Walton's workshop:

> With that curious devotion to duty, which sometimes possesses composers, William Walton suddenly took to doing a bit of copying of the orchestral parts for the first London performance (25 November) of his oratorio Belshazzar's Feast. The work had already been performed at Leeds (8 October) but for some reason the composer undertook to rescore one or two passages and decided that it would save time if he copied the orchestral parts himself. The first subject of A Harlem Symphony [Hughes's composition] was scribbled on the back of a manuscript flute part that had gone wrong in the copying.[24]

In the absence of the autograph full score and any original orchestral parts, it is impossible even to hazard a guess as to what these first revisions could have been.

The earliest orchestral score that we now possess is in the hand of a copyist. It has been marked up by Sargent and was almost certainly used by him at the premiere. It contains some half a dozen minor corrections in the composer's hand, but as very few of these are found in a second early score, used by Constant Lambert in 1933, they must have been inserted at a later time. It was not until after his 1943 recording that Walton began to have serious second thoughts, as he so often did, resulting in a series of extensive revisions sufficient to warrant the making of an entirely new score. This daunting task was put into the hands of Roy Douglas, who had helped Walton enormously with his film scores during the war, and went on to prepare many of his works for publication, notably *Troilus and Cressida*.

Walton's principal revisions are:

1 a major reorchestration of bars 781–864 ('While the Kings of the Earth')
2 new brass and organ parts for bars 1016–71 (these are contained on three pages of autograph and represent the only part of the work that at present exists in Walton's hand)
3 redistributed parts for trumpets and trombones in bars 987–1001
4 a considerable reduction of the percussion parts
5 a completely revised ending from bar 1114 to the end

The revised ending has been the subject of much confusion. Contrary to what is sometimes asserted, it is quite clear that this was the first revision on which Walton embarked. We know this because the two early scores already cited have their three final pages pasted over with sheets containing the new orchestration, so this version must have been current before Roy Douglas made his new score in 1948. The pasting is so solid that, were it not for the existence of a third early score recently recovered from the USA, it would be impossible to determine what the original orchestration was. However, this is not quite the end of the matter. In a letter that Douglas wrote on 14 June 1987 to Stewart Craggs,[25] discussing the rescoring of the final bars, he adds something that he must have heard from the composer, namely that at a rehearsal somewhere abroad—it could have been Salzburg—the organist suggested the addition of an organ chord halfway through the penultimate bar. Walton agreed and added it to the score, in the process expanding the original two bars, to five. The organ enters halfway through the five bars, and at the same time the timpani drop an octave. None of this appears in the pasted sheets, so it is clearly a later addition. It is not difficult to track down the occasion when this must have happened. We are looking for a performance taking place abroad between 1944 and 1948—not so common at that time—at which Walton was present; and if we further assume that Douglas was right about the country, but wrong about the town, then Karajan's two performances in Vienna in June 1948 fulfil these criteria. All this fits the time frame, as the alteration could have been conveyed to Douglas just a month before he completed his new score. There are also two telling pieces of evidence: in the second of the two copyists' scores, the one used by Lambert in 1933, fragments of the German translation appear throughout in a hand suspiciously like Karajan's (Walton told Walter Legge that Karajan had helped to revise the translation), and at the bottom of the penultimate page there is a sketch on two staves of the final bars in their new guise, unquestionably in Walton's hand.

Finally, mention must be made of the two alterations that Walton made to the flutes for his 1959 recording. These are noted in the second edition of the Craggs catalogue[26] and concern bar 135, where the first flute was changed from A to G sharp, and bars 535–8 where both flutes were altered from B, E, F to B, B, E. Subsequently the OUP editor Christopher Morris, wanting to amend the parts, wrote to Walton requesting confirmation of these changes and received the following reply, which should settle the matter once and for all:

> I don't know why I so-called 'corrected' the notes in question, they are quite right as they are so leave them in peace. I suppose rehearsing the orchestra alone they did stand out a bit but they are quite OK when the chorus is singing. Either way it is of little matter, one can hardly detect the changes on the record and in actual perf (in Rome where I didn't correct anything) it sounded quite alright. Sorry to have bothered you (and myself) unnecessarily.[27]

So despite these moments being different on the 1959 recording, the text of the WWE's published score of these bars is in fact correct.

Vocal score

In the spring of 1931 OUP had hurriedly dispatched 320 copies of the first part of the vocal score to Leeds, so that the chorus could begin rehearsals. Part One ended at the baritone's words 'and his kingdom divided', immediately after the choral shout of 'Slain!'. Part Two followed a fortnight later.[28] These were pre-publication copies without any cover, but perfectly serviceable none the less. The first edition of the vocal score proper was published in September 1931, just in time for the premiere, in the now-familiar black, white, and green cover designed by the Italian artist Gino Severini. This edition is readily identifiable from the wrong G clef in the first bass part on page 1, as well as by the initial metronome mark crotchet = 60. The second edition, issued within a year, corrected the clef and several other obvious mistakes, and revised some of the metronome marks; the opening, for instance, became crotchet = 54. The English and German texts were printed separately in both editions, and an orchestral list was included with asterisks specifying which instruments could be omitted. Thereafter all reprints remained the same until 1955, except in respect of the German translation which was subject to continual alteration.

Officially credited to the author and dance critic Beryl de Zoete and to Walton's girlfriend Baroness Imma Doernberg, this translation appears only in the vocal score. The translators' names are printed on the title page of all editions prior to 1955, at which time a 'new impression' was published. The separate printing of the libretto was now omitted and the translators' names were relegated to a footnote on page 1. This was the first republication to dispense with the Severini cover, replacing it with a gold cover incorporating a reproduction of the vocal staves of bars 369–71, specially copied for the purpose by Walton. The translation was g iven its final revision, and a half-hearted attempt was made to incorporate the revised ending by adding an *ottava* sign over the last twelve bars. The extended final chord was not shown, despite its having been in use since 1948. The orchestral list now specified the percussion instruments, and there was a note about the brass band parts being cued into those of the main orchestra. This note was altered for the 'revised version' of 1959 and, apart from a new final page, it constitutes the only notable difference from its predecessor. This 'revised version', still in its gold cover, is dated 1955, but that cannot be right. Later printings of the 'new impression' contain a note drawing attention to the availability of an orchestral score (imperial octavo) at 25 shillings, which was not published until May 1957, so the new impression must have been still in circulation at this time. In his *Source Book* Stewart Craggs gives a date of 1959 as the date of the publication of the 'revised version' which makes a great deal more sense.[29]

At some point the gold cover was replaced by a reproduction of Rembrandt's painting 'Belshazzar's Feast', by courtesy of the National Gallery (as was that of the orchestral score), and this cover was retained into the twenty-first century.

The 1955 new impression managed to introduce a few errors not found in earlier editions, such as the designation 'semi chorus' at fig. 9 instead of 'Chorus II', which was corrected in the revised edition. The missing text to the tenors at fig. 6 and the missing flat sign to the sopranos and tenors at fig. 11+4 are errors that occur in every edition up to the present.

Full score

Once Roy Douglas had completed copying his manuscript full score with all Walton's revisions, this became the standard issue; all earlier copyists' scores were withdrawn and some were undoubtedly destroyed. Since it was only available on hire there soon arose a demand for a score that could be purchased. OUP eventually obliged, and in May 1957 published an octavo-sized engraved edition, which faithfully reproduced the text of the Douglas, adding only the occasional direction for a change of tuning in the timpani. Even though Douglas did much of the proofreading, there are a number of errors not found in his manuscript score. Revised metronome marks which (as noted in the Douglas score) are in accordance with Walton's 1943 recording are included, but with no note as to their derivation. These will be found to be different from those in any vocal score published before the new impression of 1955, when the metronome marks were finally brought into line with those of the Douglas score. The contents of all reprints of this full score are identical, but the covers are different. The first edition features a cover that is a collage of fragments of six pages of the autograph full score (see The autograph), but at some point this was replaced by a reproduction of Rembrandt's painting. Eventually OUP yielded to pressure to print their score in a larger format and in 1981 issued one approximately two inches larger in both dimensions, making it that much easier to read.

In 1978, the 500th anniversary of the foundation of OUP, a de luxe edition was published in a limited run of 350 numbered copies, all signed by the composer, together with an article by Michael Kennedy entitled 'The Origin of Belshazzar's Feast'.

The autograph

In 1987 Oxford University Press issued an international appeal for help in locating the missing autograph full score of *Belshazzar's Feast*, offering a reward of £1000 for any information leading to its recovery. This generated an article on the front page of the *Sunday Times* of 11 October 1987, which set out the facts as then known. From this it seems that the score was sent by OUP in 1950 to the London office of the British Council for shipping to Argentina. Andrew Potter, head of OUP's music department, is quoted as saying 'We sent the original to the British Council because we expected Sargent to conduct it in South America' (he later withdrew the work from his programmes and Argentina had to wait another 40 years to hear it). There is a letter from the Council dated 1 June 1950 acknowledging receipt of the score and undertaking to send it on to its office in Buenos Aires. However, this does not make much sense. Sargent must have had his own score at this time, as three months previously he had conducted the premiere of the revised version; the autograph would have been of no use to him.

Towards the end of his life Walton began to show an interest in the whereabouts of his manuscript score. The archive at OUP contains two letters from him in which he sets out what he remembered, none too precisely it has to be said.[30] From the second letter, which is marginally the clearer, one can gather that there were originally two scores, one completely in Walton's writing and a second in the hand of a copyist as far as fig. 52, at which point Walton had written out the final section again. The first letter adds that the copyist may have been Archie Jacob, brother of the composer Gordon, and that the two scores were of a size difficult to lose. Also in this letter the scores are said to have been in three parts, which one can reasonably assume splits the opening up until fig. 52 into two. This is particularly interesting in view of what was displayed, in March 1954, at an exhibition of composer portraits and autograph scores, organized by the Museum of Art in Toledo, Ohio. Something purporting to be the autograph full score of *Belshazzar* was described in the exhibition catalogue as containing 130 pages, measuring 45×31 cm, with the first 27 pages being in another hand. If the beginning up until fig. 52 existed as two separate parts, the natural break would come at fig. 15, which would very probably be 27 pages in. Could these have been in the putative hand of Archie Jacob?

When Boult conducted the London premiere in November 1931 he specifically requested the autograph score, so one must presume that the movements that were in Walton's hand were all together. It was common practice in those days for publishers to treat a composer's unpublished manuscript full score of an extended work as just another hire copy, and when in 1937 Boult requested its use again he found it so overlaid with other conductors' markings that it was often difficult to read exactly what the composer had written.[31]

The OUP archive also contains several inventories of Walton manuscripts held by them, three of which include references to *Belshazzar's Feast*. The earliest, dated 20 September 1949, contains an interesting footnote in the hand of Alan Frank, the head of music: 'There is the possibility that the complete MS score of Belshazzar's Feast is recoverable: it seems to have got into two parts one of which is not in our hands.'

The manuscript is further mentioned in lists dated 24 November 1959 and 30 July 1962: 'BF Part original MS only'. One can therefore safely conclude that the two parts had remained separated since 1949, so only one part, if anything, could have been sent to Argentina. If this were so one can only hazard a guess that the British Council wanted to mount some sort of exhibition and needed a specimen of Walton's manuscript for display. It is also possible that this idea was abandoned when Sargent dropped the work from his programmes.

In October 1958 the Leeds Public Library mounted an exhibition of manuscript music scores and other items associated with the Festival, whose centenary fell in that year. Walton's manuscript is listed in the catalogue, along with those of other composers, but alas no details are given and, exasperatingly, it is not among those exhibits selected for a facsimile reproduction in its pages. As OUP did not by then have access to the complete autograph it remains an open question as to exactly what was on show at this exhibition.

In May 1957 OUP published a study score of *Belshazzar's Feast*, the cover of which contained a collage of sections of six pages of what is clearly the autograph full score. Although partially obscured by the title lettering, these excerpts appear to have been taken from the latter half of the score (bars 687–974), part of the section after fig. 52 that Walton had written out twice. It does not seem that OUP had any difficulty in accessing this part of the autograph, and a memo from Christopher Morris of 25 July 1956 gives no hint of any problem: 'concerning the cover of the full score; it should consist of a repro of either the original MS or printed sheets'. What has happened since, no one seems able to say, and with its appearance in OUP's inventory of 1962 all trace of the autograph disappears. To add a final twist to this sorry tale, Roy Douglas (responsible for copying the revised version) reported in the mid-1950s that he had seen two sections of the composer's own manuscript in a hire copy at OUP. It is very likely that this is the same copy that was returned to the library by the production manager on 26 November 1956 with a note: 'It seems a pity to let this one out on hire, containing as it does a great many pages in Walton's own handwriting.' Considering that the revised version, in Roy Douglas's fine copy, had been in circulation for over six years, it does seem strange that the old full scores of the original version were still being sent out.

NOTES

1. BBC Written Archives, Cavershan.
2. Osbert Sitwell, *Laughter in the Next Room* (London, 1949), p. 312.
3. William Walton Museum, Forio, Ischia.
4. Quoted in Michael Kennedy, *Portrait of Walton* (Oxford, 1989), p. 55.
5. BBC Written Archives.
6. The contents of Walton's letter were communicated to Richard Howgill, one of the BBC music department's senior administrators, and quoted in Stephen Lloyd, *William Walton, Muse of Fire* (Woodbridge, 2001), p. 102.
7. Harriet Cohen Papers, BL Deposit 1999/10. The ABs presumably refer to Arnold Bax and Arthur Bliss.
8. Property of Michael Kennedy.

9. Letter of February 1933, quoted in Duncan Hinnells, *An Extraordinary Performance* (Oxford, 1998), p. 56.

10. Minutes of the Leeds Triennial Festival management committee, 19 February 1931. Housed in the West Yorkshire Archive Service, Sheepscar, Leeds.

11. Minutes of the Leeds Triennial Festival management committee, 15 April 1931.

12. Interview with Peter Lewis, *Daily Mail*, 28 March 1972.

13. In the interview, Walton told Lewis that it was Beecham's idea to include two brass bands. Doubtless this was because four were required in the Berlioz *Grande Messe des Morts* in the same festival.

14. *Yorkshire Evening News*, 7 October 1931.

15. Letter dated 22 July 1942 written from Renishaw Hall, Nr. Sheffield, and addressed to Norman Peterkin of OUP, OUP Archive, Oxford.

16. Beecham made this pronouncement to his assembled visitors after a performance at the Royal Festival Hall as Strafford entered to pay his compliments. This anecdote was kindly provided by his daughter Claire Strafford.

17. Quoted in Lloyd, *William Walton*, p. 104.

18. Quoted in Lloyd, *William Walton*, p. 105.

19. *Yorkshire Evening News*, 9 October 1931.

20. Brotherton Library, Leeds, Special Collections, MS 8022.

21. OUP Archive.

22. Elizabeth Schwarzkopf, *On and Off the Record* (London, 1982), p. 230.

23. Quoted in *The Selected Letters of William Walton*, ed. Malcolm Hayes (London, 2002), p. 327.

24. Spike Hughes, *Second Movement* (London, 1951), p. 140.

25. Stewart R. Craggs, *William Walton: A Catalogue* (Oxford, 1990), p. 52.

26. Craggs, *Walton: A Catalogue*, p. 52.

27. Postcard from Forio, Ischia, OUP Archive.

28. In a letter to *The Gramophone* of May 1943, Herbert Bardgett recalls that it came out in fortnightly instalments. None of the original scores consulted gives any evidence of more than two parts. Page 70 of the first edition of the vocal score has a repeated copyright line.

29. Stewart R. Craggs, *William Walton: A Source Book* (Aldershot, 1993), p. 121.

30. OUP Archive.

31. Letter from Sir Adrian Boult to Leslie Boosey, 2 December 1937, quoted in Lewis Foreman, ed., *From Parry to Britten* (London, 1987), p. 208.

Osbert Sitwell's text for *Belshazzar's Feast*

Thus spake Isaiah:　　　　　　　　　　　　　*O. Sitwell*

> Thy sons that thou shalt beget,
> They shall be taken away
> And be eunuchs
> In the palace of the King of Babylon.　　*Isaiah 39, v.7*

> > Howl ye, howl ye, therefore:
> > For the day of the Lord is at hand.　　*Isaiah 13, v.6*

· · · ·

By the waters of Babylon,
There we sat down: yea, we wept
And hanged our harps upon the willows.　　*Psalm 137, vv.1–2*

For they that wasted us
Required of us mirth;
They that carried us away captive
Required of us a song.
'Sing us one of the songs of Zion'.
How shall we sing the Lord's song
In a strange land?　　　　　　　　　　　*Psalm 137, vv.3–4*

If I forget thee, O Jerusalem,
Let my right hand forget her cunning.
If I do not remember thee,
Let my tongue cleave to the roof of my mouth;
Yea, if I prefer not Jerusalem above my chief joy.　　*Psalm 137, vv.3–4*

By the waters of Babylon,
There we sat down: yea, we wept.　　　　*Psalm 137, v.1*

O daughter of Babylon, who art to be destroyed,
Happy shall he be that taketh thy children
And dasheth them against a stone.　　　*Psalm 137, vv.8–9*

For with violence shall that great city Babylon be thrown down,
And shall be found no more at all.　　　*Revelation 18, v.21*

Babylon was a great city,　　　　　　　*O. Sitwell*

Her merchandise was of gold and silver,
Of precious stones, of pearls, of fine linen,
Of purple, silk and scarlet,
All manner vessels of ivory,
All manner vessels of most precious wood,
Of brass, iron and marble,
Cinnamon, odours and ointments,
Of frankincense, wine and oil,
Fine flour, wheat and beasts,
Sheep, horses, chariots, slaves,
And the souls of men.　　　　　　　　*Revelation 18, vv.12–13 (abbrev.)*

· · · ·

In Babylon　　　　　　　　　　　　　*O. Sitwell*

Belshazzar the King
Made a great feast,
Made a feast to a thousand of his lords,
And drank wine before the thousand.
Belshazzar, whiles he tasted the wine,
Commanded us to bring the gold and silver vessels:
Yea! the golden vessels, which his father, Nebuchadnezzar,
Had taken out of the temple that was in Jerusalem.
He commanded us to bring the golden vessels
Of the temple of the house of God,
That the King, his Princes, his wives
And his concubines might drink therein.   *Daniel 5, vv.1–3*

Then the King commanded us:
'Bring ye the cornet, flute, sackbut, psaltery,
And all kinds of music'. They drank wine again,
Yea! drank from the sacred vessels.
And then spake the King: *Daniel 3, v.5 & O. Sitwell*

'Praise ye
        The God of Gold.
Praise ye
        The God of Silver.
Praise ye
        The God of Iron.
Praise ye
        The God of Wood.
Praise ye
        The God of Stone.
Praise ye
        The God of Brass.
Praise ye the Gods!'   *Daniel 5, v.4 (adapted)*

Thus in Babylon, the mighty city,   *O. Sitwell*

Belshazzar the King made a great feast,
Made a feast to a thousand of his lords
And drank wine before the thousand.
Belshazzar, whiles he tasted the wine,
Commanded us to bring the gold and silver vessels
That his Princes, his wives and his concubines
Might rejoice and drink therein.   *Daniel 5, vv.1–2*

After they had praised their strange gods,
The idols and the devils,
False gods who can neither see nor hear,
Called they for the timbrel and the pleasant harp
To extol the glory of the King.
Then they pledged the King before the people,
Crying, 'Thou, O King, art King of Kings   *mostly O. Sitwell*

O King, live for ever' . . .   *Daniel 3, v.9*

And in that same hour, as they feasted,
Came forth fingers of a man's hand
And the King saw
The part of the hand that wrote.   *Daniel 5, v.5 (abbrev.)*

And this was the writing that was written:
'*MENE, MENE, TEKEL UPHARSIN*'   *Daniel 5,v.25*

'Thou art weighed in the balance
and found wanting'.   *Daniel 5,v.27*

In that night was Belshazzar the King slain   *Daniel 5,v.30*

And his Kingdom divided.

. . . .   *Daniel,v.28*

Then sing aloud to God our strength:
Make a joyful noise unto the God of Jacob.
Take a psalm, bring hither the timbrel.
Blow up the trumpet in the new moon,   *Psalm 81,vv.1–3 (abbrev.)*

Blow up the trumpet in Zion,   *Joel 2,v.1*

For Babylon the Great is fallen.
Alleluia!   *Revelation 14,v.8*

Then sing aloud to God our strength:
Make a joyful noise unto the God of Jacob,   *Psalm 81,v.1*

While the Kings of the Earth lament
And the merchants of the Earth
Weep, wail and rend their raiment.
They cry, 'Alas, Alas, that great city,
In one hour is her judgement come'.
The trumpeters and pipers are silent,
And the harpers have ceased to harp,
And the light of a candle shall shine no more.   *Revelation 18,vv.9–11,22–3*
    (adapted)

Then sing aloud to God our strength:
Make a joyful noise to the God of Jacob.   *Psalm 81,v.1*

For Babylon the Great is fallen.   *Revelation 14,v.8*

Alleluia!

> *Selected and arranged from*
> *The Bible by*
> OSBERT SITWELL

5

Choral Works with Orchestra *(Vol. 5)*

Timothy Brown

The award of a probationer choristership at Christ Church Cathedral, Oxford, in 1912 proved to be the start of a momentous new life for the young William Walton, who abruptly swapped the northern parochialisms of Oldham for the sophisticated and heady atmosphere of the 'dreaming spires'. Composition quickly became a passion, and, naturally enough, vocal music featured strongly among his juvenilia. His earliest surviving composition is *A Litany*, written when he was perhaps only 13, a remarkably accomplished setting of an early seventeenth-century poem. Though the focus of his subsequent life as a composer was mainly instrumental music, writing for voices was never far away—be it the quasi-*Sprechgesang* of the early 'entertainment' *Façade*, the songs, church music, works for choir and orchestra, or the operas. If *Façade* made the musical establishment sit up and take notice of the young composer, *Belshazzar's Feast* was the work that convinced the choral world that here was a true successor to Elgar and Vaughan Williams. That his eventual output of choral works with orchestra was not especially large is partly due to the fact that instrumental commissions predominated. But in any case he was not a prolific composer, not least because of his innate meticulousness.

With the possible exception of the *Coronation Te Deum*, the four works in this volume do not figure strongly in any list of works on which Walton's reputation is based. In the case of *In Honour of the City of London* and the Gloria, which have never achieved anything like the popularity of *Belshazzar*, their current neglect cannot be put down merely to perceived musical shortcomings. Perhaps the circumstances of their early performances had something to do with it; neither piece has quite recovered from the initial mixed reception. *The Twelve* is undeniably an effective church anthem, but as a work with orchestra it is, like the *Coronation Te Deum*, so comparatively brief as to be difficult to programme. There is a further point common to all the works under consideration: despite Walton's familiarity with the human voice, his vocal writing is often awkward to master, and the musical rewards are not always immediate. However, despite uneven quality, they deserve to be performed more often. They are all pieces that contain the hallmarks of Walton's mature style: powerful melodic lines and musical imagery, infectious rhythms, but above all moments of engagement that reveal the passion that beat behind the sardonic exterior that Walton so often presented to the world.

In Honour of the City of London

Genesis

The 1930s were golden years for Walton. Early successes, most notably the overture *Portsmouth Point* (1926), Sinfonia Concertante (1928), the Viola Concerto (1929), and

Belshazzar's Feast (1931), led to the First Symphony (1935), all acclaimed by the public and critics alike. He tackled film scores for the first time, producing four in as many years, and he found this a genre not only musically conducive but also financially rewarding. London society and the musical establishment increasingly lionized him, almost conferring on him an unofficial laureateship. Given this success, it was perhaps inevitable that Walton should be the natural choice for an orchestral march to be played at the coronation of King George VI on 12 May 1937. The new march, written in true Elgarian tradition but with a character all of its own, proved immensely popular. Entitled *Crown Imperial*, it carried the superscription 'In beawtie beryng the crone imperiall', a quotation from the poem *In Honour of the City of London* by the early Scottish poet William Dunbar. Dunbar (?1460–*c*.1525) is known to have come to London in 1501 as part of an ambassadorial delegation sent by King James IV of Scotland to negotiate a political settlement with Henry VII of England; to cement the treaty, Henry proposed that James should marry his eldest daughter, the 14-year-old Margaret Tudor. It was almost certainly this visit that inspired Dunbar's paean to London. Walton set the first six of the seven verses of this poem (which he found in an early edition of the *Oxford Book of English Verse*) for a new cantata, commissioned in 1936 for the following year's Leeds Triennial Musical Festival, whose organizers doubtless hoped for a successor to *Belshazzar*, the work premiered at the festival so triumphantly five years earlier.[1]

Whether Walton would have chosen to set such a text, or the festival would have accepted it, had it not been coronation year remains a moot point. On the face of it, one wonders why a northern city, proud of its own heritage, would want to celebrate the nation's southern capital; perhaps loyalty to the monarch overrode regional pride. The fact remains that the seemingly inappropriate title of Dunbar's ode did not yield a poem with the kind of dramatic and narrative possibilities that Osbert Sitwell's biblical libretto for *Belshazzar* had offered the composer. And so Walton, who by 1936 was an acknowledged master of orchestration, and whose music was known for its mixture of rhythmic incisiveness and powerful lyricism, chose in his new piece to write not so much in the style of his own earlier cantata as in that of the current 'English' school, encompassing the symphonic style of Vaughan Williams's *A Sea Symphony*, the Delius of *Sea Drift* and *A Mass of Life*, or even George Dyson, who in 1928 had achieved considerable success with his own setting of *In Honour of the City of London*.

Composition

As so often, Walton found the going tough when it came to putting notes on paper. For one thing, the cantata was not the only work on his mind. The film *Dreaming Lips* (the third of four consecutive collaborations with Paul Czinner) had to be completed and recorded, and he had also begun to think about a violin concerto for Jascha Heifetz. By mid-May 1937, while staying in Ravello, south of Naples, he had completed the vocal score of three of Dunbar's verses, and he posted them to Hubert Foss, his editor at Oxford University Press, requesting that they be engraved as quickly as possible and sent to 'the Leeds people to be going on with ... as they are getting clamourous, with the warning there will be more to come later'. In June his vocal score of two more verses arrived in Oxford with the promise that 'the last will follow I hope at the end of the week', and accompanied by the confession that 'this work has turned out to be by no means easy'.[2] OUP finally published the complete vocal score in August and dispatched it to Leeds. This left just over a month for the festival chorus to complete the preparation of the new piece in time for the first performance in early October. Meanwhile, Walton was still working on the orchestration of the cantata, which was eventually finished in London on 5 September.

The music

Doubtless some of the difficulties Walton experienced with the composition of *In Honour of the City of London* hinged on the unforgiving nature of Dunbar's wordy and unrelentingly eulogistic poem that, in the words of the *Yorkshire Post*, had 'more than a hint of poet-laureate pomp'. The work also had to contend with Dyson's setting, which had become popular with choral societies around the country.[3] Like Dyson, Walton employed no soloists and set the poem in distinct sections for SATB (divisi) chorus and a full symphony orchestra, for which the proficient Leeds Festival Chorus was more than a match. However, compared with the more immediately appealing shorter, plainer version by Dyson (who set five of Dunbar's verses to Walton's six—both composers omitted the final verse), Walton's score was chorally more polyphonic and orchestrally more elaborate. The impulse that guided Walton was description rather than narration, and he responded with gestural music that had resonances of the film scores that were increasingly occupying his attention. He found difficulty in making clear sense of his own music, as we can see from his sketchy analytical notes in the OUP Archive, headed 'QUICK CLUES TO "IN HONOUR OF THE CITY"'.[4] Alan Frank, later to become Walton's publisher at OUP, wrote perceptively in *The Chesterian* in 1939 when he said: 'It is the quieter moments…that seem most successful in Walton's… choral work *In Honour of the City of London*…This is not, frankly, a work that appeals to me: it seems as if Walton is here persistently striving to be full-blooded, whereas in *Belshazzar* he is naturally so.'[5] Though trademark Walton can be heard throughout the cantata, there is, alongside all the pomp and circumstance, a genuine English lyricism that had no place in *Belshazzar's Feast*.

Rehearsal and performance

In 1937 the Leeds Festival was extended from the customary four days to five, substantially increasing the amount of rehearsal required by the chorus. The Festival Chorus had no fewer than thirteen choral items to prepare, including Bach's *St Matthew Passion*, Beethoven's *Missa Solemnis*, Rossini's *Petite Messe solennelle*, and Berlioz's *The Childhood of Christ*, in addition to Walton's commissioned piece and a new cantata, *Jonah*, by Lennox Berkeley. The arrival of Walton's music in instalments—the last of them well after rehearsals of the cantata had begun—gave little time for preparation by the chorus, experienced and competent though it was, and made it difficult for the singers to comprehend the music as a whole until close to the performance.

In the weeks prior to the festival there was considerable interest in the progress of the new Walton piece, with frequent reports and photographs in the local press. An article in the *Yorkshire Post* stated: 'Its preparation has involved unusually strenuous rehearsal, as the music has come from the press in instalments. Walton's work is physically and musically exacting, largely by reason of energetic syncopations and cross rhythms, which may be commonplace to musicians accustomed to finding them dished up as an indispensable condiment to the banalities of jazz, but which singers of the choral classics find sufficiently unfamiliar to be somewhat disconcerting, when found along with unaccustomed skips and rapid arpeggios more germane to flute or clarinet.' The article remarks that at least the music is diatonic and concludes: 'Saturday's rehearsal of the praise of London has brought the chorus to the stage of precision upon which to build a brilliant performance.'[6]

On 21 September the *Sheffield Telegraph* stated that in his latest choral work, 'Walton shows all the brilliance and resource that one expects from the composer of *Belshazzar's Feast*.'[7] However, by 2 October there was still some way to go before *In Honour* was secure. According to the *Yorkshire Evening News*, 'William Walton's brilliant and difficult new piece...needed a good deal of castigation [from the conductor]. On Saturday, Dr Sargent, always cool and master of the situation, removed most of the chorus's fears and trepidations.'[8] Final chorus rehearsals were public, and Walton himself attended several. Referring to the dress rehearsal of the new work, another reporter wrote: 'Dr Sargent reappeared and all turned to the final polishing up of Mr Walton's new work, *In Honour of the City of London*, which is going to be one of the prominent features of the Festival. It gains with every hearing and the chorus have mastered its difficulties surprisingly well. At the close Sargent asked the composer, who was seated in the hall, "Well! Are you happy?" and Mr Walton smilingly admitted his satisfaction.'[9]

The cantata received its first performance at the Leeds Festival in the morning concert on Wednesday 6 October 1937 in Leeds Town Hall, given by the 280-strong Festival Chorus and the London Philharmonic Orchestra, conducted by Sargent. The programme note by Hubert Foss declared the new work to be 'in the true line of succession to *Belshazzar*, with its bold vocal writing and exuberant orchestral accompaniment combining to form a masterly and high-spirited choral work in the modern style.' A scrapbook dedicated to *In Honour*, created by Alice, Lady Wimborne, includes many enthusiastic reviews of the premiere, from which one might surmise that Walton had indeed produced a worthy successor to *Belshazzar*.[10]

Reception

Initial reactions to *In Honour* seemed positive. An unattributed report in the *Yorkshire Evening Post* of 6 October set the tone: 'The performance was a rousing one. Now that it is over, there is no need to make a secret of the fact that at the first public rehearsal it seemed doubtful if the music would go at all. But Dr Sargent has not only smoothed out the difficulties, but literally roused up the chorus, by his ardour and confidence, to a pitch quite above their average level. The vitality of this morning's performance was three parts due to him.' A report in the *Yorkshire Post* the following morning is equally enthusiastic: 'With the first performance of William Walton's *In Honour of the City of London* the chorus without a doubt added a new line to festival history.' The critic of the *Birmingham Post* commented: 'Strenuous as Walton's choral writing is, the Leeds choir did not shout. Even at its loudest and highest it still made perfect music, and one came away from the performance feeling a kind of exultation over a masterly new short choral work.' Richard Capell, writing the same day in the *Daily Telegraph*, was complimentary about the performance and also the music, describing it as 'an intensely spirited and gorgeously coloured example of a modern composer's treatment of the chorus, the only or most obvious drawback of which is that it wants nothing less than the Leeds choir to bring it off'.

Other reviews, not influenced by partisan local loyalties, were more qualified in their praise, several hinting at relentlessness in the performance that did the work no favours. A reviewer in the *Glasgow Herald* wrote: 'Dr Sargent's vitality as conductor is admirable in many ways, but in this performance it was applied too generously and too consistently for justice either to Dunbar or to Walton. The six verses of Dunbar's poem have been approached by Walton with a due appreciation of what the poet and the musical audience ask for in regard to variety of treatment, and it is essential to enjoyment that the more quietly poetic references should be controlled in delivery so as to give the right weight and civic importance to the big periods. In the final proclamation of Dunbar's closing line, "London, thou art the flower [*sic*] of cities all," there was no longer any thought of a song of praise but rather the declaration of a dictator who dared us to disagree.'[11] Neville Cardus, writing in the *Manchester Guardian* on 7 October, referred to 'a vigorous, not to say strenuous, setting of William Dunbar's poem *In Honour of the City of London*. The music wastes no time: the rhetoric is emphatic and a little brassy. A more yielding interpretation than Dr Sargent's might have drawn more salience out of the few quieter passages.'

The cantata was heard again in London on 1 December in Queen's Hall, performed by the BBC Choral Society with the BBC Symphony Orchestra, conducted on this occasion by Walton himself. An unattributed review in *The Times* of 2 December stated that the performance of the cantata was 'more happily heard than at Leeds because of the lighter tone of the choir, which gave relief from the vociferousness and brought the gentler poetry of the Thames scene into greater prominence', but it insisted that 'Walton [does] not yet seem to have realized the dangers of over-emphasis…mostly in the direction of insisting on tone and yet more tone'. Walter Legge, then a music critic on the *Manchester Guardian* as well as a producer at EMI, commented that the London premiere of the cantata, 'at once showed up the shortcomings of the first performance and the intrinsic worth which the first performance partly obscured'.[12] William McNaught of the *Evening News* was more reserved: 'Walton's piece is an exercise in the craft of composition, astute, brilliantly clever and exhilarating; but it never suggests that the composer was really interested in the glories of sixteenth century London.'[13]

If it is true that the problems of rehearsal and the questionable quality of the early performances of *In Honour* contributed to a mixed critical response, it is equally true that Walton took few hostages in the writing of the choral parts, which is not as straightforward as that of the usual choral society repertoire. Little wonder that the work received a less than totally persuasive first performance, despite the best efforts of Malcolm Sargent, who had achieved such a triumph with *Belshazzar* in the same festival only six years earlier. The cantata's first performance was broadcast, but plans to issue the recording on 78 rpm discs were firmly quashed. Foss wrote to Legge at EMI:

'The records taken from the air at Leeds of Walton's *In Honour of the City* have now been heard by Malcolm Sargent and William Walton himself, as well as by me, and I must say that we are all unanimous in our disapproval of them. I think it would be bad for you, bad for him, bad for Sargent, and bad for us if they were issued, and I am not therefore able to pass you Walton's consent to their issue. I am so sorry: it was an interesting experiment.'[14]

With the onset of war in 1939, there was little opportunity to revive the cantata; with peace came a new musical dawn, in which *In Honour of the City of London* seemed staid and out of date. However, in 1989 Richard Hickox conducted an award-winning recording of the cantata. In the accompanying liner note by Christopher Palmer we read a more contemporary assessment of Walton's music, defending the 'strenuousness' with which earlier critics found fault: 'What Walton evokes is a teeming cityscape athrob with expectancy, excitement, variety and sense-of adventure, [with music] which so well complements the vigour and picturesqueness of the words and the life of the times they depict.'[15]

Coronation Te Deum

Genesis

In November 1943 Sir Henry Wood invited Walton to contribute a work to the 50th season of his celebrated Promenade Concerts. In a letter of 23 December to Wood, Walton reported that he was 'safely launched' on a Te Deum for chorus and orchestra. However, by the spring of 1944 the pressure to complete the score for Laurence Olivier's film of *Henry V* forced him to abandon the Te Deum. He returned to a setting of the same text eight years later when, in 1952, he was commissioned to write the work that would conclude the coronation service of Queen Elizabeth II in June 1953. In the intervening years came the death of his companion Alice Wimborne, the composition of the String Quartet in A minor, his marriage to Susana Gil Passo, and a move to Ischia in order to concentrate on his opera *Troilus and Cressida*. In 1946 there was talk of a work for chorus and orchestra for Liverpool or Huddersfield, but that came to nothing.[16]

Initially there was some doubt as to the choice of composer to be invited to provide the obligatory Te Deum for the coronation, a contemporary setting of which had been sung at each ceremony since 1902. In his private notes on the 1953 coronation music Sir William McKie, organist of Westminster Abbey and director of music for the occasion, records that on 16 September 1952 he had met Walton and got him to promise to write a new Te Deum should it be needed. He goes on: 'On October 23 I spent the afternoon with Vaughan Williams at Dorking. I told him that a new Te Deum was desired, but he replied he did not wish to write another one.' (Vaughan Williams had provided a Festival Te Deum for George VI's coronation in 1937.) By early November, McKie's proposals for the coronation music had received royal assent, and on 14 November, in a letter from Alan Frank, Walton officially received the commission, with the request that the manuscript be forthcoming by the end of the year.

The Te Deum, to be sung by the specially assembled choir and orchestra, was to come at that point of the ceremony when the Queen, newly crowned, prepared to process out of the Abbey to greet her subjects. Walton responded to the commission with music that was at once regal, celebratory, and restrained, couched in a language that was both sacred and profane, a mixture of *Belshazzar*, *Crown Imperial*, his music for *Henry V*, Stanford's *Gloria in excelsis* (composed for King George V's coronation in 1911), and the intimacy of such partsongs as 'Where does the uttered Music go?'.

Walton had been gratified by the attention he had received from the composition of *Crown Imperial* for the coronation of King George VI in 1937 and the pageantry surrounding the event. The invitation to compose the Te Deum for the forthcoming coronation, not to mention a new coronation march, *Orb and Sceptre*, for the following June, would have appealed to this side of his character. It was a commission that he must have relished, inviting as it did music with a wider scope than that of the English cathedral tradition, which he was able to write with such instinctive ease. It also came as a welcome diversion from the seemingly all-absorbing work on his first opera, *Troilus and Cressida*.[17]

Composition

There is no evidence to suggest that, after ceasing work on Henry Wood's commission in early 1944, Walton gave the idea of a Te Deum any further thought until he received the invitation to set the text for the 1953 coronation. For once, however, the process of composition was relatively straightforward. He was prompt—he had no option— and the writing went more or less without a hitch. Extensive correspondence between Walton and McKie reveals something of the film composer at work.[18] Thanking him on 18 November 1952 for a letter laying out what was required, Walton replied: 'I suggest from 6 to 8 mins. [as a ideal length], but of course can make it more or less fit exactly what is needed.' He put forward the possibility of concluding the text at 'And we worship thy name…adding perhaps an "Amen"'. He went on: 'It has struck me that I might want to use the Queen's Trumpeters for an added effect, but it may not be practicable. But just in case could you let me know their number & your views about it[?] It might be overstepping the mark!' McKie responded on 22 November that the length should be 'no longer than necessary, but it must be long enough for you to have freedom to make the work the grand climax of the whole service'.[19] He reminded Walton that the text, if shortened, must conform to liturgical practice, and that it should contain no '"Amen", or addition of any kind'. In the same letter he encouraged the use of the Kneller Hall musicians, suggesting points in the text where they might be used (advice that Walton followed), adding: 'And by the way, may we have an organ part too?' He continued: 'I think I suggested that it would help if the chorus parts have no undue rhythmic complications; partly because these are not heard in the Abbey—the sound needs plenty of time to unroll, and the clearer the choral texture, the better it carries; partly because most of the choir are church singers, and can do better in a style more nearly what they are accustomed to.' The draft of an unusually fulsome programme note by Walton, preserved in Ischia, reveals the care that he took with the composition:

> A setting of the Te Deum should reflect the jubilant praise of the words—no other canticle, not even the Jubilate Deo, is so filled with Christian joy…The [Coronation]

Te Deum is naturally a more extended work, although I think I am right in saying that it is actually shorter than most other modern Te Deums. It is cast for double choir, full orchestra, and organ. The first problem in setting these magnificent words is naturally one of form—how to equate a satisfactory musical shape with the structure of the prayer. Unfortunately nothing obvious suggests itself, as a rereading of the Te Deum will show. Now[,] it would destroy the design to force it into a ready-made musical device, but on the other hand to ignore the question altogether would result in shape-lessness. I have tried to solve the problem by casting my work in three main sections: there is a long opening section, a quite separate middle section, and an abridged recapitulation in which fresh words are set to music that has already been heard. The idea is that praise and prayer should, by being set to the same music, both be made to seem joyful acts of worship. I can see no reason why a prayer that comes from a Christian heart need not be as confident as the voice of praise. Thus the music that you hear at the beginning to the words 'We praise thee, O God, we acknowledge thee to be the Lord' opens the recapitulation accompanying 'O Lord, save thy people, and bless thine heritage', and one or two other similar passages will be noticed. Nevertheless the work has a quiet ending, partly because its place in the coronation service made this advisable, and just as much because it seemed to me effective to repeat the *marcatis-simo* shout of 'let me never be confounded', more simply and peacefully. Faith can be expressed with vigour, but it is essentially a peace at heart.[20]

On 28 November 1952 Walton wrote to Christopher Hassall, the librettist of *Troilus and Cressida*: 'I've got cracking on the Te Deum. You will like it, I think, and I hope he [McKie presumably, or perhaps the Archbishop of Canterbury] will too. Lots of coun-ter-tenors and little boys Holy-holying, not to mention all the Queen's Trumpeters and sidedrum[mers].' On December 17 Walton wrote to McKie: 'Though I hesitate to haz-ard an opinion when I am so near to a work, but [*sic*] I think it is going to be rather splendid. I have made use of the extra brass, but have arranged it, so that it can be dis-pensed with, if impractical for any reason. There is quite an important & indispensable organ part!'[21] A day or two later he wrote on a postcard to Alan Frank: 'The "De Te" will appear shortly as [I am] now about half way in the scoring. Rather good in spite of being liable to break forth into BF [*Belshazzar's Feast*] every now and then.' In a second letter to Hassall, Walton wrote: 'After a spot of bother with the "virgin's womb" (the kind of trouble I always get into—don't tell the Archbishop) the Te Deum is complete. It is not too bad for an occasional piece and should be right for the ceremony.'[22] The reference to the 'virgin's womb' was probably more a reflection of Walton's inability to resist a risqué comment than a true reflection of the situation—namely, that there had indeed been a problem to solve at this stage in the piece, which had more to do with an awkward shift of tonality than any difficulty in word-setting.

On 22 December 1952 Walton reported to McKie that he had dispatched the vocal score to OUP, with a request that a copy should be forwarded to him. He added: 'I hope the setting will meet with your approval. It is not at all difficult, no awkward intervals or rhythms & in fact should be fairly plain sailing.' The full score followed shortly after-wards. For once, he was genuinely pleased with his efforts, as is shown in a letter to David Webster, the general administrator of the Royal Opera House, Covent Garden: 'T&C...had to be abandoned for some six weeks, while I indulged in an orgy of

Coronation music—a superb Te Deum, a spanking March & a piece for Aldeburgh. Quite a feat for me to have got it over so quickly!'[23] In a letter to Frank of 22 January 1953, Walton remarked: 'I've heard from McKie who seems very pleased (as indeed he ought to be!) with the T.D.'

Proofs of the vocal score of the Te Deum were sent to McKie at the end of January; it was published by Novello (who were the printers of the official 'form and order' for the coronation) early in March, in time for it to be distributed to the singers, so that they would have ample opportunity to master the notes before the start of the extensive schedule of choral rehearsals in May.[24] In a letter to Stewart Craggs seventeen years later, McKie recalled that he 'put the Te Deum into rehearsal at once. Its first actual performance took place in the Abbey Song School [in mid-March], with Sir William conducting the Abbey Choir and myself at the piano. Sir William was most helpful (and most successful) in showing us exactly what he wanted. He also came later to one or two of the final rehearsals in the Abbey and again was most helpful in his comments and suggestions. Both singers and orchestra were delighted with the work.'

Performance and reception

Walton was gratified by the response that greeted the exuberant first performance, given by the coronation choir and a composite symphony orchestra, assembled for the occasion, together with the fanfare musicians from the Royal Military School of Music, Kneller Hall. Sir William McKie (whose knighthood was announced on coronation morning) conducted, assisted by two sub-conductors who relayed the beat to those singers who were unable to see him; the 'important & indispensable organ part' was played by the sub-organist, Dr Osborne Peasgood.[25] The *Coronation Te Deum* made a stirring climax to a programme of music that by unanimous acclaim was a triumph of programming and performance. It created a fitting climax to the long coronation ceremony, catching the required mood perfectly. The masterstroke was to end the work, after a snatch of 'last judgement' trumpet call in the manner of Berlioz or Verdi, slowly and *pianissimo*. The contrast with Sir Arthur Bliss's brazen fanfare that followed, announcing the new queen's departure from the Abbey, was electric, as can be heard in the original recording of the ceremony.[26] Though Sir Adrian Boult, who conducted the non-liturgical music, including *Orb and Sceptre*, was said to be shocked by the Te Deum's 'pagan' sound, the general response was enthusiastic.[27] In his book on the music of Walton, Frank Howes called the Te Deum a 'shatteringly apt' display of pomp and circumstance. Eric Blom, reviewing a concert performance later that year by Sargent and the BBC Symphony Orchestra in the Royal Festival Hall, described it in *The Observer* on 15 November as 'suitably and beautifully functional... now that it has come out into the everyday light'... [it] shows its composer's unfailing ability to coin striking phrases that, once heard, cling to the memory for ever.... A special quality of the Te Deum is that it is somehow convincingly liturgical without ever becoming conventionally "churchy".'

In its first year, the *Coronation Te Deum* received many performances in England and around the British Empire, including its first concert performance on the evening of coronation day in Edinburgh. In order to encourage performances in Europe,

OUP published a vocal score with a Latin text underlaid by John Warrack, at that time working in the OUP music department. Walton approved the minor musical amendments that were necessary. Over fifty years later, the Te Deum remains fresh and vivid, a highly effective and tightly structured work that has become a benchmark for anyone faced with the prospect of composing choral music for a ceremonial occasion.

Gloria

Genesis

With the coronation out of the way, Walton could concentrate on the musical enterprise closest to his heart, the opera *Troilus and Cressida*. This lengthy undertaking finally reached fruition in December 1954, after which he turned his attention to a cello concerto for Gregor Piatigorsky, a second symphony, and other orchestral works. In 1957 the Huddersfield Choral Society, perhaps aware of Walton's laborious birth pangs when it came to the creation of new works, invited him to compose a work for the society's forthcoming 125th anniversary celebrations in 1961, which would also mark Sir Malcolm Sargent's thirtieth year as its conductor. The invitation was irresistible to the northerner, who had enjoyed such a long and rewarding connection with choral music in Leeds, and who now perhaps felt it was time to write something for Huddersfield, that other great centre of choral singing in Yorkshire. Equally, the respect (if not affection) that he had for Sargent, who had championed so much of his music, must also have been a factor.[28] Walton had already enjoyed an association with the Huddersfield Choral Society, for it was this choir that he conducted in 1943 with the Liverpool Philharmonic Orchestra in the first recording of *Belshazzar*. However, in a letter to Alan Frank of December 1957 Walton announced that the oratorio was sixth on his list, after a second symphony (fourth) and a piece for Hindemith (fifth), and he indicated that he did not think he would 'get through the oratorio before the end of '60'.

In November 1957 Walton reported to Frank that Osbert Sitwell, his first patron and the librettist of *Belshazzar*, 'was quite keen on doing a libretto for the oratorio for 'Uddersfield. He however lacks a Bible (with Apocrypha) in large enough type for him to read (so do I for that matter) so perhaps the O.U.P. could go as far as presenting us both with one.'[29] A Bible was presumably forthcoming, because in January 1958 Walton received a text from Sitwell with the title *Moses and Pharaoh*. 'Not very satisfactory at first glance—very diffuse. It's about the plagues & the exodus through the Red Sea etc. In fact a bit of Cecil B. de Mille! But I think that something can eventually be made from it,' he reported. Walton, following his long-established custom of looking at other composers' solutions to a current compositional challenge, made a request to be sent a copy of Handel's *Israel in Egypt*, adding 'It might prove useful to look at the libretto!'[30]

In June 1958 Walton informed Frank: 'I wrote to Malcolm Sargent withdrawing from writing "Moses" for the Huddersfield centenary. He's written very kindly about it and suggests I might do a smaller-scale work. Thinking it over, & while making no rash promise of delivery, I have suggested that a "Gloria in excelsis" might fit the bill. I think it would; at least one knows w[h]ere one is regarding the words—I propose doing it in Latin so there will be no bother about it if some other countries should happen to want to do it. So would you send me a Latin version of the Prayer book also the English prayer book so I know what it is all about!' A month later he requested copies of settings by Beethoven, Bach, and Mozart, 'not so much for the music as to [see] how the words are split up, as there seem to be precious little of them'.

Why Walton changed his mind about *Moses* is not clear. On a domestic front, in 1956 he had purchased a plot of land in Ischia, and plans for La Mortella (the house and garden that were thereafter to be the Waltons' home—and lifelong project) became a constant concern while building proceeded. Pressing commissions also got in the way of the Huddersfield piece, including one for a song cycle for the tenor Peter Pears and guitarist Julian Bream. More significant, though, was the fact that during the years 1957–60 Walton struggled with a successor to the First Symphony; the Second Symphony eventually received its first performance at the Edinburgh Festival in September 1960. But ultimately, it was perhaps the 'diffuseness' to which Walton had alluded when he first received *Moses and Pharaoh* that proved insurmountable—and the brief 'Gloria' text enabled him to construct a rounded, ternary structure, as in the *Coronation Te Deum*, that would perhaps be more likely to succeed than the freer, strophic form of *In Honour of the City of London*.

Composition

Once embarked on the Gloria in the autumn of 1960, Walton characteristically found the going tough. To begin with, he envisaged a work with a semi-chorus, but he wrote to Frank that 'soloists would be better'.[31] Frank replied that the Gloria would be coupled with Elgar's *The Dream of Gerontius* at the first performance. He added that Sargent thought he might wish to include a part for solo tenor, as the renowned singer Richard Lewis (who had created the role of Troilus) would be one of the soloists. Walton accordingly adopted the same line-up of soloists as in *Gerontius*, adding parts for alto, tenor, and baritone, and informing Frank that the orchestration would be virtually the same as that of Elgar's oratorio. In January 1961 he instructed Frank to tell the secretary of the Huddersfield Choral Society that the work was 'getting on now & if nobody else likes it the chorus will, & anybody would know the composer sang in St Johns [*sic*] Werneth when he was 6! It stinks of religion—pagan somewhat however [with] bars from Barnby & Belshazzar. Walton does not progress, I fear.' On 31 January he dispatched 'a baker's doz. of pages to be getting on with'.

Despite his optimism, by 14 March Walton still had only sent OUP pages 1–14 of the vocal score and had much left to write. Substantial alterations to his initial ideas slowed his progress. For instance, the surviving sketches reveal that he had originally conceived the work for double chorus (though notated SSAATTBB); was he perhaps thinking of the double choruses in *The Dream of Gerontius*? Some sense of that still occurs (for example in bars 506 ff.) but in the main the Gloria was eventually laid out for SATB divisi. Walton suggested to Frank that it would save 'an immense amount of time & physical labour' if Roy Douglas (OUP's chief freelance copyist) would supply him with a blank full score into which the chorus parts could be copied. By the end of May, having complied with Walton's request, Frank was obliged to inform the secretary of the choral society that Walton had still some way to go. More significantly he reported that

Walton had decided to amend and rewrite some passages in the section already being rehearsed by the choir.[32] The vocal score of the *Gloria* was finally finished at the end of July, and 300 printed copies were dispatched to Huddersfield on 29 August. Unfortunately, Walton's habit of revising and amending as he went along meant that the vocal lines of the eventual full score differed occasionally from those of the vocal score.

On 8 August 1961 Walton confided some of his thoughts about the completed *Gloria* to Frank: 'I think it will prove to be an effective if not a very good piece. It will certainly be set on, perhaps with a certain amount of truth, as to not breaking fresh ground etc, in fact, being in an idiom "which is no longer valid"...On the other hand an idiom is valid as long as one convinces it is [*sic*], & I think that it does convince in this particular case. Anyhow for 'Udd & Sir M. it would have been futile & ridiculous to dash into 12 tones.' Frank obviously approved of the new work, for in September Walton thanked him for his comments, adding 'I was not too fond of the "hearty" parts—particularly the "glorificamus" section but I've come round to it rather, now. I think from 256 to 415 to be pretty good & the rest, on the whole, does not let one down. The coda maybe is a bit abrupt, but isn't Beethoven's [in the *Missa Solemnis*]? In fact, yes it is. Dramatic!' By 5 September he had finally completed the full score, and on 19 September he again wrote to Frank: 'The end I think is all right after looking at it again. Anyhow if it isn't, the only thing that could be done is to repeat the last eight bars ad lib till they feel like stopping!'

In the early stages of the printing of the vocal score, there was confusion about the intended quickening up from bars 12 to 13. Walton originally wrote ♩ = 58*c*. and ♪ = ♪. When Roy Douglas, preparing Walton's vocal score for publication, queried this, Walton defended his markings vigorously. It took a prolonged correspondence between him, Douglas, and OUP to clarify the issue. Eventually, in a telegram and also a letter, both dated 16 August 1961, Walton gave way, just in time for the publication date for the vocal score of 21 August. The result was the inclusion of ♩ = ♩ from bars 12 to 13, and the deletion of ♩ = 58.

Sometime during the composition of the piece (but after printing of the vocal score had begun), Walton decided to alter the pitch of bars 415–68, the section preceding the recapitulation of the work's initial musical material. A telegram to OUP (undated, but probably towards the end of June) reads 'Hold everything[.] New version from 415 in transit[.] Sorry[.] William'. That this new version involved altering the pitch of an entire self-contained section can be deduced from portions of the original autograph that have survived, together with revisions (marked 'final version') that are included with the (incomplete) autograph piano score. No documentary evidence has been discovered to explain Walton's change of mind at this point in the work, but there is no doubt that the original version would have created an uncomfortably high tessitura for the sopranos and altos. It is possible that Sargent, who was to conduct the first performance, and whom Walton consulted during the composition of the *Gloria*, advised caution. On the other hand, the resulting harmonic transition from bars 414 to 415 is arguably less convincing than the original version, and the entry in bar 470 is awkward. Indeed Sargent, in a letter to Walton of 18 January 1962 following the London premiere, wrote that the first note at bar 470 'always seems a little doubtful for some reason' and recommended that trumpets and trombones should double the voices for ten bars—a suggestion readily accepted by the composer.

Performance and reception

Sir Malcolm Sargent conducted the first performance of the Gloria, given by the Huddersfield Choral Society and the Royal Liverpool Philharmonic Orchestra in Huddersfield Town Hall on 24 November 1961. The soloists were Marjorie Thomas, Richard Lewis, and John Cameron. Walton was in the audience. Given that the choir and orchestra had met for the first time only on the day of the concert, as was then the custom, and that preparatory rehearsals, according to one account, had been 'shambolic', it is remarkable that the premiere, which was broadcast live on the BBC Third Programme, was as successful as it was.[33] However, at a civic reception afterwards, Walton declared himself dissatisfied, blaming Sargent for failing to give the chorus sufficient rehearsal time. A more successful London premiere, again under Sargent, followed on 18 January 1962, with Marjorie Thomas, Ronald Dowd, Owen Brannigan, and the London Philharmonic Chorus and Orchestra. On 10 June Walton himself conducted the US premiere in Los Angeles, with the Roger Wagner Chorale and the Los Angeles Philharmonic Orchestra, in a concert that also included the West Coast premiere of the Second Symphony.

Writing in the quarterly *Music and Letters*, Bernarr Rainbow was enthusiastic: 'The composer's idiom is unmistakable, but he cannot be accused of not moving forward with the time, for the harmonies are more pungent than in his earlier works and there is virility on every page.'[34] Arthur Jacobs in the *Musical Times* was more blunt: 'Walton's setting is plainly not intended for church use, nor does it attempt to reproduce a devotional atmosphere. *Belshazzar* tells a story. So does *Gerontius*. That is part of their appeal. Perhaps unfortunately, Sir William evidently did not feel inspired to set some similarly direct text for this festive occasion. Instead, the words serve him as simply a peg for sounds... This Gloria must be judged simply as a study in abstract music, vocal and orchestral. As such, it is a lively, resourceful, exciting piece. The skill of *Belshazzar*, particularly the interweaving and piling-up of short vocal motives into big climaxes, is recaptured here.'[35] Frank Howes, chief music critic of *The Times*, was glowing in his appreciation. In his article, subtitled 'Bold, Thrilling and Grand', he noted that the work was 'as invigorating and substantial' as Walton had written for a long time: 'The spirit of the music, its impetus and its specific gravity, is altogether fresh... There is no sensation of old ground retilled, but of new ground made more fruitful by an old, still vigorous hand.'[36] Howes makes mention of an 'Italianate' atmosphere, owing something to late Verdi and late Puccini, and also notes (as did Walton himself) connections with the Beethoven of the *Missa Solemnis*.

Walton's comments to Alan Frank about the reviews were typically forthright: 'Except for not too much malice from Miss Porter, and a really spiteful mean & bitchy one from Mrs Heyworth the notices seem to be pretty good. I also heard from M.S. today... who said the concert was a triumph for me!'[37] However, the timing of the premiere was not altogether propitious for the Gloria. Not only had Poulenc produced his own, much-acclaimed Gloria earlier in the year,[38] but Britten was working on his *War Requiem*, amid much publicity, for the celebrations surrounding the consecration of the new Coventry Cathedral in 1962. Against the international success of two contemporary works (one of which had the same text and was similar in length and scoring), Walton's

Gloria, which is substantially harder to sing than its French counterpart, stood less chance than it might otherwise have done of attracting the interest of choral societies looking for new music. Nevertheless, despite the composer's subsequent self-deprecating remarks, 'I'm not sure that it is at all a good work, in fact not perhaps worth the hard labour necessary to make it really come off,'[39] the Gloria unquestionably contains many of the qualities that permeate the best of his compositions.

The Twelve

Orchestration

Walton's anthem *The Twelve* was the result of a joint commission with W. H. Auden (1907–1973) for the choir and organist of their alma mater, Christ Church, Oxford. (For a fuller note on this work, see Vol. 6, Shorter Choral Works without Orchestra.) It was an immediate success at its premiere on 16 May 1965, when it was performed by Christ Church Cathedral Choir, directed by Dr Sydney Watson. Less than a month later, Walton had completed its orchestration for a projected performance the following March with the Oxford Bach Choir, of which Watson was conductor. However, having been invited to write a new work to mark Westminster Abbey's 900th anniversary the following January, Walton asked Watson if he might offer the Abbey the orchestral version instead. Watson readily agreed, writing on 20 September: 'You didn't write it for the Bach Choir, after all, and Christ Church has launched it. We will let the Abbey have its fling.'

Walton could not easily revise the anthem or provide an instrumental prelude or coda (which the weightier orchestral accompaniment would seem to invite), as it would have necessitated a new vocal score. The orchestration of *The Twelve* was therefore, by comparison with composing afresh, a simple task. In any case, though he had played the organ while a student at Oxford, he had a lifelong reluctance to write for that instrument and almost certainly would have thought in orchestral terms when composing the accompaniment of the original anthem. Apart from occasional revisions (i.e. the additional orchestral chords in bars 178–9), the score remains faithful to the organ accompaniment.

Performance and reception

Walton himself conducted the first performance of the orchestral version of *The Twelve* in Westminster Abbey on 2 January 1966, in a programme that included the *Coronation Te Deum*. The performers were the London Philharmonic Choir and Orchestra, with soloists Ann Dowdall, Shirley Minty, Robert Tear, and Maurice Wakeham.[40] Musical ideas could be traced back to Walton's previous choral works with orchestra (the central soprano duet is clearly foreshadowed in the alto solo of the Gloria) and, as before, the taut structure and strongly contrasting textures and varied emotions, inspired by Auden's powerful poem, found immediate favour with most critics. Martin Cooper wrote in the *Daily Telegraph* the following day: 'Sir William has written a miniature cantata, complete with introductory recitative (but no extended instrumental prelude), short solo passages and a big fugal chorus, which debauches into a *Belshazzar*-like final jubilation. In the duet for two women's voices, ['O Lord, my God'] the composer gives a new and subtle twist to the old convention of singing in 3rds, and the final consonance of "I shall be there," echoed by the orchestra, forms a telling middle-point to the work.'

Postscript

After *The Twelve*, Walton failed to complete any further works for chorus and orchestra, though over fifteen years elapsed before his death. He did compose a number of smaller choral works, one of which, *Cantico del Sole*, he considered elaborating and orchestrating for the centenary of the Bach Choir; the idea came to nothing, as much due to his increasing infirmity as to his almost pathological sluggishness in the business of putting pen to paper.[41] Among the projects that 'might have been' were a potential commission for the 1977 Three Choirs Festival in Gloucester, an orchestral mass, and a collaboration with his old friend Paul Dehn on a work for Queen Elizabeth's silver jubilee celebrations in 1977 to be entitled *Peace*, which was curtailed by Dehn's death. He was invited to compose a work for the 1977 St Alban's International Organ Festival.[42] Nothing came of that commission, but it did result in a request from him to Christopher Morris, Frank's successor at OUP, to send him a copy of Palestrina's *Veni sponsa Christi*.[43] Walton's rekindled interest in sixteenth-century vocal polyphony remained with him until his death. A commission in 1979 from the Llandaff Festival for a work to be performed at the 1982 festival turned into a protracted correspondence; the original proposal, to set translations of Horace odes for a cappella choir, was eventually rejected in favour of Psalm 150, to be composed for brass and organ. No music appeared, and negotiations about the composition were continuing at the time of Walton's sudden death in 1983.

One particular commission, the final one as it turned out, appealed strongly to him. When invited to compose a setting of the Stabat Mater for the Huddersfield Choral Society's 150th anniversary celebrations, Walton's response was positive. On 7 March 1983 he rang the choir's conductor to confirm his enthusiasm for the project, mentioning that he knew how he might proceed with it. He died the following morning.

NOTES

1. According to Stewart Craggs in *William Walton: A Catalogue* (Oxford, 1990), p. 68, Walton had previously declined an invitation to compose a choral work for the 1936 Norwich Triennial Musical Festival.
2. Letters 14 May and [? June] 1937, OUP Archive, Oxford.
3. Also published by Oxford University Press. In retrospect, it seems strange that OUP did not discourage Walton from setting the same text for similar forces, thereby creating what amounted to rival works from the same publishing house.
4. The notes, in the OUP Archive, were almost certainly written to assist Hubert Foss with his programme note for the first performance.
5. Alan Frank, 'The Music of William Walton', *The Chesterian*, vol. 20 (1939), pp. 153–156.
6. A. H. Ashworth, *Yorkshire Post* (20 September 1937).
7. F. H. Shera, 'Musical Topics', *Sheffield Telegraph* (21 September 1937).

8. J. R. Williams, *Yorkshire Evening News* (4 October 1937). Sargent, only 42 yet widely championed as a charismatic choral director, had since 1931 shared the conducting at the Leeds Triennial Festival with its conductor-in-chief, Sir Thomas Beecham.

9. Frank Toothill, *Leeds Mercury* (5 October 1937).

10. Alice, although married to Ivor Guest, Lord Wimborne (1873–1939), was involved in an affair with Walton that lasted until her death in 1948. The beautifully bound scrapbook is preserved in the Walton Archive, Ischia.

11. *Glasgow Herald* (7 October 1937).

12. *Manchester Guardian* (2 December 1937).

13. *Evening News* (2 December 1937).

14. Letter from Hubert Foss to Walter Legge, 29 October 1937.

15. Liner note for a disc of Walton's choral music (CD–EMX 2225).

16. See letter of 22 March 1946 from Walton to Norman Peterkin, successor to Foss at OUP, in the Walton Archive, Ischia.

17. In a letter of 18 November 1952 to McKie, he confesses to being 'delighted [at the prospect of composing the Te Deum] as I'm beginning to feel the need of a break'. A letter to Frank of 23 November 1952 expressed similar sentiments. Telling him that he hoped to have the Te Deum and *Orb and Sceptre* 'polished off by Christmas', Walton added that 'then I can settle down again to T. and C.—am rather grateful to be having a busman's holiday away from it for a week or two'.

18. Letters of 18 November and 22 December 1952, and 22 March 1953, between Walton and McKie, as well as undated postcards, are held in Westminster Abbey Library.

19. Perhaps it was the exhortation to write the 'grand climax' that prompted Walton, in a letter of 17 December 1952, to ask McKie to intercede with the Archbishop of Canterbury, who had initially wanted the shortened version of the canticle, 'to allow me to set the whole of the Te Deum…With the addition of the last stanza it will work out the form & be properly rounded off.'

20. In a letter to Alan Frank of 17 April 1953 the choral conductor Charles Proctor, who had been sent an advance copy of the Te Deum, suggested that Walton might consider an alternative *fff* ending, as 'the *pp* ending does rather spoil the chances for concert performance'.

21. Walton's remark about the extra brass is somewhat misleading. Unlike *Belshazzar*, in which the two extra brass bands were expertly cued into the orchestral brass by the composer, the Kneller Hall brass and side drum parts in the Te Deum were intended to be independent of the main orchestra and to create an antiphonal effect. Walton's assistant Roy Douglas incorporated these parts into the full orchestra ensemble for concert performance, finishing the task in March 1953. To retain the antiphonal effect, Douglas was obliged to use woodwind, horns, and even organ, as well as trumpets and trombones.

22. Letter to Christopher Hassall, 29 December 1952.

23. 22 January 1953. The Aldeburgh piece was the finale of the composite Variations on an Elizabethan Theme.

24. This information is taken from the comprehensive notes on the musical preparations for the coronation made in July 1953 by McKie (Westminster Abbey Library).

25. The coronation choir was made up of singers from 24 British choirs, members of the Royal Schools of Church Music, and representatives of the British Dominions. Additional singers were drawn from a wide circle of well-known musicians, bringing the total number in the choir to 400. The orchestra was assembled from representatives of the principal British orchestras. See *Musical Times*, vol. 94, July 1953, pp. 306–307.

26. *The Coronation Service of Her Majesty Queen Elizabeth II*, EMI 5 66582 2.

27. Michael Kennedy, *Portrait of Walton* (Oxford, 1989; rev. edn, 1998), p. 166.

28. The Leeds Festival had attempted to commission from Walton a successor to *Belshazzar* and *In Honour* but in 1949, while on honeymoon in Argentina, Walton wrote to Alan Frank (Peterkin's successor as head of the music department at OUP), requesting that he 'get in touch with Leeds & Cheltenham Festivals & tell them that I don't want to write works for them' (OUP Archive).

29. Walton to Frank, 7 November 1957.

30. Walton to Frank, 4 January 1958.

31. Letter to Frank, 12 January 1961. About this time, he indicated to Frank that he hoped to have the short score complete by the end of March, and that 'it will come in batches [which] will give [the choir] something to get on with'.

32. Frank to David Crawshaw, 31 May 1961. Such was Walton's haphazard method of supplying initial copy and revisions to OUP that there were times when he had to ask OUP to send him copies of the piano score revisions, in order to incorporate them into the full score.

33. See Richard Aldous, *Tunes of Glory* (London, 2001), pp. 210–212.

34. Bernarr Rainbow, *Music and Letters*, vol. 43, no. 2 (1962), p. 184.

35. *Musical Times*, vol. 103, January 1962, p. 24.

36. Frank Howes, *The Times* (25 November 1961).

37. Andrew Porter, music critic of the *Financial Times* from 1953 to 1973; Peter Heyworth, music critic of *The Observer* from 1955 to 1987.

38. Walton wrote to Alan Frank on 12 February 1961: 'It is slightly boring that Poulenc has just come out with a "Gloria" at Boston—a great success it seems.'

39. Letter to Malcolm Arnold, 5 November 1970.

40. A recording of the first performance is available on disc (*BBC Legends*, BBCL 4098–2).

41. See Craggs, *William Walton: A Catalogue of Works*, p. 114.

42. Apparently Walton toyed with the idea of a setting of '*De profundis*' (Psalm 130). Given the subject matter, very different from his usual celebratory texts, it is a cause for regret that this work was never written.

43. Letter to Christopher Morris, 14 April 1977.

6

Shorter Choral Works without Orchestra *(Vol. 6)*

Timothy Brown

Vocal composition of one sort or another occupied William Walton throughout his life. It was a medium to which he constantly returned, in between the symphonies, concertos, ballets, film scores, and other instrumental music which, apart from *Troilus and Cressida*, were his predominant concern. As a fourteen-year-old, his first attempts at composition included '30 very bad works of various species, songs, motets, Magnificats etc'.[1] In the last weeks of his life, seven decades later, when composition was more or less beyond him, he toyed with ideas for a motet. In the intervening years, he set both sacred and secular texts, ranging from the intimate unaccompanied wedding anthem 'Set me as a seal upon thine heart' to the three-act, grandiloquent opera *Troilus and Cressida*. It was with the cantata-cum-oratorio *Belshazzar's Feast*, composed between 1929 and 1931, that Walton could be said to have come of age as a composer. As with *Façade*, composed some nine years earlier, he again took the British musical establishment by storm, this time with a work which proved beyond doubt his ability to compose for choirs. Given the unease of a man who was constantly concerned lest the world of music passed him by, and whose compositions did not always initially receive the most wholehearted reception, the warmth with which his fluent essays in choral writing were consistently greeted throughout his life, by performers and audiences alike, must have been a gratifying source of reassurance to him.

Compared with Walton's large-scale choral works with orchestra, the fourteen choral compositions included in Volume 6 of the WWE are, to a greater or lesser extent, much more modest in scope, yet all display inherent quality. The majority of them are settings of religious or semi-religious texts. Only one (the partsong 'Put Off the Serpent Girdle') is specifically secular and is, in a sense, the 'odd one out', though necessarily included by virtue of its genre. All reveal the ease and skill with which he wrote for voices and some, in their way, are miniature masterpieces. Bringing them together not only places this facility in sharper focus; at the same time it highlights a consistency of approach to this type of composition. From the outset this is quintessentially 'English' music, demonstrating its composer's innate knowledge of the national church music repertoire. Furthermore, the arching melodic lines, plangent harmonies, and drooping cadences that are a feature of Walton's mature style are evident even in his earliest known composition, the setting for equal voices of *A Litany*. Walton always wrote choral music that sounded fresh and spontaneous. It is no wonder that it remains in the catalogue and continues to receive regular performance.

Musical education

Walton's unorthodox musical apprenticeship, first as a boy chorister at Christ Church, Oxford, and then as an undergraduate at the same college, was of crucial significance to his later career as a composer. It was there, during six years at the choir school, that he first determined to compose; it was where he acquired the only formal training he ever had in harmony and counterpoint and where, as an Anglican cathedral choirboy, he soaked up the sounds and traditions that were to make his choral music so much a part of the renaissance of an 'English' school of choral composition, begun by Parry and Stanford. The familiar 'rags to riches' story—the gauche northerner who won a place in the cathedral choir, passing from there into Oxford University, only to be sent down for failing his examinations before being 'rescued' by the Sitwell family—is misleading.[2] Far from it: relatively poor and socially out of his depth he may have been, but, as a musician, he was more than the equal of his fellow 10-year-old new boys. He was gifted with perfect pitch, and singing was already in his blood by the time he took his place in the choir stalls of Christ Church Cathedral, having been a member of his father's church choir, at St John's Church, Werneth: 'It is said that he could sing before he could talk (doubtless untrue).'[3] Charles Walton, a trained singer and an ambitious, if thwarted, musician, introduced his son not only to the standard parish church choir repertoire but also to the popular choral works of the day.[4] At Oxford William found himself in an environment which from a musical point of view was remarkable (though not, according to his brother Noel, in other respects). Among his teachers were Henry Ley, the cathedral organist, Hugh Allen, organist of New College (later Heather Professor of Music at Oxford), and the historian and composer Ernest Walker. All were influential figures who contributed significantly to Walton's education and to his growing desire to become a composer. Frustratingly (in later life Walton talked little about the details of his education), it is not known what each one taught the young musician, how it was done, and when. However, by the age of 13 or 14 he was already composing avidly.[5] Although most of this juvenilia is now lost, one piece, a partsong entitled *A Litany* (a setting of 'Drop, drop, slow tears' by the seventeenth-century poet and priest Phineas Fletcher), did survive, a revised version of which was eventually published, much later, in 1930.

The Dean of Christ Church, Thomas Strong, a talented pianist with a keen interest in the new music of the day, took the budding composer under his wing, not only by taking care of the financial commitments that his parents could not meet, but also by believing sufficiently in the boy's musical promise to keep him on at the choir school after his voice broke in the summer of 1916. In 1918 he arranged for him to enter Christ Church as an undergraduate. Here Walton continued to enjoy the support of his teachers, who encouraged him to pursue his interest in composition. Just why, given such help, together with his fierce determination to succeed as a musician, Walton failed to proceed in due time to an Oxford degree (and so complete a regular musical education) has never been explained entirely satisfactorily; he was certainly intelligent enough. Maybe it was simply that the lack of a regular secondary school education denied him the opportunity to achieve the necessary academic skill in algebra or Greek. Whatever the reason, he failed to matriculate and, after five terms at the university, was sent down, thereby ending his formal musical education at the age of eighteen.

Practically all of his schooling had been spent within the rarefied atmosphere of an English cathedral precinct, where the daily musical diet was one of psalm chants, canticles, anthems, hymns, and voluntaries. He may have spoken little about this period in later life, yet his specific designation of 'treble' or 'soprano' in his choral works, and various comments about the desired vocal quality at specific points in the music, reveal that he remained to the end acutely alive to the sound of choirs of men and boys. Moreover, the traditional character of Anglican church music was so firmly ingrained that when he later came to write his own settings of familiar texts, his response was instinctive, even if the process of composition cost him, as always, much effort. Whatever shortcomings may be detected in the early instrumental music, the vocal works which survive from the same period bear testimony to the six years of Oxford tuition. Not only did they instil in Walton an infallible ability to write for voices, but they gave him the assured grasp of melodic line and feeling for counterpoint that was to infuse all his music.

A Litany

In 1930 Oxford University Press, Walton's publisher since 1925, printed *A Litany*, a short, four-part devotional partsong for unaccompanied mixed voices. Dated 'Oxford 1917' on the printed score, it has always been cited as an example of Walton's precocity as a composer, particular attention being paid to the imaginative harmony and inventive part-writing. The true facts are, however, less clear. The existing holograph (dated 1916) reveals an altogether simpler texture, which lacks the subtle phrasing as well as the most telling gestures of the 1930 printing, while being a remarkable achievement for a 14 year old. Yet another (undated) version exists, scored for four treble voices, which is even simpler in structure and style. Harmonic infelicities and elementary slips of notation suggest this to be the first version of the three. Given that treble voices would have been readily available to Walton, and that this version has survived as multiple, individual voice parts (no score exists), it is probable that a performance of the piece was envisaged, perhaps by the young composer's friends in Christ Church choir. Practically all Walton's youthful efforts at composition were destroyed; why *A Litany* survived is not known. However, in 1929, when Walton began work on *Belshazzar's Feast* (his first choral piece since Oxford days), perhaps he recalled the little partsong and decided to offer a revised version to OUP. At any rate, *A Litany* appeared in print during the period of the composition of *Belshazzar's Feast* and, as Christopher Palmer has pointed out, 'In your deep flood' in the partsong is uncannily prescient of the passage in the oratorio beginning 'By the waters of Babylon'.[6] Despite the date '1917' given at the end of the first edition, it seems likely that this indicated (albeit inaccurately) the date of the partsong's original composition (in its F minor SATB version), the revision being left until immediately prior to the 1930 publication.

The three versions of *A Litany* offer a revealing glimpse of Walton's development as a composer and provide the earliest examples of self-criticism and revision, a characteristic of his compositional method throughout his life. Each version has distinctive features (including different tonalities) while remaining fundamentally the same piece. The simplicity of the song for trebles, despite the 'exotic' harmonies of the opening and closing bars, is very different from the richness of the first attempt for four-part mixed voices. This in turn is superseded by the published version which skilfully cuts out unwanted beats, intensifies the harmonic language, and gives the phrase structure an altogether greater flexibility, features which were to remain constant in Walton's choral music.

Make we joy now in this fest

Towards the end of 1931, Walton was commissioned by the Manchester *Daily Dispatch* to write a Christmas carol. By 21 December he had still not written it, observing in a letter of the same day to Dora Foss that he had to complete it by the following morning.[7] This he did, for on 24 December 'Make we joy now in this fest', for unaccompanied mixed voices, was published in the newspaper. It is composed in a mildly dissonant and modal style that would not have been out of place among the contemporary carols in *The Oxford Book of Carols*, published three years earlier.[8] Essentially lyrical, it has, none the less, that typically robust Waltonian approach to rhythm which characterized his choral music from then on. The part-writing, though unpretentious, is assured and imaginative, and contributes greatly to the carol's effectiveness.

Set me as a seal upon thine heart

The 1930s saw the composition of the First Symphony, the coronation march *Crown Imperial*, and Walton's second major choral work, *In Honour of the City of London*. The first film scores appeared, including the music for Paul Czinner's *As You Like It*, starring Laurence Olivier. As a counterpoint to his professional life, which included an increasing number of public performances (some of which Walton conducted), he enjoyed a busy and somewhat glamorous social life among the London 'smart' set, into which he had been introduced by Sacheverell and Osbert Sitwell after leaving Oxford. In 1935, following an intense relationship with Baroness Imma Doernberg, he was introduced to Alice, Viscountess Wimborne, who was to become Walton's friend, confidante, lover, and critic, until her death in 1948. He quickly established good relations with her husband and children ('the family seemed to like me, I don't know why...I even got on very well with her husband') and spent increasing amounts of time at the family's country seat at Ashby St Ledgers, near Rugby.[9] In 1938 Walton composed a short unaccompanied anthem, 'Set me as a seal upon thine heart', as a wedding gift for Alice's son Ivor and his bride, Mabel Fox-Strangways, using words from the Song of Solomon. The first performance was given at the marriage service in St Mary Abbots Church, Kensington, on 22 November (St Cecilia's Day) 1938. Had he composed the anthem specially in honour of the patron saint of music, instead of for a marriage service, Walton could scarcely have produced a more appropriate piece. In spite of its brevity (only 38 bars), the anthem, with its perfectly placed solos for tenor and soprano, distils the essence of the evocative text (which Walton cleverly adapted to suit his purpose) in music of great beauty and expressive range.

Where does the uttered Music go?

Though much of the war was taken up with film music (most notably that for Olivier's *Henry V*) there was, for a brief period, the prospect of a Te Deum for chorus and orchestra. This was planned for the opening concert of the 1944 season of Promenade Concerts, to mark Sir Henry Wood's 50th anniversary as their conductor. But though Walton had written to Wood in December 1943 with the news that he was 'safely launched' on the piece, by February 1944 it had been abandoned when it became clear to him that delays completing *Henry V* meant it would be impossible for him to finish the Te Deum on time.

On 19 August of the same year, Wood died. To a memorial concert on 4 March 1945 Walton contributed only a fanfare, a newly revised and amplified version of one composed two years previously. But by then he had accepted an invitation from the conductor's widow to collaborate with the Poet Laureate, John Masefield, on a new work to be performed at the unveiling of a commemorative stained-glass window in St Sepulchre's Church, Holborn.[10] Walton now had the opportunity, denied him two years earlier, to pay tribute to the conductor who had been such a champion of his music. Agreeing a text with Masefield proved troublesome, and he very nearly abandoned a choral work altogether in favour of 'a short string piece'. However, Masefield eventually did produce a poetic tribute, entitled 'Sir Henry Wood', which Walton felt he could set for unaccompanied mixed voices, in time for the unveiling ceremony in April. The first performance of the new work, renamed 'Where does the uttered Music go?', took place on 26 April 1946, in a service which included Vaughan Williams's *Serenade to Music*. The BBC Chorus and Theatre Revue Chorus were conducted by Leslie Woodgate. 'Where does the uttered Music go?' was later recorded by HMV (C 3503), its release coinciding with a performance at the Henry Wood Promenade Concert on 18 September 1946.

The fact that Walton had been commissioned to compose a work to a text by the Poet Laureate for such an 'establishment' event gives some indication of his standing in London's musical and social circles at that time, and doubtless Walton felt that the new piece should be worthy of the occasion. Certainly, the work's multiple divisions and dissonant, chromatic harmony are technically demanding, but the solemn, elegiac quality of the piece (somewhat in the tradition of the medieval/Renaissance *déploration*) has an immediate appeal. In the partsong Walton demonstrates yet again an innate ability not only to write strong melodies but also to spin them into textures of great expressive warmth. The *Times*'s critic, in a somewhat bland review (27 April 1946), was none the less generous enough to suggest that it was 'sure to survive its occasion'. It has done, though an idiosyncratic text, which is neither sacred nor overtly secular, and which refers obliquely to Henry Wood ('This Man with Music touched our minds …'), makes it a difficult piece to programme in church and something of a curiosity in the concert hall. Nevertheless, this secular 'requiem', characterized by a more lyrical, less overtly rhythmic texture than Walton had previously produced, is as eloquent a piece as any of his choral music.

Put Off the Serpent Girdle

After his marriage to Susana Gil Passo in 1948, Walton left England to make his home on the island of Ischia, in the Bay of Naples. Compositionally, Walton was preoccupied during the early years of his self-imposed 'exile' with the opera *Troilus and Cressida* and, more briefly, with the Te Deum, composed for the coronation of Queen Elizabeth II in 1953.[11] The original version of the start of Act II of the opera contained a short trio for female chorus, 'Put Off the Serpent Girdle', an evening song which Cressida's serving women sing to their mistress as she prepares for bed. When Walton, stung by the lack of success of *Troilus*, began to revise the opera in 1972, Cressida's attendants were dropped and the song was thus cut from the score.

However, some years before this, Walton, who was fond of the song, had expressed a wish to publish it separately as a chorus for women's voices, though this would necessitate the writing of a second verse to make it of adequate length. Since Christopher Hassall, the opera's librettist, had died in 1963, Alan Frank, Walton's publisher at OUP and a lifelong friend, wrote on the composer's behalf to Paul Dehn on 14 February 1967, inviting him to undertake the small 'chore' of writing a second verse. Dehn, a friend of Walton's and the librettist of *The Bear*, replied by 22 February, enclosing a 'first bash', which became the second verse. The additional words proved both a perfect complement to Hassall's poem and a neat parody of his style. To complete the revised song, Walton added a brief linking passage between the two verses, and a coda. The partsong was published, in the Oxford Choral Songs series, later the same year.

What Cheer?

Over the next seven years, Walton was much involved in the writing of major orchestral works, including the Second Symphony. Between 1960 and 1961 he returned to choral composition with the Gloria, composed for the 125th anniversary celebrations of the Huddersfield Choral Society. At the same time he was invited by Christopher Morris, then Music Editor at OUP and, from 1975, Frank's successor, to contribute a carol to OUP's new anthology, *Carols for Choirs*. The result was 'What Cheer?', a buoyant, typically Waltonian offering with its jazzy rhythms, oblique harmonies, and sharply articulated dynamics. *Carols for Choirs* proved such a success that over the next seventeen years two further volumes appeared, to which Walton also contributed.

The Twelve

In 1964 W. H. Auden, like Walton a former undergraduate at Christ Church, accepted an invitation from the Dean, Cuthbert Simpson, to write a poem on the subject of the twelve apostles, the intention being that Walton should then be invited to set it to music. Christ Church had so far commissioned nothing from two of its most distinguished living alumni, and Simpson was aware of the scarcity of good anthems suitable for the feasts of the apostles. He presented the idea initially to Auden, who was at that time a frequent visitor to Oxford. Auden sent a draft of his text to Walton in Ischia. The composer's response was typically dry and superficially unenthusiastic, as revealed in a letter to Frank, written in early January 1965: 'Wystan Auden sometime last year at Oxford let himself and me in for writing an anthem for Ch. Ch. Choir. He said he must have been in his cups! Anyhow a few days ago what he calls "this bloody anthem" arrived, so I suppose I must do it. It is a somewhat obscure and difficult-to-set-text.'[12]

Some weeks later he admitted to Frank that it was 'difficult to keep from being difficult to sing and I know b- all about the organ!' In fact the text is written with an attention to rhyme, rhythm, and metre, as well as with a powerful imagery, which makes it highly suitable for musical setting.[13] Frank later wrote that 'Auden's text is surely one of the most distinguished and telling of any written expressly for musical setting in our time'.[14] Walton worked hard at the music, but felt unsure of himself when it came to the organ part. Though he had once learnt the organ, and as an undergraduate in 1918 had stood in briefly for the organ scholar of Balliol College before the latter returned from war service, he was always uncertain about writing for the instrument. On this occasion he relied on the organist of Christ Church, Dr Sydney Watson, to advise him on the playability of the organ part and on matters of registration. The anthem, scored for two treble soloists, ATB solos, double choir of 'not less than 16 trebles, 4 altos, 4 tenors, 4 basses', and organ, was finished section by section. Alan Frank received the last part in March 1965, preceded by a letter, dated 10 March, in which Walton wrote, 'It is to be hoped that there are two good little boys, otherwise I don't think it will be found too difficult…It is not anything like as difficult as Tippett, Berkeley or Rubbra!' *The Twelve* received its first performance at Evensong in Christ Church Cathedral on 16 May 1965.[15]

The 'miniature cantata', as Martin Cooper later described it,[16] was an immediate success, both with performers and audiences, and the critical response was highly favourable. Its scale certainly justifies Cooper's epithet. Its three principal sections reflect Auden's poem, and encapsulate a lyrical duet for two trebles, recitative, and dramatic choral writing that recalls the vivid immediacy of *Belshazzar's Feast,* especially in the concluding fugal section for double chorus. In the same way that the scope of the vocal writing in Berkeley's *Festival Anthem* or in Britten's *Hymn to St Cecilia* (also using an Auden text) goes beyond the realm of a mere 'anthem', so Walton scales heights in *The Twelve* that are otherwise found only in his choral works with orchestra. It is scarcely surprising then that Walton subsequently orchestrated his new anthem. In that version it was first performed in the concert held on 2 January 1966 to commemorate the 900th anniversary of the founding of Westminster Abbey.

Missa Brevis

While at work on *The Twelve*, Walton was also composing another sacred piece, a Missa Brevis ('very brevis') for Coventry Cathedral—'but don't think I've got a religious mania,' he wrote to Malcolm Arnold, an old friend who shared his scepticism of matters spiritual.[17] Coventry Cathedral, rebuilt after its wartime destruction to the design of the architect Basil Spence, was re-consecrated in 1961.[18] The new cathedral's first organist was David Lepine, a lively and energetic musician who set about establishing a choir worthy of such a major building. On 17 March 1965 Walton wrote to Alan Frank: 'I'm also on to the Missa Brevissima. I doubt if there will be more that 8 to 10 mins. of it. Remembering the boredom I suffered as a dear little choirboy, I've made it or am making it as brevissima as poss. It should be v. popular among Communion takers. But how uninspiring are the words!' Walton scored the Missa Brevis, commissioned by the Friends of Coventry Cathedral, for the new choir and the Harrison & Harrison organ, whose pipes, facing directly into the nave, decorate the entire height of the massive columns framing each side of the chancel. Despite the composer's unease at writing for the organ, to have composed a work without involving this magnificent instrument would have been a wasted opportunity. Walton nevertheless reserves the appearance of the organ until the closing Gloria, where it plays as significant a role in the music as it does in *The Twelve*. Maybe it was his innate dislike of the instrument which encouraged Walton to leave the organ out of the earlier movements, but by keeping his powder dry until the final movement the effect of the organ's entry is undoubtedly all the greater.

The Missa Brevis was to have been sung on Easter Day 1966, but on 23 March Lepine was obliged to write to OUP to explain that illness had prevented the boys from learning the work in time, and the performance was postponed. Sadly, Coventry Cathedral thus lost its opportunity to give the first performance of the mass. It was published in 1966 and quickly entered the repertoire of cathedral choirs. On 29 March 1967—the year in which Walton received the Order of Merit—it was first broadcast as part of a 65th birthday concert by the BBC Chorus, conducted by Alan G. Melville. In June 1967 Diana McVeagh reviewed the work for the *Musical Times* and wrote perceptively: 'It is spare in everything but invention . . . The music sounds hard—not to sing, or to listen to, but as though it had been composed out of hard thinking and strong feeling. A brief work certainly, but not a small one.' In 1968, Walton, at the suggestion of John Birch, the organist of Chichester Cathedral, made a small revision to enable the Sanctus and Benedictus, originally intended to follow one another without a break, to be sung as separate entities. In this form the work was first performed as part of the Southern Cathedrals Festival, held at Chichester in July 1968.

All this Time

As the 1960s drew to their close, Walton was preoccupied with more film music and with the *Improvisations on an Impromptu of Benjamin Britten*. In 1970 he composed a new carol, 'All this Time', for *Carols for Choirs 2*. It taps the same rhythmic and modal vein as the earlier 'What cheer?'. The choral refrains, which alternate with verses for sopranos and tenors, are reminiscent of Holst's 'Lullay my lyking' and are similarly effective. When it was published, David Willcocks (joint editor, *Carols for Choirs 2*) requested some clarification of the break before verses 1 and 2, and suggested the inclusion of pauses between verses. Walton obliged, noting on a postcard from Ischia to Christopher Morris at OUP on 30 December 1970: 'Herewith the carol duly marked with the (to me quite unnecessary) pauses. However, why not—what are a couple of ⌢s between friends at this festive season?'

Jubilate Deo

In 1971 Lina Lalandi, Director of the English Bach Festival, approached Walton with the idea of commissioning a work from him with which the Festival could celebrate his 70th birthday. Instead of a commission, he wrote a short Jubilate Deo for double choir and organ, a sequel to the Missa Brevis, as a present for her. Once again, having committed himself, he had second thoughts about a religious text: 'The Jubilate is not the most inspiring bit of nonsense—in fact the only thing to be said for it is its brevity.'[19]

A typical response maybe, but the resulting music was, equally typically, to the point. It captures the essence of the text in a score which, though less than four minutes long, embodies characteristically strong melodies and rhythms, hauntingly beautiful passages for both treble solo and solo ensemble, and harmonic colour which is tonal but never bland. As in *Belshazzar's Feast*, the *Coronation Te Deum*, and *The Twelve*, Walton's response to a 'joyful' text is to set it antiphonally, in short bursts of sound which practically fall over one another in their excitement. On 22 April 1972 he attended the first performance of the Jubilate Deo in the cathedral, where it was sung by the choir in a concert of his choral works, as part of the English Bach Festival. For all its brevity, the piece captured the attention of the *Times*'s critic, William Mann, who referred to its 'enchanting quiet sections, typical in their rhythmic vitality'.[20] Hugo Cole, writing in *The Guardian* on 24 April, highlighted the confident technique of Walton's choral writing: 'This is a brief, fairly impersonal work... Yet it speaks in every bar of inside knowledge and affection even for the mannerisms of the traditional idiom.' The treble solo he described as 'beautifully placed, simple, touching, and perfectly imagined in terms of a boy's voice'.

The 70th birthday tribute consolidated Walton's position as a major twentieth-century British composer of Anglican church music. Given his scant regard for established religion, it is an accolade that would doubtless have produced a wry smile on Walton's urbane countenance. Even so, he was sufficiently moved by the 1972 Christ Church recording of his church music, directed by Simon Preston,[21] to arrange for a copy to be sent to the Dowager Viscountess Wimborne, for whose wedding he had composed 'Set me as a seal upon thine heart' twenty-four years previously.

Cantico del Sole

Plans for a third symphony occupied much of 1973, but towards the end of the year Walton was invited by Professor Aloys Fleischmann to compose a work for the Cork International Choral Festival's 25th anniversary which was to be commissioned by Lady Mayer, wife of Sir Robert, the noted musical philanthropist. Three other composers, Boris Blacher, Roman Vlad, and Brian Boydell, had also been invited to submit compositions, all of which were to be performed by an amateur choir.[22] Unhappy about this stipulation, Walton was reluctant to accept the invitation. Eventually Lady Mayer, a long-standing patron of the festival, persuaded Walton to accept the commission, but only after it was agreed that the BBC Northern Singers—a choir that Walton knew and admired—would give the first performance, under their conductor Stephen Wilkinson.[23] In a letter to Malcolm Arnold dated 9 August 1973, Walton mentions the 'Cantico del Sole' by St Francis of Assisi (known as the Prayer of St Francis) as a possible text. Finishing the composition in early 1974, he revealed in another letter to Arnold typical misgivings about the piece, describing it as 'deplorably dull and unexciting', although he had previously referred to it as 'good', though needing 'the addition of a small orchestra'.[24] None the less, it was received enthusiastically at its première on 25 April 1974 in University College, Cork, and was subsequently recorded by the choir on an LP of contemporary British choral music.[25] The work was published in the same year.

Walton sets the prayer in the form of a dialogue between women's and men's voices which, except when they combine in the opening and closing sections, offer separate praise to the Lord for the bounty of the natural order. No doubt the composer, aware that the *Cantico del Sole* might be perceived as an unofficial doctoral 'exercise' for the honorary degree that was to be awarded to him during the festival by the National University of Ireland, felt that this piece should pull no punches. In view of its comparative difficulty, it is no wonder that Walton was alarmed at the original intention to have the work sung by an amateur choir. Despite the apparently characteristic jazzy rhythms and angular melodies, the vocal writing is of a different character from that of his other choral music, rather as, in its own way, is 'Where does the uttered Music go?', his other 'semi-secular' composition. Immediately striking is the sensitivity with which the Italian words, the language of the composer's adopted country, are set. The personal and prayer-like quality of the text evokes in Walton a subtler, more lyrical approach than usual, which finds its most telling expression in the climax on the final page.

The critical response to the premiere was favourable: Charles Acton, writing in the *Musical Times* (August 1974), referred to it as 'a miniature of beauty and feeling for the words, one of the festival's many successes', and Felix Aprahamian, writing in the *Sunday Times* (5 May 1974), mentions the 'eloquent antiphonal exchanges between opening and closing tutti'.[26]

Magnificat and Nunc Dimittis

Though now over 70 and in ailing health, Walton continued to compose, albeit with increasing trepidation. Among the invitations to undertake commissions which continued to arrive on his desk was one from Walter Hussey, Dean of Chichester, suggesting a set of canticles for the cathedral's 900th anniversary celebrations. It was just over thirty years since Hussey, then Vicar of St Matthew's, Northampton, had invited Walton to compose an anthem for the church's golden jubilee, in September 1943. Somewhat uncharacteristically, given his ongoing financial anxieties, Walton had at that time declined, possibly because of the seemingly 'parochial' nature of the commission. He was unaware of Hussey's enlightened patronage of the arts and of the fact that the distinguished sculptor Henry Moore had accepted a commission for a statue of the Virgin and Child to commemorate the same jubilee. In the event the 1943 musical commission went to Benjamin Britten, who composed *Rejoice in the Lamb* for the occasion. Walton was at the first performance and regretted not having fulfilled the commission himself. Consequently, when Dean Hussey's letter arrived in Italy in 1974, Walton readily accepted the new commission, especially in view of the proposed fee (£500). 'As the queer dean has been very generous, I feel I must try to do something at least respectably good,' he wrote to Alan Frank on 10 July 1974. Originally intending to write a Te Deum, Walton eventually agreed to write a set of evening canticles, though once again he was disparaging about the liturgical text: 'How I dislike the words of Mag. and Nunc.,' he wrote in the same letter. He found the realization of this commission more troublesome than he expected. In particular, he reported to Dean Hussey that he had got stuck with the text, receiving the reply that 'it was obviously the bit about "the rich being sent empty away" that was causing the mental block!'[27] By November 1974 he had completed the composition, coming up with a strong, characteristically robust, and singable work. Again, he needed help with the organ part and this was provided by John Birch, the cathedral's organist.

The first performance of the completed set of canticles took place in Chichester Cathedral on 14 June 1975, at the Evensong to mark the cathedral's anniversary.[28] Walton was, however, dissatisfied and as soon as he could set about revisions, readily accepting suggested emendations from Birch. He subsequently admitted to Christopher Morris that the corrections and emendations for the 'Mag. and Nunc.' had become slightly more than either of them had envisaged. However, although he was not in time to prevent the first engraving from going to press, he viewed the changes as being of sufficient importance to persuade OUP to withdraw the first edition before it was put on sale, and to reset it. He was even prepared to bear a proportion of the cost of re-engraving the canticles. As with the revisions of *A Litany*, some loss of spontaneity may be perceived in the process of improvement. Even though the revised Magnificat and Nunc Dimittis is undoubtedly the better for the corrections, comparison with the first version is illuminating.

Antiphon

After Chichester, Walton felt increasingly unable to accept all the commissions that came his way. He was forced to decline a request for a work for the Three Choirs Festival and a choral piece for the choir of St Alban's Abbey. But in 1977 he did complete two commissions—an anthem and a little carol, 'King Herod and the Cock'. The anthem, a setting of George Herbert's poem *Antiphon* ('Let all the world in every corner sing'), was for the 150th anniversary of St Paul's Church, Rochester, New York. Writing to Alan Frank on 13 June, Walton admitted that 'it has taken me a lot of bother. How stupid I am to worry, but I find I've a great antipathy for the organ and don't know how much to write for the bloody thing.' Remembering, perhaps, the pauses in 'All this Time', he expressed further doubts about the new piece in a scribbled note to Christopher Morris on 24 June. In the event, Walton completed the piece, and the work, exuding an upbeat brashness which belied his increasing age and infirmity, received its first performance in St Paul's Church on 20 November 1977.

Though true to the terms of the commission, for a 'festive' anthem with 'little or no divisi', and despite its reliance on ideas from the past (there are echoes of both the Jubilate and the Chichester canticles), *Antiphon* lacks those haunting melodic ideas that permeate Walton's earlier choral works. Forever nervous of writing for organ, his suggestion to OUP that Simon Preston 'might do the registration' came to nothing, and the work was printed with just one instruction, 'Full Organ', for the final bars.

King Herod and the Cock

Just over a month after the premiere of *Antiphon*, the choir of King's College, Cambridge, directed by Philip Ledger, gave the first performance of 'King Herod and the Cock' at the annual Service of Lessons and Carols on Christmas Eve. Walton was clearly bothered by the composition of this miniature, despite its slight nature. First of all he could not decide on a text. On 21 April 1977 he wrote to Christopher Morris: 'What about that there Carol? Or has it completely lapsed? I enclose a rather out of date letter from David Wilcocks [sic] but have found no trace of "Love came down at Xmas" or at any other time for that matter.' Morris provided him with some possible texts and he chose the traditional carol 'King Herod and the cock'. By June he had produced three different settings, all of which he forwarded to Morris: 'I am sending by Gillian [Widdicombe] that there carol & don't ever ask me to [do] anything like it again! You can choose which one you like—there are 3 now! Owing to the "passing notes" the Mss would suggest that both D.W. [David Willcocks] & alas, myself had contracted measles—German measles from the look of the spots. I'd give it up if I were you.'[29] In the event John Rutter, David Willcocks's co-editor of *Carols for Choirs 3*, in which the carol was published, was invited to conflate the three into one version, of which Walton presumably approved, writing in subsequent letters to Morris: 'Here is the final version of this blasted Carol. I'm having no more to do with it. Publish at your peril!' and, eventually, 'Carol Ok. at last and I hope honour is satisfied all round!'

With this short carol Walton's choral composing came to an end. There were other plans, including the composition of a Stabat Mater for Huddersfield and a potentially major commission for the Llandaff Festival, but advancing age and illness left him with little will and less energy to realize any of these projects.

Postscript

Walton was not religious in a conventional sense. In his church music there is a complete absence of the religiosity that was a feature of the repertoire that made up his staple diet as a chorister at Christ Church. His approach to the words that he set to music was not theological, rather, dramatic or even theatrical. Thus, despite the initial aversion to religious texts which may readily be detected from the various quotations in this Preface (too much exposure as a chorister to the Bible and the Book of Common Prayer, perhaps?), his initial, downbeat reaction gave way, once he put pen to paper, to an instinctive response to both language and imagery as springboards to musical composition.

Forever the professional and self-critical composer, Walton remained intrigued by the technique of composition. Despite increasing inactivity, he found diversion in the final months of his life by 'studying Palestrina like mad' with the aid of an 'excellent' recording by Michael Howard.[30] Palestrina's music, boring to him as a choirboy, now held a special fascination for him. He attempted a motet of his own. 'I'd like to think I could write something even 100th part as good [as Palestrina]. We'll see!,' he wrote to Alan Frank.[31] Indifferent as the fledgling composer might have been to Renaissance polyphony, constant exposure to its sonorities left an indelible mark. By the time he found his mature style, those transparent vocal textures that he had earlier absorbed were recreated anew, albeit in an idiom very different to that of the Renaissance masters. From the sinuous lines of *A Litany*, through 'Where does the uttered Music go?', to *Cantico del Sole*, the part-writing is as important as any harmonic gestures. Even in the more overtly homophonic pieces, the inner vocal lines often have a linear independence, and are invariably rewarding to sing. No wonder that the finer points of Palestrinian counterpoint engaged Walton's attention in the final days of his life.

NOTES

1. Letter from Walton to Hubert Foss, his first publisher, 17 May 1932, in answer to a request for an autobiographical note. The tenor of the account is self-deprecating, in a typically Waltonian way. This quotation, and others from Walton's correspondence, is taken from photocopies in the William Walton Museum, Forio, Ischia.

2. For a detailed biography of Walton, see Michael Kennedy's *Portrait of Walton* (Oxford, 1989).

3. Letter from Walton to Foss, 17 May 1932.

4. These included, according to Noel Walton, William's elder brother, Mendelssohn's *Hymn of Praise*, Gounod's *Messe Solennelle*, and Haydn's *The Creation*, as well as *Messiah* and 'lots of Anthems' (letter from Noel Walton to Hugh Ottaway, 8 April 1970).

5. Letter from Walton to Foss, 17 May 1932.

6. Christopher Palmer, 'Walton's Church Music', *Church Music*, 3, No. 19 (1973), pp. 10–13.

7. Walton's comment in the same letter, that 'it is bad to be tempted by filthy lucre', reminds us that at that time his financial state inclined him to accept all the commissions he could get; for this carol he received ten guineas. Despite eventual fame and (relative) fortune, he retained an obsession with his financial worth as a composer throughout his life.

8. One cannot help wondering why OUP, his own publisher, had not invited Walton to contribute to this important new anthology, as they were to forty years later when the *Carols for Choirs* series was devised.

9. Susana Walton, *Behind the Façade* (Oxford, 1988), pp. 79 ff.

10. Shortly before his death, Henry Wood proposed that the Musicians' Benevolent Fund should hold an annual service in St Sepulchre's on St Cecilia's Day (22 November); the first was held there in 1946.

11. He declined an invitation to contribute a madrigal to *A Garland for the Queen*, an anthology of partsongs, after the manner of *The Triumphs of Oriana*, in honour of a new Elizabethan age. This was because of an objection to an Arts Council guideline, discouraging 'brittle, sardonic, or satirical wit'—'all my best sides', as he pointed out (see Stephen Banfield, *Gerald Finzi* (London, 1998), p. 439).

12. Auden wrote to Walton on 22 December 1964: 'Here at last a draft of that bloody anthem. I've never felt so at sea before. How is one to be contemporary without becoming South Banky?... I do hope the thing will seem to you settable.'

13. In February 1966 Anthony Payne described in the *Musical Times* Auden's text as 'part poetry, part doggerel, part Biblical pastiche—and all musical'.

14. Programme note for the first performance of the orchestral version in Westminster Abbey on 2 January 1966.

15. Though Walton, somewhat disingenuously, may have underestimated the difficulty of his new piece, Christ Church Choir learnt it in time to give a successful first performance. In a letter to Christopher Morris of 17 June, Sydney Watson wrote, 'It went very well. We like it & we are doing it again this coming Saturday.'

16. In his review in the *Daily Telegraph* on 3 January 1966, following the performance in Westminster Abbey the previous day.

17. Letter to Malcolm Arnold, 20 February 1965.

18. Britten's *War Requiem* received its first performance there in May the following year.

19. Letter to Alan Frank, 2 September 1971.

20. *The Times*, 25 April 1972.

21. Argo ZRG 725.

22. See Kennedy, *Portrait*, pp. 258–259.

23. Lady Mayer died on 2 April 1974, shortly before the first performance.

24. Letter to Malcolm Arnold, 5 November 1973.

25. Abbey LPB 798, containing music by Berkeley, Britten, and Thea Musgrave.

26. For the Bach Choir's centenary Walton toyed with the possibility of orchestrating, and maybe elaborating, *Cantico del Sole*, but the idea came to nothing.

27. Letter from Dr John Birch to the editor, 5 February 1997.
28. Another commission, Lennox Berkeley's 'The Lord is my shepherd', also received its first performance in the same service.
29. Letter to Christopher Morris, 24 June 1977.
30. Letter to Alan Frank, 15 January 1983.
31. Letter to Alan Frank, 15 January 1983.

7

Façade Entertainments *(Vol. 7)*

Stewart Craggs

Façade, together with the early String Quartet (1922) and the brilliant overture *Portsmouth Point* (premiered in 1926), first brought William Walton's name before the public in the mid-1920s, earned him the immediate reputation as an *enfant terrible*, and marked the emergence of a major new talent in British music. Despite its unassuming origins, it is clear that Walton lavished considerable care and affection on *Façade*, a work to which he returned periodically throughout his life.

Just as the music of *Façade* is unique in relation to Walton's output as a whole, so are its poems to that of Edith Sitwell, who maintained that they were 'for the most part abstract patterns, difficult technical experiments'.[1] Her very first published poem, 'Drowned Suns', appeared in the *Daily Mirror* in March 1913, and the poems which were eventually to be set by Walton were printed in various volumes over the next few years: *Twentieth Century Harlequinade* (1916), *Clowns' Houses* (1918), *The Wooden Pegasus* (1920), *Façade* (1922, a privately printed limited edition), *Bucolic Comedies* (1923), *The Sleeping Beauty* (1924), *Troy Park* (1925), and *Rustic Elegies* (1927). Many of the images featured in these poems were drawn from Edith's unhappy childhood and early adult life, much of which had been spent in the oppressive atmosphere of the family seat at Renishaw in Derbyshire, or at the Sitwells' other home, Wood End, in the North Yorkshire seaside resort of Scarborough. In 1913 the 26-year-old Edith managed to break away from Renishaw to live in London under the chaperonage of Helen Rootham, her governess. In the summer of the following year they moved to a modest flat in the unfashionable district of Bayswater, which was to be her home for a number of years.[2]

Edith's younger brother Sacheverell takes the credit for 'discovering' the 16-year-old William Walton in February 1919, at which time Walton was studying music at Oxford. Within weeks Walton had met Osbert Sitwell, and by November of the same year had received the dedication of Edith's poem 'What the Goosegirl said about the Dean', when it appeared in the fourth issue of the anthology of modern poetry, *Wheels*, which she edited from 1916 to 1921. He soon became an 'adopted, or elected brother' to the Sitwells, living with Osbert and Sacheverell in London, first at Swan Walk, off the Chelsea Embankment, and later at 2 Carlyle Square, adjacent to the King's Road.[3] The Sitwells enabled Walton to attend concerts of contemporary music, brought him into close contact with leading artistic personalities of the day, and generally allowed him to imbibe the vibrant and heady atmosphere of post-war London. The mills and drab terrace houses of his Lancashire birthplace, Oldham, must have seemed to belong to another age.

Façade: an entertainment

Composition

Between 1918 and 1921 Walton worked mainly on a piano quartet, some settings of Marlowe's *The Passionate Shepherd*, and a 'pedagogic overture', *Dr Syntax*, inspired by William Combe's verses and Thomas Rowlandson's drawings; the composer waited in vain for public performance. Also belonging to this period was an early string quartet which, in its revised form, was selected for performance in August 1923 at the first festival of the International Society for Contemporary Music at Salzburg.

In the fourth volume of his autobiography Osbert Sitwell recalled the origin of Walton's *Façade* settings, noting that the idea had 'first entered our minds as the result of certain technical experiments at which my sister had recently been working: experiments in obtaining through the medium of words the rhythm of dance measures such as waltzes, polkas, foxtrots. These exercises were often experimental enquiries into the effect on rhythm, on speed, and on colour of the use of rhymes, assonances, dissonances, placed outwardly, at different places in the line, in most elaborate patterns. Some of the resulting poems were sad and serious…Others were mocking and gay…All possessed a quite extraordinary and haunting fascination.'[4] However, the fascination had not been shared by everybody. A typically negative reaction to Edith's new poems was that of a painter whose name, in the words of Osbert, 'has not attached itself to the epoch. He had passed judgement on my sister in the words, "Very clever, no doubt—but what is she but a Façade!" This had greatly delighted us, since what can any poet hope for better than to constitute a façade for his poetry? It seemed an admirable summing-up, and the very title for the sort of entertainment we wanted to present.'[5]

Edith wrote that Osbert had been 'responsible for the inception of the work', that is to say for deciding that the poems should be accompanied by music for which Walton was the obvious choice of composer. Walton was initially uncertain as to what kind of accompaniment was required and declined to write it. The Sitwells later claimed that they threatened to ask another of their protégés, the precocious Royal College of Music student Constant Lambert, and that this acted as a stimulus to Walton, who agreed to undertake the work. Osbert wrote, 'I remember so well the long sessions that my sister and William had in the rather small room he occupied upstairs [at Carlyle Square] and her going over and over the words with him, to show their rhythm and exactly how they went.'[6] According to Sacheverell, the initial writing of *Façade* took place 'in late November and December 1921, and up to the last moment on the night of 24 January 1922. I would not say that WTW, to call him by his initials, was a fervent lover of poetry, but he was attuned to them, and had, when directed to them, an instinctive understanding.'[7]

First performance

The first performance of Walton's earliest settings of Edith Sitwell's verses took place on the bitterly cold evening of Tuesday 24 January 1922 in the L-shaped, first-floor drawing room at 2 Carlyle Square. According to the reminiscences of the cellist Ambrose Gauntlett, who played in several of the early performances, three rehearsals were held there: the first on the morning of Sunday 22 January, and two more on the day of the first performance.[8] Osbert Sitwell later wrote to Frank Howes, the author of the first book on Walton's music,[9] 'The wretched players were so cold they could hardly use their lips or fingers. And this seemed to make them more cross and puzzled. Fortunately my cook had made some sloe gin the previous autumn and I brought up an old Chianti flask full of it, and dispensed in generous measure. Then they cheered up.'[10] Osbert originally suggested that Edith should recite her verses through a megaphone, but as it was considered that this would appear unsightly he then thought of the idea of presenting *Façade* with all the performers hidden behind a curtain, through which a Sengerphone[11] (Sacheverell's idea) protruded. This was, according to Edith, not only 'because it was obviously impossible for the speaker's voice, unaided, to be heard above the sound of the instruments', but also 'to *deprive* the work of any personal quality (apart from the personality inherent in the poems and music).'[12] The curtain was designed by the sculptor Frank Dobson, who at that very time was completing his celebrated brass bust of Osbert. The curtain depicted three arches; a large, half-red, half-white mask almost filled the central one, and that on its left featured a smaller black mask. Edith declaimed through the Sengerphone inserted into the mouth of the mask in the centre, while Osbert acted as master of ceremonies by speaking through that of the smaller one. Like them, invisible to the audience, Walton conducted the instrumentalists, 'holding his baton with something of the air of an elegant and handsome snipe...In the comparatively small drawing-room of Carlyle Square, the sheer volume of sound was overwhelming.'[13]

Extant copies of the typewritten programme reveal that of the eighteen numbers designated (the first being the 'Overture' and the seventh the 'Interlude') only six survived to be included in the definitive score of the 'Entertainment' published in 1951. These are 'Hornpipe', 'En Famille', 'Mariner Men [*sic*] (Presto)', 'Long Steel Grass', 'Jumbo's Lullaby', and 'When Sir Beelzebub'. Five other numbers, 'Dame Souris Trotte', 'The Octogenarian', 'Aubade', 'Water Party', and 'Said King Pompey', were to reappear over fifty years later, either in *Façade Revived* (1977) or in its revised form, *Façade 2* (1979). The five other titles were 'The Wind's Bastinado', 'Small Talk I & II', 'Switch-back', 'Bank Holiday I & II', and 'Springing Jack'.

The Entertainment was repeated two weeks later at the Montagu Square home of Mrs Robert Mathias, a notable patron of the arts and of the Russian Ballet in particular. Sergei Diaghilev was among the distinguished audience.[14]

Instrumentation

There has long been some confusion over the number of instrumentalists involved on these first two occasions. Walton, writing to Angus Morrison in the year of his 70th birthday, believed it to have been four. Happily a contemporary letter of Edith Sitwell, which only recently came to light, settles the matter conclusively. Writing on 4 April 1922 to the mother of the undergraduate poet Richard Hughes, and enclosing one of the privately printed copies of her *Façade* volume, she says, 'A good deal of the section called "Façade" [the first section was called "Winter"] was written for music; and it was set by a youth called Walton—(whom I believe most strongly to be the best composer we've had since Purcell, though he is only just twenty) and I recite them down a kind of megaphone to this accompaniment, consisting of trumpet, clarinet, flute, drum [i.e. percussion] and cello!'[15] It is thought that the players were Robert Murchie (flute and piccolo), Haydn Draper (clarinet and bass clarinet), Herbert Barr (trumpet), Ambrose Gauntlett (cello), and Charles Bender (percussion).[16]

First public performance

During the next fifteen months Walton set as many as fourteen new numbers, and revised some of those already written, in readiness for the first public performance of *Façade*. He also decided to increase the number of players from five to six by adding an alto saxophone.

The first public performance of *Façade* was given at the Aeolian Hall in New Bond Street, London, on the afternoon of Tuesday 12 June 1923. Edith Sitwell again recited and Walton conducted the five instrumentalists who are believed to have performed the work in the previous year, with the addition of F. Moss (alto saxophone). A publicity handbill advertised the proceedings as 'MISS EDITH SITWELL / presents / "FAÇADE" / A New and Original Musical Entertainment / in twenty-four facets. / Music by / W. T. Walton'. In the event, 27 numbers, in eight groups, were performed, preceded by a 'Fanfare', a 'Preface—Osbert Sitwell', and an 'Overture'. The new additions were: 'Gardener Janus Catches a Naiad', 'Clown Argheb's Song', 'Trams', 'By the Lake', 'Herodiad's [*sic*] Flea', 'Through Gilded Trellises', 'The Man from a Far Countrie [*sic*]', 'Daphne', 'Country Dance', 'Gone Dry', 'The Owl', 'Dark Song', 'Fox Trot' ['Old Sir Faulk'], and 'Ass Face'. The fourth group was introduced by 'Serenade', a short, almost certainly, purely instrumental number. 'Long Steel Grass' was temporarily retitled 'Trio for Two Cats and a Trombone', as in the printed edition of the poem, and 'Dame Souris Trotte' became 'Madame Mouse Trots'. The rejected numbers that the new ones replaced were: 'The Wind's Bastinado', 'Bank Holiday I & II', and 'Springing Jack'.

Osbert, who again acted as master of ceremonies, recalled that the potent cocktail of poems, accompaniment, and performance created 'a first class scandal in literature and music; the mask on the curtain was characterised as a "meaningless, crudely-painted moonface", the music as "collected from the works of the most eccentric of the ultra-moderns", while the words were dismissed as "drivel".'[17] However, some of this seems to have been a Sitwellian invention, concocted involuntarily in order to increase the aura of notoriety with which they liked to be associated.[18]

Press comment was indeed somewhat dismissive or mocking in tone, probably in response to the social and aesthetic standing of the Sitwells, but it has to be conceded that the occasion represented, even for the time, a rather unusual form of 'entertainment', and that Walton himself considered the musical execution to have been 'a shambles'. It certainly made for good copy. There were a large number of reviews of the event, some of which are both amusing and informative. The audience in the 'half-filled' Aeolian Hall was variously described as consisting of 'nearly all Progressive London', 'most of the leaders of the Higher Thought in the arts' and 'long-haired men, short-haired women'. Osbert announced that the Sengerphone was a means of avoiding 'the usual bugbear of ordinary recitation' which generally had as its twin poles 'the rant of the old gentleman and the hysterics of the flapper'. Edith had narrated with 'sharply defined and clearly accentuated rhythm, producing an effect somewhere between a Greek chorus and the reading of a tenancy agreement'. Despite references to people leaving the hall during the performance, *Façade* was considered to have had a very warm reception, and there had been encores. The Sitwellian experiments in reinventing the art of recitation and Walton's novelties and pastiches were seen by some as a blatant attempt to *épater le bourgeois*. The hostility that was so resented by the Sitwells was shown not so much by the critics as by the feature and gossip writers such as Hannen Swaffer who, writing under the byline 'Mr. London', admitted in his notorious article in the *Daily Graphic* that he had not even been present.[19] Against this must be put the few serious reviews, such as that of Gerald Cumberland in *Vogue*, and the anonymous *Daily Mail* critic who showed exceptional awareness of the very special quality of the musical content and praised 'the extraordinarily stimulative running comment of Mr. Walton's music. His musical invention is as original and witty as Miss Sitwell's poetry and fits the rhythm of the spoken line as though words and music were cast in one mould. He manages to get a pleasing variety of colour out of the six instruments used...and this variety forms a valuable contrast to the deliberately monotonous chant of the recitation.'[20]

Constant Lambert

It was at this time that the young Constant Lambert began his close association with Walton, the Sitwells, and *Façade*. When the work was finally published over a quarter of a century later Walton dedicated it to Lambert and, in a footnote to 'Four in the Morning', declared that the number had been written 'in collaboration with C. L.'.

The 20-year-old Walton may have been precocious but, in the words of Osbert Sitwell, 'Constant Lambert, at the age of seventeen [was] a prodigy of intelligence and learning and gifted with that particularly individual outlook and sense of humour which, surely, were born in him and impossible to acquire.'[21] It will never be possible to determine the full extent of Lambert's influence on the composition, revision, and many attempts at reordering of the *Façade* numbers, but it appears to have been significant. Later, apart from being its most admired reciter, he conducted innumerable performances of the Frederick Ashton ballet (based on the two *Façade* orchestral suites), recorded, performed, and made piano transcriptions of the suites, and, six months before his death, even corrected the second proofs of the first publication of the Entertainment. As a tribute to Lambert's long involvement with *Façade* in all its guises, here is an extract from an account of the beginning of the close friendship and professional contact between the two composers that Walton wrote at the request of his former publisher, Hubert Foss, in the months following Lambert's premature death in August 1951:

> Prior to my meeting with Constant in August [1923], I had often seen him in the King's Road in his Christ's Hospital uniform and was much struck by his handsome appearance and wondered who he could be. I think I wasn't the only one who noticed him, for people used to turn round and stare at him in the street, overcome by his handsomeness. I wasn't really surprised when it turned out to be him. Even at that age one could tell that he was one of the unique personalities of one's life.

Almost immediately we became very close friends, a friendship which continued until his death. Although in later years I never saw him as much as I had in our younger days, it made no difference. At the time I met him he had just won a scholarship as a pianist to the R.C.M. [Royal College of Music] and had only just started composing. He discarded the piano in favour of the latter. Composing was really his best means of expressing himself and it always seemed to me a tragedy that his many-sided gifts, such as conducting, writing, etc. should have diverted him from his real purpose in life. At this time—in 1923—we had just done the first performance of *Façade* in the Aeolian Hall. Constant had been among the audience and was fascinated by the performance and wished to become the reciter, which he eventually did, when it was revived at Chenil Galleries in 1926. He always remained its best interpreter.[22]

1926 performances

Nearly three years elapsed before the second and third public performances of *Façade* took place on 27 April and 29 June 1926 respectively, at the recently refurbished New Chenil Galleries, Chelsea, less than half a mile from Carlyle Square and Glebe Place, where Lambert was living. There had been considerable activity in the intervening period. Edith Sitwell and Walton had again written several new numbers—eight of them were later to be included among the eleven numbers that comprised the two orchestral suites—and had continued to revise some of those that had been performed. After the 'shambles' of the Aeolian Hall performance, Walton seems to have made fair copies of many of the older numbers, and new instrumental parts would have been copied from these. Those first performed in the April performance were 'Valse', 'Polka', 'Jodelling Song', 'Scotch Rhapsody', 'Something Lies beyond the Scene', and 'Four in the Morning'. Neil Porter, an actor in the Old Vic Company, was engaged to recite. This may have been an attempt on the part of the Sitwells to make the occasion seem more professional and less of a family affair that it had been at the Aeolian Hall. After the 1923 performance Osbert had forbidden Edith to recite *Façade* at Oxford because the family had been mercilessly caricatured by Noël Coward in a sketch called 'The Swiss Family Whittlebot' in the revue *London Calling!*, in which the poet Hernia Whittlebot recites poems with her two brothers Gob and Sago; this parody provoked a furious letter from Osbert to Coward.[23]

The participation of Neil Porter in the 1926 performances of *Façade* is well documented and even well photographed; several publicity shots of him at rehearsal with the three Sitwells and Walton were taken in the courtyard of the New Chenil Galleries. Of the concert itself, Osbert recorded that 'the words were chiefly spoken by that accomplished actor Mr. Neil Porter, my sister having decided only to recite a few of the slower poems'.[24] The critic of *Musical Opinion* (June 1926) was certainly under the impression that it was Porter who 'delivered the poems through a megaphone set in a bizarre set'.

Yet a letter from the 20-year-old Constant Lambert to his mother, written from Paris shortly before he went on to Monte Carlo to attend the 4 May premiere of his Diaghilev ballet *Romeo and Juliet*, suggests a more complex situation. He wrote, '*Façade* was great fun just before I left [England]. I ended up doing about half the programme. The house was very crowded and most enthusiastic.'[25] By now Lambert had become intimately connected with *Façade*, and he would certainly have been closely involved in the preparations for the two New Chenil Galleries performances. His letter implies that he recited at the April performance and that his contribution was more than he had originally expected. This suggests that Neil Porter may have found it necessary to yield some of his numbers to someone more musically expert. The information given in Lambert's letter demands to be taken at its face value, and it would seem that either Porter, Edith, and Lambert recited or, since Ernest Newman's enthusiastic *Sunday Times* review of 2 May shows that he was unaware of a female voice, just Porter and Lambert.[26] Though the occasion attracted minimal press interest, Newman's piece more than compensated for this by giving the composer the most enthusiastic endorsement: 'Here is obviously a humorous musical talent of the first order . . . the deft workmanship, especially in the orchestration, made the heart of the listening musician glad.' However, the facetious comment of old was not lacking. *Musical Opinion* deplored the 'waste of artistic energy, even although it served as an excuse for drawing into one hall most of the men who look like women and the women who dress up and crop like men in Chelsea!'. By June it is believed that Porter was away on tour; at any rate Lambert certainly replaced him as sole reciter, and thus established what was to become his long and much admired assumption of this role. Osbert Sitwell spoke for many when he wrote, 'Constant Lambert, possessed of so many rare gifts, has proved himself to have one more: to be the perfect instrument of this performance, as speaker *sans pareil* of the verse, clear, rapid, incisive, tireless, and commanding vocally an extraordinary range of inflection, from menace and the threat of doom to the most debonair and jaunty inconsequence.'[27]

In April 1926 the numbers were arranged in eight groups of three or four, with an initial fanfare and a fanfare and introduction prefacing the second half. In June, they were similarly arranged, but in seven groups of three or four, again with the fanfare and introduction in the middle, and with the addition of 'Tarantella', 'March', and 'Mazurka', which was making its one and only appearance. Although not mentioned in the programme, 'The Last Galop' may also have been introduced. Walton conducted on both occasions.

Eighteen months later *Façade* was given three consecutive performances—on 28, 29, and 30 November 1927—at the Arts Theatre Club during the four-day run of the Sitwell play *First-Class Passengers Only*. It is unfortunate that it has not been possible to trace a programme giving the listing and order of the numbers performed, because these may have included the premieres of the last two new numbers, 'Black Mrs Behemoth' and 'Popular Song'.

On 30 April 1929 Walton, Edith, and Lambert were in Paris to give a performace of *Façade* that was promoted by the Pro Musica Society at the Salle Chopin.

ISCM Festival, Siena

What are believed to be the first *Façade* performances outside Great Britain were the two given in the Teatro Rozzi, Siena, during the morning of 14 September 1928 at an event organized by the International Society for Contemporary Music. Hubert Foss, Walton's publisher at the recently formed Music Department of Oxford University

Press, was on the committee and may be assumed to have played a part in obtaining the invitation. Lambert again recited, and Walton conducted a group of Italian instrumentalists, with the addition of Walter Lear, who had been brought over from England to play the saxophone. A new curtain was created by the Italian artist Gino Severini, who had already designed the cover and frontispiece for Edith Sitwell's 1922 private edition of the *Façade* poems, as well as the distinctive green and black cover which OUP used for Walton's published scores between 1927 and 1951. Sadly, no illustration of the curtain has ever been found.[28] Twenty-two numbers were performed, including 'Black Mrs Behemoth' and 'Popular Song'. Edith Sitwell had written the text of the latter specially for Lambert, to whom it is dedicated in her published poems, and Walton had set it during a recent visit to his home town. These two numbers brought to an end the composition of the *Façade* settings, which finally totalled 43.

First recording

On 28 November 1929 eleven numbers from *Façade* were recorded for the Decca Record Company in the New Chenil Galleries by Edith Sitwell (four numbers), Constant Lambert (seven numbers), and a chamber ensemble conducted by the composer. Those performed were 'Black Mrs Behemoth', 'Swiss Jodelling Song', 'Scotch Rhapsody', 'Polka', 'Foxtrot', 'Tango-Pasodoblé', 'Long Steel Grass', 'A Man from a Far Countree', 'Tarantella', 'Valse', and 'Popular Song'. This was the very first recording of Walton's music, and the two records soon became popular.[29] Nineteen *Façade* numbers were first broadcast by the BBC on 3 March 1930, with Edith Sitwell and Constant Lambert narrating, and, because Walton was in Italy, Leslie Heward conducting. The final item was 'The Last Galop'.

Adaptations of the music

Walton soon realized that many of the *Façade* numbers would work equally well without the spoken text, and early in the work's history both he and OUP began to exploit the potential of this music in many different ways. To begin with, Walton made orchestrations of four numbers—'Polka', 'Valse', 'Tango-Pasodoblé', and 'Tarantella-Sevillana'. These were first performed under his direction on 3 December 1926 as an orchestral interlude at an evening of Diaghilev's Russian Ballet at the Lyceum Theatre, which included the premiere of the Lord Berners/Sacheverell Sitwell ballet *The Triumph of Neptune* that Walton had helped to orchestrate. A fifth number, 'Swiss Jodelling Song', had been added by the time the suite was published ten years later. A second suite of six numbers—'Fanfare', 'Scotch Rhapsody', 'Country Dance', 'Noche Espagnola' (i.e. 'Long Steel Grass'), 'Popular Song', and 'Old Sir Faulk'—was published in 1938. Walton's HMV recordings of nine of these numbers were released in May 1936, with 'Noche Espagnola' and 'Old Sir Faulk' following in early 1939.

The first orchestral suite formed the basis of a short ballet by the German choreographer Günter Hess; his production was given in September 1929 by the Chamber Ballet Dancing Theatre in Hagen, Westphalia. However, it was Frederick Ashton's choreography of seven numbers, which included the newly orchestrated 'Scotch Rhapsody' and

'Popular Song', that definitively established *Façade* as a ballet, and in so doing popularized the music far more than the occasional performances of the Entertainment itself. Ashton's ballet was mounted by the Camargo Society at the Cambridge Theatre, London, on 26 April 1931, conducted by Lambert. An extra number, 'Country Dance', was added in 1935 when the Vic-Wells Ballet first presented the production, and two more, 'Noche Espagnola' and 'Foxtrot' ('Old Sir Faulk'), in 1940. Other balletic presentations include John Cranko's *Familien-Album* (Stuttgart, 1961), and a version by Lindsay Kemp (Milan, 1983), in which the performers recited the poems.

The 'domestic' market for solo piano, piano duet, and two-piano arrangements of orchestral and instrumental music in the 1920s was healthy, and had not yet been undermined by the mechanical reproduction of music in the home. Hence, OUP was prompt to issue the most popular *Façade* items in these forms. Only one transcription was made by Walton himself (the 'Valse', which he arranged for solo piano); the others were undertaken by Constant Lambert, Herbert Murrill, and Roy Douglas.

Another popular form of 'adaptation' at the time was the transcription of music for concert or salon orchestra. When, in 1939, OUP issued 'Four Dances from *Façade*', in an arrangement by Walter Goehr, the consequences were unexpected. In 1909 John A. Glover-Kind had written and published the song 'I do like to be beside the seaside', which soon became very popular in music halls throughout Britain. Fourteen years later Walton, believing it to be a form of folksong, innocently incorporated an eight-bar quotation from it into *Façade*'s 'Tango-Pasodoblé'. With the publication of Goehr's arrangement, the publishers of Glover-Kind's song became aware of this infringement of copyright. Legal action was threatened but narrowly avoided on payment of an undisclosed fee and the promise of an annual royalty. The song's copyright expired in 1969.

1942–9 performances

To mark the 20th anniversary of the first private performance, the 21 numbers of what was eventually to become the definitive version of *Façade* were performed on 29 May 1942 at the Aeolian Hall, but not in the final order. John Piper designed a gouache and collage curtain for the occasion, Lambert recited, and Walton conducted a new group of instrumentalists.[30] The first half of the concert was devoted to a rare British performance of Schoenberg's *Pierrot Lunaire*, which explains why Lambert suggested arranging the numbers into seven groups of three, as a parody of Schoenberg's scheme of three times seven. In the absence of a published score, and in the confusion of wartime, scores had to be reconstituted from existing parts, and this was undertaken at OUP's instigation by the composer Franz Reizenstein. A letter of 24 April 1942 from Reizenstein to Norman Peterkin (who ran OUP's Music Department during the war) states, 'I have been in touch with Mr Walton about the reconstruction of *Façade* and he has asked me *not* to make a score of "The Last Galop". I have finished the other 23 items …'[31]

Two further performances of *Façade* were given on 9 September and 27 October 1946 at the Lyric Theatre, Hammersmith, when the 21 numbers of the 1942 event were given in the same order by Lambert and a new instrumental ensemble, conducted by Leighton Lucas.

What was billed as the first performance of *Façade* in the USA was given on 19 January 1949 at the Museum of Modern Art, New York, as part of Osbert and Edith Sitwell's triumphant first visit to that country. Edith recited, omitting 'Tarantella' (Osbert's friend David Horner recited the 'Tango'), and an instrumental ensemble, drawn from the Juilliard School of Music, was conducted by Frederick Prausnitz. A commercial recording by these performers was made at the same time.[32]

Publication

In 1930 there had been plans for OUP to publish a de luxe edition of 300 copies of *Façade*, signed by Edith Sitwell and William Walton and priced at three guineas, but nothing came of it. After World War II, pressure began to build from potential performers for a published score. In 1947–8 Walton is believed to have taken another look at the *Façade* material, made various amendments, and tried to decide on the final order. OUP originally planned their publication of the score, in royal quarto size, in the summer of 1949, at which time it would appear that 'March' and 'Daphne' were also to be included, but it was not until September 1950 that the firm of Henderson & Spalding at last commenced engraving, in a slightly smaller format. By now only the final 21 numbers were required to be published. In a letter of 18 August to the printers Alan Frank of OUP stated that three of the numbers had been newly copied for the purpose, namely 'Mariner Man', 'Old Sir Faulk', and 'Sir Beelzebub', and that 'in matters of capital letters and punctuation you must follow the printed text [probably *Façade and Other Poems*] and not the manuscript'. First proofs were checked by a professional reader in October, and at the beginning of November they and the manuscripts were sent to Walton at his London home. Walton must have been in Italy by the time the second proofs arrived, as these were corrected by Constant Lambert and returned to OUP in early February 1951.

Edith Sitwell had also been given an opportunity to check the first proofs, even though this involved sending a set of photocopies to her in America. On seeing annotations in the voice part, which she clearly did not realize had been specially supplied by Lambert, she wrote a strong letter of protest to Alan Frank: ' "Black Mrs Behemoth" in "a quiet, hard voice"!!! That is not how I wish it to be done. And "Popular Song" apparently to be recited "trippingly"!! It is to be recited smoothly.'[33] The matter was soon cleared up amicably between her, Walton, and Lambert, but the directions for the reciter that Lambert had added with a view to enhancing the publication were removed from the proofs. The score of what was now called *Façade: An Entertainment* was finally published on 26 July 1951, less than a month before Constant Lambert's death, which occurred two days before his forty-sixth birthday.

Publication led to the first British recording of the definitive version which was released by Decca in October 1954; Edith Sitwell and Peter Pears recited and the English Opera Group Ensemble was conducted by Anthony Collins.[34]

The last time the three Sitwells and Walton were together at a performance of *Façade* was on 9 October 1962 at the Royal Festival Hall on the occasion of Edith's 75th birthday. She sat in a wheelchair in the royal box, dressed in a scarlet robe and golden headdress while, on stage, Walton conducted.

In March 1972 OUP marked both the occasion of Walton's 70th birthday and the 50th anniversary of the first private performance of *Façade* by publishing a de luxe limited edition of *Façade: An Entertainment*. Walton signed 250 copies, and a further 750 copies were numbered only. Besides a corrected and re-engraved score, the edition included a newly commissioned cover and colour illustrations by John Piper, together with reproductions of his 1942 curtain and of John Armstrong's designs for the Ashton ballet. New essays by Sacheverell Sitwell and Frederick Ashton, together with a reprint of Edith Sitwell's Decca sleeve note about the poems, were also included. Walton's manuscript of the hitherto unpublished setting of 'Herodiade's Flea' was reproduced in facsimile, and a new pressing on a 45 rpm disc of the 1929 Decca recording by Edith Sitwell, Lambert, and Walton (in a different order and excluding 'Valse' because of length) was included in a special slipcase. In the following year another birthday was celebrated. On 12 June 1973 the BBC marked the 50th anniversary to the day of the first public performance of *Façade* at the Aeolian Hall by arranging for Walton to conduct it in the same venue, with Mary Thomas and Derek Hammond-Stroud as speakers.

Façade 2: a further entertainment

An important new chapter in the history of the *Façade* numbers opened at the time of Walton's seventy-fifth birthday. He had been in poor health for some time, and even dangerously so in the autumn of 1976 when attending rehearsals and performances of a new production of *Troilus and Cressida* in London. His publishers realized that there was little hope of persuading him to write a new work for the celebrations, and therefore urged him to provide an alternative kind of novelty by preparing for performance a group of unpublished *Façade* numbers, some of which had been excluded from the 1951 publication of the Entertainment solely for reasons of balance. Photocopies of all the extant manuscript material from the OUP archives were sent to Walton in Ischia, and from these he selected eight settings. A few of them underwent light revision before they were recopied and, prefaced by the published 'Fanfare', arranged to form what was provisionally called *Façade Revived*. The new work was first performed at a special birthday concert organized by Lina Lalandi, director of the English Bach Festival, on 25 March 1977 at Plaisterers' Hall in the City of London. Richard Baker recited the poems and Charles Mackerras conducted. It was given again on 3 June at a concert given by the London Sinfonietta conducted by Colin Davis.

In the spring of 1978, while reading the proofs of *Façade Revived*, which OUP had engraved and was preparing for publication, Walton decided to reject three of the numbers, replace them with others, and radically rework and reorder the rest of the music. Eight numbers had been performed in the previous year: 'Daphne', 'Herodiade's Flea', 'The Last Galop', 'The Octogenarian', 'March', 'The White Owl', 'Aubade', and 'Said King Pompey'. Three of these ('Daphne', 'The Last Galop', and 'The White Owl') were dropped and replaced by 'Madame Mouse Trots', 'Gardener Janus Catches a Naiad', and 'Water Party'. The 'Flourish' which prefaced the new selection was simply an expanded version of the introduction to 'Herodiade's Flea', which was now renamed 'Came the Great Popinjay'.

The result of this extensive revision was the retitled *Façade 2*, dedicated to Cathy Berberian (a *Façade* reciter whom Walton much admired), and first performed on

19 June 1979 at the Aldeburgh Festival, by Peter Pears and members of the English Chamber Orchestra conducted by Steuart Bedford. Following a suggestion of the composer, OUP agreed to abandon its engraved edition and instead publish *Façade 2* in a facsimile of the new manuscript, just as they had done twenty-two years earlier with his String Quartet in A minor. After Walton's death, Christopher Palmer arranged for the three numbers rejected from *Façade Revived* to be made available, on hire only. The WWE volume includes the first editions to be set of *Façade 2* and these three numbers, together with the first publication of 'Small Talk'. Although there are two autographs for 'Mazurka', the only other number represented among extant manuscripts, both are unfortunately incomplete. The opening bars are of tantalizing interest; the number could have proved a worthy addition to the existing group of numbers in dance rhythm.

* * *

On 3 August 1975 *Façade* was given its second performance at the Henry Wood Promenade Concerts; Walton had conducted the first on 27 August 1965. Replying from Ischia on 24 August to a letter from Alan Frank describing the event, Walton wryly and succinctly summed up the unique achievement of his youthful collaboration with Edith Sitwell: 'From Chelsea drawing-room to the Albert Hall—who would have believed it in 1922!'

<h2 style="text-align:center">NOTES</h2>

1. Edith Sitwell, 'Some Notes on My Own Poetry', in *Selected Poems* (London, 1936), p. 26.
2. Edith Sitwell, *Taken Care Of* (London, 1965), p. 79.
3. Osbert Sitwell, *Laughter in the Next Room* (London, 1949), p. 172.
4. Osbert Sitwell, *Laughter*, p. 185, freely paraphrasing Edith's words in 'Some Notes on My Own Poetry'.
5. Osbert Sitwell, *Laughter*, pp. 185–186.
6. Unpublished letter from Osbert Sitwell to Frank Howes of 21 November 1942 (Craggs archive).
7. Sacheverell Sitwell, in *Façade: An Entertainment* (Oxford, 1972), p. xiv.
8. Unpublished letter to Stewart Craggs of 15 May 1972 (Craggs archive).
9. Frank Howes, *The Music of William Walton* (Oxford, 1965).
10. Unpublished letter from Osbert Sitwell to Frank Howes of 25 April 1943 (Craggs archive).
11. A Sengerphone was a type of megaphone invented by the Swiss singer Alexander Senger to amplify the voice of the bass singing the offstage role of the dragon Fafner in Wagner's *Siegfried*. In notes for a projected accompanying essay to the 1951 OUP score, Osbert Sitwell wrote: 'The Sengerphone is made of compressed cotton, so there is no metallic tone in it at all. Actually it beautifies rather than distorts the timbre of the human voice' (Osbert Sitwell Archive, HRHRC, Austin, Texas, notebook 38).
12. Edith Sitwell, sleeve note for the 1954 Decca recording, reprinted in *Façade: An Entertainment*, p. xi.
13. Osbert Sitwell, *Laughter*, pp. 188, 190.
14. Neil Ritchie has kindly pointed out that a programme almost identical to that of the first private performance, but with the last seven numbers omitted (and therefore containing only 9 leaves as against 15), was sold to an unknown buyer at Sotheby's in 1987. Internal evidence—such as the listing of only one 'Small Talk'—suggests that the arrangement of numbers represents a refinement of the original, but there is an outside possibility that this is, in fact, the programme of the Carlyle Square premiere, and that the Entertainment was expanded for the performance given for Mrs Mathias.

15. Neil Ritchie, 'Note 557. Footnote to *Façade*', in *The Book Collector* (Summer 1996), pp. 261–262.

16. The programmes for the 1923 performance and the April and June 1926 performances named Paul Draper as the clarinettist, but Walton stated to Angus Morrison (see n. 24) that it was Haydn Draper. The player's full name was Haydn Paul Draper, but he was far better known in the profession by his first name.

17. Osbert Sitwell, *Laughter*, p. 192.

18. This topic is considered at greater length in John Pearson, '*Façade* and the Twenties', in *The Sitwells and the Arts of the 1920s and 1930s* (London [National Portrait Gallery exhibition catalogue], 1994).

19. 'A Wonderful London / Yesterday. / Drivel They Paid to Hear', *Daily Graphic* (14 June 1923); see Stewart Craggs, *William Walton: A Catalogue* (Oxford, 1990), p. 21, for further details of the reviews.

20. 'Mask and Megaphone / Unseen Reciter / Music Accompaniment in Place of Emotion', *Daily Mail* (13 June 1923).

21. Osbert Sitwell, *Laughter*, p. 178.

22. Original in the private possession of Mrs Diana Sparkes (née Foss). A fuller text can be found in Duncan Hinnells, *An Extraordinary Performance* (Oxford, 1998), pp. 49–50.

23. See *Edith Sitwell: Selected Letters*, ed. John Lehmann and Derek Parker (London, 1970), p. 29.

24. Osbert Sitwell, *Laughter*, p. 200. In Walton's letter to Angus Morrison of 9 February 1972 (Walton Museum, Forio, Ischia) he states, 'Neil Porter was the other reciter, which incited Constant to say, quite rightly, that he was the only one capable of doing it really well.'

25. Richard Shead, *Constant Lambert* (London, 1973), p. 48.

26. The writer is grateful to Stephen Lloyd for his advice on this matter.

27. Osbert Sitwell, *Laughter*, p. 197.

28. The Severini curtain seems to have had an altogether unfortunate history; see Osbert Sitwell, *Laughter*, pp. 293–294.

29. Decca T.124/5 (later D.K. 991–2) and American Decca 25632/3, released in February 1930.

30. For further details of this performance, which was repeated, see Richard Temple Savage, *A Voice from the Pit* (Newton Abbot, 1988), pp. 97–98.

31. The two numbers additional to the definitive 21 that Reizenstein copied were 'March' and 'Daphne'. The letter is in the OUP Archive, Oxford.

32. US Columbia: 78 rpm 72806/9D; LP ML 5241. Reissued as part of a four-record box of recordings of Walton on CBS 79411. The Juilliard Music School had considered performing it in 1937 but nothing came of this.

33. See Victoria Glendinning, *Edith Sitwell: A Unicorn among Lions* (London, 1981), p. 289. These directions were intended to indicate exceptional instances of special inflection. In his article on Walton, Lambert wrote, 'The poems are recited for the most part "senza espressione", but with the utmost precision and variety of rhythm' (*The Dominant*, February 1928, pp. 16–19). Elizabeth Salter, who knew Edith Sitwell only towards the end of her life, recorded, 'If it was read for meaning, rather than rhythm, she disapproved' (*The Last Years of a Rebel*, London, 1967, p. 66).

34. Decca LXT 2977 (UK); London A.4104 (USA).

A Note on the Poems (*David Lloyd-Jones*)

It is possible to be far more precise about the details of the first publications of the 43 poems that Walton set for *Façade* than about the composition of the music itself.[1] Edith Sitwell's earliest poems had originally appeared in newspapers and periodicals, or in *Wheels*, the annual anthology of modern poetry that she edited from 1916 to 1921, before they were republished in separate volumes. The first of these were *Twentieth Century Harlequinade* (with Osbert Sitwell, Oxford, Blackwell, 1916), which contained 'Trams';

Clowns' Houses (Oxford, Blackwell, 1918), which contained 'Mariner Men'; and *The Wooden Pegasus* (Oxford, Blackwell, 1920), which contained four other titles, and in which W. T. Walton, then only 18, is named as one of the four dedicatees.

The typed programme produced for the first private performance of *Façade* on 24 January 1922 printed the texts of the sixteen poems set, and gave notice of their imminent republication, together with some additional ones, in the next collection of Edith Sitwell's verse.[2] This was a privately printed volume, entitled *Façade* and issued in February by the Favil Press, Kensington, in a limited edition of 150 numbered and signed copies. Its distinctive boards of pink-red bricks, and the coloured frontispiece of *commedia dell'arte* figures trudging through snow, had been specially designed by the Italian Futurist-turned-classicist artist Gino Severini, who had already collaborated with Edith on the 1920 issue of *Wheels*. Of the mere fourteen poems it contained, the first five—which included 'En Famille'—were grouped under the title 'Winter', and the remaining nine under 'Façade'. It was not until the following volume, *Bucolic Comedies* (London, Duckworth, 1923), that the majority of these poems became generally available. This publication also marked the beginning of a complex and continuing process of regrouping the individual poems under different headings. *Bucolic Comedies* was the most significant printed collection of the texts of the two *Façade* Entertainments, containing eighteen of the poems that Walton was to set.

The Sleeping Beauty (London, Duckworth, 1924) was not a collection but an extended poem in 26 cantos. Three songs from it, 'The Soldan's Song' (later renamed 'Daphne'), 'Through Gilded Trellises', and 'The Man from a Far Countree', had already been set and performed by the time of publication. *Troy Park* (London, Duckworth, 1925) was another important collection because it printed for the first time three newly composed numbers that had been given at the first public performance of *Façade* on 12 June 1923, as well as 'Black Mrs Behemoth', which was not to be heard until 1927–8. At this premiere, the programme contained a note which regretted that it was not possible to print the texts of the poems 'owing to copyright'—clearly an oblique reference to the publication of *Bucolic Comedies* two months previously. 'Polka', 'Valse', and 'Jodelling Song' were first published, after they had been performed, in *Rustic Elegies* (London, Duckworth, 1927). *Popular Song* appeared in 1928 (London, Faber and Gwyer) as a separate publication, illustrated by Edward Bawden. Finally, 'Scotch Rhapsody' was included in *The Legion Book*, a privately printed anthology (London, 1929). The only numbers which seem never to have been published in Edith Sitwell's lifetime, other than in programmes, were 'Tarantella', 'March', 'Gone Dry', and 'The Last Galop'.

Regrouping and, in a few instances, revision had again taken place when in June 1930 *The Collected Poems of Edith Sitwell* was first issued by Duckworth. In a preface the author stated that the volume contained only those poems, written between 1920 and 1930, that she wanted to preserve. Some of the Walton settings, including a few published in the original 1922 *Façade* collection, were among those excluded, which probably accounts for their prompt disappearance from the Entertainment. A similar, but smaller, volume appeared in 1936 under the title *Selected Poems* (London, Duckworth); it was prefaced by an extended essay, 'Some Notes on My Own Poetry', which was reprinted, with additions, in later volumes.

In late October 1950, nine months before the belated first publication of Walton's score, Duckworth brought out a volume entitled *Façade and Other Poems, 1920–1935*. It would appear that this was, to some extent, a response to the public's growing awareness and appreciation of the Sitwell–Walton Entertainment, for a tabular appendix showed the definitive 'seven times three' grouping of the Concert Version (but in the order of the 1942 and 1947 performances), and an index to the location of the poems within the volume. 'Tarantella' was shown as being unpublished, although it had in fact appeared in the programme of the performance at the New Chenil Galleries on 29 June 1926. The dust jacket stated that the texts had been 'finally revised by the author for this edition'. Even so, the surviving typescripts and galley proofs do not show many signs of textual revision. The galleys provide one point of real interest, for they include the text of the unpublished 'Tarantella'. Against this Edith Sitwell has written, 'Please omit this poem. It was never meant to be printed and is all wrong. I cannot think who gave this copy.'[3] As already stated, this number was omitted from the publication, first appearing in book form only posthumously in the anthology of Edith's writing, edited by Elizabeth Salter and Allanah Harper, entitled *Fires of the Mind* (London, 1976).

A Note on the Music (*David Lloyd-Jones*)

There are a large number of surviving autographs and manuscripts relating to *Façade* but, sadly, not one of them is dated. The approximate date of the composition of each number, therefore, can only be deduced from the occasion of its first performance or the publication of the poem. The general appearance of the autograph and the nature of the musical setting also provide clues.

The autographs of the numbers composed for the 1922 Carlyle Square premiere, which are characterized by their simplicity, spare textures, and greater frequency of unaccompanied recitation, are poorly written and lack tempo indications and dynamics. They also have no saxophone part, although two remained this way even after revision. Later autographs show a greater concern over detail and the requirements of those who had to extract the instrumental parts. Later still, apparently around the time of the consolidating 1926 New Chenil Galleries performances, Walton made what amounted to fair copies of several of the numbers. Most of these were done on the same type of manuscript paper and are notable for the very careful transcription of the spoken text in small capital letters. Even at this time Walton gave the impression that he still regarded *Façade* as an experimental 'work in progress' that only he would be conducting, for tempi are still largely missing. It is significant that when the work was engraved in 1951, the unusual decision was taken to indicate tempi with metronome marks only, even when an indication—such as *Grazioso* in 'Popular Song'—was present in the autograph. This policy continued when *Façade Revived* was assembled, for—with the exception of 'Daphne' (marked *Andante tranquillo*)—each number was shown with a metronome mark only.[4] By the time the newly written autograph of *Façade 2* came to be published in facsimile, Walton had not only supplied Italian tempi but also amended the former metronome markings.

Constant Lambert was the first commentator to point out how the choice of poem and character of the settings rapidly evolved from the sparse, gentle underpinning 'with arabesque and timbre' of the spoken text of such numbers as 'Small Talk' and 'Madame Mouse Trots' into more elaborate settings, often in dance rhythm, and much inclined to parody or burlesque. In these there was a greater wealth of thematic material, and the elements of jazz and popular music came more explicitly to the fore.[5] This new-found supremacy of the music over the spoken word found its fullest expression in 'Tarantella' (1926), in which the text can be said to be almost entirely subordinated, to the point of unintelligibility, to the music. The very fact that Walton was able to fashion two orchestral suites from the Entertainment with very little adjustment to the form and rhythm of the original (too little, in Lambert's opinion), and that eight of the suites' total of eleven numbers derived from settings first performed at the New Chenil Galleries in 1926, shows how self-sufficiently independent the music of these latter settings became.

The addition of the saxophone to the original group of five instruments also points to the increasing prominence in the *Façade* numbers of jazz and the fashionable dance music of the 1920s. It is possible that this trend was encouraged by the close friendship that developed between Walton and Lambert soon after the first performance, but it should always be remembered that Walton's interest in jazz and jazz sonorities was innate, and that, according to Lambert, he spent 1923–4 writing and scoring foxtrots for the new Savoy Orpheans Band.[6]

The decision to provide an alternative arrangement of the original single cello part for two cellos must have been made as a result of difficulties experienced by players under Walton's direction. The existence of these parts is first mentioned in a letter of 15 November 1950 (OUP Archive) from Alan Frank to a copyist, who was preparing a new set of instrumental parts from the first proofs of the printed edition that Walton was correcting. She was instructed to make two cello parts: (a) for one cello, as in the score, and (b) for two cellos, as in the manuscript part, but with any alterations as shown to the part for single cello in the proof score. No copy of the manuscript part referred to has survived. The double cello part was not given in the 1951 score, though its availability on hire is mentioned, and it is now published for the first time. There is no reason to suppose that this arrangement was not done by Walton himself, but there are some small anomalies, mainly affecting the length of final notes, such as a crotchet instead of a quaver. Walton used the two-cello version in his 1965 Prom performance.

Variations in the Order of the Numbers

The table overleaf lists the numbers in the order in which they were first presented, as shown in the relevant programmes. The performances chosen for this purpose are those that are considered to be the most significant milestones in the history of *Façade*. A number of recurring patterns emerge, such as the grouping of 'Hornpipe', 'En Famille', and 'Mariner Man', that from April 1926 onwards became established as the opening trio, and 'Sir Beelzebub' that constituted the final number from as early as 1923.

The one mystery number is 'The Last Galop'. The first known performance of this was as the last of the eighteen numbers in the broadcast of 3 March 1930. It is not shown in any of the programmes prior to this date, although it may well have been given at the New Chenil Galleries in 1926 or in November 1927 at one of the three performances at the Arts Theatre. For this reason it is listed last, but the appearance of the autograph suggests that it is, at very least, contemporaneous with 'Popular Song' and 'Black Mrs Behemoth'.

Titles in brackets show revised designations, and an asterisk denotes an unnumbered movement.

1922	24 January, first private performance, 2 Carlyle Square, London.
1923	12 June, first public performance, Aeolian Hall, New Bond Street, London.
1926a	27 April, New Chenil Galleries, Chelsea, London.
1926b	29 June, New Chenil Galleries.
1928	14 September, Teatro Rozzi, Siena, Italy (ISCM Festival).
1942	29 May, Aeolian Hall.
1946	9 September, 27 October, Lyric Theatre, Hammersmith, London.
1951	First publication of OUP score.
1977	25 March, first performance of *Façade Revived*, Plaisterers' Hall, London.
1979	19 June, first performance of *Façade 2*, The Maltings, Snape, Suffolk.

Reallocation of the voice part for two speakers

Although the first private and public performances of *Façade* were given with only Edith Sitwell reciting, from April 1926 onwards the practice developed of sharing the numbers between two speakers. Doubtless Edith had her favourite poems—often, it would seem, the more reflective and atmospheric ones—which she reserved for herself, but equally she was happy to yield pride of place of the more brilliant numbers to Constant Lambert, whose clarity and verbal dexterity were universally admired. For a time thereafter he became the sole reciter, but the practice of experimenting with different ways of sharing the narration continued, though the matter was not discussed in the 1951 first publication of the score.

While travelling to Australia early in 1964, Walton went so far as to write out his suggestions for sharing the part—the most detailed yet—on four sides of manuscript paper. By the time this came to be typed for the performers, a few modifications had been introduced. When in August 1965 Walton conducted the first performance of *Façade* at the Promenade Concerts the scheme was altered and simplified; as ever, the capabilities and requirements of the speakers must have had some bearing. For his Argo recording with Peggy Ashcroft and Paul Scofield, made in 1969 and released in 1972, the scheme was changed yet again, though this was partly because the recording was originally planned as the soundtrack for a film treatment of *Façade* that never materialized.

Order of *Façade* numbers in significant performances.

Performance	1922	1923	1926(a)	1926(b)	1928	1942–6	1951	1977	1979
Total of numbers	18	27	26	25	22	21	21	9	8
Fanfare		*	*	*	*	*	*	1	
General Salute and Prologue [Osbert Sitwell]	*	*							

Performance	1922	1923	1926(a)	1926(b)	1928	1942–6	1951	1977	1979
Total of numbers	18	27	26	25	22	21	21	9	8
Overture	1	*							
Dame Souris Trotte (Madame Mouse Trots)	2	5	11						4
The Octogenarian	3	10=	16	15				5	5
Aubade	4	22	14	10				8	2
The Wind's Bastinado	5								
Said King Pompey	6	9	6	9				9	8
Interlude	7								
Jumbo's Lullaby	8	3	12	18	7	8	7		
Small Talk I & II	9	7	4						
Rose Castles (Water Party)	10	19							7
Hornpipe	11	21	1	1	1	1	1		
Long Steel Grass (Trio for two cats and a trombone)	12	13	17	16	16	4	4		
Sir Beelzebub	13	27	26	25	22	21	21		
Switchback	14	6	10						
Bank Holiday I & II	15								
Springing Jack	16								
En Famille	17	20	2	2		2	2		
Mariner Man	18	18	3	3	2	3	3		
Gardener Janus Catches a Naiad		1							6
Clown Argheb's Song		2							
Trams		4	13						
By the Lake		8	5	8	8	10	11		
Serenade [instrumental]		10=							
Herodiade's Flea (Came the Great Popinjay)		11						3	1
Through Gilded Trellises		12	18	17	18	5	5		
The Man from a Far Countree		14	8	21	14	11	10		
Daphne		15	7	20	13			2	
Country Dance		16	9	22	15	12	12		
Gone Dry		17							
The White Owl		23						7	
Dark Song		24							
Foxtrot 'Old Sir Faulk'		25	15	11	4	9	20		
Ass Face		26							

Performance	1922	1923	1926(a)	1926(b)	1928	1942–6	1951	1977	1979
Total of numbers	18	27	26	25	22	21	21	9	8
I Do Like to Be Beside the Seaside									
(Tango–Pasodoblé)			19	19	19	6	6		
Valse			20	5	10	17	16		
Polka			21	14	12	16	13		
Jodelling Song			22	6	11	13	17		
Scotch Rhapsody			23	4	3	7	18		
Something Lies beyond the Scene			24	23	21	20	15		
Four in the Morning			25	13	5	19	14		
Tarantella				7	20	18	9		
March				12	17			6	3
Mazurka				24					
Popular Song					6	15	19		
Black Mrs Behemoth					9	14	8		
The Last Galop				?				4	

NOTES

1. This is largely due to the painstaking research of Richard Fifoot, whose *A Bibliography of Edith, Osbert and Sacheverell Sitwell* was first published in 1963 (London, Rupert Hart-Davis) and reissued in a second edition in 1971.
2. The programme treated the bipartite poems 'Small Talk' and 'Bank Holiday' as single numbers.
3. Preserved in the Edith Sitwell archive at the Harry Ransom Humanities Research Center, Austin, Texas. The galley proofs are stamped '25 May 1950'.
4. The metronome marks given in the proofs of the discontinued engraved edition had been supplied not by Walton but by Robin Langley and Stephen Wickner of the OUP Music Department. They had proposed them, in the absence of any other tempo indications, when the manuscripts of *Façade Revived* were being professionally recopied for the first performance.
5. Constant Lambert, 'Some Recent Works by William Walton', *The Dominant*, vol. 1, no. 4 (February 1928), p. 18.
6. Constant Lambert, 'Fresh Hand; New Talent; Vital Touch', *Boston Evening Transcript* (27 November 1926), section iv, p. 5 a–f.

8

Vocal Music *(Vol. 8)*

Steuart Bedford

The present volume contains all William Walton's songs for voice and piano, plus *Anon. in Love* for voice and guitar. Also included are 'Under the Greenwood Tree', written for the 1936 film version of *As You Like It*, and 'Beatriz's Song' from the 1942 radio play *Christopher Columbus*. One of Walton's very earliest settings, 'Tell me where is Fancy bred?', is published here for the first time, as are the orchestral versions of 'Beatriz's Song', *Anon. in Love*, and *A Song for the Lord Mayor's Table*.

Tell me where is Fancy bred?

'Tell me where is Fancy bred?', the second item in Stewart Craggs's definitive *William Walton: A Catalogue*, was composed when Walton was still a 14-year-old pupil at Oxford's Christ Church Cathedral choir school, and bears the date '2 July 1916'. In a much-quoted letter to his publisher Hubert Foss describing his early days, Walton lists a number of abandoned or destroyed titles;[1] 'Tell me where is Fancy bred?' is the only one of these to survive. Walton calls the composition a partsong, possibly due to its unusual combination of two voices, three violins, and piano. A piece for such an ensemble must surely have been written for a special occasion, or at least with particular performers in mind, perhaps for a school production of *The Merchant of Venice*; the song is taken from Act III, Scene 2 of the play.[2] Indeed, in a 60th birthday interview with John Warrack in the *Sunday Telegraph* of 25 March 1962, Walton is quoted as saying that, as a chorister, he made settings of Shakespeare songs 'from the plays we happened to be studying'.

Four Swinburne Songs

Walton fell very much on his feet when he entered the Christ Church choir school in 1912. The Dean at that time was Dr Thomas Banks Strong, a doctor of music as well as divinity, who took particular interest in any burgeoning musical talent among his choristers. He was a great help to Walton, not only in arranging for him to stay at the choir school longer than was usual, but also in expediting his entry into Christ Church College as a very young undergraduate in 1918. A letter of 8 January 1938 from Strong, by then Bishop of Oxford, to Hubert Foss conjures up a charming picture of Sunday mornings at the choir school: 'In those days the 5 senior boys used to come to my house every Sunday morning after Cathedral—i.e. about 11.30 a.m. It began by being a sort of little Bible class, but they gradually developed the habit of staying till 1 p.m. and messing about with my books etc. I think, but I am not quite sure, that W. [Walton] used to strum on my piano.'[3]

Bearing in mind that Walton's response to poetry was, to say the least, muted, and that later the poems for his songs tended to be chosen for him by others, it is not unreasonable to suppose that 'messing about with my books' could well have involved some advice from Dean Strong in the matter of possible song texts. At any rate it is hard to imagine the young Walton ploughing through volumes of the poetry of Algernon Charles Swinburne (1837–1909) unaided. Strong could well have been a guiding hand, especially as Swinburne was a distinguished alumnus of the university, having graduated from Balliol in 1858.

The four Swinburne settings are all taken from the second and third series of *Poems and Ballads* of 1878 and 1889; the first three were composed in July 1918, 'The Winds' probably a little later (the autograph is lost). This last was to become the first work of Walton's to be published when it was issued by Curwen in early 1921. The autographs of the 1918 songs ('Child's Song', 'Song', and 'A Lyke-wake Song') only came to light some seven years after the composer's death. They were offered for sale at Sotheby's and snapped up by the American collector Frederick R. Koch. Eventually they were published by OUP in 2002 to mark the Walton centenary in an edition, edited by Alan Cuckston, which also included a republication of 'The Winds'.

Tritons

We will probably never know where Walton found 'Tritons', by the relatively obscure poet William Drummond of Hawthornden (1585–1649), or what induced him to set it. Perhaps he had retained a certain fascination with those creatures of the sea ever since his unfinished cantata setting of Matthew Arnold's *The Forsaken Merman* in 1916, a triton being the male form of the mermaid. Drummond is a curious figure; once he had succeeded to the lairdship he seldom left his estate at Hawthornden, seven miles from Edinburgh, where he divided his time between poetry and mechanical inventions. His most famous work is 'The Cypresse Grove', a substantial prose meditation on the subject of death. Perhaps Walton chanced to see the new 1913 critical edition of his works in Dr Strong's library, or that of the Sitwell brothers.[4] The autograph is dated '1920'.

'Tritons' is styled 'a madrigal' by Drummond, and contains a cryptic reference to his lady-love, Miss Cunningham. 'Silver Ora' refers to the river Ore which starts from Loch Ore in Fife and joins the river Leven, eventually flowing into the sea at Methil. At some point the Ore passed Miss Cunningham's house.

*   *   *

Of these early songs, only 'The Winds' and 'Tritons' received a public performance during Walton's lifetime. They may well have previously been given privately, but the first recorded public performance of 'The Winds' (and therefore any work by Walton) was given by Dorothy Moulton (soprano) at a concert of English Songs on Wednesday, 14 December 1921, at the Aeolian Hall, London. Both songs featured in a chamber concert in the same hall on Wednesday, 30 October 1929, when they were performed by the soprano Odette de Foras and the pianist Gordon Bryan. The concert, which also included the first public performances of Walton's Piano Quartet (1918–21) and the Li-Po songs of Constant Lambert, was reviewed by Eric Blom in the *Musical Times*. While regretting that the music on offer was, in Walton's case, some ten years old (the Viola Concerto had been premiered 27 days previously), he found the Piano Quartet to be 'a respectable piece of work such as might have been written by any British composer of talent and some scholastic attainment...but the two early songs left one with a far clearer sense of the composer's precocious certainty of touch'.[5]

Three Songs to poems by Edith Sitwell

In 1923, following the *succès-de-scandale* of the first public performance of *Façade: An Entertainment*, Walton adapted five of the numbers for high voice and accompaniment; that is to say, he made vocal lines out of the original reciter's spoken text. He borrowed the title *Bucolic Comedies* from Edith Sitwell's 1923 collection of poems, several of which had been used in *Façade*. It is generally stated that three of the songs had an instrumental accompaniment, presumably the same combination as that used in *Façade*, and that the enterprise was eventually abandoned, re-emerging in 1932 as 'Three Songs for high voice and piano to poems by Edith Sitwell'. There is precious little evidence for this prehistory. We have no idea which poems Walton had originally selected, nor any details as to their instrumentation. However if, for argument's sake, we assume that all the foregoing is true, we can be reasonably certain that 'Old Sir Faulk' was among them, as it is the only one of the three 1932 songs to come from Sitwell's *Bucolic Comedies*.

Thanks to a series of letters from Walton to Dora Stevens (she and her husband Hubert Foss were the dedicatees of the songs and gave their first performance), we are able to trace their dates of composition with relative accuracy. Although it is never clearly stated, there is little difficulty in deciding which song is referred to in the letters. On 21 December 1931 Walton wrote to Dora: 'Here is one of the songs. Don't hesitate (because it is dedicated to you) to severely criticise it if it doesn't meet with your approval. It is not so difficult as it first looks[,] especially the piano part.' Bearing in mind Walton's reference to the piano part, this must be 'Through Gilded Trellises'. On 2 January 1932 he followed this up: 'Here is another song, alas! not the "lydian" one which is proving a little obstreperous...it is I think fairly good of its type, and at any rate ought to evoke a touch of inconsequent lunacy in any programme.' This is clearly 'Old Sir Faulk'. Finally, still in January 1932, he writes: 'Here is the last song. I am sorry to have been such a time with it, but I could not get it satisfactory—this is the 3rd version—all I can say about it is that it is better than the other two.' This last must be 'Daphne' (the 'obstreperous' one) which is a completely new setting, and musically unrelated to that composed for *Façade*. Walton told Dora Stevens that he had never been happy with the original version; he felt that the poem needed a singing voice rather than a spoken one; indeed, after 1930 the number was dropped from *Façade* altogether.[6]

'Through Gilded Trellises' and 'Old Sir Faulk' are arrangements of their originals in *Façade*. The vocal line is created from the melodic thread that runs through both pieces, more or less continuously in the latter (which is transposed down a tone), but rather less so in the former, which also contains the occasional re-composition such as bars 37–9. Walton's hardest task was to reduce the sophisticated instrumental textures to something playable by two hands at the keyboard. The result was a fairly elaborate accompaniment. Dyneley Hussey of the *Musical Times*, reviewing the first public performance on Monday, 10 October 1932 at the Wigmore Hall, felt this to have been applied to the vocal line rather than grown out of it.[7] For this reason he considered 'Daphne' to be the best of the three. He also noted that Miss Stevens's voice had grown harder than it used to be; nonetheless, in 1941 she recorded the songs for Decca with Foss at the piano.[8] In May 1933 a performance took place with a male vocalist, John Armstrong, accompanied by Willem (later Myers) Foggin, and on Friday, 13 March 1936 Sophie Wyss gave a broadcast performance of numbers 1 and 2 only with the 22-year-old Benjamin Britten at the piano.

Under the Greenwood Tree

Walton was always vehemently opposed to any attempt to extract items from his film scores, or other incidental music, for concert use. There were notable exceptions, such as the 'Spitfire' Prelude and Fugue from the film *The First of the Few*, and a Suite from the film *Henry V*; later, the conductor Muir Mathieson was allowed to plunder some of the music from the films *Hamlet* and *Richard III*. Fortunately Walton did allow two songs from this corpus to be published separately, the first being Shakespeare's song 'Under the Greenwood Tree', written for Paul Czinner's film *As You Like It*, starring his wife Elisabeth Bergner and the young Laurence Olivier. In the end the song was not used in the film, and the autograph remains in piano format, both excellent reasons for a separate publication. In 1937 OUP issued the song for both medium and low voices (the lower being the original), and later in an arrangement for small orchestra by Roy Douglas. Finally, the song was published for unison voices to be used in schools.

Beatriz's Song

This number, from Walton's score for Louis MacNeice's 1942 radio play *Christopher Columbus*, took somewhat longer to see the light of day. Ever keen to mine the Walton hinterland, Alan Frank of OUP seems to have asked the composer if there was anything to be salvaged from it. On 19 December 1966 he replied: 'About Chris. Colomb. I can't believe that there is anything worthwhile resuscitating from that vast and boring score. I don't remember a thing so I had better have a look at those songs—not that I can do much about them as I think the BBC bought the whole outright for next to nothing. But let me have a look!' It would appear that the score was sent to him because on 12 January 1967 he wrote to Frank: 'One must draw a line somewhere about the horrors of ones past being allowed to be dredged up & I am for a complete ban on those songs even to the destruction of the MSS! I'm not at all sure that MacNeice wouldn't feel the same about his lyrics!'[9]

In the early 1970s the BBC was considering a revival of the complete production. The project was unfortunately abandoned, but the idea did prompt a re-examination of the original broadcast acetates; this was repeated on Radio Three on Sunday, 8 April 1973.

A letter from Walton to Alan Frank of OUP, dated 9 May 1973, is very characteristic: 'I don't remember anything of Columbus or Macbeth but I can quote from a note I got from Gillian W[iddecombe]: "I enjoyed the music a lot. But [BBC producer] Michael Pope and I reckoned that you ought to have Beatriz's 'When will he return' published because it is very beautiful".' Walton commented, 'I feel, if it is as beautiful as all that, I should remember it.'

The song was scored for string orchestra minus double basses, muted throughout, and in 1974 OUP published it as an arrangement for voice and guitar by Hector Quine, presumably as a gesture towards the Spanish subject. The fact that a piano version was not issued at the same time is due to the OUP music department's editors' opinion (which they claimed was shared by Walton) that such an arrangement would not be appropriate. It was not until 1991 that the song appeared in a reduction for piano by Christopher Palmer. Unfortunately, this takes considerable liberties with the string quartet writing; the version presented in the WWE adheres closely to Walton's original layout.

Anon. in Love

If one discounts the theatrical numbers, which were not conceived as separate entities, there is a gap of almost three decades between the Three Songs to poems by Edith Sitwell and Walton's next entry into the field of solo song. Writing to an unknown correspondent (but probably Alan Frank) on 24 July 1959 from Ischia, he says: 'Actually at the moment I'm on a song cycle for P.P & Julian B called Anon. in love—seven [*sic*] snappy 17th cent. lyrics. I'll have most of them finished I hope before I leave.'[10] *Anon. in Love* was commissioned by the tenor Peter Pears (the original Pandarus in *Troilus and Cressida*), who had established a successful musical collaboration with the brilliant guitar player Julian Bream. Pears was indefatigable in commissioning new pieces, and works by Lennox Berkeley, Peter Racine Fricker, Thea Musgrave, and Michael Tippett were all written for this duo, as well as Britten's *Songs from the Chinese*, Op. 58. The original idea for *Anon. in Love* seems to date back to 1956. Replying to a letter of 21 April from Pears, Walton wrote: 'You are quite right in your surmise that I've my back to the wall with the 'cello Concerto, but at the moment I'm engaged on an overture for the Johannesburg Festival. But I'm all for some little songs with guitar, when I'm finished with these works.'[11]

The days of Dean Strong or the Sitwells were long past, so for assistance in finding suitable lyrics, Walton turned to a friend and colleague. Christopher Hassall was a noted poet, and author of the standard biography of Rupert Brooke; he had also provided several lyrics for Ivor Novello, but his major collaboration with Walton had been in writing the libretto for their grand opera *Troilus and Cressida*. Hassall chose some 'snappy lyrics' exclusively from *An English Galaxy of Shorter Poems*, an anthology containing a substantial section of poems which were anonymous.[12] The first three come from the Elizabethan age; all were known and set by the madrigalists of the period, respectively Tobias Hume, John Farmer, and John Wilbye. The last three are taken from the Restoration period and contain a mild salaciousness that would have appealed to Walton. One was dropped somewhere along the line, leaving six, all of which set the poems complete. In order to help Walton master the complexities of writing for the guitar, Bream sent him a sheet entitled 'Sir William's Dot Chart for the Box' (Bream always referred to the guitar as 'the Box').[13] Precisely how this worked is difficult to say; nevertheless it did the trick and Bream was delighted with the result.

On 14 September 1959 Walton wrote to Alan Frank: 'The songs are more or less in the bag at any rate five of them—two of the poems are proving a bit difficult so will probably be discarded. Five is enough anyhow.... They are not I may add very typical W.W.—being terribly English! It [the guitar] is a fiendish instrument to write for.' The songs were dispatched to OUP on 29 December 1959 with requests to have them photographed and the autograph sent to Mrs Lilias Sheepshanks—'That will give you something to ponder over!', the composer wrote to Frank.[14] Ever practical in musical matters, Walton was especially concerned that each song should fit onto two pages so that Bream would not have to turn mid-song. The cycle was published just in time for the first performance, which took place at Shrublands Park, Claydon, near Ipswich, on Tuesday, 21 June 1960 as part of that year's Aldeburgh Festival.[15]

Overnight reviews were unanimously favourable. The anonymous critic of *The Times* wrote: 'Fired by the artistry of these two musicians Walton has distilled the fruits of his experience into a concentrated musical utterance, sometimes direct and sometimes curiously subtle...a brilliant premiere and [the cycle] will be heard everywhere with delight.' John Amis, writing in *The Guardian*, was even more positive: 'Each of the six songs is compact, supremely professional, immediately hummable and thoroughly enjoyable. This is the most satisfactory music Walton has given us for a long while.'

Orchestration

A letter from Walton to Alan Frank of 27 March 1960 is interesting in that it shows how a seed may well have been planted in Walton's mind. 'He [Bream] is no good [i.e. unavailable] for an American Perf—nor is PP. However he is all for my orchestrating them sometime.'

At that stage Walton believed that it would be a mistake to 'blow them up' for orchestra. Having done exactly that for *A Song for the Lord Mayor's Table* in March 1970, however, he turned again to the guitar songs and settled on a reduced orchestra of strings, harp, and a touch of percussion (no timpani). In a letter to Malcolm Arnold of 8 June 1970, Walton wrote: 'I don't know what to do with the 'armonys [*sic*] which are so often implied on the "box"—whether to fill them in or not.'[16] In the result, Walton's orchestration represents something of a tour de force, even by his high standards.

The date of this letter is exactly two weeks before the first performance of the orchestral version of *A Song for the Lord Mayor's Table*, so Walton would clearly have been very much in orchestration mode. OUP received the autograph full score on 2 September 1970, and the first performance was given at Mansion House, London, on Monday, 21 June 1971 by Robert Tear and the London Mozart Players, conducted by Harry Blech, coincidentally exactly eleven years to the day since the guitar version was premiered at Aldeburgh. On the following day the critic of *The Times* approved of the arrangement: 'Sir William, who was happily present, has deftly orchestrated the six songs without in any way losing the intimacy or gently lyrical character of the short cycle.'

A Song for the Lord Mayor's Table

On 6 January 1962 Ian Hunter, Artistic Director of the forthcoming first City of London Festival, wrote to Walton with a formal invitation (already discussed with OUP) to write a short song cycle for the occasion. Two days later, Walton reported to Alan Frank that he had agreed to write one for Elisabeth Schwarzkopf, thus accepting a commission from the Worshipful Company of Goldsmiths. *A Song for the Lord Mayor's Table*, as the cycle was soon called, would be performed as part of the Festival in July 1962. Once again Christopher Hassall was called upon to come up with appropriate texts, and by 24 January he had sent Walton a set of poems which, as he told Frank, 'with a possible change or two I think will work out well'. All were taken from a single anthology published in London in 1898, *London in Song*, a volume of over 200 poems devoted to all aspects of London, edited by Wilfred Whitten. Hassall's choices were wide-ranging; alongside Wordsworth and Blake we find the relatively obscure figures of Thomas Jordan and Charles Morris, as well as the ubiquitous 'Anon.'. The subjects covered include The Lord Mayor's Show, the Thames, the Old Stairs of Wapping, St Paul's Cathedral, and London's church bells.

Hassall's choice for the first song could hardly be more appropriate, being the first of eight verses and a chorus that conclude a substantial entertainment—four pageants and three speeches—performed in honour of Sir Robert Vyner Kt and Bart., Lord Mayor of the City of London, on 29 October 1674. All this was written by the official poet to the corporation of London, Thomas Jordan (1612–85). Jordan also composed the Purcellian melody to which the song was sung, and everything was printed in the 'Goldsmiths' Jubile' [*sic*] for 1674.

William Wordsworth (1770–1850) wrote his poem 'Glide gently, thus forever glide' while observing the Thames at Richmond. Strangely, Whitten prints only the first of the three verses, which is exactly what Walton sets. Wapping Old Stairs still exist, located next to the pub The Town of Ramsgate on Wapping High Street, as does the post to which the bodies of hanged pirates were chained for the tide to wash over. It is hardly surprising that such a macabre landmark should attract numerous stories and ballads. The version that Whitten chose was included in a volume entitled *A British Album* (1790) where it is called 'a characteristic song' and subtitled 'supposed to be sung by a sailor's lass to her favourite who has been treating her rather badly'. The authorship is assigned to 'Arley', a pseudonym for the maverick poet Robert Merry, who was the unaccredited editor of the volume. In this form the song became extremely popular, and even found its way into Thackeray's novel *Vanity Fair*, where the so-called favourite ballad is whistled by Emilia Osborne as she goes down to dinner (chapter 25). This would presumably be the 1810 setting by John Percy, which became something of a hit in its day.

William Blake (1757–1827) wrote his poem 'Holy Thursday' as part of *An Island in the Moon* (1784). He then included it, slightly revised, in his collection *Songs of Innocence* (1789). Holy Thursday is Ascension Day, on which occasion there is a large gathering of charity schools at St Paul's Cathedral, the Beadles of the various City parishes being present in their official dress. Blake was to return to this subject in his *Songs of Experience* (1791), where he paints a far bleaker picture, exposing the hypocrisy enshrined in the social mores of the time:

> Is this a holy thing to see
> In a rich and fruitful land—
> Babes reduced to misery
> Fed with cold and usurous hand?

Not surprisingly, Whitten chose the earlier version.

Charles Morris (1745–1838) gained considerable fame as a writer of witty political songs, which he would sing after the dinners of the Beef Steak Society, an exclusive organization, then in its heyday, limited to twenty-four members. He was one of those who found life outside the city intolerable, and 'The Contrast' celebrates the joys of the capital. There happens to be an earlier version of this poem entitled 'Town and Country', which was printed in the 14th edition (1797) of *A Collection of Political and Other Songs*. This version now appears in *The New Oxford Book of Eighteenth-Century Verse*.[17] 'The Contrast', which was not published until *Lyra Urbanica* of 1840, contains several verses not found in 'Town and Country', in particular the verse commencing 'I know love's a devil'. Whitten has mistakenly given the earlier date to the later version.

'Oranges and Lemons' was originally sung to a game that ended in the mock decapitation of one of the players. This version can be found in *The Oxford Dictionary of Nursery Rhymes*.[18] Whitten, on the other hand, provided a much longer and less bloodthirsty version, taken mainly from *Gammer Gurton's Garland of Nursery Songs* of 1810. 'Gammer' means old woman or grandmother, and is a figure analogous to Mother Hubbard or Mother Goose. She bears a name that extends far back into oral tradition— her first literary outing was in 1556 where she starred in Britain's second-oldest verse comedy 'Gamma Gurton's Needle'. The first *Garland* was published in 1783, edited by Joseph Ritson, and enlarged editions appeared throughout the nineteenth century. Earlier editions of *Gammer Gurton* have the verses in a different order, and the verses beginning 'Pokers and tongs' and 'Kettles and pans' do not appear at all. These have been borrowed from a further publication, *Songs for the Nursery* (1805). In a letter from Ischia to Alan Frank of 3 June 1962, Walton signalled the end of composition: 'No. VI was dispatched yesterday—a potboiler which I fear does not boil. In fact, these innumerable couplets cost me more irritation than the whole lot.'

The premiere of the song cycle was given by the soprano Elisabeth Schwarzkopf, whom Walton had wanted in 1953 for the lead in *Troilus and Cressida*, and Gerald Moore, indisputably the leading accompanist of his generation. Schwarzkopf had requested that she have the score at least ten weeks before the premiere so that she could get it into her voice. Many postcards and slips containing corrections flowed both ways between Walton and Moore. On 21 April Moore wrote to Christopher Morris of OUP: 'These Walton songs are really terrific—everything WW does is impressive— why the devil doesn't he write more songs?' And a letter to Frank dated 28 June from Schwarzkopf's husband, Walter Legge, reports that the artists had just had a singthrough and were both delighted.

The first performance of *A Song for the Lord Mayor's Table* took place on Wednesday, 18 July 1962, in the Goldsmiths' Hall, London, and reviews were generally favourable. On the next day, *The Times* wrote of 'songs in Walton's new mature vein—texts nicely chosen matched by gay entertaining and harmonious music, each song distinguished by some attractive stroke of imagination'. However, Walton took issue with the critic Arthur Jacobs, who suggested that the songs were really for a man's voice. 'Surely,' he said in a letter to Alan Frank dated 10 August 1962, 'the "contrast" would be a bit equivocal with a man! But anyhow if some man would like to have a go, why not?' Walton seems to have been confused here: 'The Contrast', which expounds the poet's philosophy, is if anything more suitable for a man; on the other hand, 'Wapping Old Stairs', which features a woman addressing her heartless lover, would be hardly appropriate for a male singer.

Walton had some trouble with the dedication. In his letter to Frank in August he had said: 'I should like to dedicate these songs to Edith Sitwell.' Later, he considered giving it to Schwarzkopf, but then there was 'that stipulation about "In Honour of the City of London" which I would very much like to cut out as it seems overdoing it with a choral work of the same name' (letter to Frank, 8 October 1962). In the end the work was not dedicated. The score reads 'written for Elisabeth Schwarzkopf and Gerald Moore' and, placed at the head of the first song's title, 'In Honour of the City of London'.

Orchestration

In a letter to Frank of 23 February 1962, Walton had complained: 'I must say I find writing for pfte very irksome and have spent a lot of time on No. 1 which is really for orch.' A few months later, immediately after the success of the piano version's premiere, Ian Hunter wrote to Walton: 'If you think of scoring the accompaniments for orchestra please let me know as I would like to arrange the first performance on some suitable occasion in the City.'

Walton must have decided to go ahead with this idea, for by June 1963 he was requesting OUP to provide him with a skeleton score. However, it seems that the project became temporarily unstuck. Ian Hunter wanted to include the songs in a series of concerts that he was organizing for the City Arts Trust in the Guildhall some time between October 1963 and April 1964, but nothing ever came of this. In the event the orchestration was not completed until March 1970. Writing to Frank on 28 March that year, Walton said: 'Incidentally I've kept it intact—it's come up rather better than I expected. Awkward to do all the same'. The first performance took place at Mansion House on Tuesday, 7 July, with Janet Baker and the English Chamber Orchestra, conducted by George Malcolm. Stanley Sadie, writing in *The Times* on the following day, found the more intimate songs such as 'Wapping Old Stairs' less appropriate for orchestral accompaniment, but thought that the outer numbers gained from it. In all, 'an immensely entertaining cycle either way, but the different facets of Walton's inventions glitter the more in the different version'. On the other hand Anthony Payne, writing on the same day in the *Daily Telegraph*, commented that the skill of Walton's scoring 'can make the orchestration...so astonishingly idiomatic that it is the piano version...which begins to sound like an arrangement'.

NOTES

1. Duncan Hinnells, *An Extraordinary Performance* (Oxford, 1998), p. 54.

2. It is clear that Walton retained a certain affection for the song for, despite having composed it at the age of 14, he subsequently included it in the list of his compositions submitted to the Performing Right Society. The song should not be confused with Walton's later setting which is heard in his 1936 film music for, oddly enough, *As You Like It*.

3. Original in the private possession of Mrs Diana Sparkes (née Foss). Dr Strong was also a delegate of OUP from 1904 to 1937.

4. *The Poetical Works of William Drummond of Hawthornden*, ed. L. E. Kastner (London, 1913).

5. *Musical Times*, vol. 70, 1929, p. 1125.

6. All quotations in this paragraph are taken from the Sparkes collection (see n. 3).

7. *Musical Times*, vol. 73, 1932, p. 1036. This had been preceded by a private performance six months earlier on Wednesday, 9 April in a chamber music concert at Nightingale Corner, Rickmansworth, Hertfordshire, the home of the Fosses. There was a printed programme, and among the guests were Walton, Lambert, Arthur Benjamin, the singer John Coates, the Calvocoressis, the Harold Craxtons, and the Robert Mayers. Intriguingly, the clarinettist in some songs by Gordon Jacob was Alan Frank, later head of music at OUP from 1954–75.

8. Decca M489-90, three sides of two 10" 78 rpm records. The fourth side featured Warlock's 'Rest, sweet nymphs'. The Walton songs have been reissued on Dutton CDAX 8003.

9. This, and all subsequent quotations from the correspondence between Walton and Frank, are in the OUP Archive, Oxford, as are those with Ian Hunter, Gerald Moore, and Walter Legge.

10. OUP Archive.

11. *The Selected Letters of William Walton*, ed. Malcolm Hayes (London, 2002), p. 274.

12. Gerald Bullett, ed., *An English Galaxy of Shorter Poems* (London, 1933).

13. In the William Walton Museum, Forio, Ischia. For an illustration, see Humphrey Burton and Maureen Murray, *William Walton. The Romantic Loner: A Centenary Portrait Album* (Oxford, 2002), p. 151.

14. Mrs Lilias Sheepshanks was a close friend, living near Aldeburgh.

15. This was before Shrublands Park was converted into a health hydro, which was to feature in the James Bond film *Thunderball*. In 1964 Pears and Bream recorded the cycle for RCA (RB 6621; on CD, 0906 61583–2).

16. *Selected Letters*, ed. Hayes, p. 390.

17. Roger Lonsdale, ed., *The New Oxford Book of Eighteenth-Century Verse* (Oxford, 1984).

18. Iona Opie and Peter Opie, ed., *The Oxford Dictionary of Nursery Rhymes* (2nd edn, Oxford, 1997).

9

Symphony No. 1 *(Vol. 9)*

David Lloyd-Jones

Composition

After the enthusiastic reception of his Viola Concerto of 1929 and the even greater success two years later of the cantata *Belshazzar's Feast*, it was clearly going to be only a matter of time before William Walton embarked on the challenge of a symphony. A powerful incentive to start work on one came after a fine performance of the concerto in January 1932 in Manchester, when Sir Hamilton Harty invited the composer to write a symphony for his Hallé Orchestra. In a letter of 28 January 1932 to his friend and benefactor, the poet Siegfried Sassoon, Walton announced: 'Harty has asked me to *write a symphony for him*. So I shall start on that when I come to Edith [Olivier]. A rather portentous undertaking, but the Hallé is such a good orchestra and Harty such a magnificent conductor, besides being very encouraging, that I may be able to manage to knock Bax off the map. Anyhow it is a good thing to have something definite suggested and a date to work for.'[1]

Back in the spring of 1929, a time when he was putting the final touches to the Viola Concerto, Walton had met Imma Doernberg, the attractive young widow of a German Baron who was also related to the English and Dutch royal families. By July they were very much in love and an intense relationship developed which, despite frequent periods of separation, was still continuing nearly three years later when Walton arrived on 12 February 1932 at Edith Olivier's home, the Daye House, Wilton. The daily entries in Edith's journal from that date up to his departure on 7 April show that over a month elapsed before he was able to make even a tentative start on the symphony. Thus on 7 March she writes, 'Willie says he thinks he won't begin his Symphony for some time, but go on playing *round* it. He is so afraid of starting wrong or of its being about nothing at all,' and thirteen days later, 'Willie now is writing and varies between thinking he is getting going and feeling sure that all he has done must be torn up. This evening he says it is anaemic, sentimental, dull and worthless. Says he has never been inspired in his life and can't think why he writes.' From Wilton he went on to Weston Hall, the home of Sacheverell and Georgia Sitwell, where his hesitant improvisations caused his host to suggest that it might be better for all concerned if he used a room in the stable block.

Walton spent most of the late spring and summer with the Baroness in Ascona, Switzerland, where work on the symphony made very little headway. When he revisited Edith Olivier on 13 September she was able to record, 'He played me the opening two minutes of his Symphony. It is very fine.' Although it seems likely that more had been accomplished than just the beginning, her journal entry for two days later goes a long way to explain the slow rate of progress, and gives a strong indication of Walton's emotional state at the time of the composition of the first movement:

> A day of confidences from Willie who tells me that when he first went abroad [in the previous spring] he found that Imma had misunderstood something, and thinking he didn't care for her was on the verge of marrying someone else. She wrote a breaking-off letter, refusing to see him for a month. He was at Montegufoni [the Sitwells' Tuscan home] and Sir George made him go to her *that day* and lent him money. Sir G. as the good angel is a revelation. It saved the situation—though they went through tortures for two months as they could not get things straight. Willie cried every day and that is why he could not get on with his Symphony. I see it has done him good. He has learnt that she is essential to him, and he is more in love than ever. Says they can't get married as she has *nothing at all* while Germany is in this crisis. He is supporting her and he has only the £500 a year left him by Mrs. Courtauld. But for that she would starve. He made £190 by his music last year—twice as much as ever before. But not enough to marry on.

By October 1932 Walton and the Baroness were back in Ascona, and during the following months he made better progress with the symphony, for on his return to London in the spring of 1933 he was able to play the completed first and second movements to friends, including his publisher, Hubert Foss, head of the music department of Oxford University Press. He then began work on the slow movement and, as his friend the pianist Angus Morrison has recorded:

> once a start had been made the movement was completed in short score fairly quickly.... At first it was a much longer movement and contained an extended middle section recalling the malevolent mood of the Scherzo, but which was not to my mind nearly so effective, partly because he had said it all before. Willie himself obviously had considerable misgivings about this section and had already discussed removing it with Cecil Gray. Cecil Gray speaks of it in his autobiography. By the time he came to me I think he had almost made up his mind, and his playing of it then and our discussion afterwards finally clinched it. There and then he marked the cut in his copy, tore out the intervening two pages and left them behind on my piano when he left![2]

By September 1933 he was already sketching the opening and coda of the last movement, though he very soon reached an impasse over suitable material for its central section.

In February 1933 Harty had resigned from the Hallé in order to devote more time to his new position as Principal Conductor of the London Symphony Orchestra, and though the symphony was by no means finished the LSO had decided to announce the premiere for March of the following year. In January 1934 Walton surprisingly still considered this date to be an outside possibility, but by mid-February he had to inform Adrian Boult that the LSO premiere on 19 March, and a projected second performance in May by the BBC, were both out of the question.[3] In view of his difficulties with the shape and content of the last movement, Walton decided to orchestrate the three completed movements at this time.

Most of the summer was taken up with the composition of the music for *Escape Me Never*, the first of Walton's fourteen film scores. In August Imma Doernberg, who had been away in Switzerland for several months, spent a few days with him at Edith

Olivier's. For some time now their relationship had been growing more stressful, and on the 12th of that month the Baroness finally succeeded in persuading Walton that it would be better for both of them if they put all thoughts of marriage out of mind and went their separate ways. Immediately both felt liberated by the rightness of this decision, and henceforth they remained on affectionate terms. Walton's dedication of the symphony to her, already elegantly designed by his friend Rex Whistler at the head of the unfinished autograph score, was to endure, and she had the satisfaction of attending both premieres.[4] His subsequent liaison with Alice Wimborne began in early 1935, just as he was resuming work on the last movement, and continued until her death in 1948.

Completion and performance

In the autumn of 1934 it was announced that the first performance of the three completed movements would be given on 3 December by the LSO under Harty at Queen's Hall, London. A number of reasons have been put forward as to why Walton agreed to this highly unusual procedure. Certainly the directors of the orchestra were disappointed at seeing the end of another year looming without any sign of this potentially important work being finished and performed. They were also aware of the threat that was presented by the BBC, which had founded its own symphony orchestra in 1930 and was rapidly establishing a reputation as a patron of new music. The general assumption that the LSO brought pressure to bear on Walton, Harty, and Foss is confirmed by the recent discovery of Walton's letter of 9 November to the composer Patrick Hadley. As this constitutes the most extensive and revealing statement of the composer's thoughts about the symphony during the period of its composition, it deserves to be quoted at length:

> You may or may not have seen in today's D.T. [*Daily Telegraph*] that Sir H. Harty is taking the unprecedented course of giving my Symphony (if such it may now be called) minus a finale on Dec. 3rd.
>
> The great comfort to me is that the onus of this decision rests almost entirely on your shoulders, for there is little doubt I could have pumped out tolerably easily a brilliant, out-of-the-place pointless and vacuous finale, in time for this performance, or I might have got Arthur Benjamin to 'ghost' for me! (Of course, please pass this tit-bit on!) But that is where you, or rather your letter, stepped in. Instead of doing that, egged on by you, I persisted in finding something which I felt to be right and tolerably up to the standard of the previous movements. This involved me in endless trouble and I've burn't [*sic*] about 3 finales when I saw that they weren't really leading anywhere or saying anything. And it is only comparatively lately that I've managed to get going on what I hope is the last attempt. At the moment I need hardly add that I'm held up, and my blood has turned to water and see no hope etc. etc. and shall have to begin all over again. But it is more probable that I'm a bit 'oopset' on the prospects of Dec. 3rd.
>
> Whether it is a wise decision to have arrived at, I hardly dare to think. Harty, who has behaved like a lamb, was more or less willing to wait till March, but the LSO committee said that another postponement would be fatal, and that if I agreed they would do it without the finale. It being pointed out very forcibly, by my friends and advisers,

that it was the lesser of two evils, I concurred. Anyhow I'm certain that it is better for it to appear like this, than with a bad or artificial finale. After all the worst that can happen is that it is a miserable 'flop' and that I'm prepared for, having seen it staring me in the face for some time. As for success, you know what I feel about that sort of thing by now! The only point of a success is the money it brings in, and in this work, no matter how much it had, it wouldn't bring much in, considering what sort of a work it is. The only things that can be said about it are either 'Thank God, there's not a finale' or 'What a pity there isn't one' or the more subtle ones may say 'I wonder what the finale will be like'. And that is what I want to know. For it is, for want of better words, what may be called the emotional and spiritual continuity that is worrying me and not so much the actual notes (but they are bad enough).

Luckily, however, in this work, it is not a case of it being 'made' by the finale. The three existing movements, though I say it who shouldn't, are about as good as they could be and if I can bring off a finale as good as them, the whole symphony will be a 'bit of orlright' which is, for me, saying a hell of a lot …

Forgive this long egotistical epistle, but I must do something, no longer being able to look at a piece of MS paper without acute nausea, and you are, I hope, one of my few understanding friends.[5]

The performance of the first three movements by Harty and the LSO at Queen's Hall on 3 December 1934 achieved a notable success. There were two further London performances of the three-movement torso at Courtauld–Sargent concerts under Malcolm Sargent on 1 and 2 April 1935. Walton then resumed work on the last movement. He later stated that it was Constant Lambert who had suggested a fugue as a means of dealing with his impasse over the central section. When Walton objected that he did not know how to write one, Lambert replied: 'There are a couple of rather good pages on the subject in Grove's Dictionary.' Walton adopted the idea, and on 9 July wrote to Foss: 'I've been here [Weston Hall] some ten days or so and have produced this for the 2nd subject, but I am shivering on the brink about it I need hardly say.'

In a postscript to the same letter he adds: 'Has the score of the first two movements arrived safely? There are still one or two things in the 3rd I've not yet made up my mind about, but will let you have it soon for engraving.'

On 30 August Foss announced to his wife, 'I've just heard that Willie rang up to say he'd actually finished the symphony!' The eagerly awaited first performance of the complete work was given at Queen's Hall by the BBC Symphony Orchestra under Harty on 6 November 1935, eleven months after that of the first three movements. A second performance by the City of Birmingham Orchestra under Leslie Heward took place soon after on 22 November. The first performances outside Britain were given by the Chicago Symphony Orchestra under Hamilton Harty on 22–23 January 1936.

Despite its protracted gestation period, Walton's Symphony (as it was generally known until the appearance of the Second in 1960) was a remarkable achievement for the 33-year-old composer. Other masterworks lay behind and ahead, but there are many who feel that in this work Walton displays an uniquely powerful and individual emotional range which he was able to express with exceptional directness, thanks to his mature technical mastery. Critics and audiences were not slow to recognize this, and the symphony's passionate, dramatic, and virile qualities—epithets that were rarely applied to the works of Walton's British contempories in the mid-1930s—earned it the reputation of what Michael Kennedy has aptly described as a 'liberating masterpiece'. [6]

Recording

Barely a month after the premiere Harty recorded the symphony for the Decca Record Company on 10 and 11 December 1935, but with his London Symphony Orchestra instead of the BBC Symphony Orchestra. The work filled six 78 rpm discs which were released with commendable speed on 20 December of the same year.[7] This historic document has since been reissued in LP and CD format.

An interesting account of the symphony's first recording sessions in 1935 is given by Hubert Foss, in his *Gramophone* review (February 1953) of the composer's 1951 recording of the symphony.

Publication

Not long after the release of the Decca recording the symphony was published by Oxford University Press. A detailed estimate by the printers Henderson and Spalding Ltd, submitted after work had begun, included expenses already incurred for author's corrections and revisions to full score and parts.[8] One hundred copies of the folio full score were published on 21 May 1936; 1000 copies of a photographically reduced version of this in miniature score format had already appeared on 16 April. Engraved orchestral parts were issued around the same time; the fifty sets produced were available on hire only. They give every indication of having been made directly from the individual copyist's parts used for the early performances, rather than derived from the printed full score; for example, the string parts contain bowings and fingerings that are not to be found in the autograph or score. As a result they contained inaccuracies and inconsistencies from the very start. Finally, Herbert Murrill's reduction for piano duet was put on sale in September 1937. It is notable that neither in these publications nor in the autograph is the symphony described, as it often used to be, as being in B flat minor.

Walton's corrections

The three performances of the first three movements, the premiere, the Birmingham performance, and the recording sessions had given Walton ample opportunity to reconsider and revise any details of the score that he considered to be unsatisfactory. As already mentioned, those changes made before March 1936 had been incorporated into the published score. On 11 August of that year Walton conducted his symphony for the first time with the BBC Symphony Orchestra at a Queen's Hall Promenade Concert. It is highly probable that he used the newly published score and parts for the first time, and thus he would have experienced at first hand what other conductors and players were shortly to find to their cost, namely that the full score contained numerous errors and had been imperfectly proofread, and that there were a number of mistakes in the parts, making it difficult to decide which reading represented the correct text. Internal OUP memoranda between Hubert Foss and his hire librarian show that already by February 1937 complaints were beginning to come in. The librarian prepared a list of corrections and asked for it to be submitted to Walton for comment. In an undated letter to Foss, Walton states: 'I have verified all the corrections in the list, but I cannot help feeling there must be others. I did a whole set of parts for Harty's studio performance last March and if that set could be discovered it would be best to check all virgin parts from that master.' This does not appear to have been done, and when World War II intervened nothing had altered as far as the text of the symphony was concerned other than the further correction of mistakes in the score, many of which derived from the manuscript itself.

The 1951 recording

On 17–19 October 1951 Walton conducted sessions with the Philharmonia Orchestra at HMV's Abbey Road Studios for his only commercial recording of the symphony, which was eventually released in February 1953. He took this opportunity to submit the work to a thorough revision, collating all the old errors and amendments, introducing new changes and refinements and rebalancing certain sections. Despite the modest-sized orchestra that the symphony calls for, Walton and his performers had always been aware of the somewhat relentless quality of its instrumentation, certainly as far as the wind and brass were concerned, and the forthcoming recording provided the ideal opportunity to set matters right in the light of the numerous performances and broadcasts that the work had received.

An internal OUP memo dated 1 October establishes how this revision was handled. Walton personally marked up a set of woodwind, brass, and percussion, and also the front desk copies of the five string sections. These parts were then put out to a copyist who transferred the markings to the remaining desks of each section and to the duplicate wind and brass parts. A memo to the librarian from Alan Frank, the new Head of Music at OUP, states: 'A specially marked set of material is being prepared by Walton for his recording of the work. It should be known as the "Walton set" and used for his performances where he is conducting. Also he asks that it should be used for performances given by the Philharmonia Orchestra (which is doing the recording), even when not conducted by himself.' The resulting set was indeed marked in this way, but unfortunately with time it became broken up and lost. Of the authentic parts marked by Walton himself in his distinctive greenish-blue crayon only the front desk first and second violin parts survive. There are several copies of the parts that were marked up by the copyist, and comparison between these and the first and second violin parts prepared by Walton show that his markings were faithfully transferred. However, most of the surviving parts marked up by hand, prior to their 1980 photographic reproduction, belong to those from remaining sets that were subsequently amended by other copyists, with varying degrees of accuracy.

Further revisions

In retrospect it is clear that a revised printing of the full score should have been undertaken by composer and publisher once the recording had been completed, with the result that the new score and (corrected) printed parts would have been in agreement. As it was, what now resulted was that only Walton's own full score agreed with the newly corrected parts. Other conductors, unaware of Walton's 1951 revision, failed to realize that the changes in the parts had been made by the composer, for no note to that effect appeared on them. Preferring to believe what they regarded as the sacrosanct text of their printed full score they not infrequently ordered their librarians to restore the parts to conform with their (unrevised) score. It is true that an invoice exists from a copyist in June 1953 for work on marking corrections into six full scores, but by then the deadly game had been set in motion: which was correct, the score or the parts? This situation was summed up by a disgruntled letter sent to Alan Frank by Sir Adrian Boult, following his recording of the symphony in August 1956. Sir Adrian had been performing the symphony with distinction (and to Walton's admiration) since 1938, yet the frequent disparity between score and parts was new to him and had wasted a lot of time at the sessions. Matters improved considerably in 1968 when the study score (which since 1946 had replaced the almost illegible miniature score of 1936) came up for reprint. This duly appeared in the spring with the additional designation 'corrected 1968', and enlarged photographic copies of it were made for conductors. The reprint marked a great advance on anything that had existed before in terms of accuracy and agreement with the parts. Nevertheless it still contained many inconsistencies and failed to present the revisions with clarity. It has to be conceded that in the case of the slow movement this was caused by chronic lack of space, as the existing pages were tightly packed at this point.

The 1968 reprint did not put an end to the confused and arbitrary reading of the text. In October 1975 Christopher Morris of OUP was obliged to write in the following terms to the BBC librarian: 'Sir William has written to me to say that the BBC has its own set of parts with markings inspired by Sir Adrian. Sir William says that all these markings should really be included in all our material and in the printed study score when it is reprinted. He says they chiefly concern the slow movement. Would it be possible to borrow your set for a short while to put this operation in hand?' It cannot be said with any certainty whether or not this rather dubious idea was pursued, but it is known that corrections to the study score continued to be made. In 1980 the orchestral parts achieved a stability of sorts when OUP began to have them reproduced photographically. But despite the well-meaning efforts of composer, publisher, and performers to bring some sense of order to a confused situation, the damage had been done: separate parts did not agree with one another (especially in matters of dynamics), and score and parts still showed significant disagreements. A new edition became not merely desirable but a matter of some urgency, and it is hoped that the text of the WWE fulfils this need.

NOTES

1. The original is preserved at the William Walton Museum, Forio, Ischia. The letter was written from Faringdon House, Berkshire, the home of Lord Berners. Edith Olivier was a countrywoman and writer whose home at Wilton near Salisbury was much visited by Rex Whistler, Cecil Beaton, Siegfried Sassoon, and the Sitwell circle. References to her journals are taken from *Edith Olivier: From her Journals, 1924–48*, ed. Penelope Middelboe (London, 1989), or from the unpublished originals preserved in the Wiltshire Record Office, Trowbridge.

2. Part of an illustrated talk called 'Willie: The Young Walton' given by Angus Morrison (1902–89) on 31 January 1984 at the British Library National Sound Archive.

3. Michael Kennedy, *Portrait of Walton* (Oxford, 1989), p. 74. A programme advertisement for the concert of that date, which the LSO was conveniently able to turn into a memorial concert for Elgar (who had died on 23 February), carried the following announcement: 'The Directors of the London Symphony Orchestra regret to inform their subscribers and patrons that WILLIAM WALTON is unable to complete his new symphony in time for this concert. The Directors, therefore, have been reluctantly compelled to alter the programme.'

4. The authenticity of this design has been confirmed by the artist's brother Laurence.

5. A photocopy of the letter, formerly in the possession of Christopher Palmer, is now preserved at the William Walton Museum, Forio, Ischia. The letter was written from Weston Hall, Towcester.

6. For a fuller account of the symphony's composition, see the relevant chapters in Kennedy, *Portrait*, from which all unannotated quotations have been taken.

7. See Lewis Foreman, ed., *From Parry to Britten: British Music in Letters 1900–45* (London 1987), pp. 189–190.

8. This, and all subsequent details relating to publication and corrections, have been taken from OUP files at Oxford.

10

Symphony No. 2 *(Vol. 10)*

David Russell Hulme

Reluctant and perhaps temperamentally disinclined to travel the same road twice, William Walton rarely chose to compose more than one major concert or stage work in any genre. Thus *Belshazzar's Feast* and *Façade* stand alone; *Troilus and Cressida* is his only full-scale opera; there is only one mature string quartet, and no concerto inspired another for the same instrument. It is therefore not surprising that the second of his two symphonies was a long time in appearing and that, when it did appear, it should prove to be a very different work from its predecessor. The first three movements of Walton's First Symphony had been performed on 3 December 1934 and the complete four-movement work was heard for the first time on 6 November the following year. The impact and success of that symphony had a major influence upon the composer's rise in esteem at the time and on his lasting reputation.

Almost twenty years passed before Walton considered writing a second symphony. It seems that sometime in 1953 Alan Frank, Walton's publisher at Oxford University Press, suggested to Ian Hunter, artistic director of the Edinburgh Festival, that the festival might commission a new symphony from Walton.[1] A premiere at the 1956 festival was mooted but, despite the initial enthusiasm of Walton and Hunter, the plan came to nothing.[2] However, it was not long before a more concrete proposal arrived: a commission from the Royal Liverpool Philharmonic Society for a symphony to celebrate the 750th anniversary in 1957 of the royal charter incorporating the Borough of Liverpool. In November 1955 the secretary to the society's general manager wrote to Alan Frank about the rights to the first performance of the new work, and acknowledged Frank's statement that Walton hoped it would take place during the second half of the 1957–8 concert season.[3] This hope was to prove optimistic.

Most of 1956 was occupied with revisions to *Troilus and Cressida* and the composition of the Cello Concerto for Gregor Piatigorsky. When, later in that year, Efrem Kurtz (joint chief conductor of the orchestra) enquired about the second symphony, Walton said he had not started on it. In claiming, too, that he was not even sure that the commission was confirmed, he was probably simply inventing an excuse for lack of progress. Understandably, though, the manager of the Liverpool Society was concerned to learn from Kurtz of Walton's apparent uncertainty. He wrote to Frank saying as much[4] and must have been relieved to receive an assurance by return that the arrangement with Walton was indeed firm. There was one important proviso: the composer insisted 'there should be no time limit'.[5] Walton's commissioning fee of £750 was paid that same month.

Composition

The Liverpool Philharmonic Society's hopes of including the new symphony in its anniversary season were to be disappointed; a serious motor accident disrupted the composer's plans for the first part of 1957. April arrived and work on the Partita, promised to George Szell for the Cleveland Orchestra's 40th anniversary season of 1957–8, had hardly begun. Only after the Partita was finished in late October could Walton 'look a 2nd Symph. in the face!'.[6] In December 1957 Alan Frank could report nothing more to Liverpool than that the composer had begun work. In suggesting the possibility of performance in late November or early December of the following year, the publisher was unrealistically optimistic.[7] On 12 February 1958 Walton wrote to Frank:

> I think for the moment we won't do anything about Symph 2. In fact it is going so badly, that I fear I must start again.[8]

Little progress seems to have been made before the end of the year, as Walton told Frank in a letter written on 17 January 1959:

> The thing is that I have only really settled down to work in the last couple of months having frittered away a lot of time chasing the shadow of the beautiful blonde Mrs Sidney Beer! She was on her back for weeks (but alas, only because she had fractured it!) In fact, a bad workman always blames his tool![9]

Walton was due to arrive in London later in the month. He sent a manuscript of the first movement with this letter, so that Frank could look it over prior to their meeting:

> Meanwhile I've made a fairly fair copy of mov. I which I send you, so that you can tell me the worst when we meet. Actually now that I've got some sort of birds-eye view of it, it may not eventually turn out to be quite as intolerable as I have been suspecting. To me it's [*sic*] great weakness is the 2nd sub (which however can doubtless be improved when scored, which of course also goes for it all) & a certain harmonic monotony as the whole piece turns on the 1st bar almost throughout. There is also no recapitulation, strictly speaking, of the main theme (bar 222). Whether this will appear skimped I find it hard to judge. I do know how to recapitulate if necessary in full but I incline to think it is all right as it is. However we shall see.[10]

Much work remained to be done on the first movement, as clearly what Frank received was not a full score but some form of sketch or short score.

A proposal that the work's premiere might be given by the Royal Liverpool Philharmonic Orchestra not in its home city but at the 1960 Edinburgh Festival met with the composer's approval and seems to have helped restore lost momentum. In mid-July 1959 a full score of the first movement arrived at OUP.[11] However, the symphony was not the only major work occupying Walton's thoughts that year. He was seriously considering a piano concerto for his friend Louis Kentner but this came to nothing. 'So many notes,' he told Alan Frank.[12]

Hardly had the symphony's first movement reached a reasonably finished state than Walton decided that he wanted to rewrite it. His ideas for the shape of the rest of the symphony were also to change considerably. In July 1959 he wrote about following the first movement with a scherzo,[13] but in November he was still undecided:

> Symphony 2 will be I think in three movs., maybe two—the second being slow–scherzo–slow–finale all in one mov.—but maybe that will be too much to swallow and I will separate the finale.[14]

The conductor George Szell had become an enthusiastic champion of Walton's music—the commissioning of the *Partita* for the Cleveland Orchestra's anniversary was his idea. In turn, Walton admired Szell's performances of his music and was keen that he should give the American premiere of the new symphony. A photocopy of the first movement was sent to Szell in December 1959 with a note making it clear that it was to be revised. Walton, impatient for a reply, became despondent when none arrived. He wrote to Frank on 17 January 1960:

> Please don't mention perfs of Symph 2 at the moment. It fair gives me the 'willies' as it seems to get remoter & remoter. In fact I'm feeling extremely low about it. I think Szell would have replied by now if he felt any enthusiasm for mov. I. He did when I sent him only mov. I of Partita.
>   I suffer from nightmares of irate mayors & corporations!
>   Cheer up—I'll do my damndest—but—[15]

Szell had simply been busy. When he did write on 28 January 1960, however, it was with reservations about what he had seen. His response to Alan Frank was tactful:

> This movement strikes me rather as the movement of a suite or, say, a sinfonietta… Perhaps I have too set ideas about the weight, type and posture of thematic material I expect of a first symphony movement…I don't want to appear discouraging…it is quite possible that this first movement in the context of and in balance with the other movements of the work will assume a significance different from that of the traditional first symphony movement.[16]

Frank passed on a diplomatic précis of Szell's letter to the composer.

However, progress did not depend upon a favourable response from Szell. The dates in the autograph manuscript show that the score of the second movement was begun in January, before Walton had received the conductor's comments. What is more, if he had read them by the time he began his revision of the first movement in February, they do not seem to have influenced it in any way. The earlier full score survives and comparison with the final autograph full score reveals extensive differences in the orchestration. Otherwise both versions are substantially the same.

The second movement was completed in February and the first movement followed in March. On 7 March Walton wrote to Alan Frank:

> I will send you a crumb very shortly—in fact I could send you the 2nd mov now, but I'm waiting to show it to Hans [Werner Henze] who's coming for the weekend. All I can say about it is that it is very slow & very long—getting on for 10mins. It demands a Scherzo (very short about 3 mins) which is on the way out of its shell. The last mov. I think will be a Passacaglia. It may have a 'cereal' in it because up to now there's not a

cereal in the sc[ore]—not a 'Port-Toasted' or even Quaker Oats (& the wild ones seem to have been sown long ago).[17]

Walton and Henze had met in 1953 at W. H. Auden's house on Ischia and a friendship developed. Soon afterwards, Henze came to live on the island. According to Walton, Henze was 'quite enthusiastic' about both movements[18] and was 'not at all sure that a Scherzo is needed'.[19] Walton felt that once he had completed the last movement—'a Chaconne...it may be easier to judge if a scherzo is needed or not'.[20] In the event he decided in favour of a three-movement form without a scherzo—surprising, perhaps, in view of his established prowess in this form.

After receiving the full scores of the first two movements, Frank wrote to Walton with his comments. The composer's reply contains interesting insights into his struggles with the first movement, which ultimately was less extensively revised than he had previously considered necessary:

> As to [movement] I, I've gone back to what it was, more or less originally. The first scored version was a bit truncated & gave me the feeling of being so. However I stuck to the foreshortened recapitulation which I feel, works, as well as making it more interesting formally speaking. That is more or less all I've done to it except for getting rid of the brushwood in the scoring & generally gingering it up a bit....
>
> [Movement] III is getting on. It has its points & I'm not being too pedantic with working it out serially! But I'm beginning to see that there is something after all to be said for that method, even if in the end it works back to old tonic and dominant![21]

The passacaglia theme of the third movement is a twelve-note series that receives a certain amount of formal serial treatment. However, the composer played down the serial element and was anxious to avoid too much attention being drawn to it. When Alan Frank came to prepare his programme note for the work's first performance, Walton wrote to him:

> All I ask both you and Felix [Aprahamian] is to avoid the words 12, atonal & serialism! We will see if anyone notices what slight use of those methods has been made.[22]

After presentation of the passacaglia theme, the finale continues with ten variations followed by a fugato and coda. The incomplete movement sent to Frank in June lacked the two final sections.

A visit to Gian Carlo Menotti's Spoleto Festival the same month for a performance of Henze's opera *Der Prinz von Homburg* distracted Walton. It was not until the end of July that the fugato and coda were finished and despatched. The composer's manuscript records the date of completion as 22 July 1960. Writing to Frank about the recently airmailed score, Walton had this to say:

> The Fugato & Coda are effective enough, but I am conscious (perhaps too much so) that there is more than a slight likeness (rhythmically speaking) between them & the 2nd fugal episode of the last mov of Symph I also a smattering of the Scherzo, not to mention the tutti in the 1st mov of the Vln Con. & the Interlude in T&C [*Troilus and Cressida*]. In fact that kind of 6/8 is more than a mannerism—it's a vice which must be checked in the future! However there it is, it's too late now to do 'owt about it.[23]

In another letter Walton pointed out that his metronome had broken and the markings 'may very well be out'.[24] If they were, Walton never revised them beyond the single change noted in his personal copy of the published score.

Rehearsals for the premiere, and the performance itself, threw up errors in the performing material and also suggested some revisions to the scoring. Walton was receptive to conductor John Pritchard's ideas for improvements and adopted some of them—notably the change to staccato articulation for oboes in bars 175 to 180 of the third movement where the composer had written legato slurring.[25]

Soon after the appearance of the Second Symphony, George Szell approached Walton to write a third. The composer occasionally referred to spasmodic progress on this third symphony, which after Szell's death in 1970 was promised, and even dedicated, to André Previn. However, the project was eventually abandoned. The Second Symphony proved to be the composer's penultimate extended orchestral work for the concert hall, followed only by the Variations on a Theme by Hindemith of 1963.

Performance

The Liverpool Philharmonic Society's orchestra, the Royal Liverpool Philharmonic, was to give the first performance, conducted by its musical director, John Pritchard, at the opening concert of the 14th Edinburgh International Festival in 1960. Preliminary rehearsals were held at the excellent Philharmonic Hall in Liverpool, but final rehearsals in a school hall in Edinburgh proved problematic. The acoustic was poor and Pritchard could not obtain a satisfactory balance.[26] This must have frustrated the composer, unable, in such a situation, to gain a true impression of what he had written.

The premiere took place at the Usher Hall on 2 September 1960. It was relayed by the BBC and recorded for its transcription service. The programme also included the Berg Violin Concerto (a work based on a twelve-note series that, like Walton's serial passacaglia theme, commences with triadic intervals). A new symphony by a leading British composer was a major event. There was even a small exhibition relating to the work mounted in the city by Messrs Rae, Macintosh and Co., at 39 George Street. Expectations were high, sharpened by everyone's awareness of the huge achievement of the First Symphony.

Walton always considered that making comparisons between his two symphonies was unfair and meaningless because they were so very different from each other. Inevitably, though, comparisons were made—and generally these were not favourable to the new work. Some press reviews suggested that, one way or another, the composer had been 'marking time'[27] and that he had not progressed significantly since the First Symphony. In *The Observer* Peter Heyworth expressed a view of the new work that others shared. He found it

> a more adroit affair than its rather overrated predecessor, but it never gives the impression of any extension or deepening of musical language, such as a composer arrives at . . . simply in the creative struggle to pin down an inner concept of the imagination . . . There leaps from almost any bar an intense sense of character, compounded of an odd assortment of jauntiness, irony and an underlying melancholy. A creative artist often reflects

the society that gives him birth, and who are we to object if Sir William, like most of us, prefers to look backward provided that he does it in his own way.[28]

There is a hint here of a misunderstanding, of a failure to connect with the symphony's elusive inner core, that many have experienced on first acquaintance. The 'problem' of the Second Symphony, for those who find one, is summed up by Walton's most perceptive biographer, Michael Kennedy:

> The truth is that the Second Symphony is curiously reluctant to yield its secrets and inner meanings through a few hearings. Not that it is difficult music, but it does need concentrated and frequent listenings before, suddenly, the veils part and one is admitted to the inner circle of its highly distinctive sound-world.[29]

Walton was distraught at the mixed reception afforded to the new symphony. It took a trip to New York and a performance under George Szell to restore his confidence in the work. Szell had given the American premiere of the Second Symphony with the Cleveland Orchestra in its home city in January 1961. Afterwards he wrote to Walton: 'The symphony has just been performed here very well indeed and with great success.'[30] He also sent news that a recording was soon to follow. 'What a pal!' was Walton's grateful response.[31] The symphony was given again by the same performers in New York the following month, when Walton was at Carnegie Hall in person. He thought the performance superb and, in Michael Kennedy's words, 'vindicated a work he himself regarded as better than his First Symphony'.[32]

Despite its less than rapturous reception, interest in Walton's new symphony was nevertheless healthy. A note in the OUP Archive lists 24 performances up to 2 June 1961, including those under Bernard Heinze in Melbourne, Australia, and Leopold Stokowski with the London Symphony Orchestra in Vienna. The composer conducted his Second Symphony for the first time on 20 September 1960 in Liverpool. In 1963 a radio recording of the work by the Orchestra Sinfonica RAI of Rome under Massimo Freccia won second prize in a UNESCO competition to celebrate the 150th anniversary of the Gesellschaft der Musikfreunde in Vienna.

Publication

Work on the production of a full score and manuscript orchestral parts began before the symphony had been completed. Copyists' invoices in the OUP Archive suggest that the parts were in hand before May 1960. They were copied onto dyeline transfer sheets from a photographic copy of Walton's holograph full score. The published full score was also originated from a photocopy of the manuscript.

Several proof copies of the full score were produced prior to publication. Recipients of these included the conductors John Pritchard, Sir Malcolm Sargent, and Charles Mackerras. Pritchard used a large-format proof score for the first performance that has not been traced. Sargent's copy is to be found in his bequest to the library of the Royal College of Music, and another copy (marked 'A') is preserved in the OUP hire library. Possibly the others were destroyed by the publisher when they were superseded by the amended text approved for publication.

The score, printed by Halstan and Co., was published by OUP on 1 December 1960 in large study-score format. It carried a dedication to the Royal Liverpool Philharmonic Society and included details of the first performance. Parts were available on hire only from the publisher, who also provided large-format full scores with the material.

After Szell's death, Walton decided to commemorate the artist whom he considered to be the finest interpreter of his Second Symphony by re-dedicating the work. A new title page for the full score replaced the original in OUP's remaining stock in mid-1972. It reads as follows: 'Commissioned by the Royal Liverpool Philharmonic Society and re-dedicated to the memory of George Szell'. In 1975 Halstan undertook a second printing of the score. Further reprints followed in 1987 and 1995.

Revisions and corrections

The rehearsals and early performances of the symphony revealed errors and inconsistencies in the full score and parts. Alterations were made to the master transparencies of the parts and replacement copies were run off as necessary. Evidently, though, not all identified errors were corrected. No doubt it was intended that only the latest revised states would be sent out from the OUP hire library. However, because these were not identified as such on the material, old superseded copies sometimes found their way into performing sets. Similarly, alterations were made to the proof copies of the full score before publication, and discrepancies crept in between this and the parts as corrections and amendments were sent to the copyists and engravers.

Conductors, including Sir Adrian Boult and Maurice Miles, wrote to OUP about specific problems in the performing material.[33] Assurances were given that corrections would be made when it was reprinted.[34] Although it was relatively easy to alter the parts and make new copies, the published full score would have to wait until stock levels prompted another print run. Possibly hire copies in the OUP library were amended by hand in the meantime, but none survives to tell us one way or the other. When the full score was eventually reprinted, no alterations appear to have been made to the musical text.

As late as 1975, Walton was thinking about alterations to the challenging fugato variation of the third movement (bars 166 ff.). On 18 January he wrote to Piatigorsky:

> You might get Zubin [Mehta] to take it [Symphony No. 2] up! If he would, I would modify the unnecessarily difficult passage between [bars] 166 and 227 which I suspect hampers the piece from being done more often.[35]

If, as seems likely, he had simplification of the bowing in mind, he must have forgotten the alternative already suggested in the revised parts.

Recording

EMI had planned to make a recording of the Second Symphony immediately after the Edinburgh premiere. When critical response proved lukewarm, they postponed indefinitely, offering the excuse that they wished to wait until the work became better known.[36] However, disappointment must have evaporated for Walton when Columbia

Records scheduled a recording by the Cleveland Orchestra under Szell. The recording was made at Severance Hall, Cleveland, Ohio, on 24 March 1961[37] but, surprisingly, Walton did not hear it until May of the following year. The day the disc arrived he played it several times and then wrote immediately to Szell:

> Words fail me! It is a quite fantastic & stupendous performance from every point of view. Firstly it is absolutely right musically speaking & the virtuosity of the performance is quite staggering, especially the Fugato; but everything is phrased & balanced in an unbelievable way, for which I must congratulate you and your magnificent orchestra.
>
> I can only sink into banality & say that I thank you really & truly from the bottom of my heart, & for once this is not an empty phrase.[38]

The release in the USA, on Columbia's Epic label,[39] had been delayed until March 1962, partly because of Columbia's changing marketing policy that was also to play a part in holding up its issue in Britain until September 1962.[40]

Walton recorded many of his works, including the First Symphony. Unfortunately he made no recording of the Second Symphony; neither is there any known recording (official or unofficial) of a performance or broadcast under him.

NOTES

1. See subsequent letter from Alan Frank to Walton, 8 December 1953, OUP Archive, Oxford.
2. Frank to Walton, 8 December 1953.
3. Letter from Wilfred Stiff to Alan Frank, 24 November 1955, OUP Archive.
4. Letter from Gerald McDonald to Alan Frank, 5 November 1956, relating to a conversation between Walton and Efrem Kurtz, OUP Archive.
5. Letter from Alan Frank to Gerald McDonald, 6 November 1956, OUP Archive. In the notes he made to help Alan Frank prepare the programme note for the first performance (undated, OUP Archive) Walton wrote: 'Though commissioned by Liverpool the work has nothing to do with the history of that august city, in fact I've no idea what the music is supposed to be about. No composer does unless he is a Strauss!'
6. Letter from Walton to Alan Frank, 21 October 1957, OUP Archive.
7. Letter from Alan Frank to Gerald McDonald, 30 December 1957, OUP Archive.
8. Letter from Walton to Alan Frank, OUP Archive. This and the other letters from Walton are quoted in *The Selected Letters of William Walton*, ed. Malcolm Hayes (London, 2002).
9. OUP Archive.
10. Letter from Walton to Alan Frank, 17 January 1959, OUP Archive.
11. Letter from Alan Frank to Walton, 16 July 1959, OUP Archive.
12. Quoted in Michael Kennedy, *Portrait of Walton* (Oxford, 1989, rev. edn, 1990), p. 210.
13. Letter from Walton to Alan Frank, 24 July 1959, OUP Archive.
14. Typed transcription of part of a letter of 17 November [1959] from Walton (recipient not recorded but probably Alan Frank), OUP Archive.
15. OUP Archive.
16. Letter from George Szell to Alan Frank, 28 January 1960.
17. OUP Archive.
18. Letter from Walton to Alan Frank, 27 March 1960, OUP Archive.
19. Letter from Walton to Alan Frank, 31 March 1960, OUP Archive.
20. Walton to Frank, 31 March 1960.

21. Letter from Walton to Alan Frank, 16 April 1960, OUP Archive.

22. Walton's notes to help Alan Frank prepare the programme notes for the first performance (undated, OUP Archive).

23. Letter from Walton to Alan Frank, 28 July 1960, OUP Archive.

24. Letter from Walton to Alan Frank, 29 July 1960, OUP Archive.

25. Letter from John Pritchard to Walton, 11 October 1960, OUP Archive.

26. Kennedy, *Portrait*, p. 211.

27. Unattributed quotation in Kennedy, *Portrait*, p. 214.

28. Quoted in Kennedy, *Portrait*, p. 214.

29. Kennedy, *Portrait*, pp. 211–212.

30. Quoted by Walton in a letter to Alan Frank, 10 January 1961, OUP Archive.

31. Letter from Walton to Frank, 10 January 1961.

32. Kennedy, *Portrait*, p. 214.

33. Postcard from Sir Adrian Boult to Alan Frank, undated (postmarked 21 February 1962); letter from Boult to Alan Frank, 10 December 1961; letter from Maurice Miles to Christopher Morris, 27 April 1961, OUP Archive.

34. Letter from Alan Frank to Sir Adrian Boult, 16 January 1962, OUP Archive; letter from Alan Frank to Maurice Miles, 13 June 1961, OUP Archive: 'We agree with all your suggestions and have made a note of them.'

35. Letter from Walton to Gregor Piatigorsky, 18 January 1975.

36. Susana Walton, *Behind the Façade* (Oxford, 1988), p. 156.

37. Martin Rutherford, *William Walton: A Data Base Discography* (Melbourne, 2004), p. 97.

38. Letter from Walton to George Szell, 11 May 1962; photocopy at OUP Archive. The original is displayed in the music library of the Cleveland Orchestra.

39. Epic: RLP347.

40. Columbia: 33CX 1816.

11

Sinfonia Concertante (*Vol. 13*)

Lionel Friend

Walton's first large-scale orchestral work was a product of his early twenties. As will be seen, the genesis of the Sinfonia Concertante was unusual and the result was a work that, despite its undoubted effectiveness, did not fit into any clear category as a concert item and was consequently not easy to programme. Walton clearly had a soft spot for it and found its neglect, after an initial flurry of performances at home and abroad, distressing. During World War II, which he spent mostly in the seclusion of Northamptonshire, he found that he had considerable time on his hands, and while he was revising the Violin Concerto he also undertook a recasting and reorchestration of the Sinfonia Concertante. His principal intention was to make it more economical for promoters by obviating the need for a concert soloist. However, Walton never withdrew the original version which, it would seem, he later secretly preferred, though he and his publisher extolled the merits of the more practical revised version.

Composition

Before the completion of his Sinfonia Concertante in 1927 Walton had produced three scores for orchestra. One had been an arrangement of existing material, the First Suite for Orchestra from *Façade*; one was for chamber orchestra, *Siesta*; and the third was a brilliantly characteristic overture, *Portsmouth Point*. The fourth, Sinfonia Concertante, was his first orchestral composition involving a solo instrument; the choice of title was defended by one reviewer of the first performance who wrote, '*Sinfonia* is right, and *Concertante* is right; if it be wrong to use Italian words, let the objector supply the English.'[1] The three subsequent concertos (for viola, 1929; violin, 1939; cello, 1956) were each written expressly for acknowledged virtuosi, and are more traditional in concept than this unusually conceived work, which had its origins in music planned as a ballet score for Diaghilev. The pianist Angus Morrison, who was a friend and close neighbour of Walton at the time, left a vivid account of how this came about, and it deserves to be quoted at length:

> The same year [1926] also saw the composition (in short score only) of three disconnected pieces which finally became in 1927 the *Sinfonia Concertante* for orchestra with piano. It is not one of Willie's best works, and the movements do not really hang together all that well. But its history is interesting, and I feel I must tell it, if only to refute another legend—the legend that what I am about to relate never took place—when in fact I was present and it happened in my house!

I must start by explaining that in 1926 Constant Lambert, while still a student, received a lot of notoriety through being the first English composer to have a ballet score chosen by Diaghilev for his company.[2] Willie was always extremely jealous of other people's successes—an unusual form of jealousy in that he was not jealous of the *person* who had the success, Constant remained one of his closest and most dearly loved friends right up to his untimely death in 1951—but just of the success itself and the conviction that, given the chance, he could always go one better.

Osbert and Sachie [Sitwell] were friends of Diaghilev of many years standing, and Diaghilev must have been fully aware of their great prestige in both the artistic and social life of London at that time. They felt naturally that if an unknown student could be chosen as the composer of Diaghilev's first English ballet, there was no reason on earth why, with their influence and artistic backing, Willie should not be chosen as the composer for the second.[3] Anyhow, with this in mind Willie had spent the winter in Amalfi composing these three pieces—'Traveller's Samples' as one or two of their more malicious friends called them—and it was felt that if only Diaghilev could hear them the desired result would follow automatically. Elaborate plans were laid. A wonderful luncheon party was laid on at Carlyle Square [where Walton lived in the Sitwells' house] for Diaghilev and his entourage which consisted of Boris Kochno, whom Constant always called the *éminence grise* of the Ballet, Lifar, Henri Sauguet, Georges Auric and one or two others whose identity now escapes me. Finally they all trooped over to 9 Oakley Street where I was then living, only a stone's throw away, to listen to Willie and me playing the three movements on my two pianos. Everything went according to plan except in one very important particular: Diaghilev listened very attentively, said a number of very polite and charming things, BUT the fish did not rise and the bait was not taken! ... I think it was at Constant's suggestion that Willie finally turned these three pieces into the *Sinfonia Concertante*.[4]

Performance

The minutes of the council of the Royal Philharmonic Society suggest that it was the distinguished Swiss conductor Ernest Ansermet who, in June 1927, proposed that Walton's Sinfonia Concertante be included in his forthcoming concert for the society on 5 January 1928 at Queen's Hall in London. Ansermet had known Osbert and Sacheverell Sitwell since the early years of the decade due to his close connection with Diaghilev's Ballets Russes, and at that time had even given the young Walton a few conducting lessons. Perhaps some pressure from the Sitwells was brought to bear, though the council agreed to Ansermet's proposal only after examining the manuscript score.[5] It was by far the most imposing London launch so far of one of Walton's works. The pianist was a fellow composer, York Bowen (1884–1961), and the work was broadcast on nine of the BBC's new radio stations. The composer was not happy with the performance, as can be clearly seen from a letter he wrote four days later to his friend Christabel McLaren: 'I hope you didn't listen-in on Thursday [i.e. to the broadcast], the performance was bloody, though the applause tumultuous. The work was terribly underrehearsed, in fact the players just about knew the notes and that was all. There were only two rehearsals for such an enormous programme,[6] and I doubt if more than an hour and a half was given to my work which needs very careful playing. However, it went down very well…'[7]

Press reviews were mainly positive. The *Musical Times* reviewer clearly approved of the composer's advance over earlier efforts: 'Out of it all emerged a young personality that had more in its manner than grimacing and flourishing.'[8] Much the same point was made by Richard Capell (R.C.) in his review for the *Monthly Musical Record*: 'The novelty of the concert was entertaining and a work of promise—a Sinfonia Concertante by Mr. William Walton, a young musician of the vanguard. The first movement, with a great jostling of ideas, struck one as patchy, but the slow movement was beautiful and a true achievement. The colouring of the whole was bright to the point of gaudiness. Mr. Walton speaks for the new cheerfulness in music, but his is a saner, less brutal cheerfulness than that of some other members of the modern circus school.'[9] The anonymous *Times* critic (from his biography of the composer it would appear that this was Frank Howes) noted: 'The *Symphonie* [sic] *Concertante* for pianoforte and orchestra by William Walton, which was played for the first time, provided the greatest possible contrast [it followed Schubert's 'Unfinished' Symphony]. Here everything was brilliant and restless, not with the uneasy undertone of Schubert, but with the more superficial glitter of bright instrumentation or the harsh clash of dissonances. The work is in three movements, and, apart from certain faults, is the most promising thing the composer has done.'[10] The 'faults' were then described, including a reference to the supposed influence of Elgar. In his later book, Howes was rather more enthusiastic, particularly about the slow movement: 'In it,' he wrote, 'appears for the first time in a mature expression, the composer's streak of deeply romantic feeling, hitherto buried under smart and brilliant dialogue but destined to emerge even more fully developed into the light in the Viola Concerto.'[11]

Sinfonia Concertante was soon given a second British performance on 12 April 1928 at the Bournemouth Festival under Dan Godfrey, with Gordon Bryan as pianist. Its first American performance had been given already on 2 March 1928 by the Boston Symphony Orchestra under Serge Koussevitsky, who had premiered *Portsmouth Point* there sixteen months previously. On 10 March it was repeated in New York.

The two versions

Angus Morrison's account of the origins of Walton's musical inspiration as a potential Diaghilev commission goes a long way to explain the Sinfonia Concertante's rather uncharacteristic qualities. Hugh Ottoway has described the music as a blend of neo-classical and neo-Romantic elements;[12] Neil Tierney finds in it a satirical gaiety, resembling Stravinsky—'definitely antiromantic';[13] while in his *Portrait of Walton* Michael Kennedy considers the influences to be not so much Stravinsky as 'the Russians like Borodin and Rimsky-Korsakov, the Poulenc of *Les Biches* [written for Diaghilev in 1924], and, most prominently, Ravel; for many clues to Walton's orchestration at this period, listen to *Alborado del gracioso*'.[14] Diaghilev's musical taste at the time was for a clean, somewhat dry style that Lambert clearly understood and shared—witness his ballet *Romeo and Juliet* that the impresario had accepted for production. In the earliest surviving autograph of Sinfonia Concertante

Walton's orchestra is relatively modest, in keeping with the prevalent neo-classical sonority, but the forces became gradually larger up to the publication of the first edition. Ironically, when he undertook a revision of the work in 1943, Walton felt the need to reduce again.

It is clear that Walton never intended the solo piano to challenge the orchestra in the manner of the typical 'romantic' concerto; indeed the 1943 revision shows that it was possible to interchange many phrases between piano and orchestra without doing any harm to the musical substance. The earliest surviving autograph rather belittles the pianist's contribution by describing the work as 'SINFONIA CONCERTANTE for Orchestra with PIANOFORTE (CONTINUO)', although a later one designates it as being 'for ORCHESTRA with PIANOFORTE (quasi obbligato)'. For the first edition the chosen description was simply 'for orchestra with piano'; for the final 1943 revision it became 'for orchestra with piano obbligato'. The original solo part is, nevertheless, not easy to play, and one of Walton's aims in revising the work was to make it simpler. On 23 December 1943 he wrote to Roy Douglas, 'It is also true that I've re-vivified the Sin. Con. chiefly by eliminating [!] the Pfte. & making it easy enough even for Harriet Cohen to play.'[15] Two weeks later, and less than five weeks before the performance, while asking Walter Legge to forward the piano part to Cyril Smith, he added, 'He has no need to memorise it—in fact—I['d] sooner he didn't so as to try & emphasise the point that the Pfte is not really any more important than any other instrument in the orch.'[16] Later, on 10 June 1968, in a further explanation addressed to his publisher Alan Frank, he recalled, 'The revision of S.C. was largely on practical grounds—a smaller orchestra[17] & a much less complicated Pfte. part (perhaps now too easy) so that it could be played by the pianist attached to the orchestra, without having to obtain the services of a virtuoso.'[18]

Walton, while paring down the orchestral forces and relaxing the virtuosity of the piano part, took the opportunity to rethink some passages compositionally, always with the aim of greater clarity in the musical presentation. The rather frequent changes of time signature were reduced; and although there are moments that were tightened up, the overall trend was to expand. A longer breathing space was given between sections: compare, for example, fig. 17 (original version) with the corresponding fig. 16 (revised version); or the 14 beats leading from fig. 21 to fig. 22 in the first edition which were expanded to 31 beats in 1943 (figs. 20–21). The contrapuntal texture was simplified, perhaps most notably at fig. 20 (original version) in the opening movement, where the violin material is simultaneously augmented by the third and fourth horns with the tuba; at the same time the piano theme is augmented by the contrabassoon, trombones, cellos, and double basses. In the 1943 version of this section (fig. 19) both augmented voices were eliminated; the piano idea is now played in the bass, leaving the pianist to supply block harmonies. It was perhaps a regret for the richness of such passages that made Walton tell Stewart Craggs ten years later that the original version was 'better and more interesting', adding that he thought that the new version 'rather falls between two stools, not difficult enough to interest a pianist nor spectacular enough for a conductor'.[19]

The premiere of the revised version was given in Liverpool on 9 February 1944 with the Liverpool Philharmonic Orchestra and Cyril Smith under Malcolm Sargent.

Publication and recording

Walton seems to have had trouble from the beginning in orchestrating the Sinfonia Concertante to his satisfaction: the two surviving autographs that predate the first edition differ in many salient features from what in the WWE edition is called the 'original version', as engraved by Oxford University Press in 1928. The later of these two autograph scores is of particular interest as it contains a number of pencil jottings showing the composer trying out further instrumental ideas, such as the suggestion that the horn group be expanded from two to four. These experiments came to fruition: the engraved full score does indeed call for four horns, and these were retained in the 1943 revision. In addition, this autograph score contains a number of conductor's markings, and it is clear that Ernest Ansermet used it when he conducted the first performance in January 1928. Edwin Evans's analytical notes ('based on material kindly supplied by the composer') included in the programme book contain instrumental descriptions and music examples which correspond to this manuscript version but not to the one subsequently engraved. Thus it is clear that Walton undertook a thorough overhaul of the orchestration between the premiere and the engraving. Unfortunately, as with *Portsmouth Point*, the autograph used by the engraver has been lost.

When the engraved full score and arrangement for two pianos appeared in 1928, each movement was headed by a dedication to a member of the Sitwell family (I, 'To Osbert'; II, 'To Edith'; III, 'To Sachie'). At that time Walton was living with Osbert and Sacheverell at their house in Carlyle Square, Chelsea. This, and his spectacular success with the 'entertainment' called *Façade*—settings of Edith's verse—made him virtually one of the family. However, by the time he came to make his revised version fifteen years later, the ties of affection had slackened considerably and the dedications were now omitted from the published score.

The revised version was first published by OUP in 1947 in the form of a new two-piano arrangement by Roy Douglas that corresponded to the 1943 revision. The orchestral score followed in 1953. Both publications omitted the metronome marks from the 1927 version.

Phyllis Sellick was the pianist with Malcolm Sargent and the Liverpool Philharmonic on a tour of southern England for war workers just three months after her husband, Cyril Smith, had taken part in the first performance of the Sinfonia Concertante in February 1944. It was she who was chosen for the first recording in August of the following year with the composer conducting the City of Birmingham Symphony Orchestra. In April 1970 Walton conducted the London Symphony Orchestra in a second recording of the revised version, with Peter Katin as soloist. In 1989 and 1996 it was recorded twice more, now in its original version.

NOTES

1. *Musical Times* (1 February 1928), p. 165.
2. Lambert's *Romeo and Juliet* was first performed by Diaghilev's Ballets Russes at Monte Carlo on 4 May 1926.
3. It would in fact have been the third, because Diaghilev presented *The Triumph of Neptune* by Lord Berners at the Lyceum Theatre, London, on 3 December 1926. It was during the orchestral

interlude in this performance that Walton first conducted movements from his new [First] Suite for Orchestra from *Façade*.

4. Angus Morrison: 'Willie: The Young Walton and his Four Masterpieces', *RCM Magazine* (autumn, 1984), vol. 80, no. 3, pp. 122–123.

5. The minutes of the Royal Philharmonic Society, British Library, RPS MS 292 (formerly Loan 48.2/14).

6. The programme was Beethoven: Overture: *Leonore* No. 1; Schubert: Symphony No. 8 (Unfinished); Walton: Sinfonia Concertante; and, after the interval, Ravel: *Daphnis et Chloë*, the first concert performance in Britain of the complete work.

7. *The Selected Letters of William Walton*, ed. Malcolm Hayes (London, 2002), p. 43.

8. *Musical Times* (1 February 1928), p. 165.

9. *Monthly Musical Record* (1 February 1928), p. 43.

10. *The Times* (6 January 1928), p. 6.

11. Frank Howes, *The Music of William Walton* (Oxford, 1965) p. 71.

12. *The New Grove Dictionary of Music and Musicians*, ed. Stanley Sadie (London, 1980), vol. 20, p. 197.

13. Neil Tierney, *William Walton: His Life and Music* (London, 1984), p. 191.

14. Michael Kennedy, *Portrait of Walton* (Oxford, 1989), p. 45.

15. OUP Archive, Oxford.

16. *Selected Letters*, ed. Hayes, p. 149.

17. Walton reduced the orchestra by four players, subsuming the cor anglais into the second oboe part and managing altogether without the bass clarinet, contrabassoon, and third trumpet. The percussion is used more sparingly in the 1943 version, in spite of the addition of timpani to the slow movement and the telling use of a glockenspiel in the last. Another addition was that of the tuba to the final tutti of the second movement.

18. OUP Archive. The letter continued: 'Artur Rubinstein however, to whom I showed it first (1st version) was very partial to the slow movement, and if I ever see him now he whistles it to me!' It is not known whether Rubinstein ever performed the work.

19. OUP Archive.

12

Concerto for Viola and Orchestra *(Vol. 12)*

Christopher Wellington

Considering the major effect it was to have in alerting both critics and public to the true stature of William Walton as a composer, the Concerto for Viola and Orchestra had a very uncertain start in life. A perceptive suggestion from Sir Thomas Beecham that he might compose something for the great viola player Lionel Tertis encouraged the 26-year-old Walton to start working on a concerto during his annual visit to Amalfi with Osbert Sitwell in the winter of 1928. What was it, we may wonder, about the overture *Portsmouth Point* (1925), *Siesta* (1926), or the Sinfonia Concertante for Orchestra with Piano (1927) that caused Beecham to mention a concerto for Tertis to the young composer?

In the twenty-first century we are perhaps already too remote in time to realize the standing and reputation of Lionel Tertis (1876–1975) in his prime, but we can learn something from Arnold Bax's appreciation of him, written seven years before the Viola Concerto came into being:

> The technical and emotional capabilities of the viola have been developed in Mr. Tertis's hands to a point undreamed of, as I believe, before his time. [He] has extended its possibilities until it has been proved capable of almost all the nuances of the other strings besides that peculiar acrid poignancy which this great artist derives from the higher register of the A string and which no other medium known to me can produce. It must have been in my student days that a prominent British composer remarked to me 'Surely Tertis's viola playing is the best performance on any instrument to be heard in this country'. Time has only justified and solidified this judgement.[1]

In 1964 Tertis was awarded the coveted Gold Medal of the Royal Philharmonic Society, thus achieving a unique confirmation of his eminence; he had progressed from self-taught beginnings through orchestral ranks to ultimate acceptance as a true viola soloist.

A concerto for the viola was a real rarity in the early twentieth century. In his auto-biography Tertis wrote, 'When I first began to play the viola as a solo instrument, prejudice and storms of abuse were my lot. The consensus of opinion then was that the viola had no right to be heard in solos…as a student at the RAM [I played] the Mendelssohn and Wieniawski D minor concertos (of course a fifth lower but exactly as written for the violin) at two of the fortnightly students' concerts there.'[2] Almost the only acceptable major work for viola with orchestra was Berlioz's *Harold in Italy* (1834). When Fritz Kreisler invited Tertis to play Mozart's Sinfonia Concertante, K364, with him in a 1924 recital (with piano!) at the Royal Albert Hall the work was regarded as a comparative novelty by the London press. Earlier works, like the concertos by Telemann, Stamitz, and Rolla, had yet to be rediscovered. In Britain the early 1900s saw the creation of viola concertos by Cecil Forsyth, J. B. McEwen, and York Bowen, but most of the works for the instrument from this period that have survived in the repertory bear less ambitious titles like Benjamin Dale's Suite, Op. 2, Arnold Bax's extended single-movement *Phantasy*, and Vaughan Williams's *Flos Campi*.

Composition

The progress of the concerto's composition is fitfully chronicled in Walton's letters from Amalfi to his friend and financial supporter, the poet Siegfried Sassoon.[3] On 5 December 1928 he wrote, 'I have been working hard at a Viola Concerto suggested by Beecham and designed for Lionel Tertis'; by 2 February of the following year he was able to report, 'I finished yesterday the second movement of my Viola Concerto. At the moment, I think it will be my best work, better than the "Sinfonia" [Concertante], if only the third and last movement works out well—at present I am in the painful position of starting it, which is always full of trials and disappointments, however I hope to be well away with it in a day or two'. On 12 February Walton could confirm, 'Otherwise I've no news, except that I have started on the third movement and hope to complete it soon.'

The pianist Angus Morrison, who lived very near Walton at this time, received a letter from Amalfi referring to the Viola Concerto which stated, 'My style is changing—it is becoming more melodious and mature.'[4] In a memoir as part of a BBC radio programme Morrison also recalled, 'When very soon after he returned to London the following spring he came and played it to me I realised the true significance of the remark. In this work he had in fact reached complete maturity of style and given full rein for the first time to his entirely personal lyrical gift. To my astonished ears it seemed to me, in spite of his woefully inadequate piano playing, a masterpiece in the real sense of the word.'[5]

Walton acknowledged two influences on the composition of his Viola Concerto: first, Paul Hindemith's *Kammermusik Nr.* 5, for viola and large chamber orchestra (1927); and second, Prokofiev, whose First Violin Concerto (1916–17) shows a similar scheme of movements and the device of returning to the opening material in the closing pages.[6]

When Walton returned to London in the spring of 1929 he sent the completed work to Lionel Tertis who, according to the composer, rejected it by return of post without explanation. This is how Tertis recalled the incident:

> One work of which I did *not* give the first performance was Walton's masterly concerto. With shame and contrition I admit that when the composer offered me the first performance I declined it. I was unwell at the time; but what is also true is that I had not learnt to appreciate Walton's style. The innovations in his musical language, which now seem so logical and so truly in the main-stream of music, then struck me as far-fetched. It took me time to realize what a tower of strength in the literature of the viola is this concerto, and how deep the gratitude that we who play the viola should feel towards the composer.[7]

It seems likely that the harmonic idiom, with its frequent false relations, looked too modern to him; Lillian Tertis, the great player's widow, remarked that 'Lionel couldn't imagine that a chord containing C♯ *and* C♮ could possibly sound well'.[8] Walton was so downcast at this rejection that he seriously considered converting the work into a violin concerto, but changed his mind following a suggestion from a valued BBC friend,

Edward Clark. Clark knew that Walton and Hindemith (his senior by six years) were already on friendly terms and reminded the disappointed composer that Hindemith was also a well-known viola player, both as soloist and chamber musician; furthermore he was going to be in London at the time of the proposed first performance. Clark arranged to have the score sent to Hindemith and secured his agreement to play the solo part for the first performance.

Following Tertis's initial rejection, Walton abandoned all idea of acknowledging the player at the head of the score and instead dedicated the work 'To Christabel'. Christabel was the Hon. Mrs Henry McLaren who in 1934 was to become Lady Aberconway when her husband succeeded his father as second Baron. She had long been very friendly with Osbert Sitwell (to whom she remained devoted to the end of his life in 1969), and Walton would have met her regularly at the Sitwells' London house where he was a lodger and at the Derbyshire family scat, Renishaw. She was probably the first of his serious romantic attachments, but although the attraction was mutual, the relationship seems to have remained platonic.[9]

Early performances

The premiere of the Viola Concerto took place at a Promenade Concert at Queen's Hall on 3 October 1929, with Hindemith as soloist and Walton himself conducting the Henry Wood Symphony Orchestra. At the first rehearsal the orchestral parts were found to be notably inaccurate, and Walton sat up through the night correcting and rewriting. Hindemith was dismayed at having so little time to rehearse;[10] he wrote to his wife on 2 October: 'I have just come from the rehearsal (evening around 7); it should have been early this morning but wasn't because other things were being rehearsed...Walton is conducting the concerto himself. It won't be up to much. So far he has only had one rehearsal in which he managed to play the first movement just once. The orchestra is bad, consisting mainly of women, and English ones at that.'[11]

Part of the concert, which was devoted exclusively to British music, was broadcast on one of the BBC's Daventry transmitters, and this included the concerto. The performance scored an undoubted success; the concerto's lyrical and dramatic elements made a deep impression not only on enthusiasts for contemporary music but on the musical public as a whole. The anonymous critic of *The Times* (almost certainly H. C. Colles) reported on the occasion in these terms:

> After the full scoring of the elder composer [Bax], the low scale of tone, partly conditioned, no doubt, by the nature of the solo instrument, made its colour sound a little drab. Once the ear had adjusted itself to the new values, its subtlety, its rhythmic vitality, and its lyrical charm were evident enough. The mastery and the handling of the material chosen and the restraint which has been imposed upon his facility constitute a real and astonishing advance in the composer's development.[12]

In the *Musical Times* Eric Blom was even more enthusiastic:

> The success of the Viola Concerto by William Walton might almost be said to have amounted to a sensation, were it not that the music made an impression, not a mere

hit. It is one of the most remarkable of recent compositions, British or otherwise, the more so because it does not draw attention to itself by anything but sheer quality.[13]

It is very typical of Walton (with his innate modesty and ironic humour) that he should say 'I knew little of the viola when I started save that it made a rather awful sound', and then proceed to write a concerto which captures the nature of this unusual solo instrument to a superlative degree.

Walton, although extremely grateful to Hindemith for performing at the premiere, later recalled, 'His technique was marvellous, but he was rough—no nonsense about it. He just stood up and played.'[14] Along with many other viola players, Tertis attended the first performance and reacted similarly. In his autobiography he wrote, 'The notes certainly were all there, but the tone was cold and unpleasing and the instrument he played did not deserve to be called a viola, it was far too small.'[15]

Tertis lost no time in writing to Walton, apologizing for his initial rejection and promising to perform the concerto subsequently. His first appearance with the work was less than a year later, on 4 September 1930, at the ISCM Festival at Liège with the composer conducting. After a further performance that year in Germany Walton wrote to the concert pianist Harriet Cohen:

> The orchestra was bloody, the rehearsals ditto—in fact everything seemed, with the exception of Mr. Tertis, who was a saint and angel throughout—to be all wrong, till at the performance I found myself at the top of my form and behaved like Toscanini and it all went perfectly. If the orchestra had been good the performance could not have been better. It consisted of the professors and students of the Conservatoire the average age of the former being about 90 and the latter about 15. However, they did try and in fact rose a certain distance for the occasion, and the concerto made the hit of the Festival—at any rate so far. The applause—tears—and cheers, couldn't have been better, and Tertis and I were more tired by walking on and off than by playing.
>
> My arm is fatigued by autograph signing and I was touched by the number of orchestral players who asked if I had written concertos for their several instruments. You have no conception what Tertis has made out of the work—if you liked it before, you will just pass out when you hear him play it. I nearly did myself.[16]

Over the next few years Lionel Tertis made handsome amends for his hasty refusal of the first performance, playing the concerto many times. This included appearances in London, Birmingham, Manchester, and Liverpool, as well as a famous 1932 Edinburgh concert when Adrian Boult persuaded his soloist to play the entire concerto again in the second half of the programme.[17] Tertis's performance was broadcast from Zürich and Bern during a BBC Symphony Orchestra tour of Europe with Boult conducting; at least eight broadcasts took place in Britain. It has been calculated that Tertis played the Walton Concerto some thirty times, including a post-retirement appearance on 9 July 1940 at Queen's Hall, shortly before its destruction in the London Blitz.

Publication

The first publication of the Concerto for Viola and Orchestra was by Oxford University Press in 1930, in the form of full score and arrangement for viola and piano. The arranger of the piano reduction was not specified, but was almost certainly Walton himself; the separate solo part that came with it was identical with that shown in the full score. An engraved set of orchestral parts was also produced at about the same time, though never put on sale.

Within two years the OUP music catalogue included an additional item: 'Viola Solo part, edited by Lionel Tertis, obtainable separately, 1s 6d'.[18] In this, Tertis transposed several passages up an octave, or added octave doublings; he also provided his inimitable (and all but unplayable) fingerings. To judge from the great player's personal copy, what Tertis actually played—at least towards the end of his career—showed even wider variations from the composer's text than his printed version.[19]

A wish to modify the solo line also characterized the approach to the concerto adopted by the Scottish viola player William Primrose. The programme note of a Royal Philharmonic Society concert on 27 February 1936, under Beecham, at which he gave his first performance of the work, announced, 'Mr. Primrose's rendering of the solo viola part diverges occasionally from the published version.' On 2 October 1961, while preparing for the publication of the concerto's new orchestration, Walton wrote to OUP, 'William Primrose's version [of the solo part] is yet a 4th! because it differs in many respects—not the actual notes, but bits and pieces have been shoved up an octave or are in octaves, etc. And more often than not with good effect. I was just wondering what Y.M. [Yehudi Menuhin] will do with it—whether it is worth while sending him an annotated copy incorporating W.P.'s various tricks.'[20]

After hearing Primrose's 1955 recording the conductor Denis Vaughan queried the audible departures from the printed text; in a reply Alan Frank, head of OUP's music department, wrote, 'As far as I can tell William approves of what Primrose does but doesn't come off the fence sufficiently to say that they must all be incorporated in anything we print.'[21]

Recordings

Lionel Tertis was the soloist in a performance at a BBC Symphony Orchestra concert on 24 February 1937, with Ernest Ansermet conducting: the programme also included Berlioz's *Harold in Italy*. The concert marked the player's 60th birthday, and unexpectedly his retirement. Tertis had been troubled by certain bowing difficulties, notably in playing spiccato, caused by rheumatism, and commendably opted to withdraw from concert life rather than allow his public to detect the onset of imperfections. Subsequently, he played only for a few special occasions.

In December 1935 the Decca Record Company had made a highly successful first recording of Walton's new work, his First Symphony. In October 1937 Decca wrote to inform OUP that it was now planning to record the Viola Concerto and to ask OUP to reserve the first recording rights.[22] The obvious soloist would have been Tertis, but his unswerving idealism may not have allowed him to respond to a Decca invitation after having announced his official retirement.

The viola player Frederick Riddle (1913–1995) was a valued member of the London Symphony Orchestra and was shortly (in 1938) to become Beecham's principal viola in his recently formed London Philharmonic Orchestra. Riddle received a telephone call from Lionel Tertis asking if he had a copy of the concerto.[23] Riddle said he would get one, and some ten days later he found himself giving a studio broadcast with the composer conducting. On 6 December 1937, Riddle and Walton met again at the Decca Studios in Thames Street, London, to make the first recording of the concerto with the London Symphony Orchestra.[24] The resulting set of records played an important part in establishing the concerto's secure place in the repertory.

William Primrose recorded Walton's Viola Concerto twice: first in 1946 with the Philharmonia Orchestra and the composer,[25] and then in 1955 with the Royal Philharmonic Orchestra under Sir Malcolm Sargent.[26]

Walton's two orchestrations

The brilliant but challenging content and scoring of *Portsmouth Point* and the First Orchestral Suite from *Façade* promoted the general view of Walton as something of an *enfant terrible*; the lyrical idiom and subtle scoring of his Viola Concerto caused the image to be reassessed. The 1929 orchestration calls for triple woodwind, four horns, three trumpets, three trombones, and tuba, timpani, and strings. This seems a large orchestra to accompany a solo instrument whose tone is rich rather than penetrating and which is pitched mainly in the middle register, but it can be observed that the full orchestra is reserved for the tutti passages only and the forces called for are in fact there to provide a full palette of instrumental colour. Walton has also carefully specified in the score that the string desks should be reduced to 4.3.2.2.1 when the solo viola is playing. In an article previewing Tertis's 60th birthday concert, the 32-year-old Constant Lambert wrote astutely of Walton's orchestration of this work:

> Although the composer has not scrupled to use a full modern orchestra, the problem of the balance between soloist and orchestra has been most skilfully solved. While the soloist is playing the strings are...reduced to a few desks only, so that practically speaking the work is scored for two orchestras: a chamber orchestra during the solos and full orchestra during the tuttis. Apart from this the composer has had the intelligence to realize that what covers up a solo string instrument is not so much the brass as the other strings. On paper one would think trombones and trumpets too heavy an accompaniment for a solo viola, but in practice they are so different in tone that the solo instrument stands out clearly against their superior power.[27]

Nevertheless over the years Walton introduced several minor changes of detail by way of revision and refinement, and rather more major ones in 1955. These modifications, clearly shown in an OUP reference score and entered into the orchestral parts by copyists, have been incorporated in the present edition of the original version.

In 1961 Walton wrote to OUP to say that he had decided to rescore the concerto. The new orchestration specifies double woodwind instead of triple, only two trumpets and no tuba, and a harp part is added. The string desks to accompany the solo passages are shown as 4.3.3.2.2. Walton's letter to OUP dated 16 October 1961 states, 'It is I think an improvement on the old version particularly as regards clarity and definition'; his reasons for undertaking this rescoring do not appear to be documented anywhere else. In a letter of 7 September 1961 he had written to Alan Frank: 'I agree about the Viola

Concerto, that the new version need not cancel out the original—it just may be on occasion more convenient.' The word 'Reduced' appears in blue crayon on the first page of the 1961 autograph, and the revised score is sometimes referred to as the 'reduced version', which suggests that the smaller orchestra required may also have been intended to encourage more performances. The new orchestration received its first performance on 18 January 1962, with John Coulling as soloist and the London Philharmonic Orchestra under Sir Malcolm Sargent. It was published in study score format in 1964.

It has always been assumed that Walton's purpose in rescoring the concerto was to lighten the texture in the interests of balance with the solo line, but closer examination shows that this is scarcely the case. An additional desk of violas and of double basses is prescribed in the solo sections and the woodwind frequently sounds thicker than before, since the second oboe part is scored for cor anglais throughout and the second clarinet frequently takes bass clarinet. (The loss of third trumpet and tuba does not affect the solo part, as they play only in tutti sections in the 1929 orchestration.) Walton's extensive use of the harp in his 1962 score suggests that he had by then evolved a different orchestral sound; the harp is used conspicuously in his scores for Laurence Olivier's three Shakespeare films and also the opera *Troilus and Cressida*. But the new version was not to everybody's taste. A review by Ronald Crichton in the *Financial Times* of Walton's 70th birthday concert at the Royal Festival Hall, in which Yehudi Menuhin was the soloist in the Viola Concerto, made a perceptive comment: 'One wished that just this once they had gone back to the old scoring with triple wind and without harp—no doubt the revisions make life easier for the solo, but the smoothing and streamlining tone down an acerbity that was very much part of the music, while the harp brings it nearer the Tennysonian euphony of Ischia and the later period, very beautiful, yet different.'[28]

The 'Koussevitsky' version

A certain mystery surrounds an alternative autograph of the 1929 score, which surfaced when the Library of Congress was bequeathed the library of the celebrated conductor Serge Koussevitsky in 1978. A letter from Walton to Koussevitsky in Boston dated 30 December 1929 (just under three months after the premiere) states, 'I have sent to you under separate cover the score of my Viola Concerto, also a part for the player. I am so sorry that I have been unable to send it before, but my publishers insisted on its going to press, and so I have only just had the score returned to me. The parts will arrive in Boston by the end of the month. Thank you so much for giving the work its first American performance, and I only hope that it meets with your approval.' Koussevitsky's reply of 8 February 1930 to Walton in Amalfi acknowledges receipt of score and viola part.[29]

In April 1982 the Library of Congress returned this autograph score to OUP in London, and it is now part of the Frederick R. Koch Collection in Yale.[30] What is mysterious about it is that it shows certain differences from the main autograph which formed the basis for the first printed edition. It is written on larger paper, so that each woodwind instrument has its own stave throughout, and it shows numerous changes of notation, slurs, and dynamics, as well as a few errors. The most immediately striking difference is found at the very opening which, in this version, begins *pianissimo* with a crescendo for first violins and violas until a *subito pianissimo* at the moment of the soloist's first entry. In four passages several bars of the solo part have been changed, then heavily crossed out and the notes reinstated as in the printed score. The number of string desks prescribed for the solo passages is 4.3.2.2.2, which allows one more desk of double basses than is required in the 1930 publication.[31] It must be broadly contemporary with the main autograph, since the opening theme of the finale is scored for two clarinets and bass clarinet—which had already become two bassoons by the time the printed full score and piano arrangement were published in 1930. The second and third movements show blue crayon conductor's markings (tricky changes of metre in large figures). Did this autograph simply represent an alternative version (especially at the opening it has the look of a neat fair copy) or is it perhaps an earlier score to which the main autograph is a more practical successor? And why, having said that he had waited for the return of the autograph score, would Walton send a *different* version for the first American performance? Mysterious.

The solo line

The soloists in the concerto's early performances played from manuscript—Paul Hindemith at the premiere in October 1929 and Bernard Shore in the 1930 Promenade Concert with the newly formed BBC Symphony Orchestra, of which he was principal viola.[32] The solo line shown in the 1930 arrangement for viola and piano agreed with that of the published full score. The present WWE edition of the 1929 version gives this line on the smaller stave. The full-sized stave gives a version of the solo line whose provenance is slightly more complicated.

When Frederick Riddle played the work for his studio broadcast and the first recording he devised different phrasings and bowings—without changing the actual notes—and the composer is known to have found these changed articulations an improvement on the previously published ones, both his own and the Tertis version. He therefore asked Riddle to submit his edition of the solo part to OUP for publication. The existing plates were altered (a bill for £6 18s 6d from the printers is dated 13 May 1938), and the Riddle version was put on sale with the piano reduction, though for some reason Riddle's name was not credited. It remained the only version of the solo line available with the piano reduction until the appearance of the revised orchestration in 1962.

Unfortunately, when Walton was making his new orchestration in 1961 a major misunderstanding caused a change to the published solo part which the composer did not intend. Before undertaking his reorchestration he had written to OUP asking them to prepare a dummy score in which he could enter the new instrumentation. A copyist was to draw the bar lines and enter the instrument names and the viola solo line; all other staves were to remain blank. The dummy score was duly prepared, and Walton used it to create his new orchestration.[33] However, the solo line that had been copied into the score was from the 1930 published full score, that is to say the version that had been superseded by Riddle's version. Walton somewhat confused the issue by entering into the (incorrect) solo line of this score a few alternatives ('8va', 'con 8va', etc.) derived from Primrose's ideas, possibly for his own experimental purposes. And yet he had clearly been worried by the text of the solo part that he had been given, for a letter to him from Alan Frank of OUP, dated 29 September 1961, states, 'I am not quite sure what you mean by "other versions of the solo part". But since what you have in the dummy score was copied from the [1930] printed score, maybe this printed solo part is of some help.' The card that Walton enclosed when sending OUP the new manuscript score read, 'I take it that all three Viola parts agree—the Pfte. [arrangement] and full score *and the solo part as revised by Riddle*' [author's italics]. This was not understood by OUP, who replied on 31 May 1963, 'We decided that there ought to be one solo viola part for use with both orchestrations. When the reprinted copies of the piano score arrive—which will be quite soon—the inserted [i.e. separate] viola solo part will agree with the viola part in the new score.' Note OUP's reference to the score, Walton's to the part. To take the viola line from the full score would normally be correct, but OUP had forgotten that the solo line of the 1930 publication had been replaced by Riddle's 1938 version with the composer's approval—and we find Walton writing on 13 June 1963, 'The printed part which I returned with the proofs is the one revised by Fred Riddle and the one I did ask to be used for the new version.'

It was, however, too late. OUP had unfortunately allowed the wrong solo line to be copied into the specially prepared dummy score into which Walton had entered his new orchestration, and the composer seems to have realized this at a point when the misunderstanding could not be rectified. As a result, the solo part put on sale with the piano reduction from 1963 until the present day has been derived from the long-abandoned original 1930 solo part, with some thirty added instructions and changes. The solo line shown in the WWE edition is the one that the composer made abundantly clear he wanted, namely Frederick Riddle's version.

Although Walton admired the virtuoso performances given by Tertis and Primrose, and although Lionel Tertis's edition of the solo line had been available for some years, when it came to deciding on a text it was Riddle's disciplined and balanced approach that he ultimately favoured.

The Riddle version

Frederick Riddle's revision of the 1930 solo part is admired by viola players—as presumably it was by the composer—for two special qualities. First, the phrasings and articulations convey the nature of the work even more successfully than the original, and second, they achieve solutions to technical problems caused not only by legitimate musical requirements but also by the young composer's admitted lack of knowledge of his solo instrument. If we compare, for instance, the two solo lines shown in the WWE edition at the opening of the 1929 score we can see how Riddle's version succeeds in bringing out the lyrical and nostalgic character of the first statement and at the same time organizes the bowings to deliver the soloist to the appropriate part of the bow (bars 4–22). Grouping the viola's accompanying octaves in threes rather than the original pairs in bars 13–14, and also 17–18, is slightly more tranquil, less distracting. Conversely, the fourth bar of the second movement gains from Riddle's separating the first three notes and linking the fourth and fifth: the attack is crisp and the bow kept near the strongest part, at the heel, while in Walton's original the slur on the first three notes uses more bow length so that the two staccato notes have to be played less suitably further up the bow.

These are simple, isolated examples of the many changes to be found in the Riddle version. Some of them are quite small, but in detail and in perspective they add technical expertise and a stylish dimension to the writing. Riddle's playing for that broadcast and recording must have impressed Walton as being sufficiently convincing for him to encourage the immediate publication of his soloist's reworking as the version of his choice.

Just as it is clear from Walton's correspondence that he preferred Riddle's revision of the solo part, it also emerges from successive letters that his belief in his 1962 orchestration grew; from initially regarding it as a simple alternative to the 1929 score he eventually favoured it outright.[34] On the other hand, referring to the Sinfonia Concertante, first performed in 1928 but revised in 1943, Walton told his cataloguer Stewart Craggs in 1978 that he thought the original version was 'better and more interesting'.[35] Since 1962 many musicians have expressed a preference for the fuller 1929 orchestration of the concerto, among them Sir Malcolm Sargent, Norman Del Mar, and Michael Kennedy, all of whom would have been accustomed to the 1938 recording. It seems appropriate to point out that both scores have their individual merits—the 1929 score, which established the concerto's original impact and reputation, and the 1962 revision, which prescribes a somewhat smaller orchestra and reflects the composer's later preferences in instrumentation.

Whichever version is performed, William Walton's Concerto for Viola and Orchestra is surely established as a classic of the twentieth century and a major pinnacle of the viola repertory.

NOTES

1. *Musical News and Herald*, 27 May 1922.
2. Lionel Tertis, *My Viola and I* (London, 1974), pp. 16, 18. This is the revised and enlarged edition of his 1955 original, *Cinderella No More*.
3. The correspondence with Sassoon is preserved at the William Walton Museum, Forio, Ischia.
4. *RCM Magazine*, vol. 80, no. 3, p. 123.
5. 'Walton in the 20s', *BBC Music Magazine*, 26 March 1972.
6. For further discussion of these influences, see Robert Meikle, 'The Symphonies and Concertos', in Stewart Craggs, ed., *William Walton: Music and Literature* (Aldershot, 1999), pp. 70–74.
7. Tertis, *My Viola*, p. 36.
8. Conversation with Christopher Wellington.
9. Susana Walton, *Behind the Façade* (Oxford, 1988), pp. 34–35.
10. Bernard Shore, *Sixteen Symphonies* (London, 1949), p. 367.
11. *Selected Letters of Paul Hindemith*, ed. and trans. Geoffrey Skelton (New Haven, CT, 1995), p. 54.
12. *The Times*, 4 October 1929.
13. *Musical Times*, 70, 1 November 1929, p. 1030.
14. Geoffrey Skelton, *Paul Hindemith: The Man behind the Music* (London, 1975), p. 98. Walton told Skelton of his awareness of Hindemith's *Kammermusik Nr. 5* and, referring to the premiere of his own viola concerto, added, 'I was surprised he played it. One or two bars are almost identical.'
15. Tertis, *My Viola*, pp. 36–37. The need for a large viola was an article of faith with Tertis; any player whose viola measured less than $16^1/_2$ inches (41.9 cm.), length of back, was liable to be told, 'Put it on the fire, my boy—that's all it's fit for!'
16. *A Bundle of Time: The Memoirs of Harriet Cohen* (London, 1969), p. 169.

17. Tertis, *My Viola*, p. 71.

18. A letter of 13 November 1975 from Thomas Russell (a former secretary and business manager of the LPO) to Walton states, 'Soon after your Concerto for Viola and Orchestra was presented I acquired a copy of the solo part edited by Lionel Tertis. In 1932 or soon after I studied the work with him' (OUP Archive, Oxford).

19. Walton was always receptive to practical advice; as late as 1982 Rostropovitch edited the first publication of the Passacaglia for cello solo.

20. OUP Archive; all the correspondence cited between Walton and OUP is from the same source.

21. 29 April 1964, OUP Archive.

22. Letter from the Decca Record Co. of 8 October 1937, OUP Archive.

23. Conversation with Christopher Wellington.

24. Decca X199–201. Remastered for CD by Dutton Laboratories in 1993 on 'Walton Gramophone Premières' (with Symphony No. 1 and Three Songs from *Façade*), CDAX 8003. It is sometimes incorrectly stated that the recording was made in Kingsway Hall.

25. HMV AB6309–11 (autochange version DB9036–8); reissued in 1996 on CD in a William Primrose collection, Pearl GEMM CD9252.

26. Philips ABL 3045 (mono).

27. *The Listener*, 17 February 1937.

28. *Financial Times*, 30 March 1972. Quoted by Michael Kennedy in *Portrait of Walton* (Oxford, 1989), p. 251.

29. Both letters in OUP Archive.

30. Beinecke Rare Book and Manuscript Library, Yale University.

31. The RCM autograph, which acted as printer's copy for the first publication, also prescribes two desks of basses.

32. Shore's performance was on 21 August 1930, with Walton conducting. Talking about the composition of the concerto in a BBC interview with John Amis on 4 June 1977, Walton acknowledged that 'I had a sort of help from Bernard Shore'.

33. This manuscript was photographed by OUP and several copies made for use as hire conducting scores until the new orchestration was eventually published in 1964.

34. An OUP instruction to the Hire Department of 25 February 1969 reads, 'If anyone specifies the old version please advise them first that the composer infinitely prefers the new version' (OUP Archive).

35. Kennedy, *Portrait of Walton*, p. 45.

13

Violin and Cello Concertos *(Vol. 11)*

David Lloyd-Jones

These are the second and third of the three concertos for stringed instruments that Walton composed between 1928 and 1956. Although an indifferent performer on the violin, as well as the piano, it is clear that he favoured stringed instruments over keyboard or other orchestral instruments, even though he was tempted at one point to write a piano concerto for his friend Louis Kentner, and also contemplated a concerto for the clarinettist Frederick Thurston. It is true that the impetus to write his Viola Concerto came from Sir Thomas Beecham, who suggested to Walton that the outstanding British viola player Lionel Tertis deserved a modern concerto. Nevertheless it would seem that, thanks to early visits with the Sitwell brothers, it was Walton's love of Italy, with its delight in melody, that resulted in his choice of stringed instruments for the only concertos that he wrote. Furthermore, all three were designed with specific performers in mind, although only those for violin and cello benefited from the advice of their commissioners from the outset.

Violin Concerto

Genesis

The year 1937, in which it is believed Walton began to consider writing his Violin Concerto, was something of a watershed in his way of life. Following the break-up of his affair with Baroness Imma Doernberg (the dedicatee of the First Symphony), Walton had formed a new relationship with the married Alice, Viscountess Wimborne. Twenty-two years his senior, she was rich, highly intelligent, and attractive. She was a great friend of Osbert Sitwell, and the new liaison caused what Walton termed 'a slight chilliness between me & Carlyle Squ.', that is to say the Chelsea house where he had been staying with the Sitwell brothers since 1919.[1] This, and a new-found affluence, had caused him to move to a house in Belgravia in October 1935. Oxford University Press, his publishers, were not far away in central London and on the end of the phone, so relatively few letters from this period survive, certainly when compared to the number he was obliged to write after his subsequent move to the Italian island of Ischia (see Cello Concerto).

The great violinist Jascha Heifetz (often called 'the Paganini of the twentieth century') would have known about Walton if only because of the success of the Viola Concerto, written in 1928–9, which was performed and recorded by his friend and colleague, the Scottish violist William Primrose. There is no doubt about the fact that Heifetz commissioned the Violin Concerto, but exactly when this was is hard to establish. The first definite mention of it comes in an internal BBC memo, dated 27 November 1936, concerning the commissioning of the coronation march *Crown Imperial*. This states that Walton is concerned about his ability to deliver on time because he has to compose a violin concerto for Heifetz, a choral work for the following year's Leeds Festival, and music for a film. It would appear, therefore, that the accounts of the meeting with Heifetz that are given below date from some time in 1936, prior to November. Heifetz, however, did not visit the UK in 1936, but he had been there in November and December 1935. This may well be the time when the lunch at the Berkeley Hotel took place because, if we are able to believe the reminiscences of the distinguished violinist Antonio Brosa, Walton showed him the first two movements when Brosa was involved as soloist in the recording of Walton's music for the film *Dreaming Lips* towards the end of 1936. Yet against this possible dating are Walton's letters of January and May 1938 to his publisher and confidant Hubert Foss which describe the slow-going composition of these two movements. Only access to details of Heifetz's bank debits in late 1935 could possibly solve the dilemma.

There are two accounts of Walton's meeting with Heifetz. The first is given by Walton's friend Patrick ('Spike') Hughes in one of his volumes of reminiscences: 'Some years ago Jascha Heifetz asked me if I knew a young man by the name of Walton with whom he wanted to discuss a violin concerto. I said I did. Why? Well, could I bring him to lunch? I could and I did, and out of that lunch at the Berkeley [hotel] (smoked salmon and tournedos) came Jascha's commission for the Walton violin concerto.'[2] Walton, replying on 1 October 1973 to Alan Frank's request for information about the origins of the concerto, gives a slightly different version of events:

Heifetz date—1937–1938—I can't remember which, but it was thru' Willie Primrose. One Concerto begets another & Heifetz took us out to lunch at the Berkeley (the old one) (& paid for it). We discussed writing a Concerto. He'd already been disappointed by the Bax [which was written for him] & was v. wary. I wasn't all that keen knowing how difficult it could be. However we got as far as terms—1500 dollars or £300 (the £ was worth more than the dollar then). It was duly finished...I went with Alice to New York to see him. All more or less satisfactory. Not so many changes as one might have expected. They came later in the scoring [of the revised version] when I'd heard the recording of Cincinnati perf. with Heifetz and Rodzinski [*recte* Goossens]. As I was leaving the question of being paid arose. Was it £300 or $1500? I said £300, not realising by then that the pound was a bit shaky even in those days. So he then took out a bit of paper[,] rang up his bank & gave me 1493 dollars & some cents! He'd made on the deal![3]

Characteristically, Heifetz seems to have struck another hard bargain, insisting on the 'gentleman's agreement that if he did not like it he need not accept it and if he did that he would take it for a couple of seasons exclusively'.[4] He also demanded that OUP supply him with his personal full score and a set of parts.

It would appear that despite Brosa's claim, no actual composition was done until January 1938. In a letter to Hubert Foss (received on the 27th of that month from the Wimborne country house of Ashby St. Ledgers, near Rugby), Walton signs off: ' "Morning sickness" is beginning, otherwise not much progress.'[5] This can only refer to the first stirrings of the concerto, the only major work that he had on the stocks at that time. But it was not only a question of 'morning sickness' at the outset of pregnancy, for at the end of 1937 Walton had suffered a double hernia and had been in hospital for several weeks. All this delayed work on the concerto. However, once ideas began to flow it would seem that the lyrical first movement, which commentators consider may reflect the benign influence of Alice Wimborne, took shape at the leisurely pace which was normal with Walton when engaged on major works.

The British Council

However, a dramatic sideshow was about to take place. As a delayed antidote to the Great Depression, New York decided to stage an exciting, even futuristic, World's Fair in 1939. A by-product of this was to be a series of concerts performed by the BBC Symphony Orchestra under their principal conductor, Sir Adrian Boult, and the British Council therefore became involved in showcasing newly commissioned works by British composers. Accordingly, following a Council meeting on 9 March 1938, Vaughan Williams, Bax, Bliss, and Walton were selected 'to write a special composition which should be dedicated to the American people'.[6] Each composer was to be offered £250 by the Council, plus £100 should they wish to visit New York to supervise the performance of their work. Bliss, a member of the Music Committee, was delegated to write to Walton with this proposal, which he did on 15 April. In the meantime, Walton and Alice Wimborne had indulged in their mutual love of southern Italy and installed themselves in the luxurious Villa Cimbrone in Ravello, near Amalfi, recently vacated by Leopold Stokowski and Greta Garbo. On 28 April Walton wrote enthusiastically to Bliss: 'Your letter has just been forwarded to me, for which many thanks. The proposal suits me admirably, that is, if everything can be arranged.' He proceeded to inform him about the new commission '& I have just got started on it', but expressed some doubts about a collaboration between the British Council (who might insist on a British soloist) and Heifetz.[7] Matters dragged on, largely because of lack of information from the Council, but an extract from the minutes of the Music Committee's meeting on 22 September 1938 gives the interesting information that Hubert Foss had reported that 'the first two movements of Mr. Walton's Violin Concerto were at present with Mr. Heifetz in America'. A further communication of 14 October from the Chairman of the committee urged Walton to make up his mind about the dual considerations of the British Council and Heifetz, and commented: 'I understand from Mr. Foss that Mr. Heifetz has seen the first two movements of the concerto, but has intimated that he cannot decide as to the work as a whole without knowledge of the last movement, and that this is not yet ready.' In his reply of 18 October, accepting the Council's offer, Walton wrote that he would 'abide by the decision they [the Council] come to as regards the soloist, and hope that it will turn out that Mr. Heifetz will be able to see his way to give the performance. I aim at having the Concerto finished by the end of November.' A communication from the Secretary of the Music Council to Walton of 9 February 1939 includes the important phrase: 'as the Concerto which the Council commissioned from you is now finished....

Composition

The British Council saga (still to be concluded) takes us ahead of the chronology of the concerto's composition. The idyllic conditions at Villa Cimbrone clearly left their impression on the Italianate first movement. In a letter of 11 May 1938 to Hubert Foss, Walton reported that the concerto was 'developing in an extremely intimate way'.[8] In a later letter, which he omitted to date, but which probably refers to some time in May or June, Walton announced: 'I have been undergoing the usual travail & have dropped at last the 1st movement. Not too bad.' He continues: 'Having been bitten by a tarantula[,] a rare & dangerous & unpleasant experience[,] I have celebrated the occasion by the 2nd movement being a kind of tarantella "Presto cappricciosamente alla napolitana". Quite gaga I may say & of doubtful propriety after the 1st movement,—however you will be able to judge.'[9]

The third movement that Heifetz had been waiting for in September 1938 was completed back in England early in the New Year. A letter, dated 18 January 1939, from Dora Foss to her husband in the USA says that Walton had telephoned her saying 'his difficulty is making the last movement elaborate enough for Heifetz to play it'. On 4 February she wrote again: 'William isn't at all pleased with the last movement, says it wants two months' more work. Brosa not very enthusiastic.'[10] This shows that Brosa (who was to give the first performance of the Britten Violin Concerto in March 1940) was indeed consulted by Walton at some point, and it is possible that—quite apart from advising on technical matters—Brosa was able to inform the composer of the distinctive qualities of Heifetz's style that he was then able to incorporate, prior to the revisions Walton later sent to Heifetz.[11] An undated letter from Walton to Foss, probably relating to early March 1939, announces: 'Just heard that Heifetz has accepted my concerto.'[12] Unfortunately the welcome news was accompanied by the violinist's statement that it was too late for him to be interested in the World's Fair's proposal, so this put Walton in an awkward position vis-à-vis the British Council after such protracted negotiations and goodwill on their part. On 21 March Walton wrote a six-page letter to the Chairman of the Music Committee saying that 'after much thought and consultation I have come to the conclusion that although I lose financially it is only right for the sake of the work, to let Mr. Heifetz have it and abandon the World's Fair proposal of the British Council.... After all[,] having landed the biggest fish in the ocean of violinists, you will agree that it is hardly to be expected that I throw him back & take some smaller fry with obviously less advantages musically attached.' The press heard about the withdrawal and, still sore, the Chairman mischievously put it about that this was because the concerto was still unfinished.

Visit to Heifetz

In a letter of 28 March to the conductor Leslie Heward, Walton said, 'I am going over [to America] sometime soon to work with Heifetz on the concerto,'[13] and a postcard to Dora Foss from the luxury liner SS Normandie postmarked 'Le Havre à New York, 15 May 1939' announced 'Arrive tomorrow after a very good passage in this miracle of a ship'.[14] Heifetz had a farmhouse in Redding in the Saugatuck Valley, Connecticut, and it was there that Walton went to discuss details of the concerto and the solo line in particular. Two autographs of unusual interest, which Heifetz eventually presented to the Library of Congress in February 1952, give a very clear idea of what they worked from. There had been something like three months between Walton's finishing the concerto and his arrival in America; furthermore, he had sent Heifetz the first two movements at least nine months earlier. From an examination of both autographs it would appear that Walton had written what was, to all intents and purposes, a detailed violin and piano sketch, and that he had then made a form of digest from these two movements (the first with far fuller accompaniment than the more barren second) in order to give Heifetz the all-important information about the solo line. It is to be assumed that Walton in England retained the autograph violin and piano version in order to complete the orchestration, and also for the émigré composer and pianist Franz Reizenstein to make the official (though unaccredited) piano reduction, using Walton's sketch (and presumably full score) as a basis. This was completed by the time Walton left for the USA.

Two surprising facts emerge from the copy that Walton sent Heifetz. The first is how relatively little Heifetz has changed in the essence of the solo line; in other words, how well Walton has written for the violin and fully understood its technical, as well as musical, capabilities. The second is how musically imaginative and understanding Heifetz shows himself to be. Of course bowings, slurrings, phrasings, and changes from slurred to separate (and vice versa) were made, and regular bowings of convenience introduced (see bars 92 and 97 of the first movement), even when this led to inconsistencies with repetitions of phrases, as in figs. 43–44. However, right from the third and eleventh bars, in which Heifetz has deleted Walton's up and down hairpins in order to establish an immediate *sognando*, Heifetz shows himself to be interested not only in the technical aspect of the solo part (especially in those matters in which he excelled, such as his famous up-bow spiccato) but also in the expressive. The solo line of this fascinating autograph later served as the basis for Heifetz's editing of the solo line for the 1941 OUP publication of the violin and piano score.

Walton's autograph arrangement for violin and piano, although it contains some annotations and timings by Heifetz (seemingly made at the time of the first recording), remains remarkably as the composer wrote it. In other words, whatever alterations were agreed in Connecticut, Walton entered very few of them into his piano arrangement. Of greater interest is when and how he wrote the autograph full score. It would seem that the two processes went side by side—there was plenty of time for this to happen—and there is a telling internal memo from a member of staff at OUP's New York office to London saying: 'The day Walton arrived here he came into the office in a great rush to get photostat copies overnight of the third movement [full score?] and piano scores of his Violin Concerto.'[15]

Most of what Heifetz suggested appears to have been granted immediately but there were points which Walton clearly felt he wanted to consider at greater leisure. Walton returned to England on 6 June 1939, and the days spent on the luxury liner were his last taste of *la dolce vita* for some time, because on 3 September Great Britain went to war with Germany. In a ten-page letter to Heifetz of 15 October Walton says: 'Thank you for your letter, since receiving it I have heard from Mr. Foss that the first performance is to be at Cleveland on Dec. 7th & 9th, and I am delighted about it. Alas, I don't think[,] owing to this something war, there is the slightest likelihood of my being able to get over for it...As for your alteration, I approve of it & send you some alternatives on a separate sheet...The only other suggestion I've made (in the 1st movement) is also on it'. This concerns Heifetz's suggested alternative to the fourteen largely solo bars before fig. 63 in the last movement. Walton goes on to say: 'Also could you…send me a photostat copy of your violin part as you will be playing it. I ask this, as we wish to get it in print (proofs only, not to be published till the date you stipulate) before the cost of printing becomes prohibitive.' In a postscript he adds that it might be best to cut down the strings to 6-5-4-3-2 desks while the solo is playing, as he had done successfully in his Viola Concerto.[16]

Performance

As planned, the premiere of the Violin Concerto duly took place on 7 December 1939 in Cleveland, Ohio, at Severance Hall with Heifetz and the Cleveland Orchestra, conducted by Artur Rodzinski. It was repeated two days later. Writing shortly afterwards to Hubert Foss, Walton said: 'Here are the cables: Concerto enormous success. Orchestra played superbly you would have been extremely pleased. Congratulations your most successful concerto. Writing sending programme. Best greetings Heifetz.'[17] The other enthusiastic cable came from the wife of the chief conductor of the Cincinnati Symphony Orchestra, Eugene Goossens. And it was Goossens, with his orchestra, who made the first commercial recording of the concerto with Heifetz on 18 February 1941, even though the original performers, who were not contracted to record for RCA Victor, had just given the first New York performance at Carnegie Hall on 5 February.[18]

Publication and revision

Wartime conditions accounted for an unprecedented two and-a-half-year delay between the completion of composition and first publication of a major Walton work. Heifetz sent over his edited solo line, but this was sunk somewhere in the mid-Atlantic. Fortunately a photocopy had been made in New York and this finally reached London by air, so that the violin and piano reduction version of the concerto could be published by OUP in September 1941. The first British performance did not take place until a Royal Philharmonic Society concert in a sparsely filled Royal Albert Hall on the afternoon of Saturday, 1 November 1941, with the Danish violinist Henry Holst and the London Philharmonic Orchestra, conducted by Walton. On the following Monday the critic of *The Times* may have given Walton food for thought when, in the course of a generally positive review, he wrote: 'There are here many moments of distinctive beauty, though also not a few where the rapid movement, the intricate passage work and the explosive orchestration (especially when heard in the reverberating Albert Hall) may be thought to be at variance with the prevalent lyricism declared in the opening cantilena.' Eleven days later Holst and Walton repeated the performance with the evacuated BBC Symphony Orchestra in the Corn Exchange, Bedford, in a broadcast concert which also included the first British performance of his new overture *Scapino*.

Walton was an inveterate reviser, and these performances under his direction, later augmented by reference to the Heifetz recording, induced him to rethink and lighten the orchestration, especially as the full score had not been published. On 23 December 1943 he wrote to his occasional assistant Roy Douglas: 'I have been taking the opportunity during a lull in [the composition of the music for the film] Henry V to rescore the Vl. Con. I started out to do a little patching here & there but found it not a satisfactory way of doing it, so more or less I started from the beginning...I sent it to be copied next [?] week in the hope the parts will be ready for a performance at Birmingham [*recte* Wolverhampton] on Jan 17th. If they are ready you must come down & hear it. I think now that I've got it as good as I can get it.'[19] Walton used a similar-sized orchestra for his revision, except that the percussion section no longer included castanets, glockenspiel, bass drum, and tam-tam, and was used more sparingly. Instead of writing out a new full score, he surprisingly reused that of the 1939 version by rubbing out everything he wished to change. Comparison between the new autograph and a photocopy of the old shows that the pagination, barring, and solo line therefore remain identical, as do the instrumental accolades, except in those places where he required a different distribution. Six pages of the third movement were entirely rewritten. Henry Holst was again the soloist when the revised version was first given in Wolverhampton on 17 January 1944 by the Liverpool Philharmonic Orchestra (of which he was leader) under Malcolm Sargent.

In mid-1944 OUP was able to undertake the engraving of a study score of the revised Violin Concerto; this was done from a second copy of the revised full score.[20] In a letter of 21 June 1945 to Benjamin Britten, congratulating him on the success of his just-premiered opera *Peter Grimes*, Walton wrote: 'I meant to have written you before but have these last days been overwhelmed by proofs of my Violin Concerto & I fondly but vainly hope to get the score out in time for the "Prom" performance which I hope you may be able to hear. I say fondly and vainly as I have been four months getting the 2nd proofs.'[21] This was wishful thinking on Walton's part; the study score was not officially published until 29 November of that year. The solo line was not that of his autograph full score, but the one shown in the published violin and piano reduction of 1941, minus the Heifetz bowings and fingerings. Although Walton responded to a list of queries from Roy Douglas by replying simply 'Yes' or 'No', the proofreading process was far from satisfactory and, following a renewed scrutiny by Douglas, corrected impressions of the score had to be issued in 1952 and 1969. The Heifetz/Walton wheel finally came full circle when they both recorded the concerto for HMV with the Philharmonia Orchestra on 26–27 June 1950.[22]

Walton was always grateful to Heifetz for commissioning the concerto and, as conductor, aided and abetted the violinist's brilliant, pacy, though emotionally cool interpretation, one that several others have tried to emulate. However, he reserved his greatest praise for the interpretation of his friend Yehudi Menuhin, with whom he re-recorded the concerto with the London Symphony Orchestra in July 1969. The letter he wrote to Menuhin on 21 April 1970, after hearing the disc, contains feelings that are surely of considerable significance in connection with the concerto's essential poetic lyricism: 'Your playing is absolutely astounding, in fact I am unable to conjure up adequate superlatives for your interpretation & performance—nor can I thank you enough for having brought to life a dream which I thought would never come true.'[23]

Cello Concerto

Genesis

The success that Heifetz achieved in commissioning a violin concerto from Walton was doubtless very much connected with the creation of the Cello Concerto. Born three years after Heifetz in 1903, the Russian cellist Gregor (Grisha) Piatigorsky was, with Pablo Casals, Emanuel Feuermann, and Mstislav Rostopovich, one of the undisputed leading cellists of the twentieth century. As far back as the summer of 1934, Prokofiev had begun a concerto for him. After a series of highly successful appearances with various orchestras in the USA, he had become a naturalized citizen of that country in 1942. More importantly in the present context, since the mid-1940s he had been playing and recording chamber music with his friend and Los Angeles neighbour, Heifetz, and it is to be assumed that when he contemplated commissioning a concerto, the precedent of Walton's concerto for Heifetz would have been uppermost in his mind.

In his autobiography, Ivor Newton, the pianist and regular Piatigorsky accompanist, gives the following account of the origins of the Cello Concerto:

> Piatigorsky much admired the concertos for viola and violin by Sir William Walton, and wanted Walton to write a cello concerto for him. I was deputed to discuss the possibility with Sir William, a coolly elegant and at the same time entirely professional and business-like composer who prefers to keep profundities of feeling for his compositions and not waste them in conversation. 'Would you consider writing a cello concerto for Piatigorsky?' I asked him. 'I'm a professional composer,' was the reply. 'I'll write anything for anybody, if he pays me.' In a moment, came an afterthought in which Sir William's impishness, one of the qualities that audiences have learned to recognise in his music, won a minor victory. 'I write much better if they pay me in dollars,' he said. Incidentally, when Piatigorsky met Sir William, he was deeply impressed. 'I have never,' he said firmly, 'met such a rare combination of greatness and simplicity.'[24]

No date is given for this meeting, but an internal OUP memo, dated 21 December 1954, announces: 'PIATIGORSKY has commissioned a CELLO CONCERTO from WALTON, probably paying him $3000 for 2 years' rights. Possible premiere at Edinburgh Festival 1956.'[25] Also, it is possible that Ian Hunter, managing director of Harold Holt Ltd and agent to both player and composer, had played a matchmaker role in bringing the two together. A letter from Walton to his publisher Alan Frank of 18 July 1955 ends with the lines: 'I've as yet not made much progress, if any with [the] cello concerto. I must admit I've not been trying very hard, but will pull myself together shortly I hope.'[26] By 24 August he was writing to David Webster, General Manager of the Royal Opera House: 'Also I think now I'm embarked on the Vlc. Con. that I ought to finish it. It is fairly well under way & if it wasn't for my visit to the U.S. & to Milan in Dec, it would be finished by Xmas.'[27] A more pressing commission for an overture intervened and resulted in the *Johannesburg Festival Overture*, but Walton was soon back working on Piatigorsky's cello concerto.

At this point it may be stated that the correspondence with Piatigorsky on the subject of the composition and first performances of the Cello Concerto is voluminous, and contrasts greatly with the relative paucity of information about the genesis of the Violin Concerto. It so happens that the concerto was one of four works chosen to be represented at unusual length (though, even so, in very condensed form) by Malcolm Hayes in *The Selected Letters of William Walton* that was published by Faber & Faber in 2002. The interested reader is referred to pages 274–313 and 411–20 of that publication, but, nevertheless, the following facts need to be reported here.

A premiere at the 1956 Edinburgh Festival was unrealistic. However, Alan Frank was on the Council of the distinguished Royal Philharmonic Society, and on 12 December 1955 wrote to the General Manager of the Liverpool Philharmonic Orchestra: 'This is just to tell you, as I promised I would, that a letter is now on its way to Piatigorsky, inviting him to give the first English performance of Walton's CELLO CONCERTO, in London, for the Royal Philharmonic Society on 13th February 1957.'[28] The RPS also acted on a hint from Piatigorsky, relayed to Frank by Walton, that he would appreciate the distinction of being made an Honorary Member of the Society at the same time, which indeed eventually happened. Piatigorsky, however, appears to have decided on an American premiere instead. On 17 March 1956 he wrote to Walton: 'We now have a deadline to meet, viz. December 7th, when it will have its world premiere in Boston. I have just accepted invitation to play it in London January 29th. The first performance in New York will be with the New York Philharmonic, Mitropoulos, in May.'[29]

This news spurred Walton into action. Writing on 24 April 1956 to Alan Frank, he said: 'I enclose the [cello and piano arrangement of the] 1st movement. Will you have it photostatted & the Vlc. part copied…Checking it over I find it rather good & wonder why I've had such difficulty with it as it's really very simple and straightforward. Perhaps that's why?'[30] On receiving the photocopy, Piatigorsky replied by cable on 10 May: 'First movement magnificent. Not a note to change. Thanks love Grisha.' He followed this up with a letter on 17 May in which he continued to enthuse about the first movement, and continued: 'My new Stradivari [*sic*] is of such glorious quality that as a special request for his genius, I would love to have some solo spot for it in your Concerto, unmixed with any other instruments, in whatever form it be.' This request was to be granted twofold. Walton then immersed himself in the second movement. Piatigorsky suggested a number of alterations to the solo line, and on 10 August 1956 Walton wrote to him: 'Here is what I hope is the final version—as far as it goes [up to fig. 19]. I'm in a hurry to send it off so that you can have it on your journey [i.e. tour of the Far East]. This new version I think incorporates all your suggestions for which many thanks. It is as you will quickly see very different from what I've already sent you, so please destroy the former version…The cadenza can be played as freely as you like. I think I've covered most questions by alternative versions.'[31]

On 9 September he reported to Piatigorsky:'After many false starts & what is worse nothing happening at all, I'm at last launched on the finale. It opens with a solo Vlc. all on its own quite a while. Very 'robusto'.

I won't send any more in case I change it! [Walton eventually entirely rethought this opening]. I think it will end quietly with a longish coda based on themes from the 1st mov. But we will see.'[32] There was much detailed discussion, especially about the two solo 'improvisations', and Walton was quite firm in reiterating his conviction that the quiet ending 'rounds off the work in a satisfying & logical way and should sound beautiful, noble, dignified etc. though it ends on a whisper. Sometimes (& I hope this is one of them) an ending such as this one, is in every way just as impressive and evocative as a more spectacular & loud one, especially in this case, as I feel there is no other solution.'[33] On 26 October he told Piatigorsky, 'The score is now completely finished', and on 4 November, 'It is to my mind, the best of my now, three concertos, but don't say so to Jascha!'[34] All this while, OUP had been arranging for the full score to be copied by Roy Douglas who, in the process, was able to spot mistakes; he also checked the transparencies of the orchestral parts that were being made at the same time.

Performance

At this point, disaster struck on both sides of the Atlantic. First Piatigorsky, who had been quite ill in June and had just finished a particularly strenuous autumn tour, had a nervous breakdown; in consequence, the two scheduled first performances in Boston on the 7th of December (matinée) and the 8th (evening) had to be cancelled. Fortunately it was possible to reschedule the first performance for 25 January 1957, when it was given in Symphony Hall by Piatigorsky and the Boston Symphony Orchestra under Charles Münch. This was fourteen days before the long-arranged British premiere under the auspices of the Royal Philharmonic Society. Walton and his wife decided to drive from Ischia to London to attend this important event (his first major orchestral concert work since the overture *Scapino* of 1940), but en route they were involved in a serious collision with a cement lorry just outside Rome. Walton was told that he would not be able to move for forty days.

Despite this double setback, the British premiere went ahead as planned, with Piatigorsky and with Sir Malcolm Sargent conducting the BBC Symphony Orchestra at the Royal Festival Hall on 13 February 1957. Two days earlier, Piatigorsky had spent two hours with Roy Douglas at the Savoy Hotel discussing further alterations to the cello part; they were played by telephone to Walton in his Roman clinic and approved. The performance was broadcast and shown live on BBC TV, and Radio Italiana went out of its way to relay the performance, as the composer was still bedridden. The work was very well received by the press and public alike.

Recording

Even before the European premiere, Piatigorsky had recorded the concerto for RCA Victor in Boston three days after its first performance there. Although delighted with what he had heard of Piatigorsky's playing in London, Walton had been troubled by the slow tempi and, in particular, those of the two unaccompanied improvisations in the third movement, which made it some three and a half minutes longer than the timings he had envisaged.[35] He was even more worried by this when he heard a test pressing of the RCA recording, and OUP in New York and London were faced with the delicate task of asking all those concerned if it would be possible for the improvisations to be re-recorded. When Piatigorsky agreed to this Walton, by now in London, arranged for Roy Douglas to make a tape of them at his preferred tempi. This was done on 20 March and sent to Piatigorsky in America. In a letter of the following day, Walton says: 'Neither [improvisations] 2 or 4 should be regarded as "cadenzas". No 2 in fact should wake up the whole movement!…Both 2 and 4 need to have the feeling of a beat (almost as if they were being conducted).' Piatigorsky performed the concerto in New York on 3 and 5 May, and the re-recordings were planned for sometime that month. The recording was eventually released in June 1958, coupled with Bloch's *Schelomo*.[36]

OUP were keen to release the engraved study score in time for the performance of the concerto at the Proms on 21 August 1957, played by Piatigorsky's brilliant Danish pupil Erling Bengtsson. At the same time, the arrangement for cello and piano was in production. At an early stage in the concerto's composition Walton had asked Piatigorsky whether he would mind editing the solo part, in the same way that Heifetz had for the Violin Concerto. Eventually Alan Frank dissuaded him from pursuing this, saying: 'All our experience shows that solo performers tend to dislike edited parts, since they all have their own ideas.'[37] No editing was shown in the eventual publication, which bears the note: 'The composer is indebted to Roy Douglas for his help in the preparation of the piano reduction of this work.' Both publications eventually appeared in December of that year.

Alternative endings

On 2 November 1956 Piatigorsky had cabled Walton: 'Entire concerto wonderful with deeply moving and only possible epilogue…Love, congratulations and thanks Grisha.'[38] However, during the period of recuperation from his nervous breakdown, the cellist seems to have reconsidered his former opinion, especially as Heifetz, to whom he had shown the new concerto before the premiere, suggested that the ending could be more intense, and that the second improvisation in the third movement could be shortened. Walton had responded to both comments. A letter of 31 December 1956 from Alan Frank to OUP's New York office says: 'I have a note today from Sir William saying that Piatigorsky was not entirely happy about the end. He therefore has written two new endings, and has sent them over, leaving it to Piatigorsky to choose the one he likes best and to send it to you.'[39] However, writing again to New York on 21 January, Frank said: 'As far as we can make out from a note from Walton [not preserved] Piatigorsky seems to have gone back to the first ending.'[40] No trace of these early alternative endings exists, and all performances and publications up until the WWE edition have presented what Walton originally wrote.

Renewed contact between composer and player in the summer of 1974, however, emboldened Piatigorsky to ask Walton for a new piece, and later to request a new ending to the concerto. On 3 December of that year he wrote: 'I could not help wishing that the very conclusion of the Concerto, instead of resembling the mood of the ending of the first movement[,] would transform [*sic*] by your adding only a few bars the touching reminiscence, to a bright and ringing conclusion.' On 24 July Walton replied: 'Having looked at the 'Cello Concerto I feel a bit doubtful about that also. It may seem as if something had been stitched on, like adding a new hem to an old skirt! However, I will keep you informed.'[41] On 17 December Walton wrote again: 'I was so happy to receive your letter & to discover what you want for the new ending of the Concerto, but I'd got the wrong idea & thought you wished for a loud pyrotechnical ending, but your description of what you really want has been of the greatest help & I send a sketch of what I've done—but it's only a sketch & if it appeals to you I'll work it out properly.'[42]

On 6 February 1975 he wrote to Alan Frank: 'I've done a new end which I hope will be alright. I don't suppose P. will approve as it is to all purposes the same as the original— but he can't say I haven't tried.'[43] On 25 February Walton replied to an enthusiastic cable from Piatigorsky: 'I'm most happy to learn that my new ending is more or less what you want. Why it bothered me so much I don't know.'[44] Sadly Piatigorsky, who had been ill with cancer for some time, died on 6 August 1976, without ever playing the new ending of the concerto. It was published for the first time in the WWE edition.

NOTES

1. Letter to Siegfried Sassoon of 21 October 1935. Quoted in *The Selected Letters of William Walton*, ed. Malcolm Hayes (London, 2002), p. 101.

2. Spike Hughes, *Opening Bars* (London, 1946), p. 315. The question of the dating of the commission has been much revised since the publication of the WWE.

3. OUP Archive, Oxford.

4. OUP Archive.

5. *Selected Letters*, ed. Hayes, p. 112.

6. For this, and the other quotations relating to the concerto and the World's Fair concerts, see the special British Council file, later donated to the OUP Archive.

7. *Selected Letters*, ed. Hayes, p. 113.

8. *Selected Letters*, ed. Hayes, p. 115.

9. *Selected Letters*, ed. Hayes, p. 116.

10. Both Dora Foss letters are in the possession of Mrs Diana Sparkes (née Foss).

11. H. Dawkes and J. Tooze, 'A Conversation with Antonio Brosa', in *Royal College of Music Magazine* 65(1), Easter 1969, p. 10.

12. *Selected Letters*, ed. Hayes, p. 118. The telegram, dated 28 Feb. 39, read: 'Accept enthusiastically your concerto however collaboration necessary please advise earliest [possible] date your arrival letter follows greetings Heifetz' (OUP Archive).

13. *Selected Letters*, ed. Hayes, p. 118.

14. *Selected Letters*, ed. Hayes, p. 119.

15. Memo of 15 June 1939, OUP Archive.

16. Heifetz Collection, Music Division, Library of Congress, Washington DC.

17. *Selected Letters*, ed. Hayes, p. 126.

18. Victor 18414-6, in album M-808; HMV DB 5953-5. Reissued in CD format in 2000 by Naxos on 8.110939. Roy Douglas, doubtless repeating information supplied by Walton, claimed that Heifetz had a firm conviction that, commercially speaking, no concerto recording should ever occupy more than three 78 rpm records, which goes some way to explaining his generally fast tempi.

19. *Selected Letters*, ed. Hayes, pp. 147–148.

20. Letter to Norman Peterkin of 25 September 1944. OUP Archive.

21. *Selected Letters*, ed. Hayes, p. 154.

22. HMV DB 21257-9, released May 1951. Reissued as CD on RCA Victor GD 87966 in November 1988, and in the USA on album DM 1511 (78 rpm), and LM 1121 (LP).

23. *Selected Letters*, ed. Hayes, p. 389. HMV ASD 2542, released on LP in March 1970. Reissued as CD on CHS5 65003-2.

24. Ivor Newton, *At the Piano* (London, 1966), p. 128.

25. OUP Archive.

26. OUP Archive.

27. *Selected Letters*, ed. Hayes, p. 269.
28. OUP Archive.
29. OUP Archive. There were four performances, May 2–5.
30. OUP Archive.
31. *Selected Letters*, ed. Hayes, p. 274. A thick file in the OUP Archive makes it possible to follow the Walton–Piatigorsky correspondence in great detail.
32. *Selected Letters*, ed. Hayes, p. 275.
33. *Selected Letters*, ed. Hayes, p. 282.
34. *Selected Letters*, ed. Hayes, pp. 281 and 284.
35. Letter of Walton to Piatigorsky of 12 March 1957; see *Selected Letters*, ed. Hayes, pp. 295–296. Walton always had a very clear conception of the timings of his works; in a letter to Alan Frank of 26 October 1952, announcing the completion of the third movement, he says: 'It lasts about 11'–12' so the total duration will be something between 24'–26'. As the details listed below show, this is remarkably accurate. The timings of the three movements on the only recording of Walton conducting the concerto, a live performance on 23 August 1959 with Pierre Fournier and the Royal Philharmonic Orchestra at the Edinburgh Festival (BBCL 4098–2), are: I – 6.42, II – 6.04, III – 11.17, in all 24.03; these are probably the fastest ever. See Appendix 3 of Angela Hughes, *Pierre Fournier: Cellist in a Landscape with Figures* (Aldershot, 1998) for Walton's letter of 27 August 1958 to Fournier with his performing suggestions.
36. RCA RB 16027.
37. OUP Archive.
38. OUP Archive.
39. OUP Archive.
40. OUP Archive.
41. *Selected Letters*, ed. Hayes, p. 413.
42. *Selected Letters*, ed. Hayes, p. 416.
43. *Selected Letters*, ed. Hayes, p. 418.
44. *Selected Letters*, ed. Hayes, p. 419. Rafael Wallfisch, a pupil of Piatigorsky who gave him a copy of the 1975 revised ending, has performed it once in concert in Edmonton, Canada. It has been recorded by Jamie Walton on SIGCD220.

14

Overtures *(Vol. 14)*

David Lloyd-Jones

By the beginning of the twentieth century the operatic overture had virtually disappeared and given way to the prelude. Even these became increasingly shorter, and in *Salome* (1905) Richard Strauss dispensed with one altogether. The concert overture, on the other hand, continued to attract some composers as a convenient form for a short orchestral piece that did not aspire to the length or complexity of the symphonic poem, though it was consistently avoided by those of a more avant-garde persuasion, who turned their backs on anything that smacked of old Austro-German procedures. It says much for Walton's belief in the continued validity of traditional forms and reluctance to pander to fashion that he should write three brilliant concert overtures at significant moments in his long composing career.[1] His innate business sense must have told him that such pieces would always be welcome as concert openers, as long as the conventional symphony orchestra flourished. They also suited his lifelong inclination towards concision rather than expansion.

Portsmouth Point

Composition

The title of Walton's first extant orchestral work, the overture *Portsmouth Point*, derives from an etching by the English artist and caricaturist Thomas Rowlandson (1756–1827), which portrays an amusingly animated nautical scene on the waterfront of the Point at Portsmouth.[2] Curiously Lord Berners, a friend of Osbert and Sacheverell Sitwell and therefore of the young composer who then lived with them, had already written a piano piece of the same name, probably in 1918, and in 1920 had also contemplated a ballet on this subject. Walton later claimed that when he came to write the overture in 1925 he was unaware of this fact, but it seems highly probable that the Berners precedent and the artistic tastes of the Sitwells somehow sparked off the idea of basing an overture on the Rowlandson print.

However, this may have happened obliquely. The Berners connection with Rowlandson could have been responsible for the fact that some five years earlier the 20-year-old Walton had written a 'pedagogic overture' for full orchestra to accompany Rowlandson's well-known series of drawings of the adventures of a certain Dr Syntax. Only one page of the original score exists, and though it is most unlikely that this overture contained any of the thematic material of *Portsmouth Point*, it is interesting to note that the wind and brass forces that Walton employed were exactly the same as those used in his later overture.[3]

It is believed that Walton began the composition of *Portsmouth Point* at the Sitwells' house in Carlyle Square, Chelsea, during the first months of 1925, and that he continued to work on it while holidaying with them in Spain in the spring of that year. In a BBC interview given in June 1977, Walton declared that the main theme had come to him while riding on the top of a number 22 bus (a route that travels along the King's Road past Carlyle Square to this day), and that he nearly had to get off to write it down.[4]

Very little else is known about the circumstances of the overture's composition other than that on 9 November 1925 Walton wrote to Sacheverell to say that it was finished. Next came the arrangements for its first performance. Walton submitted his overture to be considered for inclusion at the 1926 Festival of the International Society for Contemporary Music, which that year was being held in Zürich. Professor E. J. Dent, from whom the young composer had received some lessons a few years previously, was the society's president, just as he had been when the revised version of Walton's String Quartet (1922) had been given during the very first ISCM Festival at Salzburg in 1923. Walton wrote the words 'British Section' in the top right-hand corner of his autograph, sent it in, and was successful in having the overture accepted. Since he lacked a publisher and was reluctant to pay a copyist when he had time on his hands, it is believed that he personally wrote out a full set of orchestral parts.

Performance

The first performance of *Portsmouth Point*, the work in which Walton's highly distinctive voice as a composer for the concert hall can be heard for the first time, was given in the Tonhalle, Zürich, on 22 June 1926 by the Tonhalle Orchestra, conducted by Volkmar Andreae. Prior to the festival, Dent had written from Zürich to the pianist Harriet Cohen (at that time undergoing treatment for tuberculosis in Geneva): 'I have just had tea with Dr. Andreae....He is very much pleased with William Walton's overture *Portsmouth Point* which we are doing—and it is so full of force that you feel as if the orchestra ought to play in their shirtsleeves!'[5] Dent's words were virtually echoed in a long article on the whole festival by the 'special correspondent' of *The Times* who reported: 'Among the new orchestral works none made a more favourable impression than Mr. W. T. Walton's overture "Portsmouth Point". Suggested by a colour-print of the time of the Napoleonic wars, it came like a stiff sea-breeze and braced the audience for the rest of the programme.'[6]

The first British performance was given under less than ideal conditions a mere six days later on 28 June 1926, when it was played as an orchestral interlude during an evening of the Diaghilev Ballets Russes season at His Majesty's Theatre, during which the Auric/Balanchine *La Pastorale* received its first performance in England. It is to be assumed that Diaghilev calculated that because of the necessary rehearsal for the ballet premiere, the resident orchestra, conducted by Eugene Goossens, would have some spare time in which to prepare another novelty. On this occasion *The Times* was unimpressed: 'In one of the intervals Mr. William Walton's Overture "Portsmouth Point" was played. We should like to hear it under more favourable conditions. For it needs a greater virtuosity of performance than was forthcoming, and it is a little difficult to make much of new music when it is heard through the hum of conversation.'[7] On 19 November of that year Serge Koussevitsky, ever the lover of novelty, was the conductor of its American premiere given by the Boston Symphony Orchestra. As a corollary to this, eight days later the *Boston Evening Transcript* published an article on Walton by the 21-year-old Constant Lambert which contained an assessment of *Portsmouth Point* that would be hard to surpass for insight and acumen:

> Here, if you like, is English music, English as the *Water Music* of Handel or as the horn-pipes of Purcell, English as the print by Rowlandson from which the title is taken. The clear air is displayed unclouded by the least suspicion of Celtic Twilight and the sparkling gaiety is undimmed by any pretentious moralising. Wisely refraining from striking the deeper note, the composer has nevertheless succeeded in producing a work of profundity, if we use that word as it might be applied to a Scarlatti sonata or a rondo by Haydn. Though lasting only a few minutes this overture is one of the most sustained efforts I know of, unlike so many modern works where the utmost ingenuity on the part of the composer cannot disguise the fact that the piece is a mere pot-pourri of fragmentary scraps of material. *Portsmouth Point* has a clear and sweeping line that is only too rare in contemporary music. Though some attempt may be made to analyse the overture as sonata form, the impression we receive is of one breathless section, an effect in no way mitigated by the profusion of themes, which take their place in the order of things like so many sudden views of the sea from the window of an express train. Technically speaking we may notice the influence of jazz on the exhilarating syncopation of the tunes, but nothing could be further removed from the soulful chromaticisms of the jazz-composer than the rollicking high spirits of this work.[8]

In a 1962 newspaper interview Walton acknowledged the influence of Stravinsky on his overture: 'No young composer could escape the great man's influence and I certainly showed it in the rhythmical complexities of *Portsmouth Point*.'[9]

Publication

The overture marked another turning point in the career of W. T. Walton (as he styled himself in those days, both in autograph and print), for it was to be the first work to be accepted by the newly founded music department of Oxford University Press, who thereafter published everything he wrote. Hubert Foss was the music editor; like Dent, he was also to become closely involved with the ISCM and may have attended the Zürich premiere. However, it would appear that the connection with OUP was brokered by Walton's friend and benefactor Siegfried Sassoon. A letter of 5 October 1926 to the poet reads: 'I am letting you know about the fruits of your labours. Foss has taken not only those songs but also P.P; also he has made a contract for 5 years to publish my works. Thank you so much for the trouble you've taken.'[10] First to appear was Walton's own transcription of the overture for piano duet; his inscribed copy to Eugene Goossens is dated 23 June 1927.[11] By the time the full score was issued exactly a year later the composer (now calling himself William Walton) had dedicated the overture to Sassoon.

He had also subjected the work, and especially its orchestration, to a careful revision, possibly in consultation with Lambert. Walton's mastery of orchestration is usually taken for granted and yet, like Elgar, he never received any instruction in this highly technical discipline. Furthermore, whereas Elgar was an experienced orchestral player and thus fully aware of the complexities of the orchestra from within, Walton never mastered an orchestral instrument. His sole guides were his fine ear (made more acute by the gift of perfect pitch), his love of listening to music of all styles—in which he was much helped by the newly burgeoning gramophone and BBC—and his ready ability to absorb the secrets of modern orchestration from reading scores. His scoring of *Portsmouth Point*, as shown by his original autograph and as performed at Zürich, is highly accomplished, but by the time the overture was published in 1928 it had been significantly strengthened and given increased brilliance by further doublings and the rewriting of instruments in more effective registers, while the percussion parts had been both extended and refined.

Lambert's reduced orchestration

As with several other early works of Walton, his younger friend, colleague, and admirer Constant Lambert played a significant part in promoting the success of *Portsmouth Point*, which, it could be said, is the Walton work that he would most like to have written himself. To begin with he copied out the entire full score, faithfully keeping to the layout of each page of Walton's autograph and occasionally making discreet but significant amendments. The manuscript contains extensive conductor's markings, and it is reasonable to suppose that this copy was made for the use of Eugene Goossens on 16 June 1926, since Walton's original had served as the conducting score for the Zürich premiere six days previously. Lambert, a great devotee of the music of Boyce and Dibdin, whose nautical style is so strongly evoked in the overture, was determined that Walton's overture should reach a wider audience, so in 1932 he made a simplified version, doubtless with Walton's agreement. It is best described in the words with which Lambert prefaced his score:

> This edition has been prepared with the intention of making William Walton's 'Portsmouth Point' available to those many orchestral societies who (in view of its heavy scoring and rhythmic difficulties) have hitherto been prevented from performing the work. In this version the orchestra has been reduced to the minimum required by a symphonic body (viz. 6 woodwind, 5 brass, 2 or 1 percussion players and a moderate number of strings) while the many changes of time signature which, in the original version, afforded a certain source of vexation to both orchestra and conductor, have here been replaced (whenever possible) by a series of comparatively simple time signatures (4/4, 3/4, and the like) with the cross rhythms indicated by marks of phrasing and accentuation.
>
> It is hoped that the present edition will not only render this glorious masterpiece accessible to all but will become a welcome companion in the concert-room and a treasure and ornament for the home.

Lambert was possibly not telling the whole truth; it would seem that another reason for making this 'simplified' reduction was because the overture was played at six performances during June and July 1932 of the small-scale Camargo Ballet Society, of which Lambert was musical director. The orchestral forces are virtually identical with those of his reduction of Vaughan Williams's *Job*, first performed in July 1931.

For all its brevity, *Portsmouth Point* is something of a milestone in the development of British music in that it heralded a new muscular style that doffed its cap at contemporary harmonic and rhythmic innovations, yet remained quintessentially native. The chief influence was clearly the Franco-Russian idiom that had been brought to universal attention by Diaghilev's sensational commissions for his Ballets Russes. Lambert again best sums up the achievement:

> It has many of the qualities one associates with the Diaghilev ballets of that time; breezy diatonic tunes supported by a very free use of diatonic discords, restless syncopated rhythms and clean but rather acid scoring.
>
> *Portsmouth Point*, however, has both more personality and more ability than the other works of its type and has deservedly outlasted them.[12]

Scapino

Composition

Information about the genesis of Walton's next overture, *Scapino: A Comedy Overture*, is equally scanty, partly due to the fact that it was composed during the early months of World War II. However its cause is quite certain. In July 1938 Dr Frederick A. Stock, the redoubtable principal conductor of the Chicago Symphony Orchestra, visited London, met Walton and discussed the possibility of his writing an orchestral work that could be given during the 1940–41 season celebrating the 50th anniversary of the orchestra's foundation.[13] Nothing appears to have been finalized on this occasion, but by the time of Walton's return from a short visit to the USA in the spring of 1939 to work on the final revisions of his Violin Concerto with Heifetz, matters had been settled. An internal memorandum dated 21 June 1939 from Hubert Foss to Sir Humphrey Milford, the OUP Publisher, reveals that Walton had now signed a contract to write an orchestral work for Chicago. For this he had been offered 750 dollars and an invitation to conduct the piece at its premiere. There were four conditions: the work was to be delivered by 1 July 1940, it was to be dedicated to the Chicago Orchestra Association, the orchestra was to be allowed to play the piece as often as it liked without payment during the 1940–41 season, and Walton's autograph score was to be presented to the orchestra's library. Foss added that Walton was contemplating an overture lasting about fifteen minutes.[14]

Fifteen minutes may have been Walton's calculation of what 750 dollars bought, but the extended overture (possibly he had in mind something between the length of Elgar's *Cockaigne* and *In the South*) soon gave way to the idea of a suite in five movements. In a letter to Foss dated 9 September 1939 Walton wrote:

> Meanwhile I am trying not too successfully to get going on this work for Chicago. But I've got quite a good scheme for the work. It is not to be an overture, but a suite which I am entitling *Varii Capricci*. There are to be five pieces, thus:

I Intrada   (full orch.)
II Siciliana   (Woodwind)
III Sarabanda   (Strings and Harps)
IV Marcia   (Brass and Percussion)
V Giga   (full orch.)

The idea of displaying the three sections of the virtuoso Chicago orchestra, framed by sonorous tuttis, is appealing and intriguingly foreshadows Britten's more adventurous *Young Person's Guide to the Orchestra* of 1945; it is a great pity that, having conceived such an original plan, Walton never returned to the idea.

In a later letter to Foss, dated 7 November of the same year, Walton gives a surprisingly full list of future compositional plans. This again includes the title *Varii Capricci*, but by now the projected work has become 'portraits from the *commedia del'arte* [*sic*] for orchestra'; Walton adds: 'This is to be a rather more ambitious work than the original plan I had for it.' By the following month OUP learned that he was anxious to write an orchestral piece with the title *Monsieur Mongo*; the idea could well have been suggested by Lambert, who had come across this patron saint of topers when making his choral setting of texts from Thomas Nash's *Summer's Last Will and Testament* some five years earlier. Nothing further was heard of any of these ideas.

Commedia dell'arte

Walton is believed to have begun the composition of his overture *Scapino* in July 1940, that is to say at precisely the time that he had agreed to deliver it to Chicago. Before this he had still been casting round for a theme and a title, though by now these had assumed an antique and Mediterranean aspect, as his undated letter to Foss, probably relating to the early months of 1940, shows: 'I'm still exercised in my mind about the title for the overture. What do you think of "The triumph of Silenus" or "(T'was) Bacchus and his crew". I incline to the latter. See Oxford B[ook] of V[erse] p. 723 at verse starting "And as I sat," Keats. If this and the following verse were quoted it might give enough of a clue without involving one in a "tone poem"?'[15]

The work was probably completed in late November or December, for the copy that he made and retained of the autograph delivered to Chicago is dated 'London, 28:12:40'. In an undated letter to Foss, received by OUP on 5 November, Walton wrote: 'I send under separate cover what there is of the overture. I hope that the title will meet with your approval; on the whole I think it best meets with the content'. This suggests that although the *commedia dell'arte* idea was clearly still at the back of his mind, the particular character of Scapino had not necessarily been the original starting point of the overture. Italy, in all its manifestations, had always been a source of delight and inspiration for Walton ever since his first memorable visit to Amalfi with the Sitwell brothers in the spring of 1920. This, combined with his love of Rossini and the world of the Ballets Russes, would have made the whole culture of the *commedia dell'arte* particularly attractive. Another influence could have been the Italian futurist artist Gino Severini (1883–1966), who was designing covers and frontispieces for the Sitwells when Walton first met them and who, in his new neo-classical phase, was very much preoccupied with *commedia dell'arte*. The bookplate that he produced for the young W. T. Walton, with its clown's costume and mask, is a perfect example of this and, it would seem, consciously harks back to the famous series of prints on the subject by the French engraver Jacques Callot.

Callot (1592–1635) was born in Lorraine and spent some formative years in Florence, which explains his interest in *commedia dell'arte* and why he came to produce a total of 32 plates on the subject. Of these 24 are devoted to the series entitled *Balli di Sfessania*, and the twelfth engraving depicts two characters conversing animatedly, who are designated as 'Scapino' and 'Cap[itano] Zerbino'. The *Balli* sequence is the source that Walton quotes on the title page of his autograph and also that of the first printed edition, but the statement proves to be a half-truth. As already described, Scapino is indeed represented in this series but he is almost indistinguishable from the other characters. However, the Callot print that undoubtedly inspired Walton was an earlier, larger etching that was devoted wholly to Scapino and suggested his character to marvellous effect. This etching was one of a group of three, produced in 1618–19, called *Les Trois Pantalons* and was designated '*Le Zani* [clown] *ou Scapin*'.[16] Walton appears to have believed that this formed part of the sequence, because he stuck a reproduction of the *Balli* title page on that of his 'Chicago' autograph, following his subtitle 'after an etching from Jacques Callot's *Balli di Sfessania* 1622', and then one of the '*Trois Pantalons*' Scapino a page later. The misattribution, still perpetuated by the 1950 first publication of the overture, was corrected when the score came up for reprinting. The published score goes on to give the following note: 'SCAPINO is one of the less familiar characters of the Commedia dell' Arte, the hero of Molière's 'Les Fourberies de Scapin', who may figure in the complicated ancestry of Figaro. We owe him the word 'escapade', which is descriptive of the character's stock-in-trade. Callot's etching, reproduced on the cover, portrays him in his traditional costume.' To this may be added the facts that the name derives from the Italian *scappare* ('to flee', as in the slang word 'scarper'), and that the character's speciality was scheming in the pursuit of money or revenge and then running away. Scapino was also said by P. L. Duchartre, in his classic book on Italian comedy, to be 'as amorous as birds in spring, and for him it is spring the whole year round',[17] which explains the A♭ middle section of the overture.

Performance

Despite the fact that it was delivered considerably later than agreed, the overture was still able to be included in the Chicago Symphony Orchestra's golden jubilee season. It received its premiere at Orchestra Hall on 3 April 1941 and was repeated the following night. The programme stated that Walton had composed the work 'with some difficulty for he was, and is, serving with the British forces in the present war'. Walton may have given some such excuse for his late delivery of the overture; if so it was a rather high-flown way of describing his short-lived employment as an ambulance driver for an Air Raid Precautions unit in the English Midlands. As the wartime conditions made it impossible for Walton to travel to Chicago to conduct, as originally envisioned, Dr Stock took his place. The composer's absence emboldened him to make a 21-bar cut which was restored when he and the orchestra went on to record *Scapino* for American Columbia on 20 November of the same year.[18] In Britain the overture received its first performance as a studio broadcast on 12 November 1941 at the Corn Exchange, Bedford, to where the orchestra, the BBC Symphony, had been evacuated. Walton conducted, and a photograph exists of him in rehearsal for the occasion. London first heard *Scapino* on the afternoon of 13 December when Walton conducted the London Philharmonic Orchestra at the Royal Albert Hall. Two days later *The Times* reported that it was 'comedy music in the composer's best vein' and that it had been 'excellently played'.

Revision

No printed score was issued at this time; instead OUP made a few photocopies of Walton's exceptionally neat 'London' autograph for the use of conductors. This may have had something to do with paper shortage and the severely curtailed activities of the OUP music department under wartime conditions, but was possibly also due to the fact that Walton was already considering revision. His letter to OUP of 8 February 1941 from the home of Alice, Viscountess Wimborne at Ashby St Ledgers reads: 'Would you send the photostat score of Scapino so I can look into the question of cutting down the scoring.' Eventually, urged on by Alan Frank of OUP, Walton made a revision in the autumn of 1949, shortly before he and his wife left London for their first stay on Ischia. While adding a third trumpet and dispensing with the contrabassoon, two cornets, and fourth percussion of the original, the revision introduced seven cuts amounting to a total of 61 bars. At the same time certain passages were transposed and the orchestration was revised. Great care was taken with the first publication of the score, which nevertheless contained a number of errors. Walton personally inspected three sets of proofs, including the transparencies of the orchestral parts, and for the first time the cover of an important new Walton work was not that designed by Gino Severini for *Portsmouth Point* in 1927 but the Callot engraving of *Le Zani ou Scapin*, which Walton himself provided. The study score, with its elegant and distinctive rust-brown cover, appeared in December 1950; a limited number of full-sized conducting scores were put on sale shortly after. The revised version of *Scapino* was given its first performance on 13 November 1950 at the Royal Albert Hall by the Philharmonia Orchestra under Wilhelm Furtwängler.

Few people listening to *Scapino* will have failed to be struck by the *giocoso* passage in 3rds for trumpets, first heard in bar 110, which appears to be a virtual quotation from the second movement of Rimsky-Korsakov's *Sheherazade*. The conductor Boyd Neel certainly believed this to be the case and commented on it in the course of a BBC gramophone record programme called 'Where have I heard that before?', presented by him on Sunday 19 April 1942. Walton privately countered with the rejoinder, 'Ass, don't you know *Tancredi* when you hear it?!!' Frank Howes made the same observation in his 1943 analysis of the work, though he appears to have already discussed this with Walton for he writes: 'There is no significance in the fortuitous resemblance, but as the phrase is repeated one's attention is diverted from what is going on by a puzzled search for its congener, and such distraction is bad for the apprehension of music so fleet as this. The similarity certainly never entered the head of the composer who considers it more like a phrase from the overture to *Tancredi* and certainly treats it more in the manner of Rossini than of Rimsky-Korsakov.'[19] Walton may have become sensitive on this point. At any rate Ralph Hill's programme analysis for the 1950 first performance of the revised version included sentences that sound as if they were prompted by the composer himself: 'It is the kind of thing one might imagine Rossini writing had he lived today. Indeed, Walton is a great admirer of the old Italian master and has actually quoted the second subject of Rossini's Overture "Tancredi" as a counterpart to the second subject of "Scapino." Walton says that the reason for this quotation is because he is inordinately fond of Rossini's music and also because he hoped it would help "point" the character of Scapino—"Rossini being the most Scapinoesque of composers".'

Scapino was the only concert work that Walton wrote between the Violin Concerto of 1939 and the String Quartet in A minor, completed in 1946.

Johannesburg Festival Overture

There is little to be said about this attractive and effective work. In January 1956, while Walton was in Milan attending rehearsals of the new production of his opera *Troilus and Cressida* at La Scala, he was approached in person by Ernest Fleischmann, the director of music and drama for the forthcoming Johannesburg Festival, with a commission to write an overture for the occasion.[20] The festival was being held to celebrate the 70th anniversary of the foundation of that city, and was planned to take place in the autumn of the same year. Despite the fact that he was already working on his Cello Concerto, the composer readily accepted.

Walton always responded well to tight deadlines—that for *Scapino* had perhaps been too slack—and after listening to some records of African music sent to him at his own request by the African Music Society in Johnnesburg,[21] he composed the overture between February and 31 May at his home in Forio, Ischia. In delivering it Walton wrote to say that he had introduced a number of Bantu melodies 'with considerable effect'. He continued, 'It is a very gay, one might almost say hilarious piece which, I trust, is needed to brighten up the Festival—if it needs it!'[22] The overture received its broadcast world premiere on 25 September 1956 at the City Hall, Johannesburg, when the South African Broadcasting Corporation Symphony Orchestra was conducted by Sir Malcolm Sargent, who thus was giving the third of his four Walton premieres.[23] In England the *Johannesburg Festival Overture* was first heard on 13 November in the Philharmonic Hall, Liverpool; the Liverpool Philharmonic Orchestra was conducted by Efrem Kurtz.

The overture was published by OUP in 1958 in study score format. By then Walton had made a 34-bar cut, which accounts for the lack of rehearsal figures 20 and 21. The cut music is merely a repeat of two bars before fig. 1 to two before fig. 3 (bars 27–57), with a link into fig. 22. After publication he also decided that the 16 bars of harp from fig. 16 to the bar after fig. 17 (bars 256–71) were better omitted.

The overture has proved to be a fine piece of semi-light music and is notable for what Frank Howes has aptly called its 'sleek elegance'; only the less than alluring title has in any way checked its unqualified appeal. Walton's own evaluation of it may be judged from a letter he wrote to his New York friend Dorle Soria from Ischia on 9 April 1963 in connection with the programme for a forthcoming concert he was to conduct: 'I would like to start off with "Johannesburg Festival Overture" rather than "Scapino". It is easier to play and rather a better and more popular piece'.[24]

NOTES

1. It is noteworthy that the first performances of all three overtures took place outside the British Isles.
2. *Portsmouth Point* was drawn by Rowlandson on 14 July 1814 and published by T. Tegg. It measures 33.3 × 22.8 cm, and is often seen in coloured copies. It is not to be confused with his watercolour of the same name of 1782.

3. The page was seen by Stewart Craggs at OUP when he was working on *William Walton: A Catalogue*, but its whereabouts at present are unknown.

4. 'A Portrait of William Walton', presented by John Amis, 4 June 1977.

5. Harriet Cohen, *A Bundle of Time* (London, 1969), p. 106.

6. *The Times* (30 June 1926), p. 14b.

7. *The Times* (29 June 1926), p. 14c.

8. Constant Lambert, 'Fresh Hand; New Talent; Vital Touch', *Boston Evening Transcript* (27 November 1926), section IV, p. 5 a–f.

9. *Sunday Telegraph* (25 March 1962).

10. William Walton Museum, Forio, Ischia. Walton omits the year, but it is obvious from the context.

11. Walton Museum.

12. Constant Lambert, 'Some Angles of the Compleat Walton', *Radio Times* (7 August 1936), p. 13.

13. Among the numerous other works commissioned for the same occasion were Kodály's Concerto for Orchestra, Stravinsky's Symphony in C, Milhaud's Symphony No. 1, and Myaskovsky's Symphony No. 21.

14. OUP Archive, Oxford. All other letters to Foss quoted derive from the same source.

15. *The Selected Letters of William Walton*, ed. Malcolm Hayes (London, 2002), p. 129.

16. The Callot etching measures 24 × 15.2 cm. Scapino is sometimes described as holding a sword, but it is so broad that the alternative suggestion that it is a slapstick (*battocchino*) is more convincing. Walton may have believed this because in the longest cut section of his original version (following on the present bar 106) he employed a slapstick in his percussion section.

17. P. L. Duchartre, *The Italian Comedy*, trans. Randolph T. Weaver (London, 1929), p. 168.

18. American Columbia 11945D, Columbia LX 931 (78 rpm); Biddulph WHL021/2 (CD).

19. Frank Howes, *The Music of William Walton*, 2 vols., Musical Pilgrim Series (London, 1942–3), vol. 2, p. 70; rev. and enlarged edn (London, 1965, rev. 1974), p. 114.

20. Fleischmann was later to become executive director of the London Symphony Orchestra and general director of the Los Angeles Symphony Orchestra.

21. See article by David Rycroft in the *Bulletin of the British Institute of Recorded Sound*, 3 (winter 1956), pp. 19–21. The theme played by horns at fig. 16, accompanied by an exotic array of percussion, is the one usually identified as having been influenced by the African recordings.

22. Quoted in the programme of the first performance.

23. Due to popular demand, the overture was repeated at Sargent's next concert on 2 October.

24. Walton Museum.

15

Orchestral Works I *(Vol. 15)*

James Brooks Kuykendall

On 30 March 1956 the trustees of the Cleveland Orchestra met with music director George Szell to discuss how best to commemorate the 40th anniversary of the orchestra during the 1957–8 season, with the aim both to increase the orchestra's national and international reputation and to strive for the greatest artistic merit in their performances and programming. In a memo of this meeting, orchestra president Frank E. Taplin recorded their conclusion that 'it would seem desirable to commission works from contemporary composers of the highest rank in order to achieve these twin objectives'. The five anticipated commissions, each worth approximately $2000, would be for works for full symphony orchestra only (with no soloists), and should include at least one American composer. Taplin's memo lists the names of the eighteen composers proposed at the initial meeting, categorizing them by nationality. At the head of the list is 'England: Walton, Britten'.[1]

The Cleveland Orchestra under Szell was to become particularly associated with Walton's later orchestral works, earning the composer's enthusiastic praise more than once. Walton's position as one of Szell's top choices for the Cleveland anniversary commissions is not surprising given the conductor's previous important connections with the composer.[2] Walton's penchant for carefully calculated scoring and brilliance would have been attractive to Szell as a mechanism to display the virtuosity of his Cleveland ensemble, which at that moment was becoming internationally recognized as a major American orchestra. The orchestra's first European tour in the early summer of 1957 garnered astonished reviews: 'no finer orchestra playing has yet been heard in the Festival Hall, and I doubt whether anything superior is to be heard anywhere else' was the reaction of the distinguished critic Desmond Shawe-Taylor.[3]

The Partita, the Second Symphony, and the Hindemith Variations are the works most closely associated with Szell because of his premieres, recordings, and repeated programming. At first glance they may seem strange bedfellows, but there is an integral kinship between these works. For example, the 'Toccata' from the Partita for Orchestra foreshadows the musical gestures of the first movement of the symphony; and in the Variations on a Theme by Hindemith Walton explores more ambitiously the compositional challenges of the variations–fugato–coda form of the symphony's finale, with remarkable echoes of the earlier piece in this later one (as at the transition into the fugato, bars 145–65 of the symphony finale becoming bars 445–55 in the Variations). The Partita's 'Pastorale Siciliana' mood and scoring continued to haunt Walton, recurring in the third of his unpublished Granada TV call signs (1962),[4] and finally in the lyrical Variation 3 of his tribute to Hindemith. Despite these and other common threads, there is a marked change in the composer's attitude—from the almost flippant experiment of the Partita, through the serious study of the symphony, to the devoted homage embodied in the Variations. Most importantly, these works bear witness to Walton's vital mastery of his craft at the height of his maturity and reputation.

Partita for Orchestra

Composition

After the initial meeting about the 40th anniversary celebrations, the Cleveland Orchestra sent telegrams on 30 April 1956 offering commissions to three composers: Samuel Barber, Paul Hindemith, and William Walton. Barber and Hindemith both declined, so the scheme was expanded to include a total of ten commissions.[5] In a letter of 10 May, George Smith, the orchestra's assistant manager, requested 'an orchestral work in one movement of not less than ten minutes' duration'. Walton was not enthusiastic about this stipulation, as he wrote on 17 May to his publisher Alan Frank at Oxford University Press: 'What I had in mind to do was a short Sinfonietta or Suite with 4 or 5 movements of 3–4 minutes each. Also I've had a letter from Szell not mentioning what kind of work I was to write, but dwelling on matters of the Horn[,] Oboe[,] etc.'[6] Once the contract was negotiated, it was some months before Walton gave any further thought to the project. On 17 November, however, he requested Frank to send scores of works by Berlioz, Mahler, Prokofiev, and Roussel (including the *Suite en Fa*, which would turn out to be significant), remarking, 'I'm on the track of the work for Cleveland.' The Waltons' serious car accident in January 1957 delayed all progress, and as late as April 1957 Walton could write only that he was 'about to begin' the Partita.[7]

By early July Walton had completed the score of the first movement, and the second followed in early August ('no great shakes, but I think it will pass,' the composer wrote to Alan Frank on 11 August); the finale was delayed until late October. Szell was pleased with the first movement when he saw it, writing that it would be 'by far the finest of our commissions'. Responding to a request from Cleveland for 'whatever description, analysis, or comments you would care to make about the work', Walton wrote to Frank on 13 November that 'it has no programme or any ulterior motive behind it either deep or shallow (save perhaps making $2000!)'. From this Frank assembled the following note, to be published in the Cleveland *Plain Dealer* above Walton's signature which, when used subsequently, was always attributed to the composer:

> Two major difficulties confront me in responding to your kind invitation to contribute a few words about my new <u>Partita for Orchestra</u>. Firstly, I am a writer of notes and (to my regret) not of prose. Secondly, it is surely easier to write about a piece of creative work if there is something problematical about it. Indeed—so it seems to me—the more problematical, the greater the flow of words. Unfortunately from this point of view, my Partita poses no problems, has no ulterior motive or meaning behind it, and makes no attempt to ponder the imponderables. I have written it in the hope that it may be enjoyed straight off, without any preliminary probing into the score. I have also written it with the wonderful players of the Cleveland Orchestra in mind, hoping that they may enjoy playing it. If either of these two hopes is fulfilled, I shall be more than happy.
>
> The work is in three shortish movements, and their titles explain themselves: 1. Toccata; 2. Pastorale Siciliana; 3. Giga burlesca. The orchestra used is normal, with no unusual 'extras'. Since the first and third movements are predominantly vigorous

and use full orchestra for a good deal of the time, I have designed the middle movement, the Pastorale Siciliana, which opens with an unaccompanied duet between solo
viola and solo oboe, as a complete contrast in mood and texture.

Finally, I want to say how touched and delighted I was when, in May 1956, I received
at my home in Ischia, Italy, a cable from George Szell, offering me this commission.
The execution of it has given me the greatest pleasure, particularly so since it was also
in Cleveland, nearly twenty years ago, that the world première of my Violin Concerto
was given.

'Bravo—I couldn't have done it better it better myself,' Walton responded on 24
November. 'It says everything that is needed.'

Premieres

On 30 January 1958 Szell conducted the world premiere at Severance Hall in Cleveland;
a televised rehearsal in the preceding week had given the Cleveland audience a fore-
taste of the work. The next day *Cleveland News* critic Ethel Boros assessed the work as
'a jolly, tongue-in-cheek affair which takes a musical poke at composers who try to
cloak themselves in the mantles of old forms'. Szell was delighted, writing on 31 January
to Walton (who was not present at the premiere) that 'it is not quite possible for me
to express adequately my delight over this splendid work. The performance its-self
[*sic*] confirmed my initial, very sanguine expectations to the fullest extent. I think all
orchestras owe you a great debt of gratitude for this significant enrichment of their
repertoire.'

The Hallé Orchestra presented the British premiere in Manchester on 30 April, under
the baton of the composer. Malcolm Tillis, then a violinist in the Hallé, recalled numerous frustrating errors in the orchestral parts. (There were so many, in fact, that three
weeks before Walton's performance the OUP editorial staff recalled all the materials
sent to Manchester in order to correct mistakes and update readings standardized during the preparation of the printed full score.) There were still more changes to come, as
Tillis later described:

> Walton, smiling rather diffidently, took his place on the rostrum; he decided to keep
> the chair that had been placed there. Sitting very erect, he put on a pair of thickrimmed
> glasses and took off his tie. I was surprised to see how grey his hair had become. He
> took hold of his baton awkwardly, paused for a moment, and said 'You know, I haven't
> heard this piece through yet but before we start would you all mark an alteration one
> bar after seven?'.... The last rehearsal found Walton in a much more serious frame of
> mind; the chair was dispensed with; he made far more stops to clear up untidy pas-
> sages. At one point he even became annoyed, 'Someone is still not sure about the rests
> at figure two. I'm giving you a very strong up-beat [*recte* down-beat?] so do sort it out.
> Surely there can't be anything wrong with the parts after all this time.' He took the
> whole section very slowly, his head buried in the score. Suddenly he decided to alter
> some of the dynamic marks; it is never to late to make insertions or deletions if they
> clarify the composer's intentions. The passage was then taken at the correct tempo; it
> came off perfectly. The Siciliana was played straight through; Walton's face took on a
> placid mask: it seemed completely detached from and unaffected by the exotic sounds

that were coming from the orchestra.... At the end of the rehearsal he was all smiles, 'No questions? Any complaints? Don't worry, I'll be all right tonight', were his last words as he flicked the score closed.[8]

A conductor more different from George Szell can hardly be imagined.

Szell continued to conduct the Partita, using it again at the inaugural concert of the newly remodelled Severance Hall on 8 October 1958.[9] He had also reserved exclusive recording rights for a year after the premiere, an agreement which delayed Walton's own recording. Szell recorded the Partita with the Cleveland Orchestra on 21 January 1959, although it was not released until September 1962 (paired with Symphony No. 2); Walton's recording with the Philharmonia Orchestra (February 1959) was issued in December 1959.

Several commentators have noted similarities between Walton's Partita and the *Suite en Fa* (1926) by Albert Roussel. The proportions of the outer movements are strikingly similar. Roussel's 'Prélude' is an *Allegro molto* of 194 bars, compared with Walton's 196-bar *Brioso*; the gigue finales of both works extend to exactly 341 bars, although the internal dispositions do not coincide. There is sufficient evidence to confirm that Walton used the Roussel work as a model. The correspondences between the two works are most clear in the first movements where, as Stephen Lloyd has written, 'for a few bars the composers could almost be interchanged'.[10] Not only the general bustling mood of the piece, but even as ostensibly idiosyncratic a melodic figure as Walton's bars 35–42 seems clearly derived from Roussel's bars 22–32. It is at the climactic moments where the resemblance between the movements is perhaps most striking: Walton's memorable bars 67–94 (reprised at bars 160 ff.) achieve the same effect with very nearly the same means as Roussel's bars 61–87 (bars 159 ff.); the same is true of the transition into the recapitulation (Walton, bars 118–121; Roussel, bars 119–122). Even the inclusion of the tamtam and celesta suggests Roussel's influence. At least for the first movement, Michael Kennedy's charitable description (a 'brilliantly creative paraphrase') is apt.[11]

Variations on a Theme by Hindemith

Genesis

By his middle age, Walton must surely have had time to realize the full extent of his indebtedness to Paul Hindemith. The German composer was six years older than Walton, and they had been acquainted since 1923. In 1929 Hindemith had been the soloist for the premiere of the Viola Concerto and thus helped to establish the junior composer's career at a crucial moment. Walton's gratitude to Hindemith was expressed in two significant ways: one was by following Hindemith's example in encouraging and assisting younger composers (particularly Hans Werner Henze and Malcolm Arnold); the other was by documenting his appreciation by composing a piece in tribute to the senior composer. Walton's letters have vague references to a promise that would ultimately come to fruition in the Variations on a Theme by Hindemith. 'I shall eventually produce something new for him, before not too long, I hope,' Walton wrote to Gertrude Hindemith on 10 May 1955; some thirty months later, having just completed the Partita, Walton repeats, 'Don't think I've forgotten about the work I intend writing for you!'[12]

Indeed Walton had not forgotten, and told Alan Frank on several occasions that time would have to be set aside for the Hindemith project.[13] Commissions for Symphony No. 2 and the Gloria crowded Walton's schedule, and it was not until August 1961 that an opportunity presented itself. The Royal Philharmonic Society offered a commission for a programme scheduled for 8 March 1963, the exact date of the sesquicentennial of the society's first concert. On 2 August 1961 Alan Frank wrote to Walton 'could it in fact be the Hindemith Variations?'; Walton replied on 8 August that 'it would be quite an idea to do the Hindemith Variations. But as I said before the trouble is to find the suitable themes. Perhaps you could ask [Howard] Hartog [at Schott, Hindemith's publisher] to send me all the works of H that have variations. It would be I think wise to work on a theme that one knows can be varied.' Scores of *Der Schwanendreher*, 'A Frog he went a-courting' Variations, *Philharmonisches Konzert*, Septet, Viola Sonata (Op. 11, No. 4), Solo Violin Sonata (Op. 31, No. 1), and *The Four Temperaments* were dispatched to Walton's home in Ischia.

Composition

When on 12 December Walton next mentioned the Variations in his correspondence, he had selected a theme not from any of these works, but from the middle movement of Hindemith's Cello Concerto (1940). 'If you know the theme you will see that it is not entirely my fault if it turns out to be a late Vic. or early Edwardian work,' he warned Frank on 22 December 1961.[14] Walton set to work promptly. Once he was sufficiently satisfied with his sketches, he obtained permission from Schott in January 1962 for the Hindemith theme to be used. Walton opted to borrow not only the theme, but its accompaniment as well: bars 1–36 of the two works are nearly identical. Even in rescoring the melody (originally given to the solo cello), he takes his cue from Hindemith's reprise (compare bars 207–221 in the concerto).

For most of the first half of 1962 Walton was occupied with other matters: completing *A Song for the Lord Mayor's Table*, making a British concert tour to celebrate his 60th birthday, and moving into his long-awaited new home, La Mortella, and in August he was 'somewhat lazily settling down to the Variations'. The Variations on a Theme by Hindemith is one of Walton's very few works of which at least some compositional sketches survive, and only because he had come to realize that even the sketches might be of some commercial value. Indeed, on 22 January 1962 the solicitor Stanley Rubenstein had written to Walton about the '"fancy prices" which the University of Texas [home to the Harry Ransom Humanities Research Center] is paying for authors' and composers' manuscripts, providing they are full of corrections so that the University Professors can deduce from such corrections how the work has developed in the mind of the author or composer'. On 5 April Alan Frank replied to Rubenstein offering the autographs of both the first symphony and the early string quartet, as well as 'the first sketch score of Sir William's next orchestral work, together with the final fair-copied manuscript....Hitherto the composer's first sketches seem to have disintegrated, but this would be possible, as I say, for the work he is engaged upon at present, which is in fact the VARIATIONS ON A THEME OF HINDEMITH.'

Although this offer was not taken up, at least some of these sketches have survived, and form part of the Frederick R. Koch Collection at Yale University. The sketches are in full score (though with all instruments at concert pitch) and with a great amount of orchestral detail—although not always with the same scoring as the final version. The sketches for any given movement are written on one side of a page only, suggesting that Walton preferred to be able to lay them out in such a way that he could see an entire movement at a glance. There are several false starts to Variations 2 and 6; Variations 3 and 5 are sketched very thoroughly; the sketch of Variation 4 is patchy at best, and there are no extant sketches after Variation 6. (In his rough index of these papers, Walton notes, 'The rest seems to be lost, or maybe I had no longer any need to make sketches!'[15]) The most striking difference between the sketches and the text of the autograph score is the substantial number of metrical adjustments and re-barrings, very often with neither version more complicated than the other but with a subtle shift of emphasis.

On 16 October 1962 Walton started work on the autograph manuscript, and in early November he posted to London the first instalment (the theme and first two variations). By early December the third and fourth variations had followed, and Walton was able to respond to Frank's request for a commentary that might be mined for programme notes:

> I've not indulged in 'indeterminacy' but started with a perhaps too rigid key-scheme which we had perhaps not better mention, in case I fail to adhere to it! It is in fact a quite simple one that there's a variation for each note of the main theme. The 1st starts on E & the 2nd G#—the 3rd F# (we miss out the A as it repeats as No. 7) & so forth, which explains the somewhat arbitrary change of keys (or tonal centres if you must have it so)[.] V goes backwards & arse over tippett as well & of course the inversion of bar 24 produces that fetish B.A.C.H. Why it has this mystic significance beats me. For my part it is purely a fluke & has about as much interest to me as Boo-Cee And Hawkes! However the coda of this var. is very obscure. I find it so myself so what anyone else will think, I dread to contemplate.[16]

In the same letter, Walton expressed concerns about the looming deadline: 'If necessary I shall have to cut Vars 8 & 9 & dash for the Finale. That is why no mention should be made of the key scheme.' On 19 December Alan Frank was nervous, too, though able to jest about it: 'I agree that the number of variations should be governed by your rate of progress and that the work might well be terminated on the last day of January, even if you are halfway through a bar.' Walton's progress continued throughout January, despite a comedy of errors prompted by false reports of Szell's death. When the second bar after fig. 46 crossed Frank's desk on 28 January, he wrote, 'I always cheer up—no doubt you do too—when I see the word "stringendo", assuming that this means the end is in sight.' On 7 February—barely a month before the premiere—the autograph was complete.

Performance

Walton then turned his attention to preparing to conduct the first performance. He had spent several months working on each variation separately, and he now made adjustments to the transitions from one section to the next, becoming increasingly less satisfied with the whole piece. Walton wrote to Frank on 15 February, 'Having to learn my beats I've been going thro' it daily & must confess I find it a trifle dull. I don't think I've got far enough away from the Theme especially the form. On the other hand the Theme has such a well defined form that it would be very difficult—even wrong to have tried to have done so.' Indeed, the theme has so many segments that it proved a challenge to vary *each* of them in each variation. He had complained in December that 'there [are] certain bars for instance that are most intractable, 5 & 6, 10–15 & one can practically only repeat them which is bad'; a comparison of bars 10–15 with the corresponding passage in some variations suggests that Walton was reaching the limits of his creative energy for this particular motive.

In general, however, the work displays a startling abundance of invention. Perhaps the most striking example is his treatment of the conspicuous sequence of arpeggiated triads a major 3rd apart (Theme, bars 29–32). Walton regularly exploits the tonal ambiguity of the figure in order to finish one variation in the tonality which will begin the next, contributing to the sense of inevitability in the work as a whole. Sometimes this is a matter of cycling through the 3rds until he arrives convincingly at the 'wrong' one (bars 94–100); at other times the whirling repetitions act as a sleight of hand, obscuring an abrupt shift that will allow an easy path to the new tonic (bars 220, 263). In Variation 5 the motive is inverted and then re-inverted (bars 301–8). The masterstroke is in Variation 7, where Walton unmasks the motive with a pointed quotation—complete with quotation marks in the score at bars 394–7—from Hindemith's opera *Mathis der Maler*, first performed in 1938.[17] Hindemith seems to have been unaware of this resemblance, but Walton had found his theme 'naggingly familiar'.[18] Walton may have recognized the motive because he had used an almost identical figure in bars 84–95 (at the text 'We made it not in vain') of 'Glory to God' in *Christopher Columbus* (1942), a movement which seems to culminate in another *Mathis* reference.[19] Critical reaction after the premiere was mixed. Writing in the *Musical Times*, Andrew Porter declared,

> Ear tells me that [the variations] are well-contrasted yet coherent in total effect; that each of them immediately captures the interest, but not all sustain it for the whole length—the idea of each is fascinating, but its working out tends to be protracted; that the work is scored in a new 'functional' way, without the ripeness, but not without the enjoyment and command of orchestral colour that marked, say, the Second Symphony.[20]

By far the most negative review was that in *The Observer*, by Walton's 'tormenter-in-chief', Peter Heyworth. Under the headline 'Walton Free-Wheels', Heyworth is unrelenting:

> In their youth both [Walton and Hindemith] for a while passed as bright young sparks, but since the war the tides of taste have moved so decisively away from their sort of music that today they appear rather as companions in misfortune, isolated and beleaguered bastions of a tottering order....Agreeable though it would be to salute these Variations as a successful sortie against contemporary conformities and as an effective expression of the order for which both Walton and Hindemith stand, it is, alas, nothing of the sort. One seeks in vain the sort of cross-fertilisation (such as Stravinsky has never scorned) that might issue from handling material so markedly individual as Hindemith's. There are indeed isolated Hindemithian passages. But they provide an intermittent flavour rather than a real enrichment of idiom, and for the rest there is only an intensely depressing sense of familiarity and routine.[21]

Heyworth cites 'the usual manifestations of Waltonian vitality: the nervous syncopations, the garish, fussy orchestration, the whirligig joviality, the Scapino-like bustle'.

Perhaps it is understandable that on one hearing only Heyworth would latch onto Walton's mannerisms—manifest throughout the work—particularly as these would strengthen the critic's oft-repeated theory that Walton's creative facility was stagnant.[22] Save for his remark that 'This is a work that will appeal primarily to those who like what they know', Heyworth surely could not have anticipated that the Variations would come to be regarded as one of Walton's most impressive late works.

Hindemith himself—who, unlike the critics, had the benefit of repeated listening to a private recording of the premiere—was almost inordinately pleased, as he wrote to Walton on 29 July:

> I am particularly fond of the honest solidity of workmanship in this score—something that seems almost completely lost nowadays. Let us thank you for your kindness and for the wonderfully touching and artistically convincing manifestation of this kindness (even old Mathis is permitted to peep through the fence, which for a spectre like him seems to be some kind of resurrection after artificial respiration!).... I shall do my best to become a worthy interpreter of W.W.[23]

Despite his intention, he never conducted the work, and Walton's long-intended tribute was only just in time: Paul Hindemith died on 28 December 1963.

George Szell conducted the American premiere in Cleveland on 18 April 1963 and immediately took the work on a tour to New York State (Ithaca and New York City) and Ontario (Ottawa and London). On 6 May 1963 he wrote to Walton, 'In every instance the reception was an exceedingly warm one and I was particularly impressed by the fact that the applause set in spontaneously in full force after the last chord, in spite of the quiet close after an exciting climax—or perhaps because of it? We, as performers, have found continuous pleasure in playing and replaying the piece.' In the same letter he includes 'observations and suggestions' about details of scoring, almost always having to do with balance; in each case Walton made some adjustment, almost always adopting Szell's suggestion. When Walton heard Szell rehearse the Variations in Amsterdam with the Concertgebouw Orchestra in November 1964, he was at a loss for words: 'It was stupendous. After rehearsing it he turned to me and asked for any comment. I could make none as there was nothing to say except a rather tame "Thank You". How can one comment on a performance which is flawless in every aspect?'[24]

Walton was fortunate to have found a champion with such an established international career. Szell continued to conduct Walton's works regularly, and it was largely due to the conductor that in 1959 Walton ranked behind only Stravinsky and Copland in a list of most-performed modern composers by American orchestras during the 1958–9 season.[25] Szell's death on 30 July 1970 was a great blow to Walton; as he wrote on 18 August 1970 to John Owen Ward, head of the music department at OUP's New York office, '[Szell's] demise is a great loss to me as it is of no use pretending that [Pierre] Boulez will continue his good work or anyone else for that matter.'[26] But in the happier days that produced these works, the composer had every reason to be more optimistic:

> The pendulum swings so fast these days that—who knows?—any minute we may well find ourselves in for a real neo-romantic revival. In which case I may find myself in the unlikely position of being abreast of the times for a change. So 60 seems to me just the beginning. In fact, I like to regard myself as rather a promising composer.[27]

NOTES

1. Taplin memo (6 April 1956), General Manager's Records—Office Files 1957/58; quoted by courtesy of the Cleveland Orchestra Archives.
2. In 1938–9 Szell had conducted the Scottish, Continental, and Australian premieres of Walton's Symphony No. 1. The Cleveland Orchestra under Artur Rodzinski premiered Walton's Violin Concerto on 7 December 1939, with Jascha Heifetz.
3. 'A Great Orchestra', *New Statesman and Nation* (18 May 1957), pp. 638–639. For an assessment of the tour in a larger context see Donald Rosenberg, *The Cleveland Orchestra Story* (Cleveland, 2000), pp. 291–296. See also Michael Charry, *George Szell: A Life in Music* (Urbana, 2011), pp. 170 ff.
4. Beinecke Rare Book and Manuscript Library, Yale University, Frederick R. Koch Collection, MS 601, Granada TV Call Signs, p. 2 [p. 41].
5. In addition to Walton were Boris Blacher, Paul Creston, Henri Dutilleux, Alvin Etler, Howard Hanson, Bohuslav Martinů, Peter Mennin, Robert Moevs, and Gottfried von Einem; Dutilleux's *Cinq Métaboles* was delayed until 1965, but all the other premieres occurred in the anniversary season as intended.
6. Except where stated, all subsequent quotations are taken from the production files in the OUP Archive, Oxford.
7. Walton to Gregor Piatigorsky, 4 April 1957; quoted in *The Selected Letters of William Walton*, ed. Malcolm Hayes (London, 2002), p. 297.
8. Malcolm Tillis, *Chords & Discords: The Life of an Orchestral Musician* (London, 1960), pp. 131–133.
9. Rosenberg, *Cleveland Orchestra Story*, p. 302.
10. Stephen Lloyd, *William Walton: Muse of Fire* (Woodbridge, 2001), p. 231.
11. Michael Kennedy, *Portrait of Walton* (Oxford, 1989; rev. edn, 1998), p. 208.
12. *Selected Letters*, ed. Hayes, pp. 266, 308.
13. *Selected Letters*, ed. Hayes, pp. 286, 308.
14. When the work was finished, Walton wrote to Alan Frank on 9 February 1963 fearing that the coda 'may sound like the Salvation Army outside the "pub" on a cold and frosty Sun. morn. with a long Sullivanesque "Great Amen" at the end'.
15. Beinecke Rare Book and Manuscript Library, Yale University, Frederick R. Koch Collection, MS 600, Variations on a Theme by Hindemith, Sketches p. [1].
16. Walton to Alan Frank, 12 December 1962.
17. Walton quoted *Mathis* from the vocal score; Hindemith's harmony is retained, but the orchestration follows the simplified piano reduction.
18. Quoted in Frank Howes, *The Music of William Walton* (2nd edn, London, 1973), p. 60.
19. See Zelda Lawrence-Curran, ' "All the things that might have been": *Christopher Columbus*', in Stewart R. Craggs, ed., *William Walton: Music and Literature* (Aldershot, 1999), p. 172. Walton had almost certainly heard the BBC's concert performance of Hindemith's opera conducted by Clarence Raybould at the Queen's Hall on 15 March 1939.
20. *Musical Times*, vol. 104 (April 1963), p. 265.
21. *The Observer* (10 March 1963), p. 27.
22. For a perceptive discussion of the Walton–Heyworth relationship see Kennedy, *Portrait*, pp. 199–202.
23. Quoted in Howes, *William Walton*, pp. 54 f.
24. Walton to John Owen Ward, 16 March 1965; Beinecke Rare Book and Manuscript Library, Yale University, John Owen Ward papers, Uncat. MSS. 106.
25. 'Annual Orchestra Survey: Conservatism Gains', *Musical America* (June 1959), pp. 14, 26. Significantly, Walton's position in the list rested on the strength of only three works (*Belshazzar's Feast*, the Violin Concerto, and the Partita for Orchestra) which together garnered 25 performances.
26. Beinecke Rare Book and Manuscript Library, Yale University, John Owen Ward papers, Uncat. MSS. 106.
27. William Walton, 'My Life in Music' (interview with John Warrack), *Sunday Telegraph* (25 March 1962), p. 8.

16

Orchestral Works 2 *(Vol. 16)*

Michael Durnin

From the beginning of Walton's career, listeners noted in his music qualities of the astringent, the sardonic, even the malicious. Through the years the remarks came to attach less to the music, though still to the man. Part of the high repute in which he was held as an 'institution' in British musical life depended on his good value as a provocateur, as someone who would puncture certain pomposities, who would undermine received ideas of good taste.

Though the successes of his early career had bred in Walton a confidence about his own skill and professionalism, he found it progressively harder to retain the same confidence in his fertility. The perceived failure to make a profound impact on the opera scene with *Troilus and Cressida* in 1954 had certainly taken its toll, as had the less than adulatory responses to his Second Symphony and the Cello Concerto. By the middle of the 1960s—by the middle of *his* sixties—Walton was experiencing severe self-doubt. He drew very strongly on the warmth and widespread regard which his fame had brought him, even if he continued to be stung by accusations that his music had failed to evolve, that it had 'gone soft'.

A report on Walton's critical standing was given by Stephen Walsh in *Tempo* in the autumn of 1965:

> In the preface to his 'Musical Pilgrim' booklets on William Walton's music, published in 1942, Frank Howes was able to assert that the then forty-year-old Lancastrian had 'established himself as the leading English composer of his generation.' Arguably true in the harsh days of wartime, with Britten scarcely back from America and Tippett little more than a newcomer to the musical scene, it is a judgment that would be inconceivable today. Walton is by nature a slow, careful worker and one who takes little part in the rough and tumble of day-to-day musical life; he has receded from the public view, to the extent that new works from his pen are greeted with mild surprise rather than eager anticipation, and, from the critical standpoint at least, tend to be regarded as guilty until proven innocent.[1]

Walsh did point out in the same article that Walton's achievement was 'far in advance of anything with which he is nowadays popularly credited'.

Nevertheless, Walton became progressively disheartened by the critical response to his music. In her memoir, Susana Walton said that her husband liked to perplex interviewers with remarks such as that his eraser was more important than his pencil, or that he lived abroad to prevent people in England from finding out that he couldn't read or write![2] But what had been provocative playfulness perhaps became in later years a joke that consoled. Sometimes one senses that his jocularity did not quite disguise a real bitterness; in 1968 he wrote to Alan Frank, head of music at Oxford University Press: 'Thank you for the Elgar book [Michael Kennedy, *Portrait of Elgar*] which I found excellent & very interesting. I was so pleased to discover that he hated music almost as much, if not more, than I do.'[3]

The titles in this volume have in common a certain tentativeness about the grand gesture or the major statement: no longer symphony, concerto, even sinfonia concertante, but 'capriccio', 'improvisations', 'varii', 'fantasia'. Three of the pieces were commissions from the United States, where Walton's music had been enthusiastically received.

Capriccio Burlesco

Commission

In May 1963 the New York Philharmonic inaugurated a series of early summer concerts at Philharmonic Hall in Lincoln Center, New York. They were called 'Promenades', after the series in London, and were successful in bringing in audiences somewhat different from those of the winter subscription concerts. The guiding spirit behind the concerts was André Kostelanetz, who conducted most of them. Kostelanetz was a pioneer of what became known as 'easy listening'. Although he would have been best known to British audiences from his arrangement of the Rodgers and Hart song 'With a song in my heart' from the musical *Spring Is Here*, other extremely creditable compositions owe their commissions to Kostelanetz, including Aaron Copland's *Lincoln Portrait* (1942) and William Schuman's orchestration of Charles Ives's *Variations on 'America'* (1963). Kostelanetz was known to be a supporter of Walton's music; in 1959 he had made the first recording of the *Johannesburg Festival Overture*.

The managing director of the New York Philharmonic, Carlos Moseley, wrote to OUP, and to Walton himself, on 29 June 1965 proposing the commission of a work for the Promenade series of 1967, 'of the length and type of the *Johannesburg Festival Overture*... orchestras everywhere would welcome a "twin brother"'. He suggested a fee of $2500, plus $1000 towards the cost of preparing the score and parts.

On 12 July Alan Frank encouraged Walton to accept ('should be a money-spinner'), and the composer agreed with alacrity, though Frank's letter contained a hostage to fortune: 'there's a good deal of time'.

Walton was simultaneously engaged in preliminary work on his second opera, *The Bear*, and John Ward, OUP's representative in New York, though enthused by the commission, wondered how it would fit with Walton's work on the opera (the commission for that was already seven years old). He was understandably reluctant to advertise the new commission until it was 'all set'.

Composition

In the later part of 1965 Walton was diagnosed with lung cancer, and the extended treatment delayed his work on the opera and prevented his starting the work for New York. By August 1966 he at least had an idea for the title—the less than startling 'Philharmonic Overture (N.Y. '67)'—but he had made little progress on the music. On 4 November

1966 Walton asked OUP to explain to the orchestra that there was no realistic prospect of his completing the work by the scheduled date. On 14 November Moseley replied that Kostelanetz and the orchestra would be 'most happy to receive the new work at any time when you find it convenient to complete it'. They hoped it could be included in the 1968 season.

By the end of December 1967 Walton was becoming dismayed at his lack of progress: 'It will I fear have to be burn't & I must make a restart. It's too bad even for A.K. In fact, I [am] most depressed & seem to find it almost impossible to find a good idea.' Alan Frank was sympathetic about the intractability of Walton's muse and on 15 February 1968 tried to encourage him with practical suggestions: 'I wonder if it would help—it sometimes does—if you had some idea at the back of your mind for this overture, not necessarily programmatic, perhaps literary or pictorial, thinking of SCAPINO and PORTSMOUTH POINT, or even near-abstract....I make the suggestion most tentatively.' It plainly had some effect, since Frank was able to reply to Walton's next report: 'I'm so glad that the overture, for better or worse, is beginning to come along and I feel sure it cannot be quite as bad as you say it is.'

The new impetus proved short-lived, and on 4 April 1968 Walton wrote to Frank to say that he had informed Kostelanetz that it was most unlikely that he would have the overture finished by the new deadline, 18 June:

> It has just not occurred. I['m] trying for the fourth time & though it is slightly more promising it do[e]sn't really get off the ground. There's no material. Anyhow unless I finish the sketch by the time I come to London (the 25th) I still have the scoring to complete & the parts etc have to be done. I need hardly say in what despair I am, & how humiliated I feel & not to mention those dollars I so sorely need. But I'll go on trying till I return.

Walton received an amiable, if disappointed, cable from Kostelanetz. His relief at not being in bad odour with the conductor seems in some way to have stimulated his thoughts, since he wrote to Frank on 16 April, 'Typically I believe I may finish it in time if I haven't to stay too long in London.' He was in London in May to receive the Order of Merit from the Queen.

By now the work had been programmed for 7 December in New York, with an anticipated London premiere at a Royal Philharmonic Society concert in February 1969 by the BBC Symphony Orchestra, under Colin Davis.

On 10 June 1968 Walton wrote of his latest ideas for the title: 'I must say Kostelanetz has behaved terribly well about the OVERTURE. I've thought of renaming it AN ANNIVERSARY OVERTURE FOR A.K. AND THE NEW YORK PHIL. ORCH. what do you think? I think I may be finished by 1 December!'

Walton delivered the first nineteen pages of the work to OUP on 24 July, though he warned, 'Don't let me lead you up the garden path into thinking I am anywhere near the end—it's about half way. Maybe I shall have the rest with me when I come to London on Aug 13th but I doubt it. It is, I fear[,] not very good—it may get better—it can hardly get any worse!' However, he did feel confident enough to suggest that his 'amanuensis', Roy Douglas, should make a start on the transposing woodwind and horn parts: 'They are all written in C. Very contemporary!'

By the time Frank replied, Walton had sent a cable telling him to ignore the first four pages until he received new versions. (Frank wryly noted to Walton, 'no real need to advise caution on my part since as soon as we get any music from you it is followed by a telegram withdrawing it'.) The new pages arrived on 29 July and the full score was completely delivered by 11 September, though a revised ending, in which the last four bars were altered to six, took until the end of September.

Kostelanetz apparently thought the work was 'very lovely' and cabled Walton to tell him so. He tried to persuade OUP that his own staff at the orchestra should prepare the parts, even though OUP had already started the process. According to Frank's letter to Ward of 3 October 1968, Kostelanetz felt he knew 'Walton's mind so well that he would have absolutely no trouble in solving 90% of the musical problems that would arise', though Frank wondered whether he wanted also to be the editor of the work 'or even co-author in certain places'.

It was not only musical problems that remained, however. Walton wrote to Frank on 4 November 1968:

> Everybody is being rather trying at the moment! First I'm run[g] up from N.Y. from Kostelanet[z']s representative saying that noone [sic] including the orch likes the title of the ov. (I must say I rather agree)—that it will stop other orch's from playing [it] etc etc & and will I find another. Easier said than done.
>
> I've wracked the old brain but nothing very attractive has occurred to it. In fact I can only think of 'Anniversary Overture' (we've already rejected that, but we could try it on again)—Sinfonia Burlesca or Burlesque Overture (a bit dangerous this one, but I'm rather inclined to it—A Dithyrambic Overture—Spike Hughes suggestion of 'Long Island Sound'. In fact, I don't know & it has been the bother & impediment since the beginning. However A. K. seems to like the piece very much & I'm coming round to it myself slightly.
>
> If you have any happy thoughts please send them to A. K. direct as there is [sic] only 10 days in which to decide.

Frank agreed to propose *Burlesque, An Occasional Overture*, which in turn prompted Kostelanetz to rechristen it *Capriccio Burlesco*. That evidently appealed to Walton, or at least to his humour; on 6 December 1968 he wrote to Frank, 'I've mislaid my dictionary so I'm a bit in doubt about "capriccio" presumably something to do with a goat'.

Performance

The first performance took place on Thursday 7 December 1968 at the Philharmonic Hall in Lincoln Center. Kostelanetz cabled Walton on the 9th: 'Your wonderful *Capriccio Burlesco* tremendous exciting success thrilling reaction of audience and orchestra.' He followed with a letter the same day that began, 'The reaction of the audience was immediate, electric and overwhelming. The Philharmonic played with great élan and obvious enjoyement [sic]. Warm thanks again for your dedication... *Can we record it?*' Further performances were scheduled for 5, 6, and 7 June the following year.

Orchestras in Britain were lining up to perform the work. In November André Previn had asked enthusiastically to see the new score. But Colin Davis gave the premiere as anticipated, on 5 February 1969, with the BBC Symphony Orchestra at the Royal Festival Hall, London, at a Royal Philharmonic Society concert.

Responses to the work were generally approving. Most reviewers related the piece to one or other of Walton's earlier overtures. *The Times* reported: 'As an article of craftsmanship, the piece trips along with caprine surety. The materials are simply but satisfyingly proportioned and the scoring sparkles with touches of imaginative instrumentation that makes it an effective showpiece for a virtuoso orchestra.' But once again the question of Walton's alleged decline made an appearance: 'Gone for ever, it seems, are the brittle high spirits and pointed dry wit of Walton's musical escapades in the 1920s: only a trace of the former enfant terrible reappeared in the concluding syncopated measures.'[4]

In *Music and Letters* Michael Tilmouth, reviewing the published score, drew comparison rather with the American element of the occasion, comparing the work with Leonard Bernstein:

> The C major chord with its F♯ appoggiatura at the opening and the subsequent move to the chord with the flattened 7th has another concordance: Tony's 'Something's coming…it's "gonna be great"'. The backdrop to this piece is not the West End but West Side…Walton's earliest success, 'Façade', was a parody of music styles: now he has turned his sharp talent upon himself and made a flamboyant and enjoyable spectacle of it. There are some deliciously bad things in the piece, such as the transition to the 'big tune' on p. 28, of which any military bandleader would have been mightily proud. The sheer expertise of its execution brings the joke off, though some will cavil and complain that to write a burlesque at all is to evade the problem of doing something new.[5]

Revisions

Kostelanetz's letter to Walton two days after the first performance included a squib, exactly the sort of thing Frank had hinted at in his October letter:

> However to have smoother transitions: instead of *A Tempo* at 164 I changed to *Poco a poco Tempo I°* over 164 to 168. I advanced *Accelerando 2* [sic]

> bars to 285 [from] 288. We had considerable difficulty at the 5/8 320, 322 to 324, since the headlong rush and accelerando is so irresistible.
> I changed these bars to the following design:

> I regret to do this without talking it over with you first and I only hope you will not mind it too much.

Walton did mind very much, and replied politely but firmly to Kostelanetz that he preferred it played as he had written it. 'Please try and stick to the 5/8's at 320—2/4 is not so effective I feel.'[6]

The issue continued to bother the composer, and although he wrote to Alan Frank on 19 December that he thought the conductor rather than the orchestra was at fault ('They are getting Malcolmitis'), he added a note saying, 'Let me know if Colin D[avis] & the B.B.C. have the same difficulty. [I]f they have it had better be looked at.'

Walton remained irritated, especially since Kostelanetz intended to record the piece and OUP was pressing ahead with preparing a score for publication. The question arose about what Kostelanetz actually performed. Alan Frank wrote to John Ward on 12 February 1969:

> About Kostelanetz's alterations of the 5/8 bars into I think 6/8, William is a little confused as to exactly what K intends or indeed actually played. Although William has expostulated I am sure that he will fall in with K's wishes. It might even be that we should decide to make the published score correspond. Could you however, let us have either a note or a photograph of the page in question so that we can discuss it with William and make a decision whether to incorporate the change. William realises that the recording next month is going to be done in K's way.

Alan Frank was ostensibly supportive of Walton's position, though in a letter to him of 4 March the issue of the recording led him to waver:

> I am sure he is going to do this in the recording. Personally I think you are absolutely right that we should stick to the 5/8, particularly because if you have three bars of 2/4 (instead of 5/8), leading into the 9/8 it surely must sound so tame and square. However, Kostelanetz says that they had difficulty as it were holding back these 5/8 bars since 'the headlong rush and accelerando is so irresistible'.
>
> Unless you have changed your mind I propose that we go ahead in our score with the 5/8 retained.

Walton reluctantly did change his mind, writing to Frank on 8 March: 'I think we had better stick to Kostelanetz's change. On the whole I think it's alright especially if it's recorded. It will lead to all kinds of bother & argument—in fact it is not worth while bothering about.' Three days later Frank agreed: 'Right you are: I will make sure that Kostelanetz has recorded in his way, rather than yours, and if that is so we will incorporate the change. I still think that what you wrote is better, but I absolutely agree that people will fuss like mad if there is a discrepancy between the record and the score.'

In fact the score was changed not to Kostelanetz's preferred reading, but to something else again, as published in the WWE. Where Kostelanetz had semiquavers, the revised version turned the bars into triplets. Kostelanetz's own recording definitely has the semiquaver rhythm on the first beat, but Charles Groves's recording, which came out at the same time, has triplets throughout, as does Walton's own recording of the following year.

There is no evidence of what Colin Davis did in his performances, though in a letter of 30 September 1969 Alan Frank told the conductor that 'despite the fact that there are already two commercial recordings…yours is the only performance that pleases [Walton] so far. I had a letter from him today to that effect and in it he expressed the hope that you might one day be able to include it on a record.' Unfortunately, it did not happen.

Publication

Preparation for publication had started by the time the issue of the ending had arisen. By 14 May 1969 Ronald Finch started originating the score using Letraset and ink pens. The score was published by OUP on 27 November 1969.

Improvisations on an Impromptu of Benjamin Britten

Commission

On 28 June 1967 Joseph Scafidi, manager of the San Francisco Symphony Association, wrote to Alan Frank:

> We have been approached by Dr. Ralph I. Dorfman who is exceedingly desirous of commissioning a musical composition in memory of his first wife and which would be given its World Premiere by the San Francisco Symphony Orchestra under the direction of Maestro Josef Krips.
>
> Maestro Krips is quite eager to accommodate Dr. Dorfman, and has asked me to advise you that it would give him, Dr. Dorfman, and the San Francisco Symphony Association a great deal of pleasure and honor if you would agree to accept such a commission. The work could be any length of your choosing, or a short orchestral work would suffice.

Alan Frank replied that he would be meeting Walton in London in early July and that he would put the proposal to him. The composer was at that time in despair at his lack of progress with the New York commission, and at the meeting with Frank—for which there are no minutes—he seems to have suggested a polite brush-off, proposing a high fee for the work and a more than usually flexible timetable. Frank accordingly wrote back to Scafidi that despite the composer's 'unbounded admiration for Maestro Krips' he could not tackle such a commission because of existing commitments. 'He is also not a particularly quick worker as you probably know. I am sure he could not start to think about a work until well into next year.' A completion date of late 1969 or even 1970 was suggested, together with a fee of $5000, for a work of 12–15 minutes. Frank copied the message to John Ward in New York, and in a letter of 3 August added:

> He is totally disinclined at present to undertake any commission at all which carries a date for delivery. I think he is rightly goin[g] to wait and see how the Muse is working or failing to work. As he put it, 'I think I had better write the works first and then auction them to the highest bidder'.... Of course, if the widower in San Francisco decided, surprisingly[,] to cough up $5000 and without too rigorous a time-table, William might fall for that one.

In due course Scafidi wrote back to say that a fee of $5000 was acceptable, together with a schedule flexible enough to accommodate more or less any timetable Walton proposed.

Frank's note to Ward of 11 July had indicated his doubts about the whole project: 'In the unlikely event of this going forward ...' Nevertheless, on 29 September the orchestra board drafted a document to formalize the agreed commission. It even included the provision that in the event of Walton's not being able to compose the piece he would not in any way be beholden to the orchestra.

On 18 December 1967 Frank sent Walton a final exasperated note: 'I can do nothing with them because they agree to everything.' He then outlined the provisions of the commission, ending, 'Well, there you are: I think we ought to sign don't you?' Walton's reply of 29 December was gruff: 'Yes, I suppose you had better sign...But anyone will be lucky to get anything judging from the way this overture is working out.'

Genesis

When he finally made a start on what would become *Capriccio Burlesco* in the summer of 1968 Walton seems to have hit on an idea for the work for San Francisco. On 9 September he wrote to Benjamin Britten:

> Dear Ben,
>
> I hope that you will not think that I am making a too strange request—namely that you will allow me to attempt to write Variations (orchestral) on the theme of the 3rd movement of your Piano Concerto. I realize that you have used it as a passacaglia but not strictly speaking as a theme & variations & hope very much you will let me have a try. It is not a new idea of mine but one which I've been thinking about for some time.
>
> … a postcard with 'yes' or 'no' will suffice & I won't complain if it is the latter even if I shall be very dissapointed [*sic*].[7]

On the 22nd Britten wrote back from the Red House, Aldeburgh:

> My dear William,
>
> Of course you may 'vary' that tune from the 3rd movement of the Pft. Concerto— with the greatest pleasure. Perhaps it will be my way of going down into the future!— anyway, I feel very honoured. I will write to Boosey & Hawkes & tell them I am very willing, & that they mustn't be greedy pigs (as they once were with me when I varied a bit of Kodaly!)

Boosey & Hawkes were not 'greedy pigs', but a certain amount of negotiation went on behind the scenes between Alan Frank and David Adams of Booseys. The latter had been stung with the cost of Britten's having used a theme of Frank Bridge for a set of variations (1937), whereas Hindemith's publisher, Schott, had charged nothing for Walton's using a theme in his Variations on a Theme of Hindemith (1963). Each company was therefore proceeding from a different background. Walton was above all anxious that Britten himself should not be caught in the middle and asked that the issue be ignored until it was clear that he would actually complete the piece.

The theme Walton chose is from Britten's Piano Concerto, Op. 13. The third of the four movements was originally a 'Recitative and Aria', but in 1945, responding to advice from Clifford Curzon and Aaron Copland, Britten had replaced it with a passacaglia movement called 'Impromptu'.[8] As Britten himself pointed out, it was not a revision but a reversion, since 'the theme itself was composed in the same year as the *Concerto* (1938), and most of the rest of the material comes from the original third movement'.[9]

Benjamin Britten

It is perhaps worth a digression to consider Walton's relationship with Britten, because it was not simple or free of friction. In an interview with Hans Keller, published in 1966, Walton was asked, 'If you were woken up in the middle of the night, to name the five most important 20th century composers, whom would you name?' He answered, 'Debussy, Schoenberg, Stravinsky—after that it becomes difficult…I suppose Sibelius in a kind of way, and Mahler. If I'd been asked for seven I would have added Hindemith and Britten.'[10]

Walton had previously composed a set of variations on a theme by Hindemith, another contemporary. But between Hindemith and Walton there was never a hint of prickliness. Of course, Hindemith was seven years older than Walton, and Britten eleven years younger. Walton seems not to have felt any sort of rivalry with Hindemith, whose critical fate in some ways resembles his. But from the start of his career, Britten occupied something of the same status that Walton had initially enjoyed, and had made a conspicuous success in the area where Walton had been felt to have failed, opera.

Their first real encounter was in July 1937, when Britten was writing the Variations on a Theme of Frank Bridge. He wrote in his diary:

> lunch with William Walton at Sloane Square. He is charming, but I feel always the school relationship with him—he is so obviously the head-prefect of English music, whereas I am the promising new boy. Soon of course he'll leave and return as a member of the staff...Anyhow apart from a few slight reprimands (as to music opinions) I am patronized in a very friendly manner. Perhaps the prefect is already regretting the lost freedom, & newly found authority![11]

In September 1942 Walton had spoken on behalf of Britten at the latter's hearing as a conscientious objector, and each had fulsomely praised the work of the other. But Walton could be vulgar and somewhat malicious when talking about Britten to others. Michael Tippett for one found it irritating and told Walton so.[12]

Nevertheless, Walton's letter to Britten on the latter's 50th birthday was sincere:

> In the last years your music has come to mean more & more to me—it shines out as a beacon (how banal I'm becoming!) in, to me at least, a chaotic & barren musical world & I'm sure it does for thousands of others as well....I do understand, appreciate & love, I hope, nearly everything about your music, not only the ingenuity & technique but the emotional depth of feeling, & above all the originality & beauty of sound which permeates these works.[13]

Britten replied with equal sincerity that Walton's music had been a turning point in his musical life: 'You showed me the way of being relaxed & fresh, & intensely personal & yet still with the terms of reference which I had to have.'[14]

Composition

By January 1969 the San Francisco orchestra was keen to put in place its schedule for the 1969–70 season of concerts and wrote an enquiring letter to Alan Frank about progress. On 10 February Frank could offer something at least to reassure—'William...feels reasonably confident that the new work could be ready in time for a premiere in early 1970'—though he added that with Walton 'nothing is absolutely guaranteed until it is finished'. Evidently Frank was feeling confident enough to return to negotiations with Boosey & Hawkes with renewed vigour, settling on an arrangement that gave Booseys a small one-off payment of £40 and a modest share of performing rights.

Walton was pleased enough with his own progress that in April 1969 he permitted the orchestra to announce the commission and performance date, together with the title of the piece, *Elegiac Variations on a Theme of Benjamin Britten*.

By September the work was nearing completion and the process of preparing usable scores and parts was beginning. Pages started to arrive at OUP in the latter part of October; on the 21st Walton wrote that he was 'about halfway having reached 6'–10' including the theme! So there's only another 6 or so to go, but of course it becomes more difficult to deal with as one proceeds. There is only one interval in the whole theme & we are all sick of that already. However we'll see.'

While Walton was, as Frank said, 'staggering' through to the end, Frank told him that he wanted to show him a picture of the person who commissioned the piece, whom they both continued to refer to as 'the widower', Ralph Dorfman. According to Frank, 'He looks a thoroughly jolly character, so perhaps we shouldn't overdo the elegiac flavour.' The distinguished biochemist Dorfman was indeed jolly and regarded his deceased wife Adeline, who had been an extremely gifted pianist, as also having had a cheerful disposition. According to Michael Kennedy, he expressed a wish that the work commemorating his wife should have a joyful rather than a mournful conclusion, and it was this that prompted Walton to change the title.[15] However, a letter of 27 October to Frank suggests that it was on Walton's initiative that the title changed. While it is not impossible that Dorfman's suggestion was passed on to Walton independently, it does seem that it was the composer's decision to abandon the word 'variations' in favour of 'improvisations', which better characterized his approach in the piece's second half when, as he had implied, he had already exhausted the potential of the theme itself. He later took to referring to it by the euphonious 'Imps on an imp'.

The orchestra's management was pleased enough with the change of title, but slightly peeved that it had just sent out 300,000 leaflets containing the previous version. It asked OUP's New York office to confirm that the change was definitive.

By 19 November 1969 OUP had received all but the last six pages of the score from Walton, and Alan Frank felt it was reasonable to ask the composer to elaborate a little on the piece for the sake of the orchestra, and in particular to explain the title's change of emphasis. Frank wrote to Jonathan Kramer, who was to write a programme note for the forthcoming concerts:

> As to the change of title, the theme itself has a somewhat elegiac quality about it and when Sir William started the work he fully expected this quality would colour it. However as he said to me… 'Things don't always turn out as you expect and that goes for composition as well!' As a result, though of course an elegiac note remains in the slower music of the work, a good deal of it is in fact brisk, extrovert and resolute in character.
>
> As to the second change in the title, IMPROVISATIONS in Sir William's view suggest something freer than VARIATIONS: he points out that the theme itself is not of a type which lends itself to variations treatment in the manner of Beethoven or Brahms.

Performance

Preparations for the first performance were thrown into disarray when the orchestral materials reached San Francisco only four days before the premiere, casting the staff into tearful panic. However, Krips gave the first of its three performances on Wednesday

14 January 1970, at the War Memorial Opera House, San Francisco, with the San Francisco Symphony Orchestra. He sent Walton a telegram on 17 January: 'Your work enthusiastically received[. A]n excellent composition[. C]ongratulations.'[16] Walton's younger brother, Alexander, who lived in Vancouver, went to two of the performances in San Francisco and sent OUP two good notices from the local newspapers.

The orchestra had no plans to tour Europe, so the first performance there of the Improvisations was appropriately picked up by the Aldeburgh Festival, and Charles Groves conducted the first British performance with the Royal Philharmonic Orchestra at Snape Maltings on Saturday 27 June 1970, with Walton in the audience. Stanley Sadie reviewed the performance for *The Times* two days later and called it a 'fascinating product of the contact between two musical minds'. Later that year Groves gave the first London performance with the London Philharmonic, on 20 October at the Royal Festival Hall.

At Walton's 70th birthday concert at the Royal Festival Hall on 28 March 1972 André Previn conducted the Improvisations with the London Symphony Orchestra. At the same concert, six composers, including Nicholas Maw, Richard Rodney Bennett, and Peter Maxwell Davies, performed six miniature 'Happy Birthday' pieces they had composed, prompting Walton to quip, 'A real tribute from the avant-garde to the almost dead and buried.'[17]

Publication

The orchestral materials had been dispatched to San Francisco in such haste that there had been no time for OUP to incorporate in their copies of the scores the various changes and corrections that had arisen in checking the parts. They now had to ask for the score to be returned from San Francisco so that they could get on with publishing it.

Ronald Finch originated the score in April and May 1970. It was made ready for printing in September. Amendments had been incorporated from a score that Walton had corrected after the Aldeburgh rehearsal and performance. In a memo to John Ward of 1 December, Christopher Morris explained that 'the only corrections not passed on to you were those made by the composer after the Aldeburgh performance. They are marked in the score D which we are sending to you under separate cover, which is, as you will see, a photograph of the composer's manuscript. These corrections have been made in the printed full score.' The memo implies that corrections not taken into the full score from the Aldeburgh copy were deliberately omitted. The score was published by OUP on 5 November 1970.

Varii Capricci

Commission

In 1951 Walton was too busy with *Troilus and Cressida* to compose a work for the Festival of Britain, although he was asked and briefly considered it.[18] When it was decided to celebrate the 25th anniversary of the Royal Festival Hall, built for that occasion, the management approached Walton with an idea for a commission. The chairman of the Royal Philharmonic Society, Myers Foggin, wrote to the composer, who was staying at the Ritz Hotel in London, on 6 December 1973. The plans were still in embryo, but the lure of the commission was that the work would be performed by the Berlin Philharmonic conducted by Herbert von Karajan.

Given Karajan's public status at the time, the offer might have appeared irresistible, but the conductor's reputation within the profession gave Walton immediate doubts, as he wrote to the record producer Walter Legge on 24 July 1974: 'Even if I write a piece I[']d bet anything that H.K would squirm out of it, just as he has avoided ever doing "Belshazzar" ever since that marvellous perf. in Vienna.' Walton relayed Legge's pithy response in a letter of 17 August to Alan Frank: 'I quote—"Herbert v. K. is a shit—that I've known from bitter experience over the last 20 yrs. But it happens that he did the best perf. ever of B[elshazzar']s F[east] & and he owes to you & to me to do it as he did it in Vienna."'

Over the next eight months John Denison, managing director of the Festival Hall, spent a great deal of time trying to pin down Karajan and the Berlin orchestra. Walton spent an equal amount of time bemoaning what he would be taking on. On 28 July 1974 he wrote to Frank, 'I'm sick of writing ceremonial balls so I'm very inclined to cry off. What else am I supposed to be writing?'

It took until 27 January 1975 for the official commission to appear from John Denison. The fee was £2000 for a work, preferably 'festive and/or lyrical in character, of approximately 10–15 minutes' duration'. On 6 February Walton told Frank that he had accepted the commission: 'Now what remains is to write the bloody thing. I for one shall be v. interested to see & hear what turns up as I seem to be absolutely impotent…having committed myself I'll do my best not to let the side down.'

Even Denison was by this time admitting some doubts about Karajan; on 13 February 1975 he wrote to Frank, 'One can only keep one's fingers crossed that the Maestro will not find some insuperable reason for not performing it!' The anxiety was not without foundation: 'Did Alan Frank tell you that Karajan has suggested that you should personally conduct your piece?'[19] The idea was impossible, and by March 1975 Walton was in a mood to drop the whole idea and offer the commission to Malcolm Arnold or Lennox Berkeley, especially since both had become candidates for the position of Master of the Queen's Music, available since the death that month of Sir Arthur Bliss. On 15 April Frank tried to draw Walton's attention from Karajan to the piece itself: 'If ideas are pouring out, you should not stop work on it.' By May it had become clear to all concerned that the Karajan idea had lost whatever impetus it had ever had.

Even with the relief of the Karajan distraction out of the way, ideas about the piece could not be said to be 'pouring out'. At that time Walton was in regular correspondence with Malcolm Arnold, to whom he had dedicated his Five Bagatelles for Guitar in 1972. And it was to Arnold that, on 26 March 1975, Walton sent his most forlorn *cri de coeur*: 'I've let myself in for this fucking piece for the R.F.H. but I've still got a bit of time to get out of it if I make up my mind quickly. Ideas are sparse, bare & ugly so "per forza" I think I shall have to give it up. In fact I must face it that it is highly probably [*sic*] that I shall never write a note again. It dos'ent [*sic*] depress me too much—nor I imagine anyone else.'

Walton was briefly encouraged by Arnold's reply, but the 'dreadful R.F.H. piece which is ruining my life'[20] finally expired at the end of the summer, along with rather half-hearted plans for a third symphony.

Composition

Since it was to Arnold that Walton had expostulated, there is a mild irony in that when he did finally settle to a task for the Festival Hall he turned to the very pieces he had dedicated to Arnold, the bagatelles. In a letter to André Previn of 7 October 1975 Walton first mentioned that he was arranging them for orchestra: 'They are working out well, but not easy to do. What to add and what to leave out, those are the questions! I thought of asking you to do them, but I realized it was not fair to ask you especially as you are occupied....I don't know whether John Denison will want to do my transcriptions. They are called *Vari Caprici* [sic] in their new garb, by the way.[21] But it will be a first performance in their new garb—and much better than the pompous bore I was turning out for that occasion.'[22] On 30 October he told Christopher Morris at OUP that 'There's not got to be a whisper of a guitar in the orch. version which will be for a large orch. sparingly used for the most part.'

The title *Varii Capricci* had occurred to Walton before. While he was struggling to start the work for the Chicago Symphony Orchestra in 1939 that would become *Scapino*, Walton had written to the then head of music at OUP, Hubert Foss, of a scheme for a suite of five pieces to which he gave the title *Varii Capricci*. The movements were to show off the various sections of the Chicago orchestra. The idea stayed with him, and later that year he described the proposed work as 'portraits from the *commedia del'arte* [sic]'. That piece did not materialize, but plainly the idea stayed in his mind.

By 23 March 1976 two of the pieces had been dispatched to Christopher Morris, by now head of the OUP music department (Alan Frank retired in 1975). 'They've proved v. difficult to transcribe & I fear I've not done them at all well so please show them to André P before allowing a perf. You can always say, and it's very likely true, that they [have] been lost in the post!' The third piece arrived on 2 April, the fourth on 9 April. Since the first performance was less than a month away, Morris asked anxiously whether number 5 would be long in coming. By 16 April Walton had finished the transcriptions and wrote to Arnold:

> I've been much occupied & preoccupied by scoring those 5 Bagatelles for a large orchestra & they appear or rather re-appear under the name of "Varii Capricci". They are to be done at the F.H. on May 4th at its 25th anniversary concert. I fear I've not done them very well, in fact I should have asked you to do them, but having let myself in for something for F.H. I thought these would [be] easy. I couldnt have been more mistaken. I found them full of pitfalls especially the last one which is musically very much changed & hurriedly scored (& full of wrong notes!). I'd left it to the last minute as the O.U.P were panicking about part-copying. The only thing that is intact is the dedication!'[23]

The final pages arrived at OUP on 20 April.

Performance

The first performance of *Varii Capricci* was given at the Royal Festival Hall on Tuesday 4 May 1976 by the London Symphony Orchestra under André Previn. On the following day, Alan Blyth in *The Times* was moderately enthusiastic: 'Its five deliberately light and somewhat parodistic sections (they hardly amount to movements) pass a quarter of an hour pleasingly enough in the company of a composer who, in his eighth decade, still delights in youthful exuberance tinged with gentle lyricism, suffused by the warm Mediterranean air he now chooses to breathe.' While welcoming the new piece as a happy sign, Paul Griffiths in the *Musical Times* nevertheless thought it disconcerting 'to find a large orchestra bounding along the previously naked line of guitar melody, and the impasto treatment does vulgarize what were delicate sketches, especially when, as in the first and last pieces, breezy jamborees expend their enormous energies in the oddly brief time of three minutes'.[24] Most of the reviews were generally good, and Robert Ponsonby, head of the BBC Proms, was keen that the work should be given in the following year's series.

Publication

The parts for the first performance had been hurriedly prepared from Walton's manuscript, but arrangements were soon made for a score to be published. From May to September 1976 Ronald Finch made a fair copy.

The process generated queries which Walton was obliged to answer, and the checking dragged on into 1977. Meanwhile Sir Frederick Ashton had suggested that he would like to turn the piece into a ballet. In rethinking the piece for the ballet, Walton was forced to consider the fifth movement, about which he had had such misgivings. His first intuition was to extend it, but soon he decided to rewrite it completely. The score was by this stage ready for printing by the Scolar Press but on 18 October Morris had to call a halt. On 12 November Walton sent a brief note, saying that he hoped 'fairly shortly to send you V. C. with its new addition for the ballet. Looking at No V in any case it does need extension & is a damp squib as an end piece so have patience & do not proceed—there's time.' Two days later he had sent the revised last movement and Ronald Finch had to prepare 31 replacement pages of score, which he finished in early December. The score was finally published by OUP on 7 September 1978.

The first performance of the revised version took place only in 1981. Owain Arwel Hughes conducted the BBC Welsh Symphony Orchestra in a studio recording in Cardiff on 28 January 1981, which was first broadcast on 21 July 1981.

Ashton's ballet

Robert Ponsonby was still waiting for the opportunity to programme *Varii Capricci* at the Proms, and by this time Morris had an additional motive for making it possible. On 2 May 1978 he wrote to Ponsonby: 'One incentive that exists for Sir William is that Sir Frederick Ashton wants to make a ballet out of the work but is not really capable of reading a score and desperately wants to hear the complete work in its new form'—an odd angle, one may think, from which to entice Ponsonby to programme the work.

On 6 October 1978 Stephen Wikner, promotion manager at OUP, invited the copyist and arranger Alan Boustead to make a piano arrangement of the Bagatelles and a piano reduction of the *Varii Capricci*, the latter ostensibly so that Frederick Ashton could have a copy 'before his current enthusiasm cools'. In characteristic fashion Boustead had finished the work by 21 October, 'a little hurried, but O.K. for ballet rehearsing (i.e. literally transcribed rather than imaginative!)'. He had started each piece on a righthand page, 'so you can shuffle them all together if you want, in any order', a sensible idea, since it was not clear how Ashton would fashion the ballet. Wikner was able to send Ashton the scores and promise a special pressing from a BBC tape of the unrevised version. Unfortunately, Wikner left OUP to take up a new position, and the recording never made its way to the Royal Ballet. A year later the Royal Ballet wrote to say that the recording had still not been received, and OUP quickly arranged to send it, still with the original fifth movement, since the revised version had not yet been performed.

It took a further four years for the ballet to reach its final form. Ashton's scenario was set in Walton's garden on Ischia, and is an ironic update of Nijinsky's scandalous *L'Après-midi d'un faune* (1912).[25]

In the end Ashton did not use Walton's rewritten final movement, but reverted to the original version. As a sixth movement, he used a section of the first movement, to which, at Ashton's request, Walton added a brief short-score coda on 4 March 1983. It was the last fragment of music that he wrote. He died on 8 March, the date on which the coda arrived at OUP, and the following day Ronald Finch finished scoring it in time for a rehearsal at Covent Garden on 15 March.

The ballet was given its first performance by the Royal Ballet at the Metropolitan Opera House, New York, on 19 April 1983, conducted by Ashley Lawrence. Its first London performance was on 20 July 1983 at Covent Garden, with the Orchestra of the Royal Opera House under Lawrence. Sets were by David Hockney and the costumes were by the fashion designer Ossie Clark. The performers were Antoinette Sibley, Anthony Dowell, and a group of eight 'Varii amici'. Ashton dedicated his new ballet 'to the memory of my lifelong friend'.

Prologo e Fantasia

Commission

In 1977 Mstislav Rostropovich became chief conductor of the National Symphony Orchestra in Washington DC. On 19 November 1979 he wrote to Walton:

> I simply can't forget our meeting in Aldeburgh…You then planted a seed in my heart that doesn't give me any peace: I long for the composition for solo cello.[26] But, as always my ego knows no bounds, and I am ready to kneel before you with another request.
>
> For the past three years I have been the Music Director of the National Symphony Orchestra in Washington, D.C. I devote a great deal of my heart and time to this orchestra. Now, in the name of the National Symphony, I ask you to undertake a commission to write a composition for my orchestra.

Walton was not accustomed to this kind of effusiveness from a commissioning body, and he responded eagerly, not least because he was keen for Rostropovich to take up his Cello Concerto. As he wrote to Christopher Morris on 7 December: 'It's going to be a short piece[,] that I can assure you. It is for him to play the Vlc. Con. In fact a carrot!'

The National Symphony Orchestra was not at that time one of the very finest American orchestras. Nevertheless, under its previous director, Antal Doráti, and now under Rostropovich, its quality had improved. It had commissioned works before, though they tended to be fanfares and encore pieces. Rostropovich wanted to broaden the orchestral repertoire in the way he had done for the cello. Martin Feinstein, president of the National Symphony Orchestra, asked Christopher Morris what would be appropriate in the way of a commissioning fee. On 14 March 1980 Morris consulted Susan Brailove in OUP's New York office about 'what amount of money is around' and suggested £10,000 plus £2000 towards copying. Feinstein, who shortly afterwards left to become president of Washington National Opera, was evidently taken aback at the fee ('kind of high') and proposed that the orchestra would share in the royalties of all performances of the piece for a period of five years. It was now Morris's turn to be taken aback, since this arrangement, apparently common enough in the theatre, was an innovation in orchestral music. Negotiations continued for several months, during which a compromise was reached, in which the National Symphony would indeed derive income from performances by other orchestras. The one point on which Walton himself was adamant was that he would not give up his copy of the manuscript, which the orchestra had requested. This was, presumably, because he realized that his calligraphy had deteriorated.

Negotiations were finally concluded in November 1980, at which point both sides of the Atlantic were keen to allow Walton to start the piece, to 'jolly him along' as Christopher Morris put it. The piece was scheduled for the autumn season of 1981.

Composition

On 8 December 1980 Morris wrote to Feinstein that Walton was working on the job, 'but the dear man is notoriously slow at composition'. However, the jollying seemed to be working, so that by 6 April 1981 Walton had at least produced the first ten pages of full score of the piece. 'This is very encouraging,' wrote Morris to Feinstein on the same day, 'because once he gets going, he usually works pretty steadily.' Walton's manuscript at this stage titled the work 'Introduction and Fantasia' (the 'Fantasia' presumably to be pronounced as in English).

Perhaps too much encouraged by the news, the Washington orchestra decided to schedule Walton's new piece for 15 September 1981. On 24 June Morris asked Walton, 'Are you going to make it?' In some haste Walton rewrote the first ten pages and changed the title to *Prologo e Fantasia*. On 16 July Walton telephoned Morris to say that did not think he would be able to complete the work in time. He was evidently upset, since he believed it was the only date Rostropovich could conduct the work. Four days later he was feeling more optimistic, and phoned to say that he would contact Rostropovich directly to work out a timetable.

Meanwhile Ronald Finch started copying the score and parts for OUP. Finch must have worked feverishly, since he had finished parts and score, up to page 23, by 27 July. On 12 August Morris wrote to Robert Noerr, Feinstein's replacement in Washington.

Walton was making progress, but did not quite know whether it would be done in time. He had completed five to six minutes of music, but, as Morris explained, 'One never knows what he is going to scrap!' Noerr replied that Walton had apparently arranged with Rostropovich that the work would be performed on 26–29 January 1982, first in Washington, then on 20 February in London, where the orchestra would be touring.

Small batches continued to be sent to Ronald Finch. By the end of November OUP was becoming anxious about the deadline that the orchestra in Washington would need. A tentative suggestion was made that if the score and parts could not be produced in time for the Washington performances, perhaps the piece could be ready in time for the London date in February.

The National Orchestra was very accommodating, and replied that it would be willing to postpone the premiere until 20 February. Parts would have to be ready by 14 February, at which time the orchestra would be rehearsing in Vienna.

On 13 January 1982 Susana Walton phoned Christopher Morris to say that the piece was finally completed and on its way to London. At that point Walton asked the conductor Elgar Howarth to 'vet' the score. Shortly before, Howarth had helped Walton with a competition piece he was writing for brass band. The piece was first called 'Medley', but later developed into *The First Shoot*.[27] Walton reused the discarded first part of 'Medley' (which he had admitted was somewhat in the style of his friend Henze) as the opening part of *Prologo e Fantasia*.

Performance

The orchestra was touring Europe in the first part of 1982, and at the beginning of February the parts and scores were sent to Zürich, where the orchestra had some rehearsal time. The National Orchestra had, remarkably, not insisted that the work should be performed first on its own territory, and *Prologo e Fantasia* was duly given its premiere in London on 20 February. Walton himself made an unexpected appearance at the rehearsal and the concert, though he had initially intended to be in London only for his 80th birthday celebrations in March.

Two days later Max Harrison in *The Times* acknowledged that the work was a *pièce d'occasion*, but that it was 'genuinely felt on its own level'. Judith Nagley later wrote in the *Musical Times* that she regretted the brevity of the work which was 'likely to make a significant impact on the orchestral repertory'.[28]

Publication

Ronald Finch made an initial fair copy by hand, which was circulated as a reduced-sized study score from 1982. Judith Nagley's point about the brevity of the score seems to have been shared by the composer, since in a memo of 5 March to Christopher Morris, Barbara Gunyon, promoter of new music for OUP, wrote that Walton had phoned to say that 'he thinks he will add one or two minutes to the work but continues to be happy to allow performances'. In the event he seems to have made no such elaboration, and it was only after his death that the full score was reoriginated, by John Barkwith, and published by OUP on 26 April 1984.

NOTES

1. Stephen Walsh, *Tempo*, no. 74 (autumn 1965), pp. 29–30.
2. Susana Walton, *William Walton: Behind the Façade* (Oxford, 1988), p. 49.
3. 24 July 1968. Unless otherwise indicated, all correspondence is from the archives of Oxford University Press (OUP Archive).
4. Peter Davis, *The Times* (10 December 1968), p. 7.
5. Michael Tilmouth, 'Capriccio Burlesco', *Music & Letters*, vol. 51, no. 3 (July 1970), p. 341.
6. Walton to Kostelanetz, 19 December 1968, quoted in memo from Susan Brailove to Alan Frank, 25 February 1969.
7. The Britten–Pears Library, Aldeburgh; cited in *The Selected Letters of William Walton*, ed. Malcolm Hayes (London, 2002), p. 384.
8. For an account of the revision, see Eric Roseberry, 'Britten's Piano Concerto: The Original Version', *Tempo*, no. 172 (March 1990), pp. 10–18.
9. Letter from Britten's secretary Rosemund Strode to Alan Frank, 21 April 1970. In the same letter Strode added, 'Ben... evidently considers that the theme isn't quite as straightforward as all that!'
10. 'Contemporary Music: Its Problems and its Future: Sir William Walton and Hans Keller', *Composer*, vol. 20 (1966), pp. 2–4.
11. Diary entry for 28 July 1937, quoted in Michael Kennedy, *Portrait of Walton* (Oxford, 1989), p. 96.
12. See Michael Tippett, *Those Twentieth Century Blues* (London, 1991), pp. 213–214.
13. *Letters from a Life: Selected Letters and Diaries of Benjamin Britten*, ed. Donald Mitchell and Philip Reed (London, 1991), p. 203.
14. *Letters from a Life*, ed. Mitchell and Reed, p. 202.
15. Kennedy, *Portrait*, p. 243.
16. He wrote to Alan Frank on 2 February, 'Walton's "Improvisation's" is the work of a real master and an immediate success. The musicians adored it and played beautifully and 3 audiences were enthusiastic.'
17. Susana Walton, *Behind the Façade*, p. 215.
18. Stewart Craggs, *William Walton: A Source Book* (Aldershot, 1993), p. 54.
19. Denison to Walton, 24 March 1975. If Karajan were to remain obdurate, Denison made the extraordinary suggestion of sending 'the best English conductor we can to go to Berlin and rehearse it a few days in advance', proposing perhaps Colin Davis! Walton was appalled by the idea.
20. Kennedy, *Portrait*, p. 264; Letters, p. 425.
21. The eighteenth-century Venetian artist Giovanni Battista Tiepolo made a series of etchings with that title. It is not known whether Walton knew of the works, which seem not to have any obvious connection with the music. While the score was being prepared for publication Anthony Howell, of OUP's production department, suggested reproducing one of the images on the cover, an idea that was not taken up.
22. Kennedy, *Portrait*, pp. 264–265. In the spring of 1971 Walton had transcribed for orchestra the guitar accompaniments to the song cycle *Anon. in Love*, which had been written for Julian Bream and Peter Pears, and the process in turn prompted him to compose the bagatelles for Bream.
23. In fact the final score omitted the dedication, perhaps through an oversight. It was restored in the WWE.
24. *Musical Times*, vol. 117, no. 1601 (July 1976), p. 589.
25. See Tobi Tobias, 'Royal Caprices', *New York Magazine* (9 May 1983), p. 86; David Vaughan, *Frederick Ashton and his Ballets* (London, 1999), pp. 415–416. For a photograph of the ballet, see Humphrey Burton and Maureen Murray, *William Walton: The Romantic Loner* (Oxford, 2002), p. 173.
26. *Passacaglia*, for solo cello, composed in 1979–80.
27. See *William Walton Edition*, vol. 21, *Music for Brass*, ed. Elgar Howarth (Oxford, 2006), pp. x–xi.
28. *Musical Times*, vol. 123, no. 1670 (April 1982), p. 275.

17

Shorter Orchestral Works 1 *(Vol. 17)*

David Lloyd-Jones

Concert-giving organizations and audiences are fortunate that, in addition to his three overtures, William Walton provided the orchestral repertoire with several short works which can be programmed effectively in orchestral concerts, especially those of a popular nature. Three of these are already acknowledged as quasi-classics of their genre. Furthermore, when the occasion presented itself, and when the remuneration was sufficiently attractive, Walton was perfectly prepared to produce occasional music, including orchestrations of the most occasional works of all, national anthems. The eleven items in this volume, only three of which have been published previously, show him at his most professional, while at the same time displaying the flair and imagination that seemed rarely to fail him.

Crown Imperial: Coronation March (1937)

Towards the end of 1936 Walton must have felt himself to be on the crest of a wave of success. In the previous decade, performances of at least eight new works had shown him to be the most stimulating new voice in British music. There was further excitement in the air. In May 1937 the new young king, Edward VIII, was to be crowned in Westminster Abbey, and plans were already afoot for the programme of music to precede the service and for the service itself. Walton probably felt that this was an occasion on which he could leave an indelible mark.

The BBC (not yet fifteen years old) had already played a part in the creation of the Viola Concerto and *Belshazzar's Feast*. An informal meeting seems to have been arranged with the assistant director of music, Kenneth Wright, who sent the following perceptive internal memo to his superior, Adrian Boult, on 27 November 1936:

> Confirming my conversation with you last evening, Walton would love to be commissioned by the Corporation to write a really fine Symphonic Coronation March. No-one will doubt that his immense technical ability should produce a March of exceptional brilliance, and from the point of view of general symphonic repertoire of equal value to the existing Elgar Marches. He is the one person of the younger generation of composers most able to do this, and I should like the Corporation to give its approval in principle to the matter being gone into from the financial point of view. There should be no lack of opportunities for publishing with his own publishers The Oxford University Press, who ought to make a very good thing out of it, but Walton is at the moment engaged on a violin concerto for Heifetz, a choral work for next year's Leeds Festival and music for a film, so that he feels that some sort of immediate financial

encouragement from the Corporation would be justified in order to enable him to put some of his work on one side and get on with the March.[1]

The project seems to have been approved, and by 19 February 1937 Walton was writing to his mother: 'I am down here [Ashby St Ledgers, near Rugby, the house of Lord and Lady Wimborne] for some days trying to get going on my Coronation March for the Abbey so I'm pretty busy.'[2] Terms with the BBC were finalized in early March; Walton was to be paid an outright commissioning fee of 40 guineas for what was termed his 'symphonic march'.

The earliest recordings of Walton's music (eleven numbers from *Façade*, the Symphony, *Portsmouth Point*) had been made by Decca, but as Adrian Boult, principal conductor of the BBC Symphony Orchestra, was connected with HMV, it was this firm that decided to record the march with these forces prior to the coronation, especially as Boult was to conduct it there, together with other non-liturgical music. The session took place on 16 April at Kingsway Hall, London, and the record was released in June.[3] Though at the time Walton was in Italy with Alice, Lady Wimborne, and working on his violin concerto, he did manage to tune in to the first broadcast performance of the march on 9 May by the BBC orchestra; the *Radio Times* announced that the conductor would be Boult, but in the end it was his associate, Clarence Raybould. In a letter of 11 May from Ravello to his publisher, Hubert Foss, Walton wrote: 'Thank you for your valiant efforts on behalf of the March [this presumably refers to further financial arrangements]. I heard it very badly on Sunday. It seemed to me Raybould took the first section too slowly[;] it lacked any kick and there ought to be plenty. I hope Boult's record hasn't the same fault.'[4] Walton need not have worried; at the end of his autograph score he marks '8 mins. 10 secs.' and, remarkably, Boult's recording comes out at 8 minutes, 8 seconds.

Crown Imperial, A Coronation March (1937)—to quote the billing in *Radio Times*—received its first public performance before the coronation service in Westminster Abbey on 12 May 1937, played by the Coronation Orchestra under Sir Adrian Boult, who had been knighted in February of that year. By now, due to the dramatic abdication of Edward VIII, the new monarch was his younger brother, George VI. The march was played to accompany the procession of the Dowager Queen Mary; Elgar's *Imperial March* was used for that of the new king and queen. Mystifyingly, the extended account of all the music played at the Abbey in *The Times* on the following day failed to mention the premiere of *Crown Imperial*.

The new march became immediately popular, and arrangements for piano (by Walton himself), organ (Herbert Murrill), small orchestra with piano (Hyam Greenbaum), and military band (W. J. Duthoit) were published by OUP within the same year. Walton conducted it at the Proms on 28 August, and Sir Thomas Beecham gave it on 7 October at the Leeds Festival—the day after the world premiere of Walton's choral cantata *In Honour of the City of London*, to words by the Scottish poet William Dunbar (?1460–c.1525). It is from a line in Dunbar's poem, 'In beawtie beryng the crone imperiall', that Walton took his title and the march's inscription, although it should be noted that the same term is used, in more modern spelling, in Act IV, Scene I of Shakespeare's *Henry V*.

Unlike its younger brother, *Orb and Sceptre, Crown Imperial* has had a complex history since its first performance. Already in his arrangement of the march for piano solo (which was probably a reworking of his sketch for the work), published by OUP two days before the coronation, Walton had indicated a 65-bar cut (from letters P to T) in the recapitulation of the first section; the identical cut is shown in Murrill's arrangement for organ, published at the same time. The reason for this cut is clearly explained in a letter that the composer wrote on 8 February 1941 to the BBC music producer Julian Herbage, in connection with a forthcoming broadcast performance that he was to conduct: 'Will it be in order if I make a cut or two in the Coronation March? Knocking off about 1½ to 2 mins. It will be reducing it to its original length of about 6 mins. I must confess that I spun it out, to its detriment, in order to comply with the B.B.C. commissioned length of 8 or 9 mins.'[5]

Had the committee in charge of the coronation music asked the BBC for eight or nine minutes? The Queen of Norway and the Dowager Queen Mary were scheduled to arrive at the west door of the abbey at 10.35, and the new king and queen at 11.00 so that quite a lot of time had to be filled with music. One begins to see why the BBC had termed it a 'symphonic march'. It has to be conceded that there is a good deal of repetition in the full version, though because of the sheer quality of the music and its orchestration it can amply sustain its length and achieve a 'cumulative grandeur' (Stephen Lloyd) in an energetic complete performance. Nevertheless, the question of overall timing seems to have been much in Walton's mind from the very beginning. His metronome marking is crotchet = 126, which is almost impossibly brisk and ill accords with the direction 'Allegro reale' (royal). This figure was even increased to 132 in the 1967 publication. Boult's initial tempo is akin to 104, while that of Walton's recording is 108 (the marking for *Orb and Sceptre*). Both conductors increase the tempo as the march develops.

When Walton recorded *Crown Imperial* with the Philharmonia Orchestra in March 1953, at the same time as *Orb and Sceptre*, he made the 65-bar cut shown in his piano transcription, plus two further ones: just before letter D to just before I, and the two bars before letter N. By removing a total of 128 bars, he cut the march down to 6'40", that is to say 1'28" less than Boult's complete performance and 35 seconds less than his recording of the considerably shorter *Orb and Sceptre* (176 bars of 4/4 as opposed to 481 of 2/4).

In February 1958 Alan Frank asked his assistant editor, Christopher Morris, for information on reduced versions of the march. Morris supplied the details and ended his memo: 'It looks to me as if we could do with a normal reduced version for double woodwind and the usual other reductions.' Frank consequently wrote to Vilem Tausky, at that time conductor of the BBC Concert Orchestra, which was of exactly this size, inviting him to make such a reduction. By the end of the month, Tausky had sent OUP a marked-up photocopy of the score of the full version showing his arrangement, but nothing seems to have been done about it at this time.

In 1963 Walton conducted the march several times during his foreign concert tours, and after returning to Ischia wrote to Frank suggesting publication (the first) of the march in a further cut version. In doing so, he altered his original 65-bar cut following the 'Trio' so that it went from seven bars before letter R to three before V. It was at this point that the score containing the combination of the first three Walton cuts, two new ones (10 bars, from ten after K to two before L; and 12 bars, at bars 447–58), and the Tausky version for reduced orchestra came into being. After considerable trial and error a study score, incorporating these cuts but showing the full orchestration as well as Tausky's reduction, was eventually published by OUP in September 1967.

Crown Imperial is mostly performed these days in the 'Tausky' version, that is to say reduced for double wind etc., and with cuts amounting to as many as 151 bars out of a total of 481. It should be emphasized that the two new cuts are hardly likely to have been Tausky's suggestions, but were almost certainly demanded by Walton himself. Particularly distressing are the unnecessary reduction by two bars of the link into the 'Trio' section and the twelve-bar cut in the peroration which excludes some highly effective climactic brass and percussion chords. In a letter to OUP of 28 April 1970 this 1967 cut version was much criticized by J. W. Babb, secretary of the National Association of Youth Orchestras, who complained that 'architecturally it does not balance. The recapitulation at fig.6 P is so incomplete as to be a perfunctory adherence to form, a mere means to establish the tonality for the repeat of the "Trio" tune. The deletion of the 6 "cannon shots" [*recte* 3] robs the March of its significance associated with the Coronation of George VI.' Many others have also seen fit to censure Walton's preference for all five cuts, while approving Tausky's eminently practical reduction of the scoring for orchestras lacking triple wind. Against this, the distinguished organist Simon Preston relates that when in 1965 he told Walton, with some satisfaction, that he had just recorded the march complete, Walton replied, 'You bloody fool, it's far too long.'

Prelude and Fugue (The 'Spitfire')

In 1942, in the darkest days of World War II, British Aviation Pictures, with the support of Fighter Command and the backing of J. Arthur Rank, decided that a film should be made about the aircraft designer, Reginald Mitchell. Before his early death from cancer in 1937, Mitchell had designed the Spitfire, the iconic aeroplane that had made such a decisive contribution to the success of Allied airmen in the 1940 Battle of Britain; by the end of the war, 19,000 had been produced. The film script, by Miles Malleson and Anatole de Grunwald, was based on a book by Henry C. James and Kay Strueby. The popular film star Leslie Howard not only acted the role of Mitchell but also directed and produced the film, before, in a tragic irony, being killed by enemy action in a civilian air crash in 1943. *The First of the Few* is essentially the story of one man's vision, and his struggle with entrenched official attitudes, to get his aeroplane built and put into production; this was eventually achieved in July 1938.

William Walton spent the greater part of the war living with the recently widowed Alice, Lady Wimborne, at her imposing Northamptonshire home in Ashby St Ledgers. With three wartime film scores already to his credit and his availability as a non-combatant, it was only natural that he should have been asked to write the music for *The First of the Few*. It consisted of some eighteen cues of widely differing lengths. Leslie Ruth Howard, the actor's son, recalled: 'Sidney Cole, the supervising editor, arranged a runthrough of a rough-cut of the film for Walton. "Leslie gave me very full instructions to pass on to Willie Walton about his feelings regarding the music. These, after the showing, I dutifully relayed to Walton." ' After listening carefully, the composer observed drily, 'I see. Leslie wants a lot of notes!'[6] Walton's remark was apt because his score for *The First of the Few* is considerably more substantial than those for his previous three films. He began work during early spring 1942, and the soundtrack was recorded shortly after by the London Symphony Orchestra, conducted by Muir Mathieson. The film received its premiere on 20 August at the Odeon Leicester Square Cinema. It was very much in keeping with the mood of the time and became highly successful.

Walton later extracted and arranged the Prelude and Fugue as a concert piece, but this decision was most uncharacteristic. He was always extremely resistant to requests to exploit the scores that he wrote for films, theatrical productions, and BBC broadcasts, which he regarded as having a specific purpose (see *Film Suites*, Vol. 22). It was undoubtedly due to the special patriotic atmosphere created by wartime and, possibly, the urgings of OUP and friends, that he made an exception on this occasion. At all events, the two-part concert piece was made, using the film's title music as the Prelude, and the scene in the factory showing the production line making Spitfires, as the Fugue. As a moment of calm in this latter section (*Meno mosso*), Walton used the elegiac music with solo violin associated with the dying Mitchell's home life. Walton's fine craftsmanship is well displayed in the way he makes the theme of the Prelude combine with the Fugue towards the end of the work. The composer himself conducted the first performance on 2 January 1943 with the Liverpool Philharmonic Orchestra at their Philharmonic Hall. London first heard it at the Albert Hall on 21 February, with Malcolm Sargent conducting the London Philharmonic Orchestra.

Walton recorded the work with the Hallé Orchestra in Manchester on 24 June 1943, and its release in August brought about a sudden strong interest in the piece.[7] OUP immediately had to face a considerable demand for scores and parts, so much so that Norman Peterkin (who had succeeded Hubert Foss as head of the music department) wrote to Walton on 20 September 1943: 'Do you feel we should publish this work?' Walton replied at once from Ashby St Ledgers: 'I don't know what to think about engraving and publishing the "Spitfire". On the whole I think it may be just a bubble which by the time the engraving is done, may have burst. If it could be done in 6 weeks I'd be all for it, but I know that[,] or anything like it[,] is impossible [under wartime conditions]'. It was therefore decided that, as publication would take many months, and as by then the hire library would be well supplied with photostats of the autograph full score and manuscript parts, it would be better to mark time.

It was not until 4 March 1960 that Alan Frank (Peterkin's successor) wrote to Walton: 'I have had it in mind for some time that we ought to print a 10 x 7 score of the Spitfire PRELUDE AND FUGUE, which already gets performed quite a lot.... There is just one point: although the brass is full, the woodwind is for some reason or other only 2121. Would it be in order for me to get someone, Tausky I think, to blow this up to double woodwind?' To this, Walton replied on 7 March: 'I imagine economic reasons account[ed] for 2121 in S.P& Fugue. Do what you like with it.' Frank therefore wrote to Tausky on 11 March enclosing a score, and Tausky returned it to OUP on 9 May with his new optional second oboe and second bassoon parts notated in red ink. The score was published on 25 May 1961; in this the tuba is also marked as optional, though no such indication is shown in Walton's autograph. Much trouble was taken over the proofreading of both score and parts, and Walton responded to various queries, notably the revision of the brass in the final two bars.

The 'Spitfire' Prelude and Fugue, which was re-recorded by the composer with the Philharmonia Orchestra on 16 October 1963, has always been deservedly popular, and has been transcribed for many combinations, including brass ensemble, brass band, and military band. The Prelude has been arranged for organ in a shortened version that was approved by Walton.

Memorial Fanfare for Henry Wood

On 19 August 1944, at a time when London was being severely harassed by the V2 'flying bombs', the great conductor and founder of the Promenade Concerts, Sir Henry Wood, died. On 25 March that year the three London orchestras (the London Symphony, the London Philharmonic, and the BBC Symphony) had combined in an Albert Hall concert to celebrate his 75th birthday, just as they had done to mark his jubilee as a conductor on 5 October 1938. It was therefore only natural that they should come together again for the Henry Wood Memorial Concert, sponsored by the *Daily Telegraph*, which took place in the Albert Hall on the afternoon of Sunday, 4 March 1945, conducted by Sir Adrian Boult, John Barbirolli, and Basil Cameron. One of the purposes of the concert was to raise funds to rebuild the bombed Queen's Hall, with which Wood had been so closely associated. The only composer who was asked to write something appropriate for the occasion was Walton, who took the opportunity to revise and amplify the first of the fanfares for brass and percussion that he had written in 1943 as part of the Ministry of Information's *Salute to the Red Army*, an extravaganza produced by Basil Dean in the Albert Hall on 21 February that year.

Walton had been approached on 17 January 1945 by W. W. Thompson, concert manager of the BBC Symphony Orchestra, with the request to write a fanfare that would conclude the concert, following the Bach–Klenovsky [Henry Wood] Toccata and Fugue in D minor. The fanfare was composed quickly, and though it was finally dated 5 February, the outsized autograph was received by the BBC on 26 January. In his letter of the same day acknowledging its safe receipt, Thompson said: 'All concerned are most grateful for the gesture you have very kindly made', which suggests that Walton had waived any idea of a fee. A duplicate score and the parts were immediately put in hand with the BBC's 'best copyist', Gus de Mauny. The fanfare was conducted by Sir Adrian Boult, and the whole concert was broadcast. It was described on the following day by *The Times* as 'dignified and elegiac', and the *Daily Telegraph* considered its 'splendid harshness' to be 'majestic and impressive'.

For the *Memorial Fanfare* Walton seized his opportunity of writing for three orchestras by multiplying each instrumental line of the normal symphony orchestra, based on triple wind, by three. Thus there are three piccolos and six flutes, twelve horns, three tubas, three harps, as well as a vast array of strings (38 first violins!), which are ingeniously divided. At the same time, it is so written that it can be played by a normal symphony orchestra, although in that case the horn parts require some adjustment. It was, in fact, so performed at the opening concert of the 51st season of Promenade Concerts on 21 July 1945, when it was conducted by Constant Lambert as the penultimate item, followed by *Crown Imperial*. No later performances are known.

Orb and Sceptre: Coronation March (1953)

As has been seen, it was the BBC who had commissioned Walton to write the coronation march *Crown Imperial* in 1937. By the time of the coronation of Queen Elizabeth II in 1953, a new cultural institution had come into being, namely the Arts Council of Great Britain, which had evolved from the wartime Council for the Encouragement of Music and the Arts (CEMA). It was its secretary general, W. E. Williams, who wrote to Alan Frank on 31 October 1952 offering Walton a commission to write a new coronation march in time for the ceremony in Westminster Abbey on 2 June of the following year. Details of such a march must have been leaked previously, because the first public performance of the work had already been earmarked by the Royal Philharmonic Society for their concert at the Royal Festival Hall on 7 June, with the London Symphony Orchestra to be conducted by Sir John Barbirolli. The Arts Council stated that there was no objection to a recording being made before the coronation, providing that it was neither released nor reviewed before this date; equally, there was to be no public performance or broadcast before the ceremony. A subsequent letter of 3 November 1952 from Frank to Walton suggests that the matter had already been discussed informally between the parties concerned, and that Walton had accepted the offer and was already talking of somebody being engaged to make military and brass band arrangements of the march. Another letter of 18 November shows that he had by then chosen the title *Orb and Sceptre*.

By the middle of January 1953 Walton had informed Frank that the duration of the march would be about six minutes; around the same time he asked for information on metronome marks relating to the marching tempo of the Guards regiments. Frank replied that he had contacted the director of music of the Irish Guards and had been told that, whereas the official ruling was crotchet = 114–116, experience had taught them that this was too fast, and that they marched to 105–108. This latter figure was the one that Walton eventually indicated, even though there was no question of anybody marching in Westminster Abbey.

On 22 January Walton wrote to Frank: 'The March has been posted and I hope will duly arrive safely. It is not too bad—rather M.G.M. or perhaps Ealing Studios; a slight but not over-subtle distinction…It lasts about 6½ mins.' The letter also gives instructions about photographing pages of the autograph for the first ten pages of the repeat of the main section, following the 'Trio'. In a subsequent undated postcard to Frank, Walton added a postscript: 'I've an uncomfortable feeling that the March[,] especially the opening[,] is rather like Mendelssohn's Wedding March. At any rate it is out of copyright!'

On 19 February, by which time Roy Douglas had begun his various arrangements, Frank wrote to Walton: 'It seems to Roy and myself that the organ part in the full version of ORB AND SCEPTRE is optional, and I want your permission to mark it so, if you agree.' It is clear that Walton did so, and the part bears this designation.

On 18 March 1953, nearly three months before the coronation, Walton recorded *Orb and Sceptre* at Kingsway Hall with the Philharmonia Orchestra; as usual, Walter Legge was his producer.[8] The composer and OUP now had a more accurate timing, and this was rounded up to 7'30" in correspondence. On 27 April Sir Malcolm Sargent recorded the March with the London Symphony Orchestra for Decca.

Orb and Sceptre was duly played before the start of the coronation service on 2 June 1953, together with *Crown Imperial*, by the special Coronation Orchestra, conducted by Sir Adrian Boult. The march played as Queen Elizabeth II entered Westminster Abbey for her coronation was newly composed by the Master of the Queen's Music, Sir Arnold Bax. Unfortunately, as it preceded the service proper, *Orb and Sceptre* was not included on the recording of the occasion that was issued commercially on long-playing records soon after, and that is now available on CD. As soon as the date of the original embargo had passed, OUP published arrangements for piano solo (by Roy Douglas), organ solo (Sir William McKie), and what was described in those days as 'pierhead' orchestra (Roy Douglas). An arrangement for military band was, by agreement, issued by Boosey & Hawkes, as previously in the case of *Crown Imperial*. The march is less formal, and considerably more contrapuntal and chromatic, than its predecessor and, as the composer had perceptively noted at the time of composition, not a little influenced by his recent extensive experience with film music.

There is a final point concerning the title. Although in 1936 Walton had not yet composed his memorable score for Laurence Olivier's film of *Henry V*, it was generally recognized that the title *Crown Imperial* came not only from Dunbar's poem but also from Henry's 'ceremony' soliloquy before the battle of Agincourt. It has therefore always been assumed that the phrase 'orb and sceptre' derives from this source, especially as Walton joked that the same speech would also give him the title 'bed majestical' if he were ever required to write a march for the wedding of the young Prince Charles. But in fact the first two lines of what Shakespeare wrote are:

> 'Tis not the balm, the sceptre, and the ball,
> The sword, the mace, the crown imperial,

On the other hand, in the film of *Henry V* and the set of 78 rpm records that Walton and Olivier made in 1946 of excerpts from it, what Olivier speaks is:

> 'Tis not the orb and sceptre, crown imperial,
> The throne he sits on, nor the tide of pomp
> That beats upon the high shore of this world—
> Not all these laid in bed majestical,

In other words, for the sake of cinematic concision, somebody has made just four lines out of Shakespeare's eight. That person was almost certainly Olivier's text advisor, the theatre critic Alan Dent; little did he realize that he was thereby supplying the future title for a highly effective coronation march.[9]

Finale from Variations on an Elizabethan Theme ('Sellenger's Round')

Among the various requests that came Walton's way in connection with the forthcoming coronation of Queen Elizabeth II was an invitation from Benjamin Britten in early 1953 to provide for that year's Aldeburgh Festival a finale to round off a composite set of celebratory variations for string orchestra on the well-known dance tune 'Sellenger's Round'. The five composers who were invited to write the preceding variations were

Arthur Oldham, Michael Tippett, Lennox Berkeley, Benjamin Britten himself, and Humphrey Searle. The harmonization of the chosen theme was from William Byrd's transcription in the Fitzwilliam Virginal Book, and this was arranged for four parts by Britten's amanuensis, Imogen Holst.

Having recently put aside work on his opera *Troilus and Cressida* in order to fulfil two commissions, the *Coronation Te Deum* and the march *Orb and Sceptre*, the expatriate Walton seems to have been keen to comply with Britten's request in order to ally himself with some of his fellow British composers, especially as the project involved technique more than inspiration. He was further intrigued when he heard that the Festival intended to list the six composers alphabetically, and to institute a fundraising competition in which, for the outlay of *2s 6d*, members of the audience were encouraged to guess the authorship of the individual variations. It is said that it was Walton himself who suggested that each composer should include a self-quotation from a previous work. The composite Variations on an Elizabethan Theme ('Sellenger's Round') was first performed on 20 June 1953 at the opening concert of that year's Aldeburgh Festival with the Aldeburgh Festival Orchestra, conducted by Benjamin Britten. This premiere performance was recorded by Decca and issued on LP in September.[10]

'Sellenger's Round' is believed originally to have been a sixteenth-century dance tune, possibly a maypole dance. Its name may be a corruption of St Ledger's Round, which lends further credence to the spelling with a central 'e' (as adopted by the Aldeburgh Festival) rather than 'i', which is somewhat more usual. The tune was very popular and was included in several well-known manuscript collections of keyboard music at the time. Walton's finale variation is not only highly ingenious, based as it is on a quasi-fugal treatment of a *Presto giocoso* retrograde version of the tune, with the tune proper in augmentation in the middle section, but his self-quotation is especially clever and well camouflaged; this proves to be the opening two chords of the overture *Portsmouth Point* in the closing bars.

Boosey & Hawkes, Britten's publisher at the time, took over the performing material and put the composite work into its hire library, where it still remains. Britten himself retained the six autograph scores but, with the full agreement of the contributing composers, put them on sale at Christie's on 23 March 1961 at a fundraising auction for the Aldeburgh Festival. They were acquired by the James Marshall and Marie-Louise Osborn Collection, which is now housed in the Beinecke Library, Yale University.

March for 'A History of the English-Speaking Peoples'

On 8 July 1958 the British-born, though American-based, television and film producer Harry Alan Towers (subsequently referred to by the acronym-loving Walton as 'HAT') sent a letter from his London office to the composer in Ischia, the beginning of which is quoted as follows:

SIR WINSTON CHURCHILL'S
'HISTORY OF THE ENGLISH-SPEAKING PEOPLES'
narrated by SIR LAURENCE OLIVIER

The name of my Company [Towers of America (Inc.)] may be known to you as producers of recorded radio and film programmes. We have recently completed negotiations with Sir Winston Churchill whereby we are planning to produce five one-hour films primarily intended for television based on the above work. Sir Laurence Olivier has consented to narrate these films, and we are currently making arrangements for the transmission of the series in many parts of the world.

As you will appreciate, the music will play an important part in the production of the series. I am writing to you to see whether it might be possible to interest you in this matter. I would imagine that, in view of the time involved, you would not be prepared to consider writing a musical score for the group of films, and so my suggestion would be whether you would consider a commission to compose the principal theme for the work which would, I imagine, be a triumphal march.

Walton responded by letter four days later, and by 26 August he was writing to Alan Frank: 'If I do do the piece for HAT (by no means certain) it won't be possible to use it as a concert piece. If it is play[ed as] in & out music it can't possibly be longer than 2 mins. without becoming tedious (however good) on the screen. If I come [to London] in Oct. I will certainly be most circumspect in my dealings with H.A.T.'

Walton had lunch with Towers on 13 October when he was in England to conduct *Belshazzar's Feast* at the Leeds Festival, and a formal contract was drawn up on 31 December and signed by Walton on 17 January 1959. This stipulated that he was to compose a 'triumphal march, not exceeding four minutes', and that the manuscript was to be delivered not later than the last day of April.

On 9 March Walton was able to announce to Frank: 'Have dispatched the H.A.T. March today. Not too bad for its purpose but the tune not quite up to standard but full of "dirt" harmony by way of compensation!' On his next visit to England Walton recorded the march with the London Symphony Orchestra at the ADPC Studios, Elstree, on 25 May. No record of this performance is at present known to exist.

And there the matter seems to have rested. Nothing came of the 'series of films' which had been mentioned in the contract, and it is far from certain whether Walton ever received more than even half the commissioning fee which was payable on receipt of the signed acknowledgement of the contract letter. On 19 June Walton wrote to Frank: 'Firstly H.A.T.—writ him! He's not yet paid up and nearly got us in a nasty jam with the N.Y. Bank [Walton had arranged to be paid in the USA and Towers had already assured Frank that the money had been deposited]. . . . His word is not to be trusted & only a live cheque will convince me that he's on the level.' The outcome of this is not known, but the collapse of the venture is probably explained by the information that Frank provided in March 1961. On the 7th of that month he wrote to Walton: 'I have sent you separately a splendid cutting about Harry Alan Towers which is presumably the last we shall hear of the television series.' The separate dispatch of the cutting was probably in order to save his secretary's blushes. On 6 March H.A.T. had been charged in New York with violation of the White Slave Traffic Act, after bringing a prostitute into the USA. He managed to flee the country, and the case against him was eventually dropped. He continued his film career in Britain and the USA until his death in July 2009.

Eventually the composer and conductor Carl Davis took an interest in the march; he recorded it with the London Philharmonic Orchestra in May 1986 and subsequently performed it in concert. It was put into the OUP Hire Library in December of that year. Despite subsequent recordings, the march is possibly best known because Christopher Palmer incorporated the beginning and end of it into his *Henry V: A Shakespeare Scenario*. This was in order to introduce the speech of the Chorus, 'Now all the youth of England are on fire', before the embarkation of Henry's army for France, there being no other suitable music in the film for this purpose.

Prelude for Orchestra

The Granada television network, though based in Manchester (where its hugely successful soap opera *Coronation Street* is recorded), has its main office is in London. On 1 June 1961 Douglas Terry, a producer at Granada, wrote from there to Walton: 'I am writing to inquire whether you might consider composing a short piece of occasional music for this Company. This would be broadcast each afternoon prior to [the start of] our transmissions and would in fact be a sort of signature tune lasting about 6 minutes. At the end of the day further music, based if possible on the same material, terminates our broadcasts, but this is a mere 20 seconds or so.... You may know the Granada TV Network serves the North of England so that, if you felt able to do this, our viewers would not only be hearing music written by a great British composer but also[,] appropriately[,] by a Lancastrian.'

Walton wrote to Alan Frank on 11 June: 'I've written to Granada saying I'd like to have a shot at doing a piece for them. It will not be an easy piece to do, to hit off something which will have immediate and at the same time some enduring appeal as it would be played so often. But it would be good business if one could bring it off.' There was a lull in the negotiations, but matters were resumed in late December, by which time it had been decided that the piece was to be a march, and its length reduced to 4 minutes 55 seconds. In a more detailed letter to Walton of 14 February, Terry explained that 1 minute 55 seconds from the end of the march there would be a short announcement, and about 35 seconds from the end, the music would be faded for a further announcement of approximately 30 seconds. Terry added: 'I mention this because it is obviously desirable that at this time the musical significance should be small.' He goes on to describe the 'Call Signs' also required: short musical phrases of three to four seconds, orchestrated in different ways, to suit the type of programme that was to follow. He ended by suggesting that 'allusions to one or two of the better-known folk tunes of Yorkshire and Lancashire would not be inappropriate'. Walton asked Alan Frank to research such possible tunes; he obliged with four titles, but in the event none was used.

On 10 August 1962 Walton wrote to Frank; 'Sent off the Granada pieces yesterday. A Prelude – End Music and the Call sign with no less than fifteen variants to make up for being late! It's not too good but neither too bad and at any rate I hope it is what is desired.' A photocopy of the score was dispatched to Granada on 23 August.

And with Granada it remained for virtually four years. Frank informed Walton that the unofficial reason for this was the exorbitant Musician's Union rate demanded by symphony orchestras for recording signature tunes. In the meantime, Granada had decided to branch out into the record business (Terry had formerly worked with Pye Records) and, as one of its first releases, intended to issue a popular military band disc that could include an arrangement of the Prelude, rescored for this purpose by the well-known composer and arranger Gilbert Vinter. In a letter to Frank of 23 August 1966 Walton readily agreed to this proposal, adding 'I can't remember the piece, but I suspect it may sound best in the new version.'

Vinter duly made his reorchestration of the Prelude only, including an effective 22-bar cut of the passage where it had been requested that 'the musical significance should be small', and also cutting bars 253–4. His recording of it with the 46-piece London Symphonic Band (with members drawn mostly from the main London symphony orchestras) appeared on Pye Records in the autumn of 1967 under the title *March for Concert Band*.[11] It was this Vinter version of Walton's Prelude that was transmitted at the start of Granada's programmes; they stopped using it in September 1973. The End Music and Call Signs were never used. Because of the great popularity of marching bands in America, it was decided that OUP Inc., USA, should issue the Vinter version, and score and parts were eventually published there in the summer of 1972, not long after the death of the arranger.

Walton's original orchestration of the Prelude for symphony orchestra was not heard until it was first performed on 25 June 1977 at St John's, Smith Square, London, by the Young Musicians Symphony Orchestra, conducted by James Blair. Edward Greenfield, reviewing the concert in *The Guardian* on the following day, affectionately dubbed it 'Orb, Sceptre and Castanets', but made a more telling comment when he suggested that in Queen Elizabeth II's jubilee year, it might have been more appropriately titled 'Jubilee Prelude'.

The National Anthem (with Introduction)

According to Susana Walton, it was David Webster, General Administrator of the Royal Opera House, Covent Garden, who asked Walton to make a new arrangement of the National Anthem to precede the gala premiere of Benjamin Britten's coronation opera *Gloriana*, which was to be given on 8 June 1953 in the presence of the new Queen Elizabeth II, the royal family, and a large section of the establishment. Walton obliged with an imaginative orchestration and this was first performed before the opera by the ROH orchestra, conducted by John Pritchard. According to the Waltons, it was a fiasco. In the words of Lady Walton:

> John Pritchard, the conductor, was so overcome by the excitement of the event that he became very flustered. As soon as he saw the Queen enter the royal box, he gave the first beat for the orchestra to start up the national anthem. Alas, only half the orchestra started; the other half, knowing that the whole of the royal party had to be in their places before the music could begin, just sat and waited. Pritchard, who had his back to the orchestra, could not control the shambles that ensued.... William was beset by irate gentlemen at the ball in Buckingham Palace a few evenings later. We had to ask David Webster to write to the Queen's private secretary to explain that this discordant version of the national anthem was not William's fault.[12]

It is therefore odd that John Pritchard did not recall anything going wrong. In a letter to David Webster he stated: 'I have heard from two sources which I do not think frivolous

a) that William Walton attributes the lack of success of his version of the National Anthem to a fault of mine in the direction of the arrangement and b) that it has been represented to Buckingham Palace that the Conductor made a mistake and caused the Anthem to appear in an unfavourable light. I think I ought to say that my performance of the anthem at the Gala which I conducted was precisely the same as that which the composer heard and approved in rehearsal and which you also heard.'[13] The overnight review of the occasion in *The Times* made no reference to the new version of the National Anthem or its performance.

The arrangement seems to have been totally forgotten until somebody at the ROH discovered the autograph in 1984 and sent it to Lady Walton in Ischia. When she told Christopher Morris, then head of music at OUP, he expressed an interest in putting the arrangement into the hire library. He consequently wrote to John Tooley, Webster's successor, to find out whether there were any copyright issues at stake. The matter was eventually settled by payment of a modest lump sum to the ROH, and Lady Walton assigned the copyright to OUP, though this did not preclude her receiving royalties.

In 1986 it was decided to issue the arrangement in score and parts. By this time it had been performed at the Barbican Centre on 14 October 1985 to launch a concert in memory of Sir Robert Mayer, founder of Youth and Music, who had died in January of that year. The orchestra was the BBC Symphony, and the conductor, ironically enough, Sir John Pritchard, who had premiered it 32 years previously. By this time Walton had written the brass fanfare *Salute to Sir Robert Mayer* to precede the National Anthem at the concert in the Festival Hall on 5 June 1979 celebrating Sir Robert's 100th birthday, and this was therefore featured in the publication of the Anthem, which appeared in February 1988.

God Save the Queen

This artless orchestration (not to be confused with the previous, more imaginative, 1953 version known as *The National Anthem*) was made by Walton for the Philharmonia Orchestra, presumably at the request of his friend Walter Legge, their founder and managing director, to be played at the start of the concerts that it was to give on its first tour of the USA under Herbert von Karajan in October and November 1955.

It seems that, in the event, this arrangement was never played in the USA, possibly because it required the full orchestra or because anthems were not as customary there as they were in Great Britain. It was first heard at a Philharmonia concert under Karajan on 18 October 1955 in the Royal Festival Hall, on the eve of the orchestra's departure for its American tour. In his book on the first forty years of the Philharmonia, Stephen Pettitt records: 'It featured the horn section very prominently, and at a signal from Dennis Brain they raised the bells of their instruments in the air for maximum effect. It was a popular arrangement and was still pasted inside the music folders ten years later.'[14] What Dennis Brain had noticed was that, instead of supplying harmonic backing as was normal, the horns had for once been given the tune. It was still being played by the orchestra at the composer's Royal Festival Hall 80th birthday concert on 29 March 1982, by which time it had been slightly adapted for use with the Philharmonia Chorus.

The Star-Spangled Banner

As well as 'God Save the Queen', Walton was commissioned to orchestrate the American anthem for the Philharmonia Orchestra's first tour of the United States. Answering a query from Alan Frank in a postcard to him of 10 March 1975, Walton wrote: 'Yes I did orchestrate the S.S.B. for Karajan when he took the Philharmonia to the U.S. years ago…It was *not* my best effort of [*sic*] scoring and & I don't think it was ever played or paid for! I've no idea where the sc. & parts are but it is best destroyed if discovered.'

The origins of *The Star-Spangled Banner* (not always hyphenated) are obscure, but it is generally believed that the melody was originally known as 'The Anacreontic Song', as sung by the members of the Anacreontic Society in London, and first published there probably in 1779–80. The composer of the tune is usually assumed to be John Stafford Smith, a member of the society. However, others believe that it was composed earlier, possibly in Ireland, as a hunting or military song for valveless horn or trumpet.[15]

Title music for the BBC TV Shakespeare series

In 1975 Cedric Messina, a producer and director for BBC TV Drama, persuaded the corporation to undertake an ambitious project to produce all 36 plays in the First Folio of Shakespeare, together with *Pericles*. The idea was eventually approved, subject to American financial backing, which was subsequently forthcoming, and the resulting productions were later published as DVDs. For specially composed title music, Messina naturally turned to the British composer who was most associated with Shakespeare, namely Walton. At the same time he asked the editor of this volume to act as his music advisor.

Negotiations were handled by Walton's agent, Ian Hunter of Harold Holt Ltd, and a meeting was arranged in 1977 at the Ritz Hotel, during one of the composer's visits to London. With his tongue characteristically in his cheek, the 75-year-old Walton said: '25 seconds? That's just the sort of length I feel I can handle these days.' Later, Messina and the editor travelled to Ischia, where they found that Walton had taken the request for something vaguely Elizabethan, scored for modest forces, rather too literally. He readily agreed to revise the piece and make it more arresting.

On 7 October Walton sent the new autograph score to OUP in London, and the piece was subsequently recorded on 26 January 1978 at Lime Grove Studios by members of the orchestra of English National Opera, conducted by the present editor. The final take was played back by phone to the composer in Ischia and was approved. The title music was first heard introducing the transmission of *Romeo and Juliet* on 3 December 1978, and it preceded the following 11 plays that were recorded during Messina's time in charge of the project, but was dropped by the two subsequent producers of the series.

NOTES

1. BBC Written Archives, Caversham.
2. William Walton Museum, Forio, Ischia.
3. HMV DB 3164.
4. OUP Archive, Oxford.
5. BBC Written Archives.

6. Stephen Lloyd, *William Walton: Muse of Fire* (Woodbridge, 2001), p. 184, quoting Ronald Howard, *In Search of My Father* (London, 1981), pp. 104–120.

7. HMV C 3359.

8. A Columbia recording released in June 1953 as a 12" 78 rpm disc LX 1583, and also released in the same month on LP as 33C 1016.

9. The editor would like to thank James Brooks Kuykendall for drawing his attention to this.

10. Decca LXT 2798.

11. Pye CSCL 30174.

12. Susana Walton, *William Walton: Behind the Façade* (Oxford, 1988), p. 132.

13. Helen Conway, *Sir John Pritchard: His Life in Music* (London, 1993), p. 110.

14. Stephen S. Pettitt, *Philharmonia Orchestra: A Record of Achievement 1945–1985* (London, 1985), p. 78.

15. See James J. Fuld, *The Book of World Famous Music* (rev. edn, New York, 1971), pp. 529–534.

18

Shorter Orchestral Works 2 *(Vol. 18)*

David Lloyd-Jones

With the exception of the Sonata for String Orchestra, the works grouped together in this volume represent an important and characteristic aspect of Walton's output, namely his ability to enrich the lighter side of the orchestral repertory. Among British works, Elgar's miniatures and two *Wand of Youth* suites may have helped to establish this genre, but Walton, ever the man of his time, was quick to exploit his own distinctive combination of astringency and wit, both of which combined easily with his genius for melody and parody. Light music and dance were in Walton's blood and he never neglected his love of them, nor their ability to add welcome contrast to even the most solemn moments in his more extended works.

Façade

The background to Walton's accompaniments to Edith Sitwell's *Façade* poems that culminated in *Façade: An Entertainment* for speaker(s) and instrumental ensemble is discussed in considerable detail in Volume 7 of the William Walton Edition. For present purposes two points need to be restated: first, that 43 settings in all were composed and performed on a trial-and-error basis between 1922 and 1928; second, that Walton's accompaniments, which at first mainly underpinned the spoken text 'with arabesque and timbre', as Constant Lambert so aptly put it, gradually came to assume an importance equal to that of the poems themselves because of their greater continuity of texture and consequent melodic allure. This is especially noticeable in those poems that deal with dance forms. First performed privately in January 1922 and publicly in June 1923, the *Façade* Entertainment established itself definitively with the London public and critics at two performances at the New Chenil Galleries, Chelsea, in April and June 1926. By this time all but two of the settings had been composed, but something else of great significance had also happened. A week before the June performance of *Façade*, the premiere of the overture *Portsmouth Point*, Walton's first orchestral work, had been given at the ISCM Festival in Zürich, thereby establishing him as an avant-garde British composer of outstanding talent and promise. Equally important was the fact that the overture had already been selected to act as an orchestral interlude in a performance during Diaghilev's Ballets Russes season, and it was performed as such on 28 June under Eugene Goossens. It is reasonable to assume that Diaghilev, who had attended one of the earliest private performances of *Façade* and was closely associated with the Sitwell circle to which Walton belonged, was sufficiently satisfied with the result to request something similar from the young composer for his winter season.

The First Orchestral Suite

In choosing to make an orchestral suite out of some of the *Façade* numbers it was only natural for Walton to choose those that featured dance. The first selection was of just five numbers—'Polka', 'Valse', 'Swiss Jodelling Song', 'Tango-Pasodoblé', and 'Tarantella'. These, minus the third number, were first performed under Walton's direction on 3 December 1926 (with repeats on the 4th and 10th) as an interlude during a Ballets Russes evening at the Lyceum Theatre, which presented the premiere of Lord Berners's and Sacheverell Sitwell's ballet *The Triumph of Neptune* that Walton had helped to orchestrate. Writing to his mother after the event Walton said: 'Friday was a great night...the production of the new ballet...I conducted my "Façade" suite with good success and again on Sat. Quite a surprise my being asked to do it.'[1] All five numbers were to form what was at the time known as the Suite from *Façade*, but which was subsequently titled the First Orchestral Suite.

The Suite was first published by Oxford University Press in October 1927 as an arrangement for piano duet by Constant Lambert. In the previous year Walton himself had arranged 'Valse' for piano solo, which OUP published in 1928. He had made it for a musical soirée given by Mrs Beverley Baxter and dedicated it to her; this explains why the dedication bizarrely remains at the head of this number in the Lambert duet version. The orchestral suite was first published by OUP in study score format only in 1936. It is hard to fathom why it took them so long to bring out such an obvious sure-fire success. (It should be borne in mind that, incredibly, the *Façade* Entertainment of 1922–8 was not published until 1951.) Most people who know or perform the (First) Suite find it difficult to understand why 'Popular Song'—the one undoubted 'hit' number—was not included. There is a simple answer: in 1926, when the orchestrations were made, 'Popular Song' (1928) had not been composed. By the time of the Suite's publication in 1936 it did, of course, very much exist but, as will be seen, there was another reason why it was not published at the time.

In *Portsmouth Point* Walton had already declared himself as an exceptional orchestrator, but the altogether lighter, more playful style of the *Façade* Suite called for something with even greater character and sleight of hand. As shown by the published score, this Walton duly provided. The only known extant autograph of Walton's orchestration, now in Austin, Texas, is a very sketchy-looking score in pencil which, however, is both complete and surprisingly close to the published version. In the OUP files there is a memo of 26 September 1949 from Alan Frank, head of the Music Department, on the subject of Walton's surviving manuscript scores in the publisher's possession. Among those that it lists are 'Façade Suite No. I, 59 pages, pencil, condition not good' (this is the surviving Austin autograph) and 'Ditto, 56 pages, ink, condition not good'. This latter autograph in ink, which must have served as printer's copy for the 1936 first publication (as the pencil version has no printer's marking), has unfortunately disappeared. It is to be hoped that it may eventually resurface because, useful though the pencil autograph has proved in establishing a definitive text of the suite, the printer's copy could also help to explain a number of anomalies in the 1936 score.

Ballet versions

An important new development in the fortunes of *Façade* in its orchestral guise occurred in 1929 when the suite was used for a ballet, choreographed by Günter Hess and performed on 22 September at Hagen, Westphalia. At this time only the piano duet version had been published, so it is surprising that any of the *Façade* music should have been known outside Britain. But it is very doubtful whether this staging influenced the next use of *Façade* for a ballet because, as this was for the Camargo Society and choreographed by Frederick Ashton, the obvious connection is Constant Lambert. In 1930 Decca Records released recordings of Walton conducting 11 numbers from the entertainment, with Edith Sitwell and Lambert as speakers. These two 78 rpm discs achieved an almost cult status in certain circles, and it was the Entertainment chamber version of the music that Ashton initially wanted to use. After the notoriously prickly Edith Sitwell objected (an action that she later admitted she regretted), Ashton and Lambert were obliged to turn to the more orchestrally expensive suite. However, the ballet, as premiered on Sunday 26 April 1931 at the Cambridge Theatre with its impressive cast of dancers under Lambert's direction, comprised not five but seven numbers. The two additions to the Suite, 'Scotch Rhapsody' and 'Popular Song', had been newly orchestrated, as had the opening 'Fanfare'.

Before addressing the matter of the orchestrator of these additional items, let us finish the account of the enormously successful Ashton ballet, which has done as much as anything else to make the orchestral *Façade* music as widely popular as it is. The Camargo Society production eventually entered the Vic-Wells Ballet repertory in October 1935 when another number, 'Country Dance', was added. After the company's disastrous tour of Holland in May 1940, when sets, costumes, and music were left behind as the company fled the unexpectedly rapid German advance, a revised production, with entirely new decor by the original designer, was quickly mounted in July 1940. For this, yet another two numbers were added—'Noche Espagnola' [*sic*] ('Nocturne péruvienne'), an orchestral version of 'Long Steel Grass', and 'Foxtrot' ('Old Sir Faulk'). By this time these had been published in the Second Orchestral Suite. Both 'Country Dance' and 'Noche Española' have been dropped from time to time in revivals, but the ballet, despite yet another loss of scenery and costumes in a fire in June 1949, would seem to be indestructible and is still revived regularly all over the world.

The Second Orchestral Suite

Returning to the orchestration of the ballet's numbers that had not featured in the original Suite from *Façade*, for many years it was suspected that these—despite what appeared to be their wholly authentic quality—were the work of Constant Lambert who had invariably conducted the first performances of the new numbers in the productions concerned, and whose connection with *Façade* in all its guises was second only to that of the composer. It is now possible to be very precise about this. It would appear that it was the publication of the First Orchestral Suite in 1936 that encouraged OUP to start considering a second suite. Fortunately we have more information about its genesis than that of the First Suite. In the OUP files there is the following letter, dated

14 November 1936, written by Hubert Foss, head of the Music Department, to Constant Lambert.

> Willie and I were talking about Façade Second Suite today. I am keen to go on with it but I am not quite sure what numbers to publish in it. It appears that the only numbers that you use at Sadler's Wells which are not in the First Suite are Fanfare, which Willie does not want, I gather, to perpetuate, 'Scotch Rhapsody', a popular song [*sic*] and 'Country Dance'. Is this so? If so, I think we must find at least two other numbers to make a reasonable suite. So far Willie can only think of 'The Man from the Far Countree'. Let us meet and discuss this soon. I much want your advice.[2]

Negotiations seem to have continued in a relaxed fashion. Foss's next internal memo of importance is dated 5 July 1937, and gives some idea of the vagueness that still hung over the Entertainment:

> Decided on Saturday July 3rd that the Second Façade Suite should consist of Scotch Rhapsody, Pastoral Song [i.e. Country Dance], Long Steel Grass, Popular Song, Foxtrot. Nos. 1, 2 and 4 already exist in orchestral form, and Lambert will score Nos. 3 and 5 for similar combination as soon as I can provide the score of Façade Entertainment for which I have cabled America today. Barbirolli wants the first performance. There will have to be a preface suggesting how the two suites can be combined, and it is thought to be an advantage that they are not scored for the same combination. Piano duet arrangement will be done by Lambert with Walton helping.

Thus it would seem that the original intention was to make the Second Suite consist entirely of Lambert's orchestrations which included the opening 'Fanfare' and, of course, 'Popular Song'. In the event Walton himself scored 'Long Steel Grass' ('Noche Española') and 'Old Sir Faulk' ('Foxtrot'). As the manuscript source of the Second Suite in the Beinecke Library shows, his autographs were bound in with a copy of the other numbers to act as an early hire score for conductors. Part of the reason why Walton fortunately decided to score the remaining two numbers himself may have been financial. It was clear that Lambert (another OUP composer) was going to have to be paid by the composer for his contribution, and the amount would obviously be less if Walton undertook this task himself. A note to the finance department of 2 August 1938 states: 'Please note that we are paying Constant Lambert £30 for orchestrating Walton: Façade Suite No. 2, and that this is to be offset against Walton's general royalties'. The Second Suite was published by OUP as a study score on 28 April 1938; the Lambert–Walton (?) piano duet reduction (not credited to either) appeared on 8 September.

It is unfortunate that the autographs of Lambert's orchestrations of four of the Second Suite's six numbers have disappeared (they were possibly left behind in Holland) as they might have shown whether Walton amended them to any significant extent before the suite was published. John Barbirolli kept his word and gave the first performance of the Second Suite (for some reason replacing 'Foxtrot' with 'Tango' from the First Suite) with the New York Philharmonic Orchestra at Carnegie Hall on 30 March 1938. The British premiere was given at Queen's Hall by the BBC Symphony Orchestra under Sir Henry Wood at a Promenade concert on 10 September of the same year.

Republications

Of the two suites it is not surprising, given the early provenance of the autograph sources, that the published text of the first proved to be the most fallible. This became particularly apparent in late 1967 when, prior to the issue of an entirely re-engraved edition that OUP published in the following year, Roy Douglas and Walton tried to sort out the many misprints and mistakes contained in the 1936 edition. Eventually Douglas sent the composer his own copy of the score (showing the additions that he suggested were necessary) for Walton's approval, and asking for any further comments that he might care to make. Walton obliged and returned Douglas's score to him with annotations and corrections, adding, in one of his more dubious asides: 'Of course [Hubert] Foss never had a proof-reader about the place.'[3] The 1968 score is a considerable improvement on what existed before but is not without problems of its own.

No such process took place with the Second Suite, which remained until now much as it appeared at the time of its publication in 1938. The new 1966 edition was a straight republication of this.

Rearrangement of numbers and recordings

To conserve space, the following numbers are given to the titles contained in the two suites: 1. Polka, 2. Valse, 3. Jodelling Song, 4. Tango, 5. Tarantella, 6. Fanfare, 7. Scotch Rhapsody, 8. Country Dance, 9. Noche Española, 10. Popular Song, 11. Foxtrot.

If all 11 numbers of the First and Second Suites are to be performed together, the order suggested by the composer in the first printed score of the Second Suite (6, 7, 2, 4, 3, 8, 1, 9, 10, 11, 5) is hard to fault, and this is the order of his second recording of 1955–6. However, Walton's first recording adopts a different order. It was first made in 1936 and included all the numbers scored by then, i.e. the five of the First Suite plus 6, 7, 8, and 10 (in Lambert's unaccredited orchestrations). The order of the two records was 6, 1, 3, 2, 4 and 10, 8, 7, 5. In October 1938 Walton recorded his two newly orchestrated numbers, 9 and 11, thereby completing the full sequence.[4]

Constant Lambert recorded the suites with the Philharmonia Orchestra on 27 September 1950 (his last recording sessions) and, with one exception, his recording preserved the same unorthodox sequence as the Walton recording. The most surprising feature is that 'Fanfare' does not go into 'Scotch Rhapsody', as in the ballet and as seemingly planned by Lambert, but, most unconvincingly, into 'Polka'. Again, there is a simple explanation. Both the first Walton and the Lambert recordings were planned and first published as 78 rpm records, and the order was clearly dictated by the need to get two (in one instance three) numbers on to one 12-inch side. When the Lambert recording was put onto vinyl (one of the very earliest Columbia LP's) the order could have been changed, but the opportunity was not taken.[5] A more recent reappearance of the first Walton recording on CD has sensibly restored the recommended sequence.[6]

If a shorter selection is required, the First Suite alone is an obvious choice but for the fact that, as already noted, it lacks 'Popular Song'. Walton himself became aware of this on the numerous occasions that he was asked to conduct the suite, and after his performance of seven numbers at the 1960 Proms he and Alan Frank arranged to produce what they came to term the 'Special Suite'. This was the First Suite, but with 'Popular Song' and 'Foxtrot' from the Second inserted before the final 'Tarantella'. As an enlarged version of this, a decade later Walton proposed a selection lacking only 'Country Dance' and 'Noche Española'—for some reason always the poor relations of the *Façade* numbers both in concert and on stage. This order was 6, 7, 2, 4, 3, 1, 10, 11, 5. Thus it would seem that whatever the selection, the best versions start with 'Fanfare'–'Scotch Rhapsody' and end with the sure-fire 'Popular Song'–'Foxtrot'–'Tarantella' sequence.

Edith Sitwell's name should always be invoked whenever anything relating to *Façade* is performed, for it is her remarkably idiosyncratic and memorable poems that caused the young Walton to compose as he did. However, one does not necessarily have to be aware of the poems or even be British to believe that the *Façade* music, as represented by these two orchestral suites, constitutes some of the finest, wittiest, and most enduring light music ever composed.

Siesta

This work, which constitutes the first musical expression of Walton's lifelong love affair with Italy, is one of the shortest, but at the same time most enigmatic, of his entire oeuvre. It was composed in the autumn of 1926, published soon after in both piano duet transcription and full score, and revised and reset in 1962. Very little is known about its origins; neither in Walton's letters nor in the OUP files is there any information about the work's provenance, and the autograph is lost. Even the dedication to the notoriously effete Stephen Tennant in the original edition could be no more than a reflection of Walton's indebtedness to Siegfried Sassoon for his financial help, for Sassoon (to whom Walton would dedicate *Portsmouth Point* in 1928) was at the time the lover of Tennant.

Scored for small orchestra, the work is essentially light-hearted and charming. Yet under the deceptively beguiling title there lurk moments that cause the listener to suspect tensions and outbursts of temperament, which are suggested by the somewhat mannered false relations and sudden moments of force. There would appear to have been an underlying programme in Walton's mind, not necessarily too precise, but nevertheless outlining some form of narrative. A similar observation might be made about another short work for chamber orchestra, Hugo Wolf's *Italian Serenade*, for which several hidden scenarios have been suggested. Walton was known for being influenced by other compositions, so it is possible that the common Italian theme is not coincidental. The one person who was very close to him at the time of composition and who might have provided a vital clue about what lies behind *Siesta* was Constant Lambert, who wrote his first article on Walton in November 1926, a matter of weeks after the work had been finished. However, in discussing his friend's few works to date, he merely refers somewhat archly to 'the charming idyll for small orchestra entitled *Siesta* to which one might apply the epithet "Mendelssohnian" were it not that the texture is mainly contrapuntal'.[7]

Walton himself conducted the first performance of *Siesta*, very soon after its completion, at the Aeolian Hall on 24 November 1926. Writing to his mother early in the following month he reported: 'Unfortunately I receive nothing for it, but it is well worth doing for the experience.'[8] It was published by OUP in Walton's own transcription for piano duet in July 1928; the full score followed in October of the following year. Accounts in the OUP files point to a certain amount of last-minute revision. For instance, the cost of engraving the 29 plates for the full score and parts was £25 7s 6d, but the charge for author's corrections was an extra £5 9s 4d, a surprisingly high proportion of the total.

In 1961 Walton looked at *Siesta* again and, together with his publisher Alan Frank, started to consider a light revision. Frank wrote appreciatively of the piece and Walton replied: 'I agree with you it is a rather enchanting piece. I think it will be better "senza sord" for the most part—better balance between the w.w. and strs., as I've indicated.' They began by issuing a list of 26 corrections; this was sent in the first instance to the librarian of the BBC Welsh Orchestra prior to Walton's appearance with them on 13 April 1962 with a programme that included *Siesta* as part of his 60th birthday celebrations. All existing stock at OUP was corrected by a copyist, but it was eventually decided to re-engrave the score. Walton marked up a copy of the printed full score and, after it was newly set, answered the proof corrector's outstanding queries in February 1963. The new edition, from which the composer removed the original dedication to Stephen Tennant, was published in September 1963; the copyright line ran '© 1963 minor revisions'.

Frederick Ashton twice used *Siesta* as the basis for an occasional *pas de deux*. The first was given by the Vic-Wells Ballet at Sadler's Wells Theatre on 24 January 1936 (postponed from 21 January due to the death of George V), danced by Pearl Argyle and Robert Helpmann and with Walton conducting. The second was presented as part of a tribute to Walton on his 70th birthday at the Aldeburgh Festival on 28 July 1972, with Vyvyan Lorrayne and Barry McGrath.

Walton recorded *Siesta* with the London Philharmonic Orchestra on two occasions, once in 1938 (as a backing to his two newly orchestrated numbers for the Second Suite of *Façade*), and again in 1970.[9]

Music for Children

Music for Children began life in early 1940 as a series of nine pieces for piano solo which Walton wrote for his 12-year-old niece Elizabeth, daughter of his elder brother Noel. Not long after, he recast them as piano duets, at the same time adding a final tenth number, and for these his nephew Michael became a co-dedicatee. Walton completely forgot about the existence of his piano solo original, and it has only become known since its first publication in Volume 20 of the WWE.

In *Tunes for my Niece*, as the piano solos were called, the individual pieces were untitled and so, initially, were the piano duets. But ever since Schumann, piano pieces written for children have been notable for their descriptive titles, and OUP may have persuaded Walton to come up with the ones that he eventually provided. In 1940 they published the duets in two books entitled *Duets for Children*, six in the first, four in the second.

In 1941 Walton orchestrated the pieces under the title *Music for Children*. Walter Goehr, who in 1939 had arranged four dances from *Façade* for small orchestra, is believed to have already orchestrated six of the numbers; however, there is no doubt that the autograph of the published edition is exclusively in Walton's hand. (It is doubtful, though, that he would have undertaken this undemanding task had it not been for the exceptional atmosphere of wartime.) In orchestrating *Duets for Children* Walton suppressed the titles and changed the order of numbers, even as late as in proof. In including a tuba (in only two of the ten numbers) and harp with no 'cueing-in', he made no concessions to the many light orchestras of the time that might have been expected to have been his main customers.

Music for Children was first performed at Queen's Hall on 16 February 1941 by the London Philharmonic Orchestra under Basil Cameron; it was published as a study score in the same year by OUP. The composer recorded it with the London Philharmonic Orchestra in 1970.[10]

Walton came to feel a bit sheepish about *Music for Children*. When the question of a reprint arose in 1966 he wrote to Alan Frank: 'Consign Mus. for Chil. to the hire library, there is no point in reprinting.'

Galop Final

Boris Kochno, Diaghilev's secretary and assistant, had been at the lunch and play-through organized by the Sitwell brothers in 1927 at which they had tried (in vain) to persuade the Russian impresario to interest himself in Walton and, in particular, the three pieces that eventually became the Sinfonia Concertante. After the death of Diaghilev, Kochno continued his deep involvement with ballet and eventually co-founded the Ballets des Champs-Élysées. Kochno's talents were essentially those of a librettist for ballets. In 1932 he provided the scenario for *Jeux d'Enfants* (Massine's ballet to Bizet's music) and this may have given him the later idea of using Walton's *Music for Children* as the basis for his 1949 ballet *Devoirs de Vacances*, with choreography by John Taras and costumes and scenery by Cecil Beaton. Walton had already added an upbeat final number 'Trumpet Tune' to his *Duets for Children*, but Kochno asked him to supply yet another, even more rousing one. Walton agreed to oblige an old friend, but promptly forgot about it due to his extreme preoccupation with his opera *Troilus and Cressida*. He was therefore alarmed when a sudden telegram arrived from Kochno saying that the ballet was in its final stages of preparation. Writing from the Convento San Francesco, Forio d'Ischia, on 4 November 1949, Walton said:

> I am sorry—but I had got into my head after our telephone conversation that you were content with the finale as in the printed copy—so I got immersed with my opera & all thoughts of the new finale vanished till the receipt of your telegram. However a day & a half's work & I've produced this—Galop final (tribute to Gavarni!) which I think is not too bad though the piano part I send is, I must emphasise, but a skeleton of the orchestral version which will reach you a couple of days after this. The duration is 3 minutes & I've marked 'cuts' if needed.
>
> I hope it is not too late & I ask forgiveness for my negligence.

Three days later, having finished the orchestration, he again wrote to Kochno:

> Here is the score—effective if a trifle vulgar! The parts will need to be copied. I've done it for the small orchestra you gave me as it will save having it rearranged if you decide on cutting down the other pieces—which can easily be done.[11]

A further letter from Walton to Kochno of 5 February 1950 takes the tale of misadventure a stage further:

> We went to Naples last week in the fond hope of seeing you, but alas, you had gone on to Paris.
>
> After the performance, which incidentally went very well, we happened to have dinner at the same restaurant as some members of the company, so I bravely asked one of them who happened to be English & whose name I could not catch how 'Les Exercises' had fared, as I had heard nothing at all about it.
>
> So I heard all the bad news in full, that it was a 'flop', that the scenery & costumes were poor, likewise the choreography & worst of all my finale arrived too late.
>
> I am too sorry for words about that—I could'nt [*sic*] apologise more. However, from what I gathered, it could'nt have turned the ballet from a failure into a success. Especially as I understand the order of the pieces had been much changed, & I had made quotations in the finale from piece No. I (in the original) which would hardly have made sense, since the position of the first piece had been changed.
>
> I gather that the ballet is going to be revised at Cannes. If this is so, may I make these suggestions? Play the music in the order of the orchestral score, with the new Finale at the end. This should bring the running time to 17 minutes which is enough for a divitissement [*sic*], I think. There should on no account be any repeats of any of the pieces—they are far too tenuous for repetition. Play the first piece before the curtain goes up—a quiet beginning is just as good as a loud one & this piece would give the clue to the ballet, being a five finger exercise. I am sure this, from a musical point of view & I suspect, from the point of view of the ballet, will be a great improvement.

It is not known whether Kochno paid any attention to these well-meaning suggestions. Unfortunately all trace of Walton's orchestration has disappeared, so in 1991 the Walton authority Christopher Palmer orchestrated the Galop (in French the final 'p' is not sounded) for the same forces as used in *Music for Children*. Palmer entered his detailed suggestions for scoring into the piano score and then gave it to an assistant orchestrator, Geoff Alexander, to flesh out, in the manner that is normal in the film world in which he often worked. The autograph is Alexander's, but Palmer has added in his own hand a number of characteristic smaller touches, mainly involving accentuation and percussion. The result is certainly effective if possibly a little more exuberant than even Walton would have envisaged. As Palmer remarked in his liner notes to the first recording of the work: '[I] can only point out that if the orchestration sounds "vulgar" so (on Walton's own admission) does the music!'[12] Galop Final received what is believed to be its first public performance on 8 June 1994 in Atlanta, USA, at an open-air concert given by the Atlanta Symphony Orchestra, conducted by Richard Kaufman. It is published in the WWE for the first time.

Sonata for String Orchestra

In the spring of 1971 Neville Marriner, music director of the highly successful Academy of St Martin-in-the-Fields, wrote to Walton requesting him to compose an extended work for strings for his players. Walton's immediate reaction was to consider which of his compositions could be adapted for this purpose, and so he suggested an arrangement of his 1947 String Quartet in A minor to be made, not by himself, but by Malcolm Arnold. Marriner met Walton on one of his visits to London, and on 27 June wrote to him:

> This is just to confirm the conversation we had yesterday about the reconstruction of your string quartet into a work for string orchestra. I think we were agreed that a slight condensation of the first and third movements would be possible and perhaps preferable, for the sort of repertoire that string orchestras will be best able to place in programmes that depend on their major works being about twenty to twenty-three minutes duration. Textually, I think this would also give the work the sort of impact that is characteristic of your major orchestral pieces. With your permission, I will send Alan Frank a copy of this letter and ask him to get in touch with Malcolm Arnold, suggesting that he, Malcolm and I might meet fairly soon to discuss the changes that you would be prepared to consider, and of course the addition of [a] contrabass part and modest bits of rescoring.

On 6 July Walton wrote to Arnold:

> I hope this reaches you before a letter from Neville Marriner or Alan Frank as I should like to be the first to ask you about the proposed project of doing my String Quartet for String Orch (ie. with Double bass)....I know it is a lot to ask, but I am too involved with it myself to do it really well otherwise I'd do it (or rather try to do it). You need'nt [*sic*] do it all—just those parts which you think would gain by more volume of Strings & it might have a solo String Quart in it, as in the Intro & Allegro of Elgar.[13]

Walton had already begun to look for cuts in the quartet, and the day before his letter to Arnold had written despairingly to Alan Frank:

> It's no good. Since I saw you I've been trying to fathom how and where to cut the 1st mov. of the Str 4tet. It just won't work. I thought I'd found one from 14 to 23 some 3', but [it] involved an excruciating gear change & the 'cut' was as if one had had one's stomach out as well as other appendages, so if N.M. wants to do it for Str Orch he'll have to do it in toto. The repeat in the Scherzo could go but it's only about a minute. The slow mov. won't cut either, but could go a bit quicker than the 'Allegri' [Quartet] take it.

Replying on 21 July Frank reported: 'Neville is perfectly happy about the work being done complete. That being so it does seem to me a bit of a pity that you don't feel inclined to do it yourself. Quite honestly I think you would do it better than anyone else, even Malcolm.'[14]

On 23 July Walton informed Frank that Malcolm Arnold was 'delighted' to undertake the orchestration but only in about a year's time. He then went on to discuss the cutting of the repeat in the scherzo: 'In the first version of the H[ollywood] Quartet's recording the repeat in the Scherzo was cut and I rather po-facedly made them put it back. It is actually, though I wasn't going to admit it at the time, rather better with the cut so I think we will stick to it tho' it is only a matter of a minute or so.' Eventually Walton retained the repeat, but made the second time round *con sordino*. A year was clearly too long to wait so, as Alan Frank had hoped, Walton himself got down to work. On 26 September he informed him: '[Malcolm Arnold] is coming here on Oct. 25th, & will cast a fatherly eye over this 4-tet which is on the way. Arranging is a fearful bore, but better than doing nothing—doldrums. I know I ought to have written a new St. piece. But there it is, I havent.' Progress was good, and on 9 October Walton wrote to Christopher Morris at OUP: 'I shall be sending shortly the 1st mov. of the Qtet arr. for Str. Orch. Not up to my usual standard of caligraphy [*sic*] but I daresay Roy [Douglas] will have little difficulty in deciphering it. I think I shall do a further 2 movs and get Malcolm to do the last.' Finally, on 2 November he wrote: 'Herewith (more or less) the rest of the 4-tet transmogrified...You can see the 4th mov. has been done by M.A. bless his heart.' It is fortunate that Walton decided to arrange the first three movements himself because his reworking is undoubtedly more imaginative than Malcolm Arnold's for the fourth movement. On the other hand, this largely percussive music did not call for any special treatment in its recasting. It is noteworthy that in the first three movements there are fewer tempo and dynamic markings than in the string quartet. Most of these omissions were probably intentional on Walton's part, as he considered that a full body of strings need not be marked with the same finesse as that required by a quartet, but possibly some of the omissions can be put down to oversight.

Sonata for String Orchestra, a title that was eventually decided on in December 1971, was premiered on 2 March 1972 (not 1 March as stated in the first edition) at the Perth Festival, Australia, by the Academy of St Martin-in-the-Fields, directed by Neville Marriner; it received its first British performance on 27 May by the same performers at the Bath Festival. In welcoming a major addition to the distinguished corpus of British music for strings, most reviews were highly favourable.

Publication

Towards the end of 1972 the sonata was being prepared for publication, and it would seem that OUP involved Neville Marriner in this process, for Walton wrote to Frank on 2 October: 'I think I would like to see the proofs of the String Sonata before it is published to know what N.M. is exactly up to.'[15] Walton was indeed sent the proofs, as his despondent postcard to OUP of over three months later indicates: 'Have not received any queries from you re the Str. Son., in fact I've heard nothing about it since I returned the corrected proofs some time ago. As there is little time I suggest that Marriner can answer them. But I had better see them before it is actually printed.'[16] Around this time Marriner and the Academy recorded the Sonata for String Orchestra (released in September of that year), but the edition still did not appear. Walton seems to have continued to study the proofs, for on 28 March 1973 he wired Christopher Morris about a change that he had made to the bars one before and at fig. 63 in the third movement: 'Alterations page seventy-two imperative the rest can wait. William'. Walton was distressed to hear that the work had already been recorded and that therefore this latest change had not been included. He requested that the passage should be re-recorded with the revised text, and this was subsequently done.[17]

Another question that arose at this time was the minimum number of strings that could be used. Walton made his views very plain in his letter of 29 March 1973 to Christopher Morris: 'I still don't know exactly the number of players needed. I personally think they should be fluid & not necessarily those of N.M.'s band, but also say for the L.S.O. strings, in fact any number. All it would entail would be to print a note saying not less than so many.' Neville Marriner was consulted on this matter and an appropriate note added to the score. Proof corrector's queries continued to arrive and were answered by Walton. However, for some reason OUP did not finally publish the study score and parts until 20 December 1973. No reference was made to Malcolm Arnold's participation.

Perhaps the character of Sonata for String Orchestra has been summed up most perceptively by a notable commentator on the music of Walton, Hugh Ottaway. Reviewing the published study score in the *Musical Times* he wrote:

> Walton's precision, the keenness of his ear and his almost feline finesse are much in evidence—the workmanship is of the highest order—and yet I feel that the original is, at least marginally, the finer realization of the musical thought. The Lento, one of Walton's most heartfelt expressions, does lose something of its intimacy, and perhaps the first movement, too, is a little coarsened by the adaptation. On the other hand, the finale, and possibly the scherzo, may be held to gain by the impact of a string orchestra.... Even so, the full string version deserves to become popular.[18]

NOTES

1. *The Selected Letters of William Walton*, ed. Malcolm Hayes (London, 2002), p. 36.
2. OUP Archive, Oxford. Unless otherwise indicated, all correspondence is from the OUP Archive.
3. Letter to Roy Douglas of 21 February 1968 (property of Roy Douglas).
4. The nine numbers were issued on HMV C 2836–7; the final two were on C 3042.
5. The Lambert 78 rpm recordings were issued on Columbia DX 1734–6; the LP was SX 1003.
6. HMV C 2836–7; EMI CDH 7 63381–2.
7. *Boston Evening Transcript* (27 November 1926), reprinted in Stephen Lloyd, *William Walton: Muse of Fire* (Woodbridge, 2001), p. 269.
8. *Selected Letters*, ed. Hayes, p. 36.
9. HMV C3042; EMI CDH 7 63381–2, and Lyrita SRCS 47; SRCD 224.
10. Lyrita SRCS 50; SRCD 224.
11. Also in the OUP Archive are the orchestral parts used for the ballet and the score that had been commissioned from an arranger. These show that Walton's original orchestration was retained, though a piano part was added.
12. Chandos 8968. The London Philharmonic Orchestra is conducted by Bryden Thomson.
13. *Selected Letters*, ed. Hayes, p. 395. The volume quotes the extensive correspondence that Walton kept up with Arnold around this time.
14. In the event Walton did make some significant alterations and abridgements in the first movement.
15. Letter of 2 October 1972.
16. Postcard of 22 February 1973.
17. ZRG 711 (not ASD 2831 as given in the first edition of the score).
18. *Musical Times*, vol. 115 (July 1974), p. 582.

19

Chamber Music *(Vol. 19)*

Hugh Macdonald

This volume includes all of Walton's chamber music, including a Piano Quartet, two String Quartets, a Violin Sonata, and some miscellaneous smaller pieces. The String Quartet of 1922, the Toccata for violin and piano, and the Tema for unaccompanied cello are published for the first time, as is the first engraved edition of the String Quartet in A minor.

Chamber music makes up an important part of Walton's output and was particularly significant at the beginning of his career before he established his reputation in symphonic and choral music. Two works in this volume, the early String Quartet and the Toccata, illustrate a phase of his stylistic development which will be surprising to those familiar with his later music and which he himself tended (or pretended) to scorn in his later years. The String Quartet in A minor and the Violin Sonata, on the other hand, are major examples of his mature style, both of them illuminating a very individual aspect of his creative personality.

Walton was, by his own admission, a poor pianist, and although he also learned the violin in childhood, he made little progress. Writing chamber music was never for his own use or amusement. One of his earliest attempts at composition was a set of variations for violin and piano on a Bach chorale, which never got very far, and despite his wide involvement with vocal and choral music in his early years it is a chamber work, the Piano Quartet begun in 1918, that marks his first significant achievement in the larger forms. It was also in chamber music, as he approached his twentieth year, that he took an astonishing step into advanced modern composition, with the String Quartet (1922) and the Toccata. He quickly turned his back, however, on this cul-de-sac (as he saw it), and devoted himself for over twenty years to choral and symphonic music and then films before returning to chamber music with the String Quartet in A minor, completed in 1947. The Violin Sonata and the Two Pieces for Violin and Piano followed soon after, and these, with the addition of two minor works for unaccompanied cello from his later years, represent his mature contribution to the repertory of chamber music. Three of the larger works have retained an honoured place in the repertoire of British twentieth-century chamber music.

Quartet for Piano and Strings

When Walton's Piano Quartet was first published in 1924, the place and date 'Oxford, 1918–19' appeared on the last page of music, assigning the work's origins to the final part of his eight-year stay at Christ Church, Oxford, when he was 16 and 17 years old. It is

thus one of his earliest works to have survived, even though it was revised before publication and revised again in 1974–5 for a second edition. Writing on 17 May 1932 to his
publisher Hubert Foss giving some autobiographical details, Walton described it as his
'first composition to show any kind of talent', and said it was 'published not very much
revised...in 1924, though written in 1918'[1]. In an interview given in 1968 Walton confessed that he wrote it 'really to emulate Herbert Howells, to be quite honest, because
he'd had a great success with his Piano Quartet and I thought I'd have a go. It got the
Carnegie Award like his did, so I was justified to a point.'[2] Walton met Howells, 'the
great composer', who was his senior by ten years, for the first time in December 1918,[3]
and a month later Howells noted in his diary that he 'found W.T. Walton in his rooms
at the House, busy with his highly-coloured chords. He showed me the first movement
of a Piano Quartet.'[4] Osbert Sitwell recalled Walton playing the slow movement on the
piano at Christ Church in 1919.[5]

On the recommendation of the adjudicators for the Carnegie United Kingdom
Trust—Sir Hugh Allen, Ralph Vaughan Williams, and Sir Henry Hadow—the Piano
Quartet was selected for publication in its series, the Carnegie Collection of British
Music; in the citation it was declared to be 'a work of real achievement, clear and trans-
parent in texture, restrained in feeling, well-written throughout, and rising at moments
of climax into a strain of great beauty and nobility'.

Its publication by Stainer & Bell Ltd in 1924 came with a dedication 'to the Right
Rev. Thomas Banks Strong, Bishop of Ripon', who had earlier, as Dean of Christ
Church, encouraged and supported the young Walton's work as a musician. It was
performed, probably for the first time, in a broadcast from Liverpool on 19 September
1924. The programme, entitled 'Carnegie Night', included works by George Dyson and
Ivor Gurney. The performers were members of the all-female Liverpool-based
McCullagh Quartet who had already performed Walton's String Quartet (1922)—
Isabel McCullagh (violin), Helen Rawdon Briggs (viola), and Mary McCullagh
(cello)—with J. E. Wallace (piano); they followed this with a public performance in
Liverpool's Rushworth Hall on 30 October 1924.[6] It was first heard in London, together
with two early songs, on 30 October 1929, played in the Aeolian Hall by Pierre Tas
(violin), James Lockyer (viola), John Gabalfa (cello), and Gordon Bryan (piano). Since
Walton was by then a better-known composer, the work received reviews in a number
of newspapers and journals, several of which regretted that he was represented by
works written some ten years earlier.[7]

In 1939 the Piano Quartet, played by the Reginald Paul Piano Quartet, was recorded
by Decca Records.[8] A second recording was made on LP in 1955 by the Robert Masters
Piano Quartet,[9] and on this occasion a number of revisions were made. In a letter to
Stewart Craggs written in 1976 Kinloch Anderson, the pianist of the Quartet, wrote:

> We took up Walton's Piano Quartet shortly after the war...In the early 1950s we
> recorded it for Argo...and either then or when we were preparing it for our first per-
> formance of it, I got in touch with Walton to ask his advice about certain things. I had
> found in working at the piano part that a few bits were virtually unplayable, mainly due to
> his obvious lack of experience at the time he wrote it....He was characteristically helpful
> when I asked him if he would agree to some alterations of a purely practical nature....

I remember being astonished that he should still remember so exactly a work which he had written more than 30 years before....He had decided that the fugue subject in the last movement should have the rhythm ♪♪ ⁷ ♪| ♪♪ ⁷ ♪|♪♪♪♪| ♩ ♩ ♪⁷ in place of ♪♪♪♪|♪♪♪♪ ♪|♪♪♪♪| ♩ ♩ ♪⁷ as printed in the original Stainer and Bell score; also that at bars 25 to 30 in the slow movement the cello should take over the melody which in the S and B score appears in the L.H. part of the piano....He left me to rearrange the piano part of these bars in the slow movement so that the accompanying figures would continue in the piano without playing the melody now taken over by the cello. There were numerous other small alterations (entirely to the piano part as far as I can remember) to which he agreed and left me to work them out for myself. In this version we played the work many times, broadcast it and recorded it.[10]

On 21 November 1957 Walton wrote to Alan Frank, head of music at OUP:

To answer your questions now. About the Pfte Qt, I don't know what to say. Best perhaps leave it as it is except for correcting the vast amount of mistakes in the sc & parts. (I was only allowed one proof & it was my first experience!) Otherwise one might get involved in all sorts of cutting & re-writing & it might emerge (& is it worth it?) as an entirely different work![11]

In fact Walton did agree to a revised second edition, which he worked on in 1974–5 and which was published by OUP in February 1976. A photocopy of the first edition on which Walton entered his revisions is now in the OUP Archive. These revisions are included in the WWE.

String Quartet (1922)

Walton's first String Quartet, repudiated by the composer and never designated 'No. 1', is one of the most remarkable works to have come from his pen. Uncompromising in its modernity and unyielding in its pursuit of ambitious formal goals, it is as far from his later mature style as it is from such jazz-inspired works as *Façade* that he was writing at the same time. In this respect it shares a special place in Walton's oeuvre with the Toccata for violin and piano which followed soon after. The original purpose of the Quartet was as an Exhibition exercise at Christ Church, probably begun in 1919 soon after completion of the Piano Quartet.[12] The 17-year-old Walton was at that time open to advanced continental influences of which the String Quartet bears clear evidence, and it received its first performance (after Walton had moved to London) on 4 March 1921 at the first concert of the London Contemporary Music Centre, probably at 19 Berners Street, W1. The performers were the Pennington String Quartet, based at the Royal College of Music: John Pennington and Kenneth Skeaping (violins), Bernard Shore (viola), and Edward Robinson (cello).[13]

At that time the work consisted of two movements only, Moderato and Fuga, and was announced as an 'unfinished quartet'. It convinced the critic Percy Scholes that Walton was 'the boldest of the bold amongst the youngest of the young'.[14] The violist Bernard Shore later recalled: 'Sir Hugh Allen [Professor of Music at Oxford and Director of the Royal College of Music] asked us to play a quartet by a young lad from

Oxford—William Walton. I regret to say that having played it, the quartet considered that it would sound better played backwards!'[15]

Walton was not discouraged, for although it is possible that he revised these two movements (for example by introducing the Scherzo's motive at bar 202 of the Fuga), no source survives earlier than an autograph fair copy dated Amalfi, 23 November 1922. In this form the work now includes a Scherzo as its second movement, and the last movement is a fugue of enormous complexity and length, echoing Beethoven's *Grosse Fuge* in a wholly atonal language. Technical demands on all four players are extreme. In later life Walton regarded this phase of his career as an aberration: 'I never got far with it, though. The style was too impersonal. It didn't come naturally.'[16] Yet there is no reason to think that, at the time, he was not sincere about pursuing an atonal style. When young British composers were falling under the spell of Debussy and Stravinsky, Walton was more inclined to look to Schoenberg and Bartók, whose first two quartets he acknowledged as influential. He was also drawn to Kaikhosru Sorabji and, through Sorabji, to Busoni. On 8 November 1921 Sorabji wrote to Philip Heseltine: 'I had Willie Walton and Sachie Sitwell here the other afternoon and dosed them with Sonata II, which they said impressed them enormously.'[17] There are certainly similarities between Walton's Quartet and Sorabji's second Piano Sonata and his *Prelude, Interlude and Fugue* for piano, published in 1920. But despite undoubted influences, Walton's achievement is remarkable. As Bayan Northcott wrote in a perceptive article in 1991 after hearing the first (incomplete) recording of the quartet:

> How had the Oxford choirboy and undergraduate from provincial Oldham contrived by the end of his teens to master with such assurance a manner abreast of the most advanced composers then working in Europe?...If Walton's early assurance of style and technique really was achieved, as it seems, largely from the silent study of printed scores...then his inner ear and gift of assimilation really must have been second to none.[18]

It was through Edward J. Dent, then a London music critic and a friend of the Sitwells, that the newly founded International Society for Contemporary Music, which held its first conference in London in January 1923 under Dent's presidency, selected Walton's String Quartet (1922) for performance at its first festival, to be held in Salzburg in August of that year.[19] Perhaps no London quartet was available or willing to take on a work of such daunting difficulty, for the chosen performers were to be the McCullagh Quartet from Liverpool: Isabel McCullagh and Gertrude Newsham (violins), Helen Rawdon Briggs (viola), and Mary McCullagh (cello). A preliminary performance was given in a concert of the London Contemporary Music Centre at the Royal College of Music on 5 July 1923,[20] followed by the Salzburg performance on 4 August. This was reported in *The Times* of 14 August:

> The impression [Walton's String Quartet] gave was first, that it might be considerably condensed, and second, that some passages might be rewritten with a view to making the work more grateful for the strings to play. The scherzo is the least effective part of the work. The lengthy treatment of an apparently meaningless figure of two notes lost the attention of the hall, and this was never regained. The result was that by the

time the latter part of the fugue was reached, the restiveness of the audience made it almost impossible to listen attentively.

The *Manchester Guardian* of 6 August reported that the players received 'unanimous approval'. The review went on:

> The talent of Walton is generally acknowledged, but his quartet is rather long and contains faults—chiefly those of youthful inexperience and enthusiasm.... While the scherzo and the exposition of the fuga reveal exceptional ability, the andante has themes which often start brilliantly but are not worked out to finely logical conclusions.

Looking back twenty years later Osbert Sitwell recalled to Walton's biographer Frank Howes: 'You can't conceive how *frightful* that poor ladies' quartet was. After all the best string quartets in Europe had been playing, these poor good English girls dressed in turquoise tulle put up an abominable performance.'[21]

The set of parts used for these performances were given in 1960 by Isabel McCullagh to Gerald Abraham, Professor of Music at Liverpool University from 1947 to 1965. These may partially explain the players' problems, for although the first violin part is clearly written out, the lower parts, all in different hands, are clumsily and inaccurately copied; it is hard to imagine how the players could have given a satisfactory performance from them. The parts originally conformed more or less to Walton's autograph score, but had been marked with cuts and revisions in all three movements. These must have been inserted before one of the two 1923 performances, including the reduction of the fugue's 266 bars to 195. The passage with the 'apparently meaningless' two-note figure in the Scherzo was also shortened. These cuts and revisions were not entered in the autograph score and have not been adopted in the WWE. It would seem that they were made with the young composer's approval, however, or at least acceptance.

With the composition of the overture *Portsmouth Point* in 1925 Walton's mature style began to take shape, leaving the atonalism of the String Quartet (1922) and the Toccata behind. Neither work was played again in his lifetime. In 1936 he gave the autograph manuscript of the Quartet to his friend 'Bumps', the composer and conductor Hyam Greenbaum, who had conducted Walton's first film score, *Escape Me Never*, the year before. He probably gave the work no more thought until 22 January 1978, when he wrote to OUP to ask if they had 'any photostat copies of that horrible early Str. Quartet (the one played at Salzburg in 1923). I'd like to have them if they exist.'[22] His reason for wanting copies is not explained, but it seems that a set of photocopies, now in the William Walton Archive in Ischia, was sent. In 1989 Christopher Palmer edited the work for performance and recording by the Gabrieli Quartet. The score he worked on was a copy that had been made for OUP from Walton's manuscript in 1988. This has been modified to include the cuts and revisions shown in the early set of parts.

The Gabrieli Quartet gave a public performance of the Quartet at the Swansea Festival on 15 October 1990, and at the end of the month they made a recording that was issued by Chandos Records the following year. This, like the textually more refined

Black Box 2000 recording by the Emperor Quartet, adopts the extensive cuts shown in the early set of parts.

Toccata for Violin and Piano

The origins of this work are not clear, for the manuscript is not dated and there are no references to it in any correspondence or memoirs before 4 May 1925 when Walton mentioned its forthcoming performance in a letter to his mother.[23] That performance took place eight days later, on 12 May 1925, at 6 Queen Square, Bloomsbury, as part of the London Contemporary Music Centre's spring programme. The performers were Miss K. Goldsmith (violin) and Angus Morrison (piano), and a review appeared in *The Times* three days later. It has always been assumed that the composition of the Toccata followed that of the early String Quartet, which was completed in November 1922 and with which it has a certain stylistic kinship. Both works are written in an experimental non-tonal language on which Walton quite soon turned his back, and neither was published during his lifetime.

In an article in the *Boston Evening Transcript* of 27 November 1926 Constant Lambert spoke of the Toccata as a 'rhapsodical work showing traces of the influence of Bartók and even Sorabji'. He judged it to be a better work than the String Quartet and praised the middle section 'in which the lyrical quality we noticed in the Piano Quartet makes a welcome reappearance'.[24]

There appear to have been no further performances until 1992, when Kenneth Sillito (violin) and Hamish Milne (piano) made a recording for Chandos Records from an incomplete copy of the manuscript, lacking the first page. It was also revived at Ian Killik's Walton Festival in Oldham on 8 May 1998 in a performance given by Paul Barritt (violin) and Catherine Edwards (piano) that was also broadcast.

The work makes considerable demands on the virtuosity of its exponents. More than sixty years after giving its first performance, Angus Morrison remembered the work as being 'very complicated—but it seems to me even more so now than it did at the time'.[25]

String Quartet in A minor

Having repudiated his first String Quartet, Walton did not give a number to the second, but simply entitled it 'String Quartet in A minor'. According to a letter from the BBC received by Walton in August 1939, he had long promised a quartet to his friend Harry Blech, leader of the Blech Quartet,[26] and a quartet appears on a list of planned works sent to Hubert Foss in November of that year.[27] But he seems not to have embarked on this project until he had finished his music for *Henry V*, the last of his wartime film scores. On 7 September 1944 Julian Herbage of the BBC asked after 'the magnum opus', a Te Deum planned for the 50th anniversary of the Proms, which Walton had started. He was told, 'The magnum opus alas is no use for the symphony concert as it happens to be a string quartet, not that I wouldn't scruple to turn it into a piece for string orch. but I'm afraid it wouldn't sound so good!'[28]

In November 1944 the quartet was 'on the way', although progress was slow. On 30 January 1945 Walton reported to Roy Douglas, 'I'm in a suicidal struggle with four strings and am making no headway whatever. Brick walls, slit trenches, Siegfried lines bristle as never before.'[29] On 26 July 1945 he sent Blech a score and parts of the slow movement. 'The news of the rest of the work is very dismal & I've been at the point of chucking the whole thing. Progress is practically nil & I can only hope that my trip to Sweden next month will put some new life into me.'[30] The Scherzo was finished a year later, in June 1946, and a first performance was announced for 4 February 1947 in the Wigmore Hall. But 'this bloody quartet' (as Walton called it) was in fact not finished until early April, so that the first performance was eventually given by the Blech Quartet as a BBC Third Programme broadcast on 4 May 1947.[31] The same players (Harry Blech, Lionel Bentley, Keith Cummings, and Douglas Cameron) gave the first public performance in the Concert Hall of Broadcasting House the following day.

The score and parts were published by OUP in July 1947 with a dedication to Ernest Irving, who had conducted a number of Walton's film scores. An OUP memo of a meeting with Walton on 2 August 1946 notes: 'Walton's suggestion, with which we agree, is that after [the] first performance he should prepare a score which we would reproduce photographically, and publish as a facsimile.'[32] The resulting publication appeared with the familiar Severini cover; the parts, however, were engraved. The Quartet was first recorded by the Hollywood Quartet on Capitol Records and released in Britain in May 1951. On hearing a test pressing in September 1950 Walton was distressed to note that the repeat in the second movement had not been observed. He insisted on this being rectified, and the movement was re-recorded.

In 1971, in response to a request for a work from Neville Marriner for his Academy of St Martin-in-the-Fields, Walton arranged the Quartet as the Sonata for String Orchestra. Small cuts and amendments were made to the second and third movements, while the first movement was more extensively revised.[33] These revisions were not applied to the String Quartet itself.

Sonata for Violin and Piano

The origins of the Violin Sonata may be traced to a fortuitous meeting between Walton and Yehudi Menuhin in Lucerne in September 1947. At a time when the amount of money that British citizens were allowed to take out of the country was severely restricted, Walton was anxious to obtain hard currency to pay for medical treatment for his companion of many years, Viscountess Alice Wimborne, who was seriously ill in the city. He and Menuhin had been acquainted for some time. Diana Gould, soon to become the latter's second wife, later recorded that Menuhin agreed to produce a commission fee of 2000 Swiss francs (of which he would pay half immediately) on condition that Walton would write a piece for him. 'For instance,' Menuhin suggested, 'what about a sonata that Lou[is Kentner] and I can play together?'[34] Writing after Walton's death, Menuhin recalled that 'to ensure that there would be no delay in fulfilling my condition, we directed our steps to the music store Hug to buy staved music paper.'[35]

Walton agreed to start at once, but work on the sonata was interrupted by the substantial film score for Laurence Olivier's *Hamlet* and by Alice Wimborne's death in April 1948. It was resumed in June 1948 and completed in August of the following year. Walton wrote to Menuhin on 30 July 1949: 'The end of your Sonata is nearly round the corner...the second movement should be [complete] in about ten days.'[36] The sonata was first performed by Menuhin and Kentner in the Tonhalle, Zürich, on 30 September 1949. At the last minute Walton produced a scherzo to serve as a middle movement, but there was no time to include it in the first performance. According to Kentner, this was originally one of the two piano pieces which Walton had written in 1944 for a projected Free French Album, and of which Kentner had given the first performance; it later became the Scherzetto published in 1951 as the second of the Two Pieces for Violin and Piano.[37] This is confirmed by an internal OUP memo written by Walton's publisher Alan Frank on 14 September 1949, which states: 'The timing is about 23 minutes, but there is a possibility that a very short middle movement might be added.' The Scherzetto was engraved (though not published) at the same time as the Sonata in the spring of 1950.[38]

Some revisions were then made, but mainly adjustments to the coda of the second movement, as the composer's autograph reveals. In the autumn of 1949 Walton and his young wife Susana had gone to live on Ischia, in the bay of Naples.

Writing to him there on 4 November, Alan Frank said: 'We are still not absolutely clear which Coda you want printing...Yehudi thinks that your final verdict was in favour of the original Coda (he has fingered both).'[39] Replying six days later, Walton proposed a mixture of both versions of the coda and went on to say: 'From bar 589 to the end use the enclosed MSS.' It has not been possible to trace this small autograph.

The sonata was played by Menuhin and Kentner on 5 February 1950 at the Drury Lane Theatre, London; the performance was broadcast. The score, when published in May of that year, named this as the first performance, as if that in Zürich had for some reason to be discounted. Yet on 28 January Walton had written to Frank: 'Y.M. if I remember rightly wanted it mentioned that it was first performed in Zürich. You might ask him.'[40] Walton later described the London performance, which he did not attend, as a 'dead flop', although only two days after the concert he wrote from Ischia to the performers and their wives: 'Thank you all a thousand times for the telegrams, letters, etc. We are delighted and rapturous that the Sonata went so well & only too sorry we weren't there to hear the marvellous performance, (we've had eye-witness accounts of that from others not only yourselves) of the wonderful work—it was those three extra bars in the coda that worked it!'[41]

Just before the London performance, as the Sonata was being printed, Walton was asked by Alan Frank whether he wanted to give the second movement the title of 'Theme and Variations'. Walton replied: 'I think we will leave the 2nd movement without title of Theme and Vars. If people can't see it for themselves well—!'[42] The published edition shows that he subsequently relented.

There has always been an analytical interest shown in the theme of the variations, since the piano solo at bar 18 has a twelve-note series as its melody, stated twice. The series uses only intervals of a descending fourth (= ascending fifth) or a semitone. Each of the seven variations takes this theme up a semitone until it reaches the note F, with a return to B flat for the fugal start to the Coda at bar 289.

Writing to Alan Frank after the Drury Lane performance (which he had not been able to attend), Walton commented wryly on the somewhat mixed critical reception that the new work had provoked, and made a passing reference to the twelve-note series. 'And what about my "creative dilemma"! After all perhaps I should have made more orthodox use of my tone-row. That would have learn't 'em.'

On 8 May 1950 Menuhin and Kentner recorded the Sonata for HMV on three 78 rpm records, later issued in the USA on LP. The score was published by OUP three days later with a dedication 'To Diana and Griselda', the wives of the two players who were also sisters. The separate violin part was edited by Menuhin.

Two Pieces for Violin and Piano

I Canzonetta
II Scherzetto

A footnote to the Canzonetta in the first printed edition of this work records that the tune in the violin at bar 5 is 'based on a troubadour melody'. Since the melody at bar 16 of the Scherzetto also has an archaic flavour, it seems probable that both these pieces were fashioned out of material collected for the music that Walton composed for Laurence Olivier's film *Henry V*, completed in 1944. He included early English and French material in the film score, and the dedication of the Two Pieces 'To Vivien [Leigh] and Larry [Olivier]' supports this association. The two pieces for piano, now lost, which Walton had composed in 1944 for a projected Free French Album, may be essentially the same works; Louis Kentner recalled playing the pieces, entitled 'Lai' and 'Rondet de Carol' at a Welsh Music Festival. As mentioned above, the 'Rondet de Carol' Kentner identified as the scherzo which Walton included at the last moment in the first version of the Violin Sonata in 1949.[43] It was omitted from the final version and published in 1951 as the Scherzetto.

In the absence of an autograph no clear date can be assigned to the composition of these two short works, but there is an OUP agreement form for them marked 'accepted November 1949'. On 18 July 1950 Alan Frank wrote to the violinist Frederick Grinke: 'I am now sending you a set of proofs of Walton's SCHERZETTO, which I hope you'll like. I spoke to him of the possibility of your doing the first English performance on 3rd August, and he seemed to think he could turn out the companion piece in time, if wanted.'[44] The first known performance took place nine weeks later on 27 September in the Concert Hall of Broadcasting House, London, when the pieces were performed by Grinke with Ernest Lush (piano) for a BBC Third Programme broadcast.

The melody of the *Canzonetta* comes from the 'Chansonnier Cangé', a thirteenth-century manuscript of troubadour songs now in the Bibliothèque Nationale de France, Paris. The song is 'Amours me fait comencier Une chançon novele', composed by Thibaut IV (1201-53), King of Navarre. It was published in facsimile and in transcription by Jean Beck in 1927. Beck's transcription is as follows:

A -mours me fait co - men - cier U - ne chan - çon no - ve - le,
Qu'e - le me vuet en - soi - gnier A a - mer la plus be - le

Qui soit ou mont vi - vant : C'est la bele au cprs gent,

C'est ce - le dont je chant. Dex m'en doint tel no - ve - le

Qui soit a mon ta - lant, Que me - nu et sou - vent

Mes cuers por li sau - te - le.

Tema (per variazioni) per' Cello Solo

On 31 March 1970 Laurence Swinyard, Chairman of the Performing Right Society, wrote to a number of British composers, all members of the PRS Council, inviting contributions to a collective composition for any combination of cello, trumpet, and piano to be presented to the Prince of Wales, cello and trumpet being the two instruments that he had studied at certain points of his life. Walton responded with a seventeen-bar theme for (but without) variations for solo cello. The autograph manuscript is dated 25 April 1970.

This was bound in a handsome red leather volume along with manuscripts by fourteen other composers—Lennox Berkeley, Arthur Bliss, Ronald Binge, Vivian Ellis, John Gardner, Joseph Horovitz, Mitch Murray, Steve Race, Ernest Tomlinson, Guy Warrack, Brian Willey, Grace Williams, and David Wynne[45]—and was presented to the Prince of Wales by Sir Arthur Bliss, Master of the Queen's Music, at the PRS annual luncheon on 1 July 1970.

It was always intended that the collection should be published by OUP, but although it was assigned an ISBN number, it never actually appeared.

Passacaglia

In January 1957 Walton's Cello Concerto was premiered by its dedicatee, Gregor Piatigorsky. Even those commentators who received it with qualified enthusiasm conceded that it was a major addition to the cello's limited concerto repertoire. Walton was therefore considerably irritated when Mstislav Rostropovich gave a series of nine concerts in 1965, in both London and New York, featuring as many as thirty-one different works for cello and orchestra, yet failed to include his new concerto.

Walton and Rostropovich would have met at Britten's Aldeburgh Festival in the late 1960s, if not before, but it was probably at the 1979 festival, at which Rostropovich conducted *Eugene Onegin* on 18 June, the day before *Façade 2* was first performed in the presence of the composer, that Walton chided Rostropovich for his neglect of the concerto, and that the latter struck a deal: if Walton would write a new work for him, he would play both. The result was the Passacaglia for Solo Cello, one of Walton's last works, composed in 1979–80. Rostropovich never played the concerto.

In a letter to Christopher Morris of OUP dated 29 April 1980 Walton wrote: 'I'm plodding away at the Rostropovich solo piece—it's about 6 mins. gone—it should be about 8 mins. The plan for the perf, I gather is that it will be included in a programme in a concert for the Queen Mother's [80th] Birthday sometime in early Oct. but I have not heard for sure.'[46] Walton can be observed working at the piano on the piece in Tony Palmer's television film *At the Haunted End of the Day*, first shown in April 1981. The finished work was dedicated to Rostropovich, who first performed it on 16 March 1982 at the Royal Festival Hall, London, as part of a London Philharmonic Orchestra concert. It was published by OUP on 16 December of the same year edited by Rostropovich, who entered his own fingerings and bowings. Presumably Walton approved this publication, although he subsequently made some important changes in the autograph manuscript, which are shown in the first of the two texts of the work in the WWE. These changes removed the left-hand pizzicatos in bars 68–76 and provided a slightly shorter ending, from bar 146. The second version given here is that of the 1982 publication, with Rostropovich's editorial markings.

NOTES

1. *The Selected Letters of William Walton*, ed. Malcolm Hayes (London, 2002), p. 75.
2. *The Listener*, 8 August 1968, p. 177.
3. *Selected Letters*, ed. Hayes, p. 22.
4. Christopher Palmer, *Herbert Howells: A Celebration* (London, 1992).
5. Osbert Sitwell, *Laughter in the Next Room* (London, 1949), p. 172.
6. Percy Scholes previewed the broadcast with an analytical summary of the work in *Radio Times*, 12 September 1924.
7. See Stewart Craggs, *William Walton: A Catalogue* (Oxford, 1990), p. 15.
8. Decca AX 228/41.
9. Argo RG 48.
10. Craggs, *Catalogue*, pp. 15–16.
11. *Selected Letters*, ed. Hayes, p. 305.
12. The autograph fair copy dates the work '1920–22'.
13. The concert was reported in the *British Music Bulletin*, vol. 3, no. 4 (April 1921), p. 96.
14. *The Observer*, 17 June 1923.
15. Told to Guy Warrack and cited in Michael Kennedy, *Portrait of Walton* (Oxford, 1989), p. 21.
16. The Oldham Chronicle, 12 September 1959, p. 12; cited in Stephen Lloyd, *William Walton: Muse of Fire* (Woodbridge, 2001), p. 26.
17. Paul Rapoport, ed., *Sorabji: a Critical Celebration* (Aldershot, 1992), p. 238.
18. 'Closet Modernist', *The Independent*, 31 August 1991, p. 29.
19. In *The Music Bulletin*, vol. 5, no. 6 (June 1923), Dent gave an account of the difficulties he had in getting the members of the jury together, and of his wholly dispassionate role in the selection process.

20. Reported in the *Monthly Musical Record*, vol. 53 (1923), pp. 226–227, and *The Music Bulletin*, vol. 5 (1923), pp. 194 and 213. In the *Sunday Times* Ernest Newman declared that 'Mr. Walton has attempted something quite beyond his present powers, both imaginative and technical'.

21. Letter of 21 November 1942 to Frank Howes, Walton Archive, Ischia; cited in Kennedy, *Portrait*, p. 25.

22. *Selected Letters*, ed. Hayes, p. 444. Nearly thirty-four years before this, a page showing bars 175–193 of the Scherzo had been shown in facsimile, described simply as 'Page from a manuscript by William Walton', in the September 1944 issue of *Tempo* in connection with an article that discussed the composer's recent music for the film of *Henry V*.

23. *Selected Letters*, ed. Hayes, p. 33.

24. Lambert's article is reproduced in full in Lloyd, *William Walton*, pp. 267–270.

25. Letter to Bruce Phillips at OUP, 29 October 1987, cited in Craggs, *Catalogue*, p. 38.

26. Lloyd, *William Walton*, p. 205.

27. *Selected Letters*, ed. Hayes, p. 126.

28. Lloyd, *William Walton*, p. 205.

29. *Selected Letters*, ed. Hayes, p. 152.

30. *Selected Letters*, ed. Hayes, p. 155.

31. *Selected Letters*, ed. Hayes, pp. 158–162.

32. OUP Archive, Oxford.

33. See Hugh Ottaway, 'Walton Adapted', *Musical Times*, vol. 115 (1974), p. 582. The fourth movement was scored by Malcolm Arnold.

34. Diana Menuhin, Classic FM interview quoted in Humphrey Burton, *Yehudi Menuhin: A Life* (London, 2000), pp. 280–281.

35. Yehudi Menuhin in the brochure inaugurating the William Walton Archive, Ischia.

36. *Selected Letters*, ed. Hayes, p. 183.

37. Craggs, *Catalogue*, p. 101.

38. Letter from Walton to Alan Frank, 19 April 1950, in *Selected Letters*, ed. Hayes, p. 204.

39. Craggs, *Catalogue*, p. 110.

40. Letter of 28 January 1950, OUP Archive, Oxford.

41. Quoted in Burton, *Yehudi Menuhin*, p. 304.

42. Letter of 28 January 1950, OUP Archive, Oxford.

43. Craggs, *Catalogue*, p. 101.

44. OUP Archive, Oxford.

45. A detailed list of the works by the other composers is given in Craggs, *Catalogue*, p. 152.

46. *Selected Letters*, ed. Hayes, p. 458.

20

Instrumental Music *(Vol. 20)*

Michael Aston

As William Walton approached his 80th birthday he took part in a film profile of his life, *At the Haunted End of the Day* (a quotation from his opera *Troilus and Cressida*), directed by Tony Palmer.[1] At the beginning of the film Walton is shown composing at an upright piano in the music room of his home, La Mortella, Forio, on the island of Ischia. In his uniquely wry manner he is discussing the issue of whether composers should use a piano in the process of composition. He says, 'When I was much younger I always composed without a piano; but everyone said "Oh, that's a great mistake. You must hear what you're writing." In the end I started to use the piano, and as I can't really play the piano it's rather buggered the whole thing up! If I was really a good composer I should be able to do without a piano at all, but all the other composers I know who write without pianos write far too much.' The comment is disarmingly self-deprecatory, but it is also a statement of fact: Walton never acquired any significant skills as a pianist, or indeed on any other instrument. His only experiences of performing music proficiently were restricted to choral singing, first in his father's choir in Oldham and then as a chorister at Christ Church Cathedral, Oxford.

As a boy Walton received tuition on the piano and the violin, but when faced with the need to find a way of making himself 'interesting' (as he put it in the film) in order to stay on at Oxford after his voice had broken, he knew that composing was the only possibility. Since he was immersed in the cloistered world of an English cathedral choir school, Walton's earliest compositions were mostly choral, with the needs of the Anglican liturgy in mind. The unpublished Choral Prelude on 'Wheatley' for organ is an impressive achievement for a 14-year-old boy, and references in letters suggest that there were other organ pieces written during Walton's time at the choir school. The organist of Christ Church, Dr Henry Ley, had auditioned the young Walton for a place in the cathedral choir, and followed his progress with interest. He gave the boy lessons on piano and organ, and in May 1918 Walton was able to write to his mother that he hoped to be playing the organ for services at Brasenose College; in the event he played at only three services until the regular organist returned from army service during the war.

After Oxford there were to be no further attempts to acquire instrumental skills. Walton was happy to use the piano when working on his compositions, but he had no interest in becoming even a competent player. Years later Walton's older brother Noel described him as a 'very bad pianist', and Sacheverell Sitwell remembered him making 'the most terrible din on the piano' during the composition of *Belshazzar's Feast*.[2] In her memoir of Walton, Dora Foss remembered occasions when her husband, Hubert Foss (head of the music department at Walton's publisher, Oxford University Press), and the composer spent long periods at a piano, 'sometimes Willie playing with his "composer's" technique.'[3] It was a perceptive comment and Walton might well have taken the same view; he regarded the piano as being essentially a tool for composition, but had no need to use it in a strictly pianistic way.

Only a small portion of Walton's oeuvre is given over to instrumental solo music. Apart from Duets for Children and Three Pieces for Organ from the film *Richard III* the only previously published keyboard music consists of arrangements made by the composer. The WWE makes available for the first time Walton's original solo version of Duets for Children and the 'Galop Final' (the finale for the 1949 ballet *Devoirs de Vacances*). The Five Bagatelles for Guitar are also included in this volume.

Tunes for my Niece

Walton's links with his family in Oldham were changed for ever following his acceptance as a choirboy at Christ Church Cathedral, Oxford. His subsequent 'adoption' by the Sitwells was the final step in the distancing process, and from the 1920s onwards communication was largely by letter rather than personal visits. Walton's younger brother, Alec, ended up living in Canada, and his sister, Nora, found her way to New Zealand. Only Noel, the eldest of the four Walton children, stayed in Oldham. He became a music teacher, married, and had two children—Elizabeth and Michael. In 1940 Elizabeth Walton was 12 years old, and Walton composed for her a series of nine short piano solos. They are inscribed simply 'for Elizabeth', and the individual pieces are untitled.

At some point Walton must have shown these pieces to his friend Dora Foss, for she is believed to have suggested that they were too difficult for a young pianist. Walton then had the idea of rearranging them as piano duets, and the duet version, with its extra concluding number, was completed on 15 May 1940.

Walton orchestrated the duets in 1941 under the title *Music for Children*. In 1945 Roy Douglas wrote to Norman Peterkin at OUP: 'On looking through the "Music for Children" recently it struck me that it would be "child's play" to arrange these duets for piano solo if you think there might be any demand for them in that form.'[4] Clearly Roy Douglas was unaware of the existence of Walton's own solo version of these pieces, and Walton does not appear to have made any attempt to press for their publication at that time or even to have recalled their existence. In July 1945 Walton wrote to Roy Douglas: 'Peterkin informs me you wish to do the Childrens Pieces as solos. Please do so whenever you like.'[5] The Douglas arrangements were published by OUP in 1949, and the titles applied to the piano duet version of 1940 were incorporated.

The Douglas solo arrangements follow the order of the piano duet version and were published in two books. For the present volume the editor has decided to publish for the first time the original nine Walton solos, and to preserve the order in which they appear in the autograph.

Duets for Children

Elizabeth and Michael were the only members of the Walton family to have compositions dedicated to them. Michael was included as a co-dedicatee when Walton embarked on the idea of turning the 'Tunes for my Niece' into piano duets. Walton presented the autograph to his accountant Alfred Chenhalls, and added an inscription: 'in celebration (surtax!)'. By 1940 Walton's income would have been substantial, with regular royalties coming in from his established masterpieces and occasional large payments for projects such as the music for the film *Escape Me Never*, and the remark could be an expression of relief that the tax had been paid, or it might be recognition that Chenhalls had in some way managed to find a way of avoiding it.

The autograph of the duets contains a new, tenth piece, but all the pieces remained untitled. The order of the pieces in the published version of 1940 differs from that of the manuscript, and titles were added at some point. The duets were published by OUP in two separate books, with six pieces in the first volume and four in the second.

When the orchestrated version of the duets, titled *Music for Children*, was premiered on 16 February 1941 at Queen's Hall, London, critical reception was mixed. Writing in the *Daily Telegraph*, F. Bonavia praised Walton's orchestration: 'Mr Walton's use of orchestral colour is that of a composer who knows well and loves his medium. Every one of these ten short, graceful pieces has its special virtue; the most attractive of all being perhaps No. 5 with its captivating five-eight lilt.'[6] The anonymous reviewer for *The Times* was less impressed. Placing Walton's pieces in the tradition of Schumann's *Kinderszenen* and Bizet's *Jeux d'enfants*, the reviewer went on: 'It is, perhaps, unfair to complain of a lack of substance in such slight pieces, but Walton's predecessors managed to invest their children's music with a tenderness and charm that seem to have eluded him.'[7]

Walton had no children of his own and perhaps found it difficult to enter fully into the fantasy world of a child's imagination. In the duets he avoided a false attempt at adopting the mantle of childhood, and instead gave the musical images a gloss of adult sophistication. Young players were not patronized in any way; instead, Walton endowed them with maturity and experience. In terms of notation and performance instructions he made no concessions whatever to the fact that the pieces were intended to be played by children.

Galop Final

At the time that Osbert Sitwell was trying to engineer a collaboration between Walton and Diaghilev in the 1920s (out of which emerged the composer's Sinfonia Concertante) one of Diaghilev's closest colleagues was Boris Kochno. Twenty years later Kochno co-founded a new company in Paris, the Ballets des Champs-Élysées. He became aware of the orchestrated version of the Duets for Children and devised a ballet based on that score. The choreography was by John Taras and the scenery and costumes were designed by Cecil Beaton. In the summer of 1949 Kochno asked Walton to compose a new finale for the ballet, called *Devoirs de Vacances*, which was premiered by the company at the Théâtre des Champs-Elysées, Paris, on 8 November 1949.

In early 1949 Walton returned to London from Buenos Aires where he had been attending a conference of the Performing Right Society. He had gone to Argentina as a 46-year-old bachelor, but he left as a married man following a whirlwind romance with Susana Gil Passo, 24 years his junior. He was determined to devote his energies to the composition of the opera *Troilus and Cressida*, and the newly-weds quickly established what was to become a pattern of life which involved spending about half of the year on Ischia, where Walton could work away from the distractions of London life. So involved was he with *Troilus and Cressida* that he had forgotten the matter of the finale for Kochno's ballet until a telegram jolted his memory. In a letter written to Kochno from Ischia on 4 November 1949 Walton apologized for his oversight and went on to say, 'However a day and a half's work and I've produced this—Galop final (tribute to Gavarni!) which I think is not too bad though the piano part I send is, I must emphasise, but a skeleton of the orchestral version which will reach you a couple of days after this.'[8] The piece cannot have arrived in time for the premiere of the ballet as it was not used. It is possible that the orchestration of the piano score, to which Walton refers, may never have been made once he was informed that the Galop had arrived too late; at all events it has never been found. In writing to Alan Frank Walton said 'it's a rather gay, if slightly vulgar piece'.[9] It was never published during his lifetime.

According to the autograph the 'Galop Final' lasts for three minutes; its closing section uses material from the first piece in *Music for Children*. The piece was later orchestrated by Christopher Palmer for inclusion with *Music for Children*; it uses the same orchestra as the rest of the suite, and is available on hire (see Vol. 18).

Valse, from Façade

In its original form, 'Valse' was first performed as part of *Façade: An Entertainment* at the Aeolian Hall, New Bond Street, London, on 12 June 1923. After inclusion at the performance given at the New Chenil Galleries, Chelsea, London, on 27 April 1926, the 'Valse' became one of the 'core' items in the entertainment, and it appears as number 16 in the 1951 published edition of the score. It is the most substantial number in *Façade*, and Walton orchestrated it, along with three other numbers, in 1926.

The arrangement for piano solo seems to have been made with a particular performer and occasion in mind. Angus Morrison, a good friend and close neighbour of Walton in the 1920s, recalled: 'when I was asked to play pieces by Lambert and Walton at a musical party he [Constant Lambert] made an exquisite little transcription of it [the Siciliana from *Pomona*] for two hands as a companion piece to the Waltz from *Façade*, arranged by Walton for the same occasion.'[10] The arrangement, made in 1926, was dedicated to the hostess of the party, Mrs Beverley Baxter, wife of the managing editor of the *Daily Express*.

The description 'concert arrangement' is apt; only a highly accomplished pianist could cope with the technical complexities of performing the piece. The 'Valse' was arranged again for piano solo in 1942 by Roy Douglas. Constant Lambert's arrangement of it for piano duet (as part of the First Suite from *Façade*) was published in 1927, and Herbert Murrill made a two-piano version which was published in 1934. It is the only number from *Façade* to be arranged for piano by the composer himself.

Choral Prelude 'Herzlich thut mich verlangen'

This arrangement was made in 1931 and published a year later as part of *A Bach Book for Harriet Cohen,* an album of arrangements of J. S. Bach dedicated to the pianist

Harriet Cohen. In her autobiography, *A Bundle of Time* (London, 1969), the pianist states that several composers had decided to make arrangements in recognition of her special love of Bach's music, and that OUP decided to publish them. As well as William Walton the contributors were Granville Bantock, Arnold Bax, Lord Berners, Arthur Bliss, Frank Bridge, Eugene Goossens, Herbert Howells, John Ireland, Constant Lambert, Ralph Vaughan Williams, and the Bach authority W. Gillies Whittaker.

For his contribution, Walton took Bach's chorale prelude for organ 'Herzlich thut mich verlangen', BWV 727. This chorale was clearly a particular favourite of Bach's; in Riemenschneider's collection of 371 chorales there are eight harmonizations of the melody. Walton's arrangement retains the key of Bach's organ chorale prelude and, apart from the exclusion of most ornamentation, there is little change to the original.

Harriet Cohen gave the first performance of the complete set on 17 October 1932 at Queen's Hall, London, as part of a concert which also included viola sonatas played by Lionel Tertis. The anonymous reviewer for *The Times* next morning praised the idea of paying a tribute to a noted Bach interpreter, but had little to praise about either the actual transcriptions or their performance. With the exceptions of the Bax and Lambert contributions, 'All the rest,' he wrote, 'involved jumps which separated notes that should have been played together. Since the book was made for Miss Cohen the arrangers might have borne in mind that she has not a big stretch, and in any case it is not the slightest use arranging works for piano unless they are going to sound like piano music.' Harriet Cohen's playing of the arrangements was equally dismissed: 'Without experience of the organ she tried to "register" her part-playing, and in so doing gave a false prominence to the chorale melodies, shattered the rhythm to pieces, and destroyed all horizontal feeling of counterpoint.'

Walton knew enough about organ-playing to realize the problems involved in making a piano transcription, but he seems to have succeeded for the most part in avoiding excessive stretches which could have led to the separation of notes within chords. The comments of the reviewer for *The Times* on this issue are not, therefore, wholly justified in the case of Walton's transcription. It is sensitive and tasteful, qualities to be found similarly in his later transcriptions of Bach's music for the 1940 ballet *The Wise Virgins*, in which 'Herzlich thut mich verlangen' appeared again as the fourth number.

Ballet, from the film *Escape Me Never*

Walton's first venture into the world of film music came at an exciting time in the history of the cinema. In America the transition from silent films to those with sound had taken place during the late 1920s, and by 1930 most cinemas were wired for sound; at about the same time Hollywood stopped making silent films. Europe was not far behind, and by 1933 cinemas in Great Britain, Germany, Denmark, and the Netherlands were wired.[11]

Christopher Palmer has described the year 1935 as 'something of a milestone in the history of the development of film music'. In that year Arthur Bliss composed the score for *Things to Come*, Max Steiner's score for the Hollywood film *The Informer* appeared, and Walton made his film music debut with the score for *Escape Me Never*. The invitation to compose this music came in the summer of 1934, a difficult time for Walton both professionally and personally. He had completed the first three movements of his

First Symphony, but the final movement had progressed no further than sketches. There was turmoil in his private life following the break-up of his relationship with Baroness Imma von Doernberg, although it was not long before he became involved in a new partnership with Alice, Viscountess Wimborne.

The film *Escape Me Never* was directed by Paul Czinner, produced by Herbert Wilcox, and starred Elisabeth Bergner, Czinner's wife. It was based on a play of the same name by Margaret Kennedy, who had enjoyed a huge success with a dramatization of her novel *The Constant Nymph*, produced by Basil Dean in 1926. When Czinner started work on *Escape Me Never* he consulted his assistant Dallas Bower about the choice of composer for the film score, and Bower unhesitatingly suggested Walton.

The film included sequences involving the production of the screen composer's ballet, and the music for that was completed in the early autumn of 1934. In November 1934 Hubert Foss corresponded with R. J. Cullen at British and Dominion Films, and the letter makes it clear that Walton had been approached about composing additional background music for the film. Foss, on Walton's behalf, stated the terms of the arrangement: 'For the Russian Ballet and the background music together, the whole not to last more than three quarters of an hour, you will pay Mr Walton the sum of £350.'[12] The film company accepted the terms and contracts were signed.

The ballet sequence was choreographed by Frederick Ashton, and Margot Fonteyn appeared with members of the Vic-Wells Ballet Company; the filming took place at the Theatre Royal, Drury Lane, London, in December 1934. The ballerina Lydia Lopokova appears to have had a hand in the engagement of Ashton as choreographer; she was a close friend and, along with her husband John Maynard Keynes, was keen to help Ashton in the early years of his career. (Lopokova had taken a leading role in Ashton's ballet *Façade* in 1931.) Ashton's biographer Julie Kavanagh has suggested that neither choreographer nor composer treated the *Escape Me Never* project very seriously, and she quotes Lopokova as remarking: 'When they asked Willy and F to compose something à la Massin W whispered to F, "What they want is bad Russian ballet, let's do it." '[13] Whatever his private views, Walton was shrewd enough to see the potentially high profile of the film, and any worries over his lack of experience in the medium would have been counterbalanced by the very substantial fee on offer.

Work on the music for *Escape Me Never* did not proceed smoothly, and Walton reported to Osbert Sitwell: 'I have had, as you may imagine a very rough time lately. The film people kept me hanging about chiefly owing to their stupidity & inefficiency & in the end I had to write all the music in four days. Luckily while the house was being painted I was able to go & stay with "Bumps" [Hyam Greenbaum, a friend and colleague who conducted the soundtrack of the film] who helped me out with the orchestration.'[14]

Spike Hughes, a close friend from the 1920s, considered Walton's involvement in film music to be a vital factor in having incidental music taken seriously within the film industry: 'Until *Escape Me Never* film music had been provided by the studio's Musical Director, and was no more important in the scheme of things than the lighting and the make-up and the usual acknowledgements to Abdulla [cigarettes]. Now producers fall over themselves to sign up Eminent Composers.'[15]

It appears that Harriet Cohen must have known about Walton's music for the ballet sequences in *Escape Me Never* and was interested in performing it. In June 1935 she wrote to Hubert Foss: 'Very many thanks for ... your great kindness in consenting to let me have the first performance of Willie's film music. If I like it (which I am sure to do) and my hands can fit it, I shall very much want to have the first performance for England and America and should like to take it to Russia next year.' There are no further references to the project.

For the publication of this excerpt of music from the film, OUP opted for a new style of cover; Walton's works since 1927 had used a design by the Italian artist Gino Severini (1883–1966), but for this publication, that was replaced by a montage of black and white shots from the film, including one of the ballet sequence. It is one of two arrangements of music from Walton's fourteen film scores to be made by the composer himself. The ballet music, in its original orchestration, is available on hire separately, and also as the third and last movement of the suite *Escape Me Never*, arranged by Christopher Palmer.

Portsmouth Point

The overture *Portsmouth Point* was composed in 1925, and Walton's arrangement of it for piano duet, completed in London in November of that year, was the first of his works to be published by OUP, in the spring of 1927. OUP's music department had been set up in 1923 with Hubert Foss, then only 24 years old, as its founding editor. The link between Walton and the publisher began in 1926 with the signing of a five-year contract. In a letter to Siegfried Sassoon dated 5 October 1926 Walton wrote: 'I am letting you know about the fruits of your labours. Foss has taken not only those songs but also P.P.' In another letter Walton spoke of dedicating the full score of *Portsmouth Point* to Sassoon 'as a small tribute'.[16] The orchestral version of *Portsmouth Point* was published in 1928.

The publication of the duet arrangement also marked the first appearance of Severini's striking cover design, which was to distinguish Walton's scores until 1951. Severini had, like Walton, benefited greatly from Sitwell patronage; during the 1920s he received many commissions from the Sitwells, ranging from covers and frontispieces to a series of frescoes featuring *commedia dell'arte* subjects for the family's castle, Montegufoni, in Tuscany. Severini designed a new curtain for the 1928 performance of *Façade* in Siena (now lost) and created a bookplate for the composer.

English audiences were introduced to the orchestral overture in June 1926, and it seems likely that Hubert Foss would have been keen to publish a piano duet version soon after the work's introduction. There was still a good market in the 1920s for piano arrangements. Constant Lambert, writing in 1928, described the overture as 'the first composition by which William Walton became known to the general public'. He praised its 'spirit of clarity and decision combined with a robust good humour'.[17] The piano duet, which probably derives from Walton's composition sketch, represents a slightly earlier version of the overture than the orchestral score in matters of dynamics, accentuation, and notation of changes of metre.

Siesta

The original version of *Siesta* is scored for a small orchestra and was composed in 1926. In this work, as the pianist Angus Morrison has pointed out, Walton gave expression to his love of Italy for the first time.[18] The Sitwells had first taken Walton to Italy in 1920, and there were many further visits while he was living as an 'adopted' member of the family. A favourite location was Amalfi, where they often spent the winter months working on their various projects. Walton was particularly drawn to the quality of light in Italy, and never forgot his first encounter with it. Over the years commentators have spoken repeatedly of the Italian atmosphere of many of Walton's works, but his own 1963 views on the subject are worth quoting: 'One might try to connect the colour and clarity I seek in orchestration with the qualities of the Mediterranean atmosphere, but I must say I have never been consciously stimulated by the Italian climate or geography.'[19]

In *Siesta* Walton showed a side of his musical personality that contrasted sharply with the brittle, nervous energy of *Portsmouth Point*. The style is altogether more lyrical and relaxed, but with hints of the streak of melancholy that would be developed further as Walton's musical language matured. Constant Lambert perceptively saw that *Siesta* amounted to more than superficial charm and evocation: 'The nonchalant waltz-tune with which the work ends might have come out of *Façade*, for there is a sadness underlying its apparent frivolity that is reminiscent of much in Miss Edith Sitwell's poetry.'[20]

Siesta was dedicated to Stephen Tennant, fourth son of Lord and Lady Glenconner and companion of Siegfried Sassoon. The version for small orchestra was first performed at the Aeolian Hall, New Bond Street, London, on 24 November 1926 under the composer's direction. It is not known exactly when Walton made his piano reduction for four hands. The cover of the published arrangement bears the date 1926 (the year of its composition), and, following the precedent of *Portsmouth Point*, it appeared in print in July 1928, fifteen months before the full score. When Walton slightly revised the orchestral version in 1962 the dedication to Stephen Tennant was removed; the arrangement for piano duet, which remains as Walton left it in the 1920s, retains the dedication.

Sinfonia Concertante

It was in 1926 that Walton's younger friend and fellow composer Constant Lambert enjoyed his first notable success when his ballet score *Romeo and Juliet* was taken up by Diaghilev for performance by the Ballets Russes. It seems likely that Osbert and Sacheverell Sitwell were encouraged by this to make efforts to secure a similar opportunity for their protégé. The winter of 1925–6 had been spent at Amalfi where Walton composed three movements of a ballet. Angus Morrison recalled that some of the Sitwells' friends referred disparagingly to these pieces as 'Traveller's Samples', designed as they were to attract Diaghilev's attention.[21]

Back in London, Osbert Sitwell hosted a lavish lunch party at Carlyle Square for Diaghilev and his entourage. Angus Morrison remembered the occasion clearly: 'Finally they all trooped over to 9 Oakley Street where I was then living, only a stone's throw away, to listen to Willie and me playing the three movements on my two pianos. Everything went according to plan except in one very important particular; Diaghilev listened very attentively, said a number of polite and charming things, BUT the fish did not rise and the bait was not taken!'[22] It is probable that what Morrison and Walton were playing was essentially the present two-piano arrangement of the music.

Following Diaghilev's rejection of the pieces as a ballet score, Walton took Lambert's advice and reworked them, and they became the Sinfonia Concertante, which was premiered and published in 1928. At that time Walton was still heavily involved in the world of the Sitwells, and he dedicated a movement to each of the trio—Osbert, Edith, and Sacheverell. York Bowen was the soloist and Ernest Ansermet conducted the Royal Philharmonic Orchestra for the work's first performance at Queen's Hall, London, on 5 January 1928. Writing in *The Dominant* in February 1928, Constant Lambert praised the work for its 'concision and originality of form, the wealth of vigorous thematic material and the ease, reminiscent of Borodin at his best, with which these themes are combined'. The end of the work, where the themes of the earlier movements are brought back, was considered by Lambert as 'no mere academic device but the natural consequence of the ideas themselves'. In contrast, Angus Morrison dismissed the coda as 'contrived', and described the whole work as 'not one of Willie's best…and the movements do not really hang together all that well.'[23]

The arrangement for two pianos was published in 1928, the same year as the full score; it takes the form of 'Solo Pianoforte' (first piano) and a reduction of the orchestral accompaniment for the second player. In 1943 Walton undertook a revision of the work which included a change of title: it became Sinfonia Concertante 'for orchestra with piano obbligato'. When the revised score was published the dedications were removed—Walton's relationship with the Sitwells had cooled in the mid-1930s, but there was not a complete breakdown in communication as has sometimes been suggested. In 1947 Roy Douglas prepared a two-piano reduction of the revised version which was published.

Crown Imperial

The first of Walton's two coronation marches, *Crown Imperial*, was commissioned by the BBC and played on 12 May 1937 in Westminster Abbey as the Dowager Queen Mary took her place at the service for the coronation of King George VI and Queen Elizabeth. No doubt in anticipation of heavy demand for the march, OUP judiciously published Walton's arrangement for piano solo and Herbert Murrill's arrangement for organ just two days before the coronation service.

With *Crown Imperial* Walton took over the mantle of Elgar, at least as far as the composition of music for great state occasions was concerned. In terms of his own standing, this commission also suggested that the *enfant terrible* of the 1920s was quietly being ushered into the halls of the musical 'establishment'. Comparisons with Elgar's earlier marches were inevitable, but the quality of Walton's craftsmanship ensured that his coronation march could stand beside the finest of the genre. Elgar's structural formula for a rousing, grand march was too good to discard; Walton wisely opted to write a march which would be seen as a natural successor to the Elgar examples, rather than risk conceptual experiments that might have failed.

The arrangement for piano contains the option of a 65-bar cut at the start of the full recapitulation of the opening material. The cut is also marked in Murrill's organ arrangement. The present arrangement is essentially a reworking of Walton's composition sketch held in the Frederick R. Koch Collection at the Beinecke Rare Book and Manuscript Library, Yale University.

Three Pieces for Organ, from the film *Richard III*

Walton composed scores for Laurence Olivier's film versions of *Henry V* in 1944 and *Hamlet* in 1947. The two men were close personal friends over many years, and their collaboration on the Shakespeare films produced exceptional artistic results. In the early 1950s Olivier was keen to embark on another Shakespeare film. He recalled that 'Alexander Korda welcomed me with relatively open arms when I took the idea of *Richard III* to him, and I was able to gather my trusted team of Roger Furse, Carmen Dillon and William Walton, with Anthony Bushell as associate director.'[24]

The composition of the score for *Richard III* came immediately after Walton's emergence from years of work on *Troilus and Cressida* which was premiered at Covent Garden in December 1954. The film score was finished in March 1955, and Olivier was pleased with the music. Walton, however, feared that he was starting to repeat himself, and Susana Walton recalls his saying: 'Of course, Shakespeare repeats himself the whole time, battle after battle after battle. And that was rather the way I was feeling about *Richard III*. I can't do any more battle music, I told Larry, or charges, or anything of that kind.'[25] Perhaps it was this sentiment that caused Walton to add this tongue-in-cheek instruction to the score of the final reprise of the Prelude's 'big tune' at the end of the film: 'con prosciutto, agnello e confitura di fragole', meaning 'with ham, lamb and strawberry jam'.

The music of two of the three organ pieces is used also in orchestrated form in the film. The March is first heard on the organ during the coronation of King Edward IV at the beginning of the film. The Scherzetto is played as the king greets his queen and homage is paid to the new king. Later, as Edward IV lies dying in his bedchamber, the death of the Duke of Clarence is announced; during this scene the second organ piece, Elegy, is heard quietly in the background. Stewart Craggs was told that the pieces were recorded on the organ of Denham Church (close to the film studios), and then incorporated into the film soundtrack.[26]

Apart from the youthful, unpublished Choral Prelude on 'Wheatley', these three pieces are the only organ solos in Walton's oeuvre.

Five Bagatelles for Guitar

In 1960 Walton composed the song cycle *Anon. in Love* for Peter Pears and the guitarist Julian Bream. The guitar writing impressed Bream greatly, and ten years later he commissioned Walton to compose some pieces for solo guitar. Walton decided that the pieces should be edited by Bream, but dedicated to his old friend Malcolm Arnold. Arnold was staying with the Waltons on Ischia over Christmas 1970 and observed how Walton was struggling with the pieces. In a letter dated 15 April 1971 Walton wrote to Arnold, 'In a few days I shall be sending you a copy of the Bagatelles. Julian on the other hand when he saw the dedication was very pleased. After all what is important to him is his rake-off as Editor!'[27]

As so often happened with Walton, he began to have doubts about his guitar pieces as composition progressed. In another letter to Arnold dated 1 June 1971 he wrote: 'I'm beginning to have cold feet about dedicating the "Bagatelles" to you—I don't think they are good enough or worthy enough for you—from which you may gather they are not going at all well. I shall dedicate something else if these aren't up to the mark'. Work continued, and on 30 August 1971 Walton was able to write: 'I've finished the Guitar pieces (5) with dedication to yourself. I'm inclined to think they are rather good, but Julian will let you know about them. He's coming to inspect them on Sept. 1st.'[28]

In Bream's recollection the pieces were subjected to two revisions before publication: once at La Mortella, and then at the Savoy Hotel in London. The published version seemed to him to reflect the composer's wishes completely. The first performance of the complete set was given by Bream at the Bath Festival on 27 May 1972.

In 1976 Walton orchestrated the Bagatelles as his contribution to celebrations marking the 25th anniversary of the Royal Festival Hall in London. The arrangements were called *Varii Capricci*. Writing about the orchestration of the pieces Walton stated: 'There's not got to be a whisper of a guitar in the orch. version which will be for a large orch. sparingly used for the most part.'[29] In 1991 Patrick Russ made a further arrangement known as 'Five Bagatelles for Guitar and Orchestra', which incorporated the solo guitar version into Walton's orchestration.

Two lost pieces

Finally, mention should be made of a work, now unfortunately lost, that Walton contributed to a projected album that had been planned by Tony Meyer, *chargé de mission* at the French Embassy in London. Acting on Meyer's behalf, the francophile critic Felix Aprahamian wrote to Walton on 15 June 1944 with the following proposal:

> The French Committee of National Liberation have asked us to assist them by compiling an album of works by British composers, to comprise piano pieces or settings of French verses, as an 'Homage à la France'.
>
> The idea of such a volume is to further musical understanding and collaboration between the two countries and I presume that it will be widely distributed in France as soon as possible. In any case, it is hoped to have it ready early in the New Year. Naturally we are most anxious to secure your collaboration. Would you be willing to help?[30]

Walton appears to have agreed, for in a letter of 1 September of the same year to Norman Peterkin at OUP he wrote: 'I hope to let you have a set of small piano pieces shortly. One of them will be published in an album which is being got up by the French Committee of National Liberation to which all the composers have been asked to contribute.' On 9 November Walton informed Peterkin: 'I've sent my pianoforte pieces to Aprahamian direct. Up to now, I've completed 3—I hope to do 12 and suggest they might be divided into 2 books.'[31]

This 'Free French Album' project was eventually abandoned when Meyer went back to liberated France, and Felix Aprahamian returned the single sheet containing a piece entitled 'Lai' to OUP. Walton appears to have composed a companion piece 'Rondet de Carol'. At any rate, an undated newspaper cutting, which according to Stewart Craggs came from the *News Chronicle*, gives this account of a performance of both pieces by Walton's pianist friend Louis Kentner in Cannes: 'Both are placed against a French background. The one called *Lai* is effective piano writing and music of an appealing lyrical quality. The *Rondet de Carol* is in the same style as *Façade*.'[32]

No trace of either piece has been found, but it seems highly probable that Walton later reworked them as the Two Pieces for Violin and Piano, first performed in 1950.

NOTES

1. Transmitted by London Weekend Television on 19 April 1981.
2. Interview, *At the Haunted End of the Day*.
3. Duncan Hinnells, *An Extraordinary Performance* (Oxford, 1998), pp. 51–53.
4. Letters to and from OUP are contained in the OUP Archive, Oxford.
5. Letter from Walton to Roy Douglas, dated 25 July 1945, and quoted in *The Selected Letters of William Walton*, ed. Malcolm Hayes (London, 2002), p. 154.
6. F. Bonavia, *Daily Telegraph* (17 February 1941), p. 3c.
7. *The Times* (18 February 1941), p. 6e.
8. Frederick R. Koch Collection, Beinecke Rare Book and Manuscript Library, Yale University. The lithographer and painter Paul Gavarni (pseudonym of Guillaume-Sulpice Chevalier, 1804–66) was a contemporary of Henri Daumier. He specialized in scenes of everyday Parisian life.
9. Letter from Walton to Alan Frank, 10 November 1949.
10. Richard Shead, *Constant Lambert* (London, 1973), p. 50.
11. Geoffrey Nowell-Smith, ed., *The Oxford History of World Cinema* (Oxford, 1996), p. 207.
12. Letter from Hubert Foss to R. J. Cullen, 29 November 1934.
13. Julie Kavanagh, *Secret Muses: The Life of Frederick Ashton* (London, 1996), p. 175.
14. Letter from Walton to Osbert Sitwell, quoted in *Selected Letters*, ed. Hayes, p. 98.
15. Spike Hughes, *Opening Bars* (London, 1946), p. 316.
16. Letter from William Walton to Siegfried Sassoon, undated, William Walton Museum, Forio, Ischia.
17. Constant Lambert, 'Some Recent Works by William Walton', *The Dominant*, no. 4 (February 1928), p. 16.
18. In Angus Morrison, 'Willie: The Young Walton and his Four Masterpieces', talk given at the National Sound Archive, 31 January 1984. An abridged version of the talk is printed in the *Royal College of Music Magazine* (1984), pp. 119–127.
19. R. M. Schafer, *British Composers in Interview* (London, 1963), p. 78.
20. Lambert, 'Recent Works', p. 18.
21. Morrison, 'Willie', p. 122.
22. Morrison, 'Willie', p. 123.
23. Morrison, 'Willie', p. 122.
24. Laurence Olivier, *On Acting* (London, 1986), p. 204.
25. Susana Walton, *Behind the Façade* (Oxford, 1988), p. 143.
26. Stewart R. Craggs, *William Walton: A Catalogue* (Oxford, 1990), p. 127.
27. William Walton Museum, Forio, Ischia.
28. *Selected Letters*, ed. Hayes, p. 397.
29. Quoted in a letter from Christopher Morris to Alan Frank, 30 October 1975.
30. OUP Archive.
31. OUP Archive.
32. Craggs, *Walton Catalogue*, p. 101.

21

Music for Brass *(Vol. 21)*

Elgar Howarth

William Walton was born into brass band country. During his childhood there would have been within a twenty-mile radius of his family home in Oldham at least 25 to 30 bands of varying standards, from the heights of the local Besses o' th' Barn, under their legendary conductor Alexander Owen (himself an Oldham man), to the most modest of village bands.

It is unlikely that he would have been much influenced. His background was the family choral tradition through his father's involvement with this, not only as a musical northerner but also as a choirmaster and singing teacher. Oddly, these two main streams of amateur music-making rarely overlapped, then as now.

Nevertheless, Walton heard bands often (he told me so), and the sound—memorable, even unique—remained in his ear. In fact it would have been difficult not to be aware of the 'banding' input into the various annual festivities of pre-World War I northern England. Staple fare for all bands were Christmas carolling, Whitsuntide church parades, summer garden parties, and concerts in the park or on the seaside pier where, in the words of the well-known song of the time, 'the brass bands play tiddly-om-pom-pom'. The attention created by the Besses' 1906 and 1909 world tours of the USA, Canada, Honolulu, Fiji (!), New Zealand, Australia, and South Africa would certainly have been remarked on in the Walton household.

It is a lasting pity that Walton never composed a major piece for the medium. The brass band has a bitter-sweet, nostalgic, melancholic lyricism which would have been ideally suited to his late-Romantic style, and the scores he finally produced late in his life—*The First Shoot*, preceded by its close sibling, the Medley for Brass Band—are not the heavyweights that the bands were seeking, though they are excellent entertainment.

As early in his career as August 1937 Walton had been approached by the National Brass Band Championships of Great Britain to write a test piece. Elgar, Holst, Ireland, Bliss, Bantock, and Howells had already provided fine serious works throughout the 1920s into the 30s. But 1937 was not a convenient time for Walton; his energies were concentrated on a more compelling project, Heifetz's request for a violin concerto. One feels that Walton's priorities were perhaps correct.

If he was little engaged by offers from the bands, his writing for orchestral brass emphasizes how striking his feel was for these instruments; indeed it is one of the glories of his style. His scores bristle with pungent brass sonority, often used sparingly but in a very telling manner. There are spectacular climaxes and witty interjections, and the relatively new muting possibilities are brilliantly incorporated, showing the influence of the French school, Stravinsky, and his early experience arranging foxtrots for Debroy

Somers's Savoy Orpheans. The trumpet writing in *Façade: An Entertainment*, a lovely mix of lyricism and jazz-style figures, is a joy to play and, with Stravinsky's *L'Histoire du Soldat* (a cornet part), presents the performer with opportunities to display a technical and expressive range to satisfy all but the most egocentric. The final wistful trumpet solo of the First Symphony is an inspired moment, focusing the climax of the work's great coda.

Walton also had a sure sense of ceremonial. The fanfares that he wrote for a variety of occasions are hardly his best music, but they are sure-footed, colourful miniatures capable of raising goose-pimples with their sheer vitality.

The music

On 12 June 1973 I played the trumpet part in *Façade* in a BBC concert at the Aeolian Hall celebrating the 50th anniversary of its first public performance there. Walton conducted, and having recently been made music advisor of the Grimethorpe Colliery Band I naturally asked him if he would write a piece for us. I met with an elusive refusal in his driest Lancastrian manner. At that point he had clearly not realized the potential of the music he had written decades earlier for the short ballet entitled *The First Shoot* for a C. B. Cochran revue.

Follow the Sun

Shortly after his completed symphony was successfully premiered in autumn 1935 and he had composed his first film score, *Escape Me Never*, Walton was asked to provide the music for a ten-minute ballet sequence in the latest of Cochran's lavish revues, *Follow the Sun*. The scenario had been devised by Osbert Sitwell, the choreography was by Frederick Ashton, and Cecil Beaton designed the sets and costumes—his first for the theatre.[1] Sitwell, who may have been responsible for suggesting Walton to Cochran, provided the following synopsis for *The First Shoot*:

> The action takes place in a woodland glade, during a fashionable Edwardian shooting party, the first given by Lord de Fontenoy since his marriage to the lovely Connie Winsome, late of Musical Comedy. After an opening dance of pheasants Lady de Fontenoy enters, soon followed by her admirer, Lord Charles Canterbury, who performs a dance for her pleasure. They are interrupted by the rest of the party, who march around firing in the air, and then dance off to luncheon. Lord Charles lingers, fires at another bird and accidentally wounds Lady de Fontenoy. Dragging herself on to the stage she dies in his arms, to the intense interest of the other guests.

The revue opened at the Manchester Opera House on 23 December 1935. The first performance in London, which was delayed by the death of George V, finally took place at the Adelphi Theatre on 4 February 1936, and the revue ran until 27 June. The star of the show was the beautiful American dancing actress Claire Luce, whom Walton described in the 1981 Promenade Concerts prospectus as 'a ravishing blond'. Beaton recalled that 'Willie Walton had composed the perversely lyrical music',[2] and indeed the ballet's scenario would seem to have called for some sterner material, especially at the tragic denouement. Yet perhaps Walton was right, for on the following day the drama critic of *The Times* (Charles Morgan) described the ballet as 'a neat and witty piece of fooling'. As Cochran presented the show twice nightly for the last two and a half months of the run, Walton must have derived reasonable financial gain from the venture.

Walton claimed that the full score of the ballet had been burnt, presumably when his home in South Eaton Place was hit during the Blitz in May 1941. But a piano reduction had been made and, thanks to the enquiries of Stewart Craggs, the copy was unearthed in the Oxford University Press hire library in October 1972. On the title page it bears the name of Francis Collinson, who had conducted the orchestra for the revue; however, it is doubtful whether he himself had made the very professional-looking copy of the reduction. Alan Frank, Walton's publisher, immediately sent it to the composer and Walton replied, 'I think it had better continue to lie in the oblivion it has been in up till now',[3] though he admitted that in 1969 he had used the waltz tune from it (presumably from memory) for the dream sequence in the Olivier film of the National Theatre production of Chekhov's *Three Sisters*. In fact he had already featured the same tune in 1942 in his score for the film *Went the Day Well?* as a piece of dance music played on the radio. The 1972 date of the rediscovery of *The First Shoot* piano score should be noted, because Walton was less than candid when, in the 1981 Proms prospectus, he wrote that the music had fortuitously turned up 'only a few months ago'.

Brass band commission

In 1977, after a gap of nearly forty years, the National Brass Band Championships renewed their efforts to persuade Walton to produce a work for them. Writing to him on 24 May, the championships' director, Robert Alexander, expressed the desire to carry on a tradition started in 1913 of persuading major British composers to 'enrich' the band repertory.[4] Walton must have agreed in principle, but then mildly panicked over his total inexperience in this field. On 6 July Christopher Morris of OUP wrote to him saying, 'I have been in touch with Gary [Elgar] Howarth over Brass Bands, and he is going to send you the information you require. I shall be sending a couple of the gramophone records of Brass Bands, and I will talk to Robert Alexander about the commission.'[5] It was at this point that I sent Walton a copy of my *Fireworks* for brass band and what I hoped would be a useful set of instructions for writing for the medium.[6] At the same time the records arrived for Walton, and one of them was my Grimethorpe record containing not only *Fireworks* but also specially commissioned works by Hans Werner Henze and Harrison Birtwistle, about which Walton later enthused in a letter to his occasional assistant Roy Douglas.[7]

By the end of June 1977 Walton had formally agreed to produce a band piece. He was ever the astute businessman, and his main motivation may have been the one later expressed in a letter to his friend, the record producer Walter Legge: 'The B.B.s are tremendously popular & if one wrote the right kind of piece, it would produce the P.R.S. very vast & fast, so I'm told.'[8] At a meeting between Morris and Alexander on 1 August a commissioning fee was agreed, and the question arose as to whether he wanted to write a contest piece or a concert piece. Christopher Morris explained: 'A contest piece is what Mr. Alexander really wants, and this means that you will have to give the players some showy passages because they are tests in technique. Contest pieces should be pretty well exactly 11 minutes long. A concert piece would not need these definite requirements, but I hope you will tackle one for contests.'[9] The piece was required for the championships in October 1978.

Medley for Brass Band

On 24 August 1977 Christopher Morris was able to inform Robert Alexander that Walton had agreed to the fee, had chosen to write a contest piece, and hoped to finish it by Christmas. On the same day he wrote to Walton, 'I take it that the proposed 5 Bagatelles for Brass Band [to which Walton had presumably alluded] will be entirely divorced from the Guitar Pieces of the same name. Maybe it would be wise to have a different title.'[10] Can Walton have been thinking of arranging for band his *Varii Capricci* of the previous year, which itself was a 'free transcription for orchestra' of the 1971 guitar pieces?

However, around Christmas 1977 (his original delivery date) something seems to have made Walton go cold on the project and then write accordingly to the National Brass Band organizers. Christopher Morris subsequently recorded that on 12 January 1978, the day on which Walton had written to Alexander withdrawing from the project, the composer had also written to him about a companion piece for his one-act opera *The Bear*: 'It would take me a long time, and as I've still to do the Brass Band & Wind Band pieces, I see no prospect of taking anything else on. In fact I've written to the Brass Band people putting it off indefinitely. As I've hardly got it going at all I can see it won't be ready in time for the bands to have time to learn it—at any rate for the next Festival.'[11] Nevertheless, he continued to work sporadically on what was to become the Medley. On 21 April 1979 he wrote to Roy Douglas, 'I have done about 3 mins. of a piece for Br. Ba. Competition, which in all probability will be sent to you by O.U.P. to discover if I'm still in my right mind!...Anyway it won't frighten the Bands, for though the piece is slightly Henze-ish, it is not at all Birtwistle-ish!'[12] And there matters seemed to come to a halt.

Suddenly on 4 October 1979 Morris received a letter from Walton announcing that 'More or less simultaneously as this pages of the Br. Ba. should arrive [the first movement]. Gary Howarth has the good idea of getting his boys to do a tape (it will cost us nothing) so I can see all the blunders I've surely made. The rest of the piece will follow shortly getting vulgarer and vulgarer as it proceeds, I fear. So will you have the sc[ore] photoed & sent to him, also the parts copied.'[13] The second, third, and fourth movements arrived at OUP on 26 October, and the fifth and last was despatched to a copyist on 15 November.

On 19 November 1979 Christopher Morris took pleasure in informing Robert Alexander of the completion of the Medley and was surprised to hear back from him saying that the commissioning fee no longer applied. Walton was naturally dismayed to hear this. He wrote to Morris on 13 December: 'There seems to be much misunderstanding about the Bra. Ba. piece. It is meant as a Contest Piece & I thought well in time for the next contest in next Oct. '80...the piece towards the end of the 1st. part has cadenzas...and the shorter pieces which follow the slightly pompous Introduction (making what follows rather unexpected and comic, I hope) have lots of virtuoso solos for nearly all. I won't say that it is music of the highest standard, but not much behind "Façade"!'[14]

There followed a considerable correspondence in an attempt to mend fences and restore the commissioning fee. However, in a letter of 16 January 1980, Alexander affirmed, 'I regret to inform you that there is no question of reviving the commission fee. At the time we had outside assistance on the matter, and of course the offer was withdrawn when Sir Walton [*sic*] wrote and said he was unable to carry out the commission at that time.'[15] But Alexander still wanted to conduct the first performance of the Medley at a Gala Concert in October, so must have been disconcerted to be told on 5 February by Christopher Morris: 'I have just heard from Sir William that he has now re-written this work and has made it a version of music he wrote for a ballet that was performed at a review [*sic*] in 1936. I now await the new score but I gather from Sir William that he is rather keen that Gary Howarth should be allowed to give the Premiere.'[16]

The First Shoot

On 19 December 1979 Christopher Morris had written to me about the Medley and asked, 'Do you agree that it is suitable as a contest piece, and if so, can you use your influence to get it accepted?'[17] I may well have confessed that, much as I liked the score, I did not really think so, knowing that tongue-in-cheek, light fare would not be thought appropriate by the organizers of the competitions. Also the idea of a future Promenade Concert devoted to brass band music and given by the Grimethorpe Colliery Band under me was at a sensitive stage of negotiation, and perhaps knowing this, Walton seems to have felt that the 'contest' content of the Medley could be jettisoned in favour of a more populist piece that would go down well at the Proms. By this time he had also heard our Grimethorpe tape of the Medley and this had helped him refine his first thoughts on how to make a band treatment of *The First Shoot* music.

In its issue of 29 December 1979 the *British Bandsman* magazine informed its readers that Walton had composed a piece for brass band and that this had been 'announced by Elgar Howarth, without whose encouragement and persuasion the work might never have been written'. It goes on to say that I had visited Walton in Ischia 'some months ago' (in fact in early August), and concludes that 'although not intended as a test-piece (which in many ways is a pity), we should rejoice that at long last one of England's greatest composers has contributed to our literature'.

In the event the first public performance of *The First Shoot* at the Proms was deferred by one year, but this made it possible to have a trial run that was semi-public. On 19 December 1980 I conducted the work with the Grimethorpe band at Goldsmith's College in London. The performance was filmed and recorded, and excerpts from it were used in Tony Palmer's TV film *At the Haunted End of the Day*, a 'profile of the life and work of William Walton', which was first transmitted on the ITV network on 19 April of the following year. The long-awaited Prom public premiere was given by the same forces at the Royal Albert Hall on 7 September 1981. Two days later Edward Greenfield in *The Guardian* described it as being 'as brief as could be, popular pastiche at its most deft', but the critic of *The Times* summed it up more sourly as 'playful and finally ebullient but also bitty and thin: a damp squib'.

Publication

In April 1982 OUP decided to publish *The First Shoot*. On the 28th of that month Christopher Morris wrote to the experienced copyist Ronald Finch, sending him photocopies of Walton's autograph and another copy edited by me. Morris wrote, 'Work entirely from Howarth's edited copy. The smaller one [Walton's] is provided for your reference only.'[18] When Finch's printed copy was finished, OUP went into consultation with the Studio Music Company who were specialists in the brass band repertory. Under a specially negotiated agreement OUP agreed to put 250 scores on sale while Studio Music handled the printing and the sale of the parts.[19] I made further adjustments to the score because over a year later Morris wrote to Studio Music, 'Here at last are the parts. Our checker had a terrible time getting them right because Elgar Howarth made so many changes, but he now reports that these parts agree with the score.'[20] The score and parts were published rather belatedly in 1986.

The four versions of The First Shoot

In analysing the form and content of *The First Shoot* we need to consider four sources:

1 The piano reduction of the original revue ballet music
2 Medley for Brass Band: Walton's autograph score
3 *The First Shoot*: Walton's autograph score
4 *The First Shoot*: first printed edition of 1986

The piano reduction enables us to evaluate the extent to which Walton transformed his original in the course of preparing his two band versions. Phrase lengths, rhythms, and harmony are all changed in the course of the reworking, sometimes slightly, sometimes quite significantly, always in my opinion for the better. Whereas the Medley had opened with the challenging Prelude, *The First Shoot* begins with a spirited new piece which sets the tone immediately in a 1930s vaudeville, cabaret style. This revised version is more detailed in orchestration than its forebear, which had slightly more elaborate percussion parts,[21] and the melody lines are fragmented to provide answering phrases, particularly in the cornet section. Single melodic lines from the Medley are also occasionally fleshed out harmonically, giving more bite and tang. The second movement begins at the end of the very brief introduction in the piano arrangement, and although at times altered substantially, it is recognizably the same piece, a sauntering, soft-shoe shuffle in both band versions. Neither is ideal in orchestration, *The First Shoot* having some low grumpy tenor horn passages (in one case briefly off the instrument), but with a more effective final bar and at times a more elegant cornet line than its near neighbour.

The third and fourth movements of *The First Shoot* run continuously, curiously in three sections: a 'hesitation' waltz and an anglicized 'can-can', followed by a close relation of 'Popular Song' from *Façade*. The waltz is one of the most attractive sections of the work, lightly scored and of real charm. The 'can-can' which follows appears in both Medley and *The First Shoot*. It is the most technically difficult of the five movements; neat triple-tonguing is required and neater fingers. It leads without a break to the 'popular song'—Walton at his most droll. The final movement is a hurly-burly, boisterous circus-style march. The two works have different endings, *The First Shoot*'s being the more effective.

Overall, *The First Shoot* is clearly a better version than the Medley, including as it does the waltz and excluding the stylistically maverick Prelude.

There is a further rider. The printed score of *The First Shoot* has various re-adjustments to the original manuscript, made at my suggestion and included after the first rehearsals of the work in the autumn of 1981. These were all approved by Walton, as were my amendments at the time of publication, and thus the WWE republication of the score should be regarded as the approved final version.

It is interesting to note that Walton did not waste the Prelude to the Medley, as he later used it as the basis for the first section of his very last work, *Prologo e Fantasia*.

The fanfares

Like several of his British contemporaries Walton wrote a number of fanfares, including some that formed an integral part of his film scores, notably the ones for the Laurence Olivier productions of *Henry V*, *Hamlet*, and *Richard III*. Towards the end of his life he was also commissioned on five occasions to write fanfares for a wide variety of events, ranging from the arrival of the Queen at a NATO conference to the opening of a new lion terrace at the London Zoo.

The first fanfare (or set of fanfares) that Walton wrote was a typical product of the war years and the propaganda efforts made by the British government to boost awareness of its surprising new ally, Soviet Russia. On Sunday 21 February 1943 *Salute to the Red Army*, a celebration devised and produced by Basil Dean and partly written by Louis MacNeice, was given at the Royal Albert Hall in London. The somewhat slender cause of the celebration was the 25th anniversary of Lenin's decree setting up a Red Army of 'workers and peasants'. Walton was asked to provide a 'triumphant fanfare' (possibly more than one) to the Red Army and this was performed by the trumpets and drums of the Life Guards, the Royal Horse Guards, and the Royal Air Force, under Malcolm Sargent. All written trace of the fanfare has disappeared, but by good chance a BBC archive recording exists; the fanfare plays for 1'15". In 1945 Walton enlarged and orchestrated it for the memorial concert for Sir Henry Wood, involving three symphony orchestras (published in Vol. 17 of the WWE).

Fanfare for a Great Occasion

The first of Walton's published fanfares was derived from his 1947 *Hamlet* film music. In March 1962 Sir Malcolm Sargent and John Pritchard took the London Philharmonic Orchestra on a tour of the Far East, and for a concert inaugurating a new concert hall in Hong Kong Sargent prepared, 'with Walton's rather grudging permission,'[22] this short, suitably effective fanfare, for trumpets, trombones, and timpani only. The fanfare, for the arrangement of which Sargent waived any financial stake, was registered with the Performing Right Society, although considerable confusion was caused there and at OUP by its lack of a distinctive title.

In 1964 OUP decided to publish the work, and Sargent informed them, 'I am thinking of adding horn parts to it and, possibly, side drum.'[23] The resulting edition of what was still titled merely *Fanfare* was published on 6 May 1965 in score and parts. A note prefacing the score states, 'This Fanfare is made up of a number of isolated fanfares written by Sir William Walton for the 1947 film of Shakespeare's *Hamlet*. Sir Malcolm Sargent has grouped them into a single piece, which he has rescored.' Apart from the last remark, this is wholly misleading. The initial roll of timpani and side drum is by Sargent, as are the slower repeated bars 31–38. Otherwise the main 30-bar fanfare is played in its entirety in the *Hamlet* film at the point where the court assembles to watch the play staged by the travelling actors.

Sargent continued to play the fanfare occasionally at his concerts, and it was probably he who eventually gave it its designation *Fanfare for a Great Occasion*. This title was certainly appropriate when it was played at the official opening of the Channel Tunnel on 6 May 1994.

A Queen's Fanfare

The autograph of this fanfare is headed 'Written for the entrance of H.M. The Queen at the N.A.T.O. Parliamentarians' Conference, London, June 1959'. As the title implies, this was a high-powered international occasion celebrating the 10th anniversary of the creation of NATO, which was held in the imposing surroundings of Westminster Hall in the Palace of Westminster. Walton sent the fanfare to Alan Frank on 9 May to have the parts copied, saying, 'It is to be played by the Royal Horseguards but as yet it has not been decided whether 8 or 12 instruments are available, so I've made it playable with either number... Though offered a fee I've done it for nowt. All the same we might cash in with the P.R.S. as it will be televised etc., I believe.'[24]

The fanfare is scored for E♭ trumpet, seven B♭ trumpets, two tenor trombones, and two bass trombones. To enable the fanfare to be played by 8 rather than 12 players there is a further instruction: 'This Fanfare can be performed without B♭ trumpets 5, 6, and 7 and bass trombone 2.'

The piece is a mere 16 bars long, but even so has two tempo directions; its harmony is based on Walton's favourite piled-up 3rds, creating 7ths, 9ths, and 11ths in profusion. Its abrupt but very effective modulation to end on a D major chord at the close was presumably made to provide a dominant pivot into the National Anthem (usually performed in G), though this is not stated in the score. The anthem was doubtless played in Westminster Hall on 5 June by the State Trumpeters who had performed the fanfare. The score was published by OUP on 27 April 1972.

Anniversary Fanfare

In a letter of 22 December 1972 Peter Andry, general manager of the international classical division of EMI, commissioned Walton to compose a fanfare for a forthcoming concert celebrating the company's 75th anniversary. He flippantly suggested one 'consisting of 75 bars or 75 notes or what-have-you' and also floated the idea of a reference to 'Happy birthday to you'.[25] He may also have informed Walton that the concert was to open with his 1953 coronation march, *Orb and Sceptre*. At the same time he appears to have contacted Lt-Col Rodney Bashford, director of music at the Royal Military School of Music, Kneller Hall, requesting his services, for in a letter to the composer dated 12 January 1973 Bashford expressed his delight at the news that there was to be a new Waltonian fanfare (his arrangement of *Fanfare for a Great Occasion*, he said, they had 'played to death') and reminded him of the forces that Kneller Hall could put at his disposal. He added, 'Our instruments are rather difficult to play, and they also have heavy banners on them, so I would be grateful for no higher note that C in alt (sounding B♭) for the trumpets, and top B♭ for trombones. These trombones do not "speak" very well below F.'[26]

Walton sent the completed fanfare to OUP in late summer 1973, and on 7 August Alan Frank sent a copy of the score to Bashford with the promise of parts extracted from it. It provoked the decidedly military reply, 'Thank you for the score of Sir William's fanfare...we would welcome them [the parts] as soon as possible since it looks a bit of a snorter.'[27] Walton exceeded the numbers proposed by Kneller Hall and scored the fanfare for nine trumpets in B♭ (5, 7, and 9 are optional), four tenor trombones (2 and 4 optional), three bass trombones (3 optional), timpani, and percussion. Already on the first main beat of the 20-bar fanfare Walton's characteristic crushed 7th features in the bass. Midway, at bar 12, the style modifies from crisp semiquaver movement to a slightly broader *marziale*. The 'Happy birthday' quotation, which is so well disguised that it hardly required being credited in the published score, begins with the upbeat to bar 16 and continues to the close in bar 20. In his autograph, Walton instructs that the fanfare is to be 'immediately followed' by *Orb and Sceptre*.

The EMI anniversary concert, for which Sir Adrian Boult and André Previn were the conductors, was given on 29 November 1973 at the Royal Festival Hall, London. Lt-Col Bashford opened the event by conducting his Kneller Hall forces in the fanfare, which led into Previn's performance with the London Symphony Orchestra of *Orb and Sceptre*.

As usual, OUP proposed a more practical reduction of forces for publication. Writing to Alan Frank on 20 August 1973, Walton said: 'I see no reason why the Fanfare should not be available in a red. version (1 player to each part & the Timp. and Perc. compressed for 1 player). P.S. Or if you can get someone to reduce it still further I don't mind. It need not be used as an introduction to O&C always simply because (& noone [*sic*] will notice it) the last bars are "Happy birthday to you"!'[28] This reduction was done by the composer John Rutter in conjunction with Walton and Christopher Morris. Sending in his score on 19 February 1974, Rutter declared that 'hardly anything needed changing.'[29] The fanfare eventually appeared in print on 5 June 1975.

Fanfare for the National

The long-awaited creation of a national theatre of Great Britain finally became a reality on the evening of 22 October 1963 when a company, under the artistic direction of Walton's great friend Sir Laurence Olivier, made its debut with an uncut staging of *Hamlet*, starring Peter O'Toole. This took place at the much-loved Old Vic Theatre. A purpose-built complex of three auditoriums had been planned for the South Bank of the Thames since 1960, but escalating costs and other delays meant that the National

Theatre was opened in phases: the Lyttleton auditorium was opened in March 1976, followed by the Olivier in October, and the Cottesloe in March 1977. Between the opening of the first two auditoriums London Weekend Television made a programme entitled *Your National Theatre*, produced by Derek Bailey, which celebrated the company's move to the South Bank. It was transmitted on 21 August 1976.

The fanfare that Walton was commissioned to provide for this TV programme is scored for trumpet in E♭, six trumpets in B♭, three tenor trombones, bass trombone, timpani, and percussion. The brisk 34-bar piece is structured in simple ABA form. Walton's fingerprint 3rds again provide the harmonic motivation. The urgent semiquaver figures of the opening (the A section) contrast with the prescribed *espressivo legato* cantabile mood of section B. From bar 25 the semiquavers revive the energy to the close. Side drum, cymbals played with wire brushes, tambourine, and latterly tubular bells provide important colour.

After an initial run-through on 1 April 1976, the fanfare was eventually recorded on 20 July at London Weekend Television's South Bank studios, with Harry Rabinowitz conducting a group of London freelance players. The fanfare's first publication was in the WWE.

Roaring Fanfare

Walton had known the immensely distinguished scientist Solly, Baron Zuckerman (1904–1993), and his wife, Joan, for many years. Already laden with every conceivable award and honorary doctorate, Zuckerman was awarded the supreme British honour of the Order of Merit in 1968 (Walton had received it in the previous year) and was made a life peer in 1971. In 1975 Zuckerman, who was secretary of the Zoological Society of London, visited his old friend in Ischia and asked him to write a piece to be played at a ceremonial visit to the zoo by the Queen to celebrate its 150th anniversary in May of the following year. As so often happened with Walton, this was really too much notice, and he possibly forgot about it. At all events, the finished manuscript of *Roaring Fanfare* reached the zoo less than a month before the occasion for which it was intended. Although written two years after *Fanfare for the National*, this was in fact Walton's next composition. It is scored for three trumpets, three tenor trombones, two bass trombones, and percussion, and bears the charming dedication 'To Solly Z. that Lion of Lions'. It was played on the arrival of the Queen at the zoo, when she attended an evening reception prior to opening the new terrace at the Lion House. Its 18 bars find Walton in his most tongue-in-cheek mood. The thirds are piled up extravagantly, sometimes to optimum 13ths, the trombones roaring their leonine glissandos. The fanfare, arranged for organ, was played at the funerals of both Lord and Lady Zuckerman. The fanfare's first publication was in the WWE.

Salute for Sir Robert Mayer on his 100th Birthday

Sir Robert Mayer, CH (1879–1985) was a businessman, philanthropist, and patron of music, who in 1923 founded the highly successful Robert Mayer concerts for children. In 1954 he extended his patronage by creating Youth and Music. It was this organization, through its joint chairman Lord Drogheda, that commissioned a fanfare from Walton to open a concert on 5 June 1979 at the Royal Festival Hall, celebrating Sir Robert's centenary. The Queen, who had attended his concerts for children when young, was present.

Walton planned his fanfare as a short introduction to the orchestral national anthem and, with unlimited youthful forces at his disposal, scored it for 12 trumpets. The *Salute* was originated by OUP and read in proof by Walton, but was first published posthumously in the WWE.

Even before Sir Robert Mayer's centenary concert Christopher Morris of OUP wrote to Walton on 3 April 1979 suggesting that he recast the Mayer fanfare for three trumpets and three trombones, with a view to publication and further performances. Walton sent back his rearrangement (lightly revised, for example in the harmonies in bar 12) with the proofs of the *Salute*, and the score was published under its new title *Introduction to the National Anthem* on 5 June 1980. In 1988 it was included as an introduction to the first publication of Walton's 1953 arrangement of the national anthem. An anonymous editorial note suggests that when the pieces are played together Walton's introductory bar to the anthem should be omitted, following the roll on the side drums.

A Birthday Fanfare

This miniature fanfare was written as a 70th birthday present for Karl-Friedrich Still, the Waltons' next-door neighbour in Ischia. The autograph is inscribed 'Fanfare for Karl on his 70th birthday. Greetings from Susana & William', and dated 16 September 1981. It also contains a brief note for Karl Rickenbacher, the conductor of the Westphalia Symphony Orchestra, which provided the players for the first performance. It reads: 'Dear Mr. Rickenbacher, Herewith Karl's Fanfare. If it should be too high for your players transpose it down a tone. As it is, I've followed Schönberg's example as the parts will have to be transposed anyhow! Regards, William Walton.'[30]

The autograph is just nine bars long, but in a separate note Walton writes, 'After a quick look at K's fanfare it seems a bit short. I suggest if there is time to make the adjustment in the parts that it should read thus: at the 9th [*recte* 8th] bar the 8th [*recte* 7th] bar should be repeated making 10 bars in all.' He adds a music example making it clear that the seventh bar is to be repeated.[31]

The fanfare was scored for three trumpets, four horns, and percussion, and was performed at Dr Still's guest house, Wengerner Mühle, in Recklinghausen on 10 October 1981. At some point the fanfare was scored for seven trumpets and percussion. As Walton had written the four horn parts in C—that is to say notated at concert pitch—this involved no change of notation. It was first heard in this form on 7 June 1982 at the Royal Albert Hall, London, played by the trumpeters of the Royal Military School, Kneller Hall, conducted by Lt-Col G. E. Evans. OUP published this version, rather than the original, in 1983; in the parts the trumpets are in both C and B♭.

NOTES

1. A brightly coloured Beaton design for one of the pheasants is on public display in the museum of the Sitwell family home at Renishaw Hall, Derbyshire.
2. *Self Portrait with Friends: The Selected Diaries of Cecil Beaton, 1926–1974*, ed. Richard Buckle (London, 1979), p. 46.
3. Letter of 19 October 1972, OUP Archive, Oxford.
4. Letter of 24 May 1977, OUP Archive.
5. OUP Archive.
6. These are still to be seen at the William Walton Museum, Forio, Ischia.
7. *The Selected Letters of William Walton*, ed. Malcolm Hayes (London, 2002), p. 445.
8. *Selected Letters*, ed. Hayes, p. 450.
9. Letter of 2 August 1977, OUP Archive.
10. Letter of 24 August 1977, OUP Archive.
11. Letter from Christopher Morris to Robert Alexander of 29 November 1979, OUP Archive. The wind band pieces to which Walton is referring were a commission that he received in 1977 from the Big Ten Band Conductors' Association in the USA for the following year's convention. The project never came to fruition.
12. *Selected Letters*, ed. Hayes, p. 453.
13. OUP Archive.
14. OUP Archive.
15. OUP Archive.
16. OUP Archive.
17. OUP Archive.
18. OUP Archive.
19. Letter of Christopher Morris to Stan Kitchen of 16 May 1982, OUP Archive.
20. Letter of 17 June 1983, OUP Archive.
21. For a discussion about the way in which the percussion content of brass band pieces increased significantly in the 1970s see Elgar and Patrick Howarth, *What a Performance! The Brass Band Plays* (London, 1988), pp. 150–151.
22. Letter from Alan Frank to John Ward (of OUP, New York) of 9 January 1963, OUP Archive.
23. Letter to Alan Frank of 9 April 1964. Sargent performed the fanfare on 6 and 7 June of that year with the New York Philharmonic Orchestra.
24. Letter of 9 May 1959, OUP Archive.
25. OUP Archive.
26. Letter of 12 January 1973, OUP Archive.
27. Letter of 4 September 1973, OUP Archive.
28. Letter of 20 August 1973, OUP Archive.
29. Letter to Christopher Morris, OUP Archive.
30. Letter of 16 September 1981, William Walton Museum.
31. Letter of 16 September 1981, William Walton Museum.

22

Film Suites *(Vol. 22)*

James Brooks Kuykendall

The appearance of film music in print represents a compromise with the composer's intentions: while this music was written for public consumption, it was to be disseminated through a single recorded performance, wedded to a moving image projected on a screen. Despite Walton's great success in the field of film music, he strongly resisted the idea of publishing extracts for concert performance, which would necessarily disrupt the integration of sound and dramatic pacing as a cinematic unity. This concern is evident in Walton's March 1942 letter to the writer and radio producer Dallas Bower, describing his prospective work on Louis MacNeice's BBC radio play *Christopher Columbus*—not a film, but it raised similar issues for the composer:

> Actually from my point of view I can't treat C.C. in any way different from a rather superior film. That is, that the music is entirely occasional & is of no use other than what it is meant for & one won't be able to get a suite out of it. Which is just as it should be, otherwise it would probably not fulfill its purpose.... Film music is not good film music if it can be used for any other purpose & you've only have [*sic*] got to have heard that concert the other night [15 March] to realise how true that is. For all the music was as bad as it could be, listened to in cold blood, but probably excellent with the film. So I don't care where Major Barbara is or any other of my films. The music should never be heard without the film.[1]

These strong words notwithstanding, in the first half of his career Walton was sometimes prepared to extract and adapt select music from his films for publication and concert performance: the piano arrangement of the ballet *Escape Me Never* (1935), the 'Spitfire' Prelude and Fugue (1942), and the 1945 Suite from *Henry V*, though this last has sometimes been erroneously attributed to Malcolm Sargent. Thereafter, he became resistant to suggestions that he should derive marketable concert works from his film scores, despite considerable encouragement from Hubert Foss and Alan Frank, his publishers at Oxford University Press. Among the papers in the OUP Archive in Oxford are letters from all over the world requesting (and sometimes even making detailed suggestions for) publications derived from Walton's film scores. That the composer was eventually persuaded to make some of the music available in print—and this despite frequent misgivings—is largely due to the tenacity of a pre-eminent figure in mid-twentieth-century British film music, Muir Mathieson.[2]

In a career spanning four decades, Mathieson (1911–75) was involved as conductor, musical director, and (occasionally) composer for nearly five hundred films. He worked with Walton on four films, serving as musical director for all three of the Shakespeare projects directed by Laurence Olivier. Perhaps his chief contribution to British cinema was his vision of what non-specialists of standing could achieve in the medium, which spurred him on to attract top composers to film projects. His connection with Ralph Vaughan Williams began with *The 49th Parallel* and continued for five more films. In 1946 he coaxed Benjamin Britten to write the short film *Instruments of the Orchestra*, and Britten's score was to achieve permanent success as a concert work when retitled *The Young Person's Guide to the Orchestra*. Later in his career, Mathieson used the considerable conducting experience he had acquired in the recording studio to champion film music on the concert platform, and the Walton Shakespeare arrangements (which all date from the 1960s) are some of the most lasting products of this initiative.

Henry V

The idea of filming *Henry V* was first conceived by the Italian immigrant lawyer turned film producer Filippo Del Giudice, following his success with several early wartime morale-boosting ventures such as Noël Coward's *In Which We Serve*. He had already worked with Laurence Olivier on *Demi-Paradise*, a government-sanctioned exercise in improving Anglo-Soviet relations, but it was after hearing Olivier in a 75-minute BBC version of Shakespeare's play on Sunday, 19 April 1942 (anticipating St George's Day by four days) that he became fired up with the idea of producing an overtly patriotic film version. Olivier readily accepted the title role, but it was only after several directors (including William Wyler and Carol Reed) had rejected the undertaking that he agreed to make his first attempt at film directing, albeit with firmly stated conditions. He also became co-producer with Del Giudice. Dallas Bower, an influential presence in the background, was made associate producer, and it was he who encouraged Olivier to engage Walton, who had already written the score for the Olivier–Bergner *As You Like It* in 1936.

By the time that Walton was contracted to do the music for *Henry V* in the first half of 1943 he was an experienced film composer, with nine productions to his credit. Nonetheless, Olivier's conception for the Technicolor film made the project a new departure for the composer. Shakespeare's play itself seems to confound the cinematographer, with its frequent breachings of the 'fourth wall'. Chorus's evocative speeches were too good to cut, and Olivier's imaginative solution—a gradual metamorphosis from the 'cockpit' of the Elizabethan Globe Theatre, via scenes of quasi-fairy tale and the contemporaneous illustrations of the *Très Riches Heures du Duc de Berry*, to the 'vasty fields' of Agincourt—made demands on the abilities of a composer seeking both a unified score and a convincing musical complement to the visual images.

Walton was required to produce 58 music cues (some merely snatches of plainchant), which ranged from four-second fanfares to the seven-minute Charge and Battle. To accomplish this, he turned to a variety of musical sources: tunes from the *Fitzwilliam Virginal Book* and Joseph Canteloube's *Chants d'Auvergne* (suggested by Olivier), and the traditional French songs 'Les Bas' and 'L'Antoine', while he adopted Vaughan Williams's suggestions that he use the Agincourt Carol (with its fifteenth-century counterpoint) and the period French battle-song 'Réveillez-vous, Piccars'.[3] He succeeded beyond all expectation. However, the score is not mere pastiche, but retains throughout a characteristic Waltonian sound.

Olivier's original intention for the Charge and Battle sequence had been to edit his footage to Walton's score. Accordingly Walton employed his occasional assistant, Roy Douglas (for whom he composed the harpsichord part), to record a special 'wild track' of what he proposed. In the end the process was reversed, and Walton was obliged to rewrite what he had already composed according to the edited film of this sequence.[4] The *Henry V* soundtrack was recorded at Denham Studios between February and May 1944 by the London Symphony Orchestra, conducted by Muir Mathieson. The first public showing of the film was at the Carlton Cinema, London, on 22 November 1944. Three days later it was shown to Winston Churchill and guests at Chequers, and one of his private secretaries recorded that 'the P.M. went into ecstasies about it'.[5] Olivier received a special Oscar for his 'outstanding achievement as actor, director, and producer'.

The eclecticism of the musical idiom, which made the score so effective in the film (and which Olivier repeatedly acknowledged was a crucial factor in its overall success), made it difficult to extract the music into a coherent suite for concert use. The first such attempt is sometimes credited to Malcolm Sargent (but never published as such): a suite for chorus and orchestra, premiered at a Promenade Concert at the Royal Albert Hall on 14 September 1945 under the composer's direction. This suite was in four movements:

1. London 1600 and Overture: The Globe Playhouse
2. Passacaglia: The Death of Falstaff
3. 'Touch her soft lips and part'
4. Agincourt Song

Score and parts were produced by the BBC Music Library from the orchestral parts used at the film sessions, and later made available on hire by OUP. Walton's recording of the two middle movements with the Philharmonia String Orchestra was released in January 1946 as the sixth side of his three-record set of the *Sinfonia Concertante*. These movements were soon being prepared for publication. On 19 June Alan Frank wrote to Walton from OUP: 'As regards the two Henry V pieces, we are now ready to engrave, and as you will remember, I want you to do a bass part for the second of these. Would you like me to send you the MS., or will you just drop in here and do it on the spot?'[6] Two Pieces for Strings was eventually published on 10 April 1947. Two years later, the Passacaglia was published in an organ arrangement by Henry Ley, who had been the young Walton's tutor at Oxford.

More significantly, in the autumn of 1946 the composer was involved in a different sort of project to exploit the film's success; for HMV he recorded a 34-minute selection of the *Henry V* music on four 78 rpm discs with the Philharmonia Orchestra, the BBC Choral Society, and Croydon Philharmonic Society, and featuring Laurence Olivier in speeches taken from several roles. While not unprecedented, these discs represent a change in attitude about the value and marketability of film music when removed from the film itself.[7] Whether the idea came from Walton's friend at EMI, the producer Walter Legge, or someone else is not known. Walton sketched out a scheme for the project on a page of his manuscript, and this list corresponds closely to the eventual release. The records relied to some extent on a listening audience familiar with the film as first screened in 1944, because there are several large stretches of music. Significantly, the Charge and Battle sequence is played virtually intact, nearly six minutes long, with the sole extra-musical cue being a sound effect taken from the film, the celebrated launch of the flight of arrows of the English archers.[8] The appearance of this section on the recording (not at that time a part of any other musical extract) highlights the remarkable role the music plays in the film, where Walton's score turns the battle into the dramatic climax rather than being merely an extravagant interpolation, replacing Shakespeare's battle vignettes. Even without images, the highly successful HMV release did ample justice to the Olivier–Walton collaboration.[9]

Hamlet

Walton did nothing further with the *Henry V* music; he had other commitments, including a commission in February 1947 that was to become the opera *Troilus and Cressida*. But almost immediately he was back at work with Olivier on another Shakespearean film project—*Hamlet*. His remark in a letter to the writer and composer Cecil Gray that this was 'not uninteresting—I've had to do nearly an hour of appropriate but otherwise useless music' is consistent with his strong feelings about what constituted good film music.[10] Although Olivier did a considerable amount of cutting and reordering of the Shakespeare text, *Hamlet* (1948) was a much more straightforward cinematic endeavour, and rather than writing a period score to evoke a series of colourful scenes, Walton had the luxury of delving into the psychology of the characters. Where Henry's introspective moments had received little or no music, the Danish prince broods to the accompaniment of the full Philharmonia Orchestra, and Walton's score resounds for one-third of the 150-minute film.[11] At the recording sessions at Denham Studios in November and December 1947 and January 1948, Mathieson did not do all of the conducting; he had recently broken an arm in a riding accident, and so had to be assisted by John Hollingsworth. The film was first shown at the Odeon Leicester Square Theatre, London, on 6 May 1948. It received four Oscars, including Best Actor for Olivier.

EMI again issued extracts on three separate 78 rpm discs, though this time these were taken directly from the film soundtrack (i.e. not newly recorded); the first contains two of Hamlet's great soliloquies, the second the scenes around the play-within-the-play, and the last the gravedigger scene and final funeral march. Perhaps because Olivier's cinematic concept for *Hamlet* (in black and white) is both more subdued and more subtle than that for *Henry V*, these scenes are very effective even with the images removed.[12] Indeed, to the ear alone Walton's music for the two soliloquies ('O, that this too too solid flesh' and 'To be or not to be') gives the impression of being midway between the calculated recitation over understated accompaniment of some of the early *Façade* numbers and the more passionate moments of *Troilus and Cressida*. In his treatment of *Hamlet*, Walton showed himself ready for the challenge of opera.[13]

Richard III

The intervening years devoted to *Troilus and Cressida* may indeed be the reason why Walton's score for Olivier's 1955 adaptation of *Richard III* 'does not quite scale the height of its eminent predecessors', in the words of Christopher Palmer, otherwise a staunch champion of Walton's film music.[14] The scope of Shakespeare's play allowed Olivier to return from the relative claustrophobia of his *Hamlet* to something like the diverse spectacle of *Henry V*. Furthermore, unlike *Henry V* and *Hamlet*, the concept for the *Richard III* film was closely connected to the celebrated 1944 Old Vic production at London's New Theatre, in which Olivier had made his sensational debut in the role. The sets, costumes, and props are notably more 'stagey' than those of the two previous films, a fact accentuated by the Technicolor and VistaVision presentation. *Richard III* thus necessitated a certain amount of neo-Tudor establishing music from Walton, which must have frustrated a composer who had spent the last eight years attempting to portray musically the innermost workings of his operatic characters. It is true that he had some opportunities for this in the film, but both of the most extensive introverted sequences in the score (the soliloquy 'Now is the winter of our discontent' and the nightmare scene before the battle) are truncated in the final cut of the film.

As with *Henry V*, the score mixes 'period' music with Walton's most mature idiom, but *Richard III* also includes a portentous sample of the English ceremonial style. At first the expansive march over the main titles seems incongruous, as it is anachronistic in the extreme, being unmistakably in the tradition of the 1953 coronation march *Orb and Sceptre*. However, no sooner has the melody begun than the following preamble scrolls across the screen:

> THE STORY OF ENGLAND
> like that of many another land
> is an interwoven pattern of
> history and legend.
>
> …
>
> HERE NOW BEGINS ONE OF THE MOST FAMOUS
> AND AT THE SAME TIME
> THE MOST INFAMOUS
> OF THE LEGENDS
> THAT ARE ATTACHED
> TO
> THE CROWN
> OF ENGLAND

Thus the reason for the *nobilmente* march is clear, and the anachronism intentional; the melody serves as a leitmotif not of a character but of the rightful succession to the crown, which extends from Edward IV and V, through Henry Tudor, down to the latest coronation. Significantly the march is never used when Richard dominates the screen. The leitmotif technique that was used sparingly in the earlier films became as a matter of course Walton's primary method of organization in *Richard III*, with motifs assigned to every character, and quoted at even the slightest allusion in the text.[15] Walton's score for *Richard III* was recorded in February and March 1955, at Shepperton Studios by the Royal Philharmonic Orchestra under Muir Mathieson. The film was first shown at the Odeon Leicester Square Theatre, London, on 13 December of the same year.

Encouraged by the success of the issues featuring selections of the previous two Shakespeare films, HMV released the complete soundtrack of *Richard III* on three LP records in March 1956, only three months after the film's premiere.[16]

Muir Mathieson's arrangements

On 12 January 1962 Alan Frank wrote to Walton:

> I have been thinking a good deal about HENRY V and HAMLET lately, and took the opportunity of having a talk with Muir. I want to put two propositions to you, both of which would be very well worth while financially. I think that, since HENRY V is internationally recognised as perhaps the outstanding film score of our time, we ought to print a 10 x 7 score of the suite. At the same time we ought to do two things: (1) reduce the scoring to double woodwind, etc.; (2) insert the Battle Music, unless you had a very good reason for leaving it out in the first place.... By the way, Muir says that the chorus throughout is optional, even in the Agincourt Song which is all doubled in the brass; this does seem to be so.
>
> Now, turning to HAMLET, Muir has produced the Funeral March, which is the only piece to be considered. Again, it should be reduced to double woodwind, etc.
>
> Muir said that both as regards HENRY V and the HAMLET Funeral March, he would be perfectly prepared to co-operate and prepare the scores for publication, including the reducing. Can we go ahead with either, preferably both, it being understood that you should see the scores before we engrave anything?

Proposals to publish music from the films had been mooted in the past, but had been consistently rejected by the composer. This time Walton was intrigued, and he replied on 17 January:

> About Hamlet and Henry V[,] I am quite willing for you to do something & for Muir to supervise.... The battle is awkward as it has neither start or finish & seems to me only understandable with the picture. There is also a snag that at L. O's request I used a copyright version of a French folksong. It was during the war & it was difficult to register it & there was a spot of bother about it after the war with I think Heugel. However I believe Rank bought the copyright of it at least for the films but whether for its inclusion in a Suite I rather doubt. But perhaps Muir would remember or could find out about that. Anyhow it would not matter a lot if it did not appear. It's not in the suite I made. Of course the Agincourt song is far better with the chorus but it would be optional.

Copyright squabbles over the opening tune in 'Tango-Pasodoblé' in *Façade* had taught Walton to be careful. In this instance, the copyright issue in question was his borrowing from Canteloube's arrangement of the Auvergne song *Baïlèro* for the Duke of Burgundy's speech about the desolation of war. It is important to note that Walton's mention of 'the suite I made' must refer to the so-called 'Sargent suite'; it cannot refer to the HMV album, where *Baïlèro* does appear. In other words, it would seem that Walton had (presumably with Sargent's permission) invoked the conductor's name as the arranger of the suite in order to camouflage his own rooted reluctance to undertake such a task himself. Frank sought permission for the tune to be used in the new suite, but experimented with other alternatives—including a newly composed but similar cor anglais solo above the existing accompaniment (still to be seen, in red ink, on the autograph manuscript). In the end, Canteloube's publisher Heugel granted permission for its use, provided that the quotation was acknowledged.

By May 1962 Frank was consulting Mathieson about what might be done with *Richard III*. 'This all comes from a remark that you made [to Mathieson] in this office about other bits and pieces from the film scores which were worth resuscitating,' Frank wrote to Walton on 29 June, and by the middle of July all parties were agreed.[17] After decades of the composer's resistance to publishing extracts from his film scores, the years 1963–5 saw the release not only of Mathieson's new *Henry V* Suite (without chorus), the *Hamlet* Funeral March, and the two adaptations of the *Richard III* score, but also Sargent's *Fanfare for a Great Occasion* derived from *Hamlet*, and the Three Pieces for Organ from *Richard III*. Even more significantly, the new Mathieson arrangements were effectively launched by the final Legge–Walton collaboration for EMI, an album of Walton's film music, entitled *Shakespeare Film Scores*, with the composer conducting the Philharmonia Orchestra, recorded in October 1963 and released in April of the following year.

It was this recording that finally settled Walton's mind about the viability of the music. On 16 September 1963, just a month before the recording sessions, the composer had been discouraged (a state only intensified by his dissatisfaction with Mathieson's conflation of different versions of the *Hamlet* Funeral March):

> I must say I rather dread the whole thing. Hen V passes more or less, but Rich III is dire. It may have been just all right on the film, but to listen to in cold blood—no—it makes an admirable & justifiable target for any mud slinging! Not that I think that Muir has not arranged them well but it is just not possible to make these odd fragments of not at all distinguished music to hang together to make musical sense. It is my own fault I admit as I should have stopped it all in the first place.

As ever, on 23 September, Frank replied with the apt practical response to assuage the composer: 'These little bits and pieces once they are available have a habit of becoming very useful in all sorts of ways—television background and so on.' As to the new version of the Funeral March, Frank assured the composer that Mathieson's performance of it at the Stirling Festival on 26 May had been successful: 'No-one was taken ill after the performance.' Walton was in a better mood at the sessions. He made a few adjustments, including a re-ordering of the *Richard III* Suite (switching Nos. 4 and 6, while also truncating the end of No. 4, which no longer concluded the set) and replacing Mathieson's original title for the Prelude ('*Richard III*: A Phantasy Overture').[18]

'Publication of your film music seems to be quite a good thing for us,' wrote Frank to Walton on 26 November 1965. 'Muir has dug out a number of bits and pieces of the HAMLET film score which he feels sure he could weld into a sequence for concert performance of perhaps 10–15 minutes.' Mathieson's 'poem for orchestra' *Hamlet and Ophelia* is a fundamentally different sort of work, a consequence of the much more substantial pieces of music that make up Walton's *Hamlet* score. Frank's description notwithstanding, Mathieson chose not 'bits and pieces' but long stretches from significant psychological moments in the score. The conception of the work is wholly Mathieson's, and the result is his very personal encapsulation of the drama as told through Walton's music. As a concert piece, it may lack distinctive character (Walton, who never recorded it, declared it to be 'terribly dull'), but the 'poem' has a certain integrity, and helps to perpetuate some of the most deeply personal music from the film.

Mathieson's Funeral March from Hamlet

A special comment is needed about Mathieson's version of the *Hamlet* Funeral March, with which the composer initially was not satisfied, although he was later prepared to record it. In the film the march is heard at both the beginning and the end, and it fits both contexts because Olivier allows the viewer to foresee Hamlet's catafalque as the opening titles end. This glimpse of the end of the film fades as we hear the midnight bell which begins the first scene. The use of this bell in Mathieson's version of the funeral march (bars 49–54) seems out of place—promising renewed energy just as the piece should be concluding. Mathieson's abrupt transition at bars 55–7 upset Walton who, in a letter to Alan Frank of 14 September, complained of the 'horrible cadence five bars from the end', and also worried that the score did not conform with the version on the recording of the soundtrack. Frank replied on 18 September:

> I am sorry you are worried about the FUNERAL MARCH. Let me say straightaway that there are indeed two scores of the piece in your manuscript which we have and that by and large the printed version—it is already printed by the way—is all your own work, even the 'horrible cadence'! Muir's job was to make a synthesis of the two and we had it in mind that for concert use the piece could afford to be longer. It doesn't seem to me to matter the least bit that the concert version is different from that on the sound track: in fact, would one not expect it to be?

This reply does not indicate that bars 55–7 were not a cadence but a transition to the anxious scene between the guards on the battlements. At this point, Mathieson seems to have been unsure of what to do: 'To ending on back of 1.M.1 ORIGINAL or Coda as taken from Record' is his note on the autograph of the revised opening titles. He opted for the former, while Walton responded: 'The version on the record (i.e. original film sound track) of the concluding Funeral March is much better than M.M.'s.' However, Mathieson and Frank's original premise was probably right; the music needed to be presented in its most expanded form if it was to make a satisfactory concert piece.

Battle of Britain

After a career of such triumphs in film music (surprisingly never recognized with an Oscar, although twice nominated), Walton's reputation as a great film composer was marred by an embarrassing defeat in later years. This is not because the music itself failed, but rather because it did not get a proper hearing during the composer's lifetime.

As far as Walton was concerned, *Battle of Britain* was a much smaller project than any of his previous post-war films. When, in a letter to Alan Frank of 2 July 1968, he mentioned that he had been asked to write the music, he remarked, 'I've seen the script & as far as I can see there can't be much more than 25 mins music if that.'[19] On 9 September Walton wrote to Malcolm Arnold, asking him to conduct the recording sessions for the film and seeking a time when the two of them could see the most recent rough cut together. In the event, Arnold's part of the project expanded considerably, from conducting to composing, basing his work at least in part on music that Walton had first sketched.[20] Additionally, jazz arranger Wally Stott supplied three versions of 'A Nightingale Sang in Berkeley Square' to be used as source music.

The Walton–Arnold score was recorded at Anvil Recording Studios, Denham, in April 1969 by a film session orchestra conducted by Malcolm Arnold, with Walton's participation. The *Guardian* critic, and ardent Walton admirer, Edward Greenfield attended the session that began with multiple takes of 'Battle in the Air', and reported that, to the delight of the orchestra, Arnold persuaded Walton to take the baton for the recording of what he termed the 'grand superdambusting march'.[21]

Only after the score had been recorded did Walton learn, when a newspaper reporter telephoned him for his response, that senior executives at United Artists in New York had rejected it. Thereafter he discovered that the march from the score had consequently been dropped from the 1969 Proms, despite having already being announced. On 12 June Walton wrote to Alan Frank:

> I know nothing about the 'Proms' switch except it[']s probably Noel Rogers['] doing.[22] He is trying & I fear has succeeded in getting my music for the B of B scrapped—owing to the fact that it won't make an L.P. & is therefore uncommercial. It seems quite idiotic—everyone on the film including the top boys Salzman, Ben Fisz, & Guy Hamilton is delighted with the music, but U.A.[United Artists] in the States say it[']s not commercial—there must be music almost all the time so they can get their money back via the record. Silly mutts have paid me in full! As it is I fear there will be a bit of a scandal, but have Lord Goodman at work on it but have heard nothing directly—only thro' Malcolm A. who has been a real pal throughout. I must say I'm feeling furious about it, because I hate the music being turned down. Though it's only 'film music' it's jolly good of it's [*sic*] kind. They are employing someone called Ron Goodwin to fill in. The name means nothing to me[.] Does it to you? Anyhow I hope to get some damages for defamation etc.!...Since writing this I've just been 'phoned by Leighton-Davis [of Goodman, Derrick & Co.]. The situation over the 'B of B' is this: the UA in Hollywood don't like my music & don't think it a commercial proposition. It is nothing to do with an L.P. So they've asked Goodwin to do another score & it will be a fight between the two scores—with the probability that I shall lose—an ignominous [*sic*] & damaging situation which I fear [is] able [to] do me a great deal of damage in all ways. But there it is, there's no redress & I can't bring action against them.

Walton's fear that his score would be competing against a new score by Ron Goodwin was at best wishful thinking. In fact, his score had been dismissed entirely, and not merely because of its brevity. A scheme contrived by Malcolm Arnold for an LP release of the score augmented by the sounds of aeroplane engines and air-raid sirens fell on deaf ears. The Walton–Arnold score for *Battle of Britain* situates the film in a highly stylized tradition of British cinema of which the Olivier–Shakespeare productions are among the most celebrated. Walton had been highly praised in the film literature of the 1940s and 50s in particular for these scores, but by the late 1960s he was no longer regularly cited as a master film composer. Although the director and producers of the film professed themselves to be satisfied with his score for *Battle of Britain*, the American executives of United Artists may have wished to use the accompanying music to distance the film from the earlier epic style—particularly as it was becoming regarded as old-fashioned and an object of parody; Peter Sellers's 1965 hit single 'A Hard Day's Night' used Olivier's portrayal of Richard III as its target, and George Martin's musical introduction employed a Waltonian neo-Tudor version of the Beatles song.[23] That Walton would have resisted a new 'American' style is suggested by a passing remark in a letter to Alan Frank of 22 January 1953, describing his new *Orb and Sceptre* as 'not too bad—rather M.G.M. or perhaps Ealing studios, a slight but not over subtle distinction'. Moreover, as Martin Hunt has argued, given the 'scrupulously authentic' approach of the producers of the film, Walton should have been the correct choice: 'Walton, so far as British films of the 1940s are concerned, was the music of the period.'[24]

From United Artists' perspective, Goodwin was a natural choice, having had notable success in 1964 with the UA release *633 Squadron*. Indeed, Goodwin's conception of the score for *Battle of Britain* follows very much that of his 1968 MGM film *Where Eagles Dare*, which has long stretches of atmospheric music under dialogue (extremely rare in Walton), punctuated by 'sting' brass outbursts that highlight a cut to an arresting image. Walton and Goodwin each use a simple leitmotif system, but Goodwin is less careful to restrict a given theme exclusively to one of the opposing sides. The complaint that there was not enough of Walton's music to fill a commercial LP was rectified with Goodwin, who was given more sequences to write, and whose cues (when they correspond to Walton's) are somewhat longer. Goodwin's score succeeds, but it yields a very different film.

It was only through the intervention of Laurence Olivier, who stars in the film with a memorably understated portrayal of Air Chief Marshal Sir Hugh Dowding, that any of the Walton–Arnold score remained in the released version of the film when it was first shown at the Dominion Cinema, London, on 15 September 1969. Appropriately, given Walton's music that underscores the battles of Agincourt and Bosworth Field, this is the 'Battle in the Air'—a gripping sequence presented, like its two famous predecessors, largely without spoken dialogue. Indeed, even the sound effects fade, and the only one that remains—the eerie throbbing engines of the planes over St Paul's Cathedral— is actually part of the score. The effect is produced by the full glissandos across the open C-string harmonics of the cellos and violas, a technique Walton may well have picked up from Stravinsky.

The Walton–Arnold manuscripts for the film were retained by United Artists even after the score was rejected. In 1972 the then Prime Minister Edward Heath secured their release (minus 'Battle in the Air') as a 70th birthday present for the composer, but UA stipulated that the music could not be published or recorded until they had recouped the sum they had paid Walton (£10,000). This terminated any hope that *Battle of Britain* could be a commercially viable score for OUP to publish in any form.

There the matter rested until 13 March 1980, when Frank's successor, Christopher Morris, approached UA again:

> I have always felt it a great pity that the music Sir William wrote for the Battle of Britain film is not available to orchestras and to audiences, both of whom clearly enjoy Walton's music. I am therefore writing to you to ask if some business deal could be arranged so that a small part of this music could be made into a concert piece.... I have in mind the Battle music, which was used in the film, combined with the March.[25]

Eventually Morris prevailed, though not until after Walton's death. On 10 May 1985, a suite of most of Walton's *Battle of Britain* music, adapted by Colin Matthews, received its premiere in the Colston Hall, Bristol, with the Bournemouth Symphony Orchestra under the direction of Carl Davis, who had suggested the suite. A year later it was issued on a disc of Walton's film music. Matthews's suite follows the pattern suggested by Morris, adding Walton's 'The Young Siegfrieds' music as a trio to the March, and an introduction (Spitfire Music) from earlier in the score. Although the soundtrack of the original recording sessions, conducted by Malcolm Arnold and Walton, was later rediscovered and released on CD, the only other portion of Walton's score to be published until now is his music for 'Gay Berlin', included in Christopher Palmer's compilation *A Wartime Sketchbook* (1989).

To some extent Walton's score has now been honoured, particularly with the special edition DVD released in 2005 by MGM–UA which features much of the rejected score included as an optional soundtrack.[26] This ought to have been a full vindication, but unfortunately almost all the music cues are misplaced, sometimes spectacularly so, with Walton's 'Young Siegfrieds' invariably accompanying triumphal scenes of the RAF. Walton's score for *Battle of Britain* still remains to be presented correctly in the context for which it was intended.[27] The Matthews suite received its first publication in the WWE.

NOTES

1. Letter preserved in BBC Written Archives, Caversham; quoted in Stephen Lloyd, *William Walton: Muse of Fire* (Woodbridge, 2001), p. 189.
2. The only extended biographical treatment of Mathieson to date is S. J. Hetherington and Mark Brownrigg, *Muir Mathieson: A Life in Film Music* (Dalkeith, 2006).
   Mathieson himself wrote very little about his craft, but his consummate professionalism is evident in his essay 'The Music Director and the Sound Recordist', chap. 4 in John Huntley and Roger Manvell, *The Technique of Film Music* (New York, 1957).
3. In 1903 Vaughan Williams had arranged his version of 'Réveillez-vous, Piccars' (published 1907). He was also very enthusiastic about Arthur Warrell's arrangement of the Agincourt Carol for male voices (Oxford, 1929). See Hugh Cobbe, *Letters of Ralph Vaughan Williams* (Oxford, 2008), p. 171.
4. See Walton's letters to Roy Douglas in *The Selected Letters of William Walton*, ed. Malcolm Hayes (London, 2002), pp. 145–147; see also Stephen Lloyd, *William Walton: Muse of Fire*, p. 197.
5. John Colville, *The Fringes of Power*, vol. 2 (London, 1985), p. 162.
6. OUP Archive, Oxford. All other quotations from Frank to Walton, and vice versa, are to be assumed as coming from this source.
7. See, for example, Ben Winters, 'Catching Dreams: Editing Film Scores for Publications', *Journal of the Royal Musical Association*, vol. 132, no. 1 (2007), pp. 115–140. He cites a May 1938 narrated radio broadcast of Korngold's score for *The Adventures of Robin Hood*, subsequently issued on disc by Columbia (MM583); two of Walton's scores received similar radio adaptations—*The Next of Kin* (C42a) and *Macbeth* (C43a)—but neither was issued on disc.
8. The composer could not have known about an astonishing coincidence concerning the Battle of Agincourt; one of the men-at-arms accompanying Sir Richard de Kyghley was a gentleman from Inskip, Lancashire, by the name of William de Walton. See Charles Kightly, *Agincourt* (London, 1974).
9. In 1956 it was reissued on a single LP (ALP 1375), though losing some seven minutes in the process. Its full length was restored in 1994 when it was reissued on CD (GHS 5 650032) as part of

EMI's 'The Walton Editon'. See Lyndon Jenkins, 'The Recorded Works', in Stewart Craggs, ed., *William Walton: Music & Literature* (Aldershot, 1999), p. 216.

10. Letter of 27 December 1947; *Selected Letters*, ed. Hayes, p. 165.

11. Essays by Walton and Mathieson (expanded from those written for Brenda Cox, ed., *The Film 'Hamlet': A Record of its Production* (London, 1948)) are reprinted in Lloyd, *William Walton*, pp. 276–280.

12. On the EMI releases, see John Huntley, 'The Music of "Hamlet" and "Oliver Twist"', *The Penguin Film Review*, vol. 8 (1949), pp. 111–113.

13. A similar point is made by Charles Hurtgen, who complains of the 'To be or not to be' music that 'the spectator is stirred, not intellectually, by means of the words, but emotionally, by means of the sounds—as in Grand Opera'. Charles Hurtgen, 'The Operatic Character of Background Music in Film Adaptations of Shakespeare', *Shakespeare Quarterly*, vol. 20, no. 1 (1969), p. 63.

14. Christopher Palmer, 'Walton's Film Music', *Musical Times*, vol. 113 (1972), p. 251.

15. By far the most discussed portion of the *Hamlet* score is the play-within-the-play. Walton's creative use of leitmotif to emphasize Claudius's pangs of guilt was singled out by Hans Keller as exemplary; see H. Keller, 'Film Music', *Grove's Dictionary of Music and Musicians* (5th edn, London, 1954), vol. 3, p. 100.

16. ALP 134 1–3; the HMV discs preserve a slightly longer version of the film than the standard release, but they were mastered after a number of cuts had already been taken.

17. Walton was to have second thoughts more than once, but the cause of his concern became increasingly financial rather than artistic; see, for example, his letter to Frank of 1 January 1963, in *Selected Letters*, ed. Hayes, pp. 330–331.

18. The quotation-titles of the individual movements for the Shakespeare Suite are Mathieson's and do not correspond to the scenes in which the music is heard. The title 'With Drums and Colours' prompted the addition of the first four bars.

19. According to the director Guy Hamilton, 'We were both in agreement that the picture did not need a great deal of music[,] which would only fight with the plentiful natural sound effects'. See Martin Hunt, 'Their Finest Hour? The Scoring of *Battle of Britain*', *Film History*, vol. 14 (2002), p. 50.

20. See *Selected Letters*, ed. Hayes, pp. 383–386. Fully half of the extant manuscript full score of the film is in Arnold's hand.

21. *The Guardian*, 29 April 1969, p. 10 b–d.

22. Noel Rogers was then Head of Music Publishing for the British wing of United Artists.

23. Parlophone R5393 (45 rpm).

24. Martin Hunt, 'Their Finest Hour?', p. 55.

25. OUP Archive.

26. 10001024 MZI (UK); 1008312 (USA).

27. James Brooks Kuykendall, 'William Walton's Film Scores: New Evidence in the Autograph Manuscripts', *Notes*, vol. 68 (2011), pp. 9–32.

23

Henry V

A Shakespeare Scenario *(Vol. 23)*
[Arr. Christopher Palmer]

David Lloyd-Jones

Although the authorized concert suite from the music that Walton composed in 1943 for Laurence Olivier's film *Henry V* is published in Volume 22, and although other arrangements made after the composer's death are not featured in the William Walton Edition, it was decided to make an exception in the case of Christopher Palmer's highly effective *Henry V: A Shakespeare Scenario*. Indeed, such was Christopher's devotion to every aspect of Walton's output, as a list of his many editions and arrangements would show, that this volume is designed to serve as a memorial to him.

Christopher Palmer, who died on 22 January 1995 at the age of 48, made a number of important and lasting contributions to the world of music. At Cambridge he read French and German before transferring to Music; this enabled him to develop further the passionate interest he had formed in twentieth-century British music. Perhaps it was the combination of his extensive knowledge of European literature (especially poetry) and his intense musicality that led to his early enthusiasm for the music of Delius (whom Walton, in a letter, once referred to as 'my most detested composer'). He followed his first sustained piece of writing, *Impressionism in Music* (1973), with *Delius: Portrait of a Cosmopolitan* (1976), which still stands in the opinion of many as the most penetrating study yet of the music and personality of this composer. Other twentieth-century British composers, sometimes relatively minor ones, were to benefit from his crusading zeal and illuminating analysis, which appeared in many forms: books, monographs, articles, recordings for which he acted as producer, reviews, broadcasts, and outstandingly readable and informative record notes. As Lewis Foreman, another expert in the same field, put it in his *Guardian* obituary of Christopher (19 February 1995), 'Range and detail were his strengths in his writing. He set his subject in the wider context and looked for meaning—discussing the words set, finding parallels, making life and art illuminate each other.'

Somewhat surprisingly perhaps, there was another side to Christopher. In addition to his love of the rarefied and poetic there was also a passionate commitment to the altogether tougher commercial world of film music. Delius and Bernard Herrmann or Miklós Rózsa might seem poles apart, but Christopher found it perfectly possible to hold his allegiances in equal balance. It was, in fact, as an outstanding transcriber, arranger, and orchestrator of film scores that he derived the greater part of his living as a musician. His success in this field enabled him to draw on his own experiences when writing *The Composer in Hollywood* (1990), one of the few authoritative books on this important subject. The film-music side of him also helps to account for his main interest outside the field of British music—Prokofiev.

It is therefore in no way remarkable that someone who was drawn both to twentieth-century British composers and to film music should find his greatest fulfilment in the works of William Walton, the composer who united both these aspects in the most comprehensive and masterly way. The Oxford University Press catalogue contains many arrangements, editions, transcriptions, concert suites, and orchestrations by Christopher, but inevitably the most impressive (and labour-intensive) were those in which he rescued the important film scores from near oblivion and reconstituted them. These include arrangements for concert performance of *As You Like It* (1936) (which Christopher called 'A Poem for Orchestra'), *Major Barbara* (1940–1) ('A Shavian Sequence'), and numbers from *The Next of Kin* (1941), *The Foreman went to France* (1942), *Went the Day Well?* (1942), and *The Battle of Britain* (1969), which became 'A Wartime Sketchbook'. *Hamlet* (1947) appeared as *Hamlet: A Shakespeare Scenario*, and *Richard III* (1955) as *Richard III: A Shakespeare Scenario*. All of these were taken into the OUP catalogue.

Christopher's finest and most imaginative achievement in this line was his reconstruction of Walton's most celebrated film score, under the title *Henry V: A Shakespeare Scenario*. Some of the *Henry V* music had been available for many years. For the 1945 season of Promenade Concerts Walton extracted a short four-movement suite for chorus and orchestra using the original orchestration; this was performed under his direction at a Promenade concert on 14 September, but the score was never put on sale. The following year brought with it a significant precursor to the idea of a speaker–chorus–orchestra presentation of the *Henry V* music. This was the set of four 78 rpm records made by HMV in the latter half of 1946, with Olivier as narrator, and the Philharmonia Orchestra and an unnamed chorus conducted by Walton. For these Olivier recited not only King Henry's set-pieces, but also three of the Chorus's speeches, the soldier Williams's reflections on a king's responsibilities in the Night-scene, the Henry/Mountjoy altercation before Agincourt, and the Duke of Burgundy's address. The records, released in July 1947, played for nearly 34 minutes, but nothing was done to preserve the material, or to present it in concert form. The recording was reissued on LP in 1956, though shorn of some seven minutes, and was transferred to CD in its entirety in 1994. The main musical gains over the 1945 suite were the Night-scene and Agincourt sequences. The two movements for strings only, 'Passacaglia: Death of Falstaff' and 'Touch her soft lips and part', were published separately in 1947. Incidentally, the familiar title of the latter number, used in the film, derives from the original 1600 Quarto edition; in the standard 1623 First Folio text of the play, Pistol, referring to the Hostess, says, 'Touch her soft mouth and march.' Then in 1963 a five-movement suite (without chorus), which made available much of the 'Battle of Agincourt' music for the first time, was made by Muir Mathieson, conductor of the original 1944 soundtrack, probably for the purpose of the LP disc of the film music that Walton recorded in October of that year. The score, published in the following year, stated that the adaptation had been made 'with the composer's authorization'; this had involved a reduction of the original orchestration. Most of the autograph scores and parts prepared for the film sessions were lost. The small number that did survive lay untouched until

Christopher undertook what amounted to a labour of love in the late 1980s: the reconstruction of the full score, and its presentation in a bold, imaginative form that was suitable for concert use.

Christopher decided to call his reconstruction *A Shakespeare Scenario*, instantly giving his work an important historic and dramatic sense. As is common in the world of film music, he was assisted in his preparation by a few trusted colleagues and protégés. These included Paul Mottram, who helped in particular with the passages that had to be transcribed from the soundtrack itself and the 1947 records, and Jeff Atmajian, who was largely responsible for the fleshing out of Christopher's detailed directions into full score. The finished manuscript was then given a final re-edit and polish by Christopher before it went to the copyists.

Neither the 1945 Walton nor the Mathieson suites had come near to representing the full extent of the music that Walton had written for *Henry V*, let alone given any idea of its additional emotive force when heard in conjunction with the Shakespearian text for which it had been composed. Christopher's inspired arrangement of a greatly expanded version of the music for speaker, chorus, and orchestra is therefore a major addition to the Walton catalogue; it was first performed and recorded in 1990, and its effectiveness and popularity are already assured. Indeed Christopher's *Henry V* arrangement has already been rearranged for both brass band and chamber ensemble by Edward Watson.

No better account of the twin achievements of Olivier and Walton in the creation of the *Henry V* film could be found than the typically engrossing essay that Christopher wrote to accompany the Chandos recording of his arrangement. This, and his synopsis of the action, are reproduced on the following pages in a slightly edited form.

Walton's Henry V: An Introductory Note
by Christopher Palmer

I first met William in 1935 on the set of Elizabeth Bergner's film of *As You Like It* in which I was doing my wretched best with Orlando. He was, I understood, writing the music. The only thing I knew of his was *Portsmouth Point*, of which I had a record, and everybody was extolling him to the skies as England's musical genius. As I looked at him, there was something about him that made me believe it. He was pale: pale-eyed, pale skinned, even pale personality plus pale green hair…the paleness and the coldness made the passionate blaze in all of his music a thing of wonder and amazement. As time went by and he brought his marvellous creations to *Henry V, Hamlet*, and *Richard III*, we got to know each other better and our relations became warmer and warmer.

(Olivier on Walton, on the occasion of the latter's 80th birthday in 1982)

They were not only professional colleagues but close friends; they understood each other. That Walton contributed the music to three of Olivier's greatest films shows how well he understood the great actor; and nobody, surely, has described the emotive force of Walton's music better than Olivier when he spoke to Tony Palmer of 'its inner vibrance, its energy which is twin to sexual energy…that exuberance, that spirit, that heart-quickening feeling, belong in the same area of human nature. Certain types of action have that quality also. It has something to do with sex, but a lot more to do with love. A vibrant sort of love, not a soft kind at all. William's music is the strong kind of love.' It is more than coincidence that those paying tribute to Olivier after his death wrote of the physical excitement he generated; of his voice now of clarion resonance, now of gentle mellifluousness; of his instinct for startling bodily gesture; of his virility, heroism, and romance, and the vulnerability, the femininity thereby concealed, or complemented; of his presence, his magnetism. And it is more than coincidence that all these qualities are precisely reflected in Walton's music. This compatibility of outlook or 'harmonious consent' (as Shakespeare's near-contemporary Thomas Morley would have termed it) lies at the root of their three renowned joint creations, of which *Henry V* is generally reckoned the finest.

Shakespeare's *Henry V* is the last of an historic trilogy, a series of chronicle plays covering the reigns of Richard II, Henry IV, and Henry V (1377–1423). In *Henry V*, the irresponsible Prince Hal of *Henry IV*, cavorting with lawless roisterers and bar-room cronies like Sir John Falstaff, is transformed into the *preux chevalier* of the English throne, a larger-than-life dramatic hero thus eulogized by Holinshed, Shakespeare's source: 'This Henry was a king of a life without sport; a prince of all men loved, that both lived and died a pattern in princehood, a lodestar in honour, and mirror of magnificence.' Now when, in 1943, he came to direct his film (in which he took the name part) Olivier had good reason for projecting this image of Henry for all it was worth. The war was on; the film is dedicated to 'the Commandos and Airborne Troops of Great Britain, the spirit of whose ancestors it has been humbly attempted to recapture in some ensuing scenes'. In other words, Olivier's *Henry V* was as much propaganda in 1943 as Shakespeare's play had been in 1600. In the opening panoramic view of medieval London the camera travels westwards upstream from the Tower over London Bridge to the point on the South Bank where the Globe Playhouse, the 'Wooden O', referred to by the Chorus in his opening speech, was located. Olivier was here—aided and abetted by Walton's glorious ode, or paean, for wordless chorus and orchestra—invoking the heroic defence of the city against the *Luftwaffe*, indeed of the whole of Britain's cultural heritage which seemed to be under threat. 'Touch her soft lips and part'—Pistol before the embarkation—would have had poignant significance, and so would the King of France's speech ('Epilogue') in praise of France's solidarity with England: for when the film was made, France was, of course, still under German occupation. Uppermost in the minds of those making and viewing the Agincourt scenes would have been the heroism of the British at Dunkirk, in the Battle of Britain, and, latterly, in the Allied invasion of Europe. Seeing the film in the context of the times we can rate it as a magnificent contribution to the war effort; at the critical moment when the tide was finally beginning to turn, the need was for a call to the nation to brace itself for whatever casualties and setbacks still remained to be faced. This need *Henry V* supplied; but that it still grips audiences today testifies not only to its intrinsic merits, and to its brilliant success as a popularization of Shakespeare (the first, and still one of the best), but also to its achievement in bringing lasting nobility to the kind of emotions that can go out of fashion almost overnight.

The idea of engaging Walton was not primarily Olivier's but that of his co-producer, Dallas Bower. Bower had worked on *As You Like It*, and the Louis MacNeice radio play *Christopher Columbus*, for both of which Walton had provided the music, and Olivier had played a leading role. Bower convinced Olivier that Walton was the right composer. Letters to his friend, the composer and keyboard-player Roy Douglas (for whom the small but important harpsichord parts in *Henry V* were written), help us to chart Walton's progress on the score. In May 1943 he was preparing a piano 'guide-track' of the Agincourt music, the original idea being to cut the film to fit the music. (In the event nothing came of this and Walton fitted his music to the edited footage in the normal way.) By January 1944 Walton was 'in the thick of' the score, and by the end of April the recording sessions (with the London Symphony Orchestra at Denham Studios, Muir Mathieson conducting) had been completed. Dubbing music, sound effects, and dialogue were undertaken between May and July, and the finished film was first shown in November of the same year.

In *Henry V* Walton for the most part neither wanted nor needed to move outside his own stylistic orbit. However, in order to shade in a little 'period' colour he made recourse to a number of sources:

1) *The Fitzwilliam Virginal Book*—the most valuable surviving collection of Elizabethan keyboard music—for the scenes set in Shakespeare's London (at the Globe Theatre and the Boar's Head). In the 'Prologue' the vocalized chorus for the two-part children's choir is a charming paraphrase or re-composition of a clavichord piece by Giles Farnaby entitled 'Rosa Solis' (it is reprised in the 'Epilogue' in a different key and with a busy harpsichord obbligato). The theme, or 'ground', of the 'Death of Falstaff' passacaglia is an anonymous drinking-song from the same collection, entitled 'Watkin's

Ale' (Falstaff, we may remember, spent much of his time quaffing in taverns). Here, however, the tune has undergone a complete personality change—from a bright beery G major to a slow funereal E minor, as if from light to night.

2) *Chants d'Auvergne*, collected and arranged by Joseph Canteloube (1879–1957), for the scenes in the Louvre Palace ('At the French Court'). In an inspired move to complement the pristine visual beauty of these scenes—modelled on the *Très Riches Heures du Duc de Berri*, the famous medieval Book of Hours—Walton, at Olivier's suggestion, drew on three melodies from Canteloube's collection, substantially transforming the first two. 'Obal, din lou Lomouzi' is the third of Canteloube's 'Trois Bourées' (Series 1, No. 3), and both introduces 'At the French Court' in bright madrigalian style, and returns at the close as a tender love song. 'Baïlèro' (Series 1, No. 2) appears as an emotive cor anglais solo, which accompanies the Duke of Burgundy's speech. The epithalamion, or bridal song, which introduces the last scene ('Epilogue') is founded on 'L'Antouèno' (Series 2, No. 2). Canteloube had not only collected and transcribed these tunes but also published them in highly skilled and elaborate arrangements of his own. These are now highly popular, but at the time of Olivier's film were almost completely unknown.

3) Two contemporary French tunes: 'Réveillez-vous Piccars' (a fifteenth-century battle-song), and the well-known 'Agincourt Song'. These were brought to Walton's notice by none other than Vaughan Williams, who had earlier used both of them in his own *Henry V*, a work for brass band written in 1933–4 but not published until 1979. Vaughan Williams' interest in the 'Agincourt Song' went back to yet another *Henry V*, a production mounted during F. R. Benson's Shakespeare season at Stratford-upon-Avon in 1913. For this, Vaughan Williams had written incidental music which included a version of the 'Agincourt Song'. 'Réveillez-vous Piccars' he had set as a solo song as far back as 1903. Typically, Vaughan Williams told Walton where to find these tunes, but *not* that he had already used them himself (presumably not to discourage him). In 1937 Vaughan Williams set the *text* of part of the 'Agincourt Song' in the last part of his *Flourish for a Coronation*; and in 1955 Sir George Dyson again used the tune—in a more straightforward setting than in Walton's 'Epilogue'—as the finale of his Shakespearian cantata *Agincourt*. For Walton, however, 'Réveillez-vous Piccars' was an even greater find; it lent itself readily to symphonic elaboration and variation, and underpins melodically almost the entire battle sequence.

Olivier once described Walton as one of the finest Shakespearian scholars of all time. Not, of course, in the limited academic sense; rather had Olivier divined that, if Shakespearian English attained to a warmth, nobility, and splendour never since equalled, let alone excelled, the one contemporary composer whose brand of musical English was rich in these qualities was Walton. For instance, the 'Prologue'—the 'London panorama'—is based on a theme developed by majestic orchestra and (wordless) chorus into a fanfare-like hymn in praise of—what? London Pride? Spirit of England? Grandeur and Glory? Whatever its symbolism, it always occurs at significant moments—at the very beginning and end of the score, always (interspersed with little harpsichord flourishes) to introduce the Chorus, in 'The Night-watch', and in the heat of the battle in 'Agincourt'. It epitomizes Walton's affinity with Olivier's Shakespeare— larger-than-life, romantic, chivalrous, great-hearted, and highly coloured.

The idea of restructuring Walton's *Henry V* score as a piece for speaker, orchestra, and chorus originated with Sir Neville Marriner and Christopher Plummer (they had, in fact, previously rough-hewn such a work, based on the published five-movement Mathieson suite, but were frustrated by the amount of missing music). My *Shakespeare Scenario* includes about 90 per cent of the complete score. A few small or fragmentary sections refused to fit in, and some judicious cuts had to be made in the already sub-stantial battle music (to play it complete would make an already long movement over-long). Conversely, there being no suitable music to introduce the Chorus' great call-to-arms in 'Embarkation' ('Now all the youth of England are on fire'), I chose a march written in 1959 for a projected ABC television series (never made) based on Churchill's *A History of the English-Speaking Peoples* (1956–8), in which Olivier was to have spoken the words of Churchill. The tone seemed right and the music too little-known to start setting up unwanted reverberations.

The new format compelled me to transpose and rearrange the text in various places, and to amend the odd phrase here and there. I do not think Shakespeare would have objected; he was above all a practical man of the theatre, used to hearing his lines delivered differently in different circumstances, and would certainly have sanctioned the making of minor changes to suit a new context. The *Shakespeare Scenario* was first performed by Sir Neville Marriner and Christopher Plummer, with the Orchestra and Chorus of the Academy of St Martin-in-the-Fields, on 11 May 1990. The venue was the Royal Festival Hall, on London's South Bank—only a stone's throw from the site of Shakespeare's Globe where, as the film shows, the original *Henry V* was first performed nearly 400 years ago.

Synopsis

1 Prologue. London, 1 May 1600. A playbill announces a production at the Globe Playhouse of 'The Chronicle History of KING HENRY THE FIFT [*sic*] with his batell fought at Agincourt in France by Will Shakespeare'. A highshot of a stylized seventeenth-century London panorama moves slowly towards the Globe, where a trumpet call announces that the theatre is in session. An Overture from the gallery commences. The Chorus enters and introduces the play.

2 Interlude: At the Boar's Head. After the quirky repartee of Bardolph, Nim, and Pistol, 'Watkin's Ale' is heard as a sombre passacaglia. The delirious Falstaff, tended by Mistress Quickly, remembers his last encounter with Prince Hal, or rather the new King Henry, and the way he had brutally rejected him.

3 Embarkation. A call-to-arms precedes the sailing of the English fleet from Southampton, as it embarks on the French campaign.

4 Interlude: 'Touch her soft lips and part'. After Falstaff's death, Pistol and his companions say farewell to Mistress Quickly outside the Boar's Head, Eastcheap, as they also set out for France.

5(i) Harfleur. The storming of the walls of Harfleur depicts the English forces hauling cannon, with Henry exhorting his men to assume a warlike and terrible demeanour.

5(ii) The Night-watch. In a scene of tense calm and hushed expectancy before battle, the French and English armies are encamped for the night. The King walks around the tents, dispensing hope and comfort, while also reflecting on the vanity of kingship. He finally prays for his men in the trial that awaits them.

6 Agincourt. At day-break the French are in high spirits, and are seen being winched into their armour. Henry climbs on to a cart and delivers the 'St Crispin's Day' speech to his men, gathered around. Preparations for the battle begin, and Henry dismisses Montjoy, ambassador for the Constable of France, who has come to demand a ransom in lieu of battle.

The French drummers beat their drums; the English archers draw their bows, and the music depicts the accelerating tempo of the French charge. Heavy fighting ensues, and the first climax shows the French infantry struggling in the morass. A new wave of French cavalry then advances over a hilltop, and as they charge through a wood, English infantrymen jump down on them from the trees. The battle turns in favour of the English, and an eerie calm succeeds the greatest climax. Henry names the battle after the nearby castle of Agincourt, after which the army walks in procession to Agincourt village to the heroic strains of the 'Agincourt Song'.

7 Interlude: At the French Court. The great hall of the Louvre Palace is the scene for both the wooing of Princess Katherine by Henry, and a successful peace treaty, negotiated by the eloquent Duke of Burgundy.

8 Epilogue. The King of France gives his daughter's hand to Henry in marriage, and after the celebrations, the scene reverts to the Globe Playhouse. The Chorus takes his leave, and the rolling credits commence, which include 'The Music by WILLIAM WALTON'.

General Index

Index of Works

A full list of works can be found in Stewart Craggs's third edition of his *Catalogue of Works*. The catalogue numbers are given below.